Corporations, Crime
and Accountability

Theories of institutional design

SERIES EDITOR Robert E. Goodin
Research School of Social Sciences
Australian National University

ADVISORY EDITORS Brian Barry, Russell Hardin, Carole Pateman, Barry Weingast, Stephen Elkin, Claus Offe, Susan Rose-Ackerman

Social scientists have rediscovered institutions. They have been increasingly concerned with the myriad ways in which social and political institutions shape the patterns of individual interactions which produce social phenomena. They are equally concerned with the ways in which those institutions emerge from such interactions.

This series is devoted to the exploration of the more normative aspects of these issues. What makes one set of institutions better than another? How, if at all, might we move from a less desirable set of institutions to a more desirable set? Alongside the questions of what institutions we would design, if we were designing them afresh, are pragmatic questions of how we can best get from here to there: from our present institutions to new revitalised ones.

Theories of institutional design is insistently multidisciplinary and inter-disciplinary, both in the institutions on which it focuses, and in the methodologies used to study them. There are interesting sociological questions to be asked about legal institutions, interesting legal questions to be asked about economic institutions, and interesting social, economic and legal questions to be asked about political institutions. By juxtaposing these approaches in print, this series aims to enrich normative discourse surrounding important issues of designing and redesigning, shaping and reshaping the social, political and economic institutions of contemporary society.

Corporations, Crime and Accountability

Brent Fisse
Faculty of Law, University of Sydney

John Braithwaite
Research School of Social Sciences,
Australian National University

CAMBRIDGE
UNIVERSITY PRESS

Published by the Press Syndicate of the University of Cambridge
The Pitt Building, Trumpington Street, Cambridge CB2 1RP, UK
40 West 20th Street, New York, NY 10011-4211, USA
10 Stamford Road, Oakleigh, Melbourne 3166, Australia

First published 1993

Printed in Hong Kong by Colorcraft

National Library of Australia cataloguing in publication data
Fisse, Brent.
Corporations, crime and accountability.
Bibliography.
Includes index.
ISBN 0 521 44130 7.
ISBN 0 521 45923 0 (pbk.).
1. Criminal liability of juristic persons. 2. Corporation law – Criminal
provisions. 3. Corporations – Corrupt practices. I. Braithwaite,
John, 1951–   . II. Title. (Series: Theories of institutional design).
345.0268

Library of Congress cataloguing in publication data
Fisse, Brent.
Corporations, crime, and accountability / Brent Fisse and John
Braithwaite.
p. cm.
Includes bibliographical references and index.
ISBN 0 521 44130 7 (hardback)
ISBN 0 521 45923 0 (paperback)
1. Criminal liability of juristic persons. 2. Corporation law–
– Criminal provisions. I. Braithwaite, John. II. Title.
K5069.F57 1993
345'.0268–dc20
[342.5268]

A catalogue record of this book is available from the British Library.

ISBN 0 521 44130 7 hardback
ISBN 0 521 45923 0 paperback

Contents

Preface

As one might expect of a work on accountability for corporate crime, this enterprise has implicated more than the usual range of suspects. Conspiracies have multiplied, much to our grateful advantage.

Five institutions especially have generously provided support during the eight years or so it has taken for this book to emerge: the University of Sydney, the Australian National University, the University of Adelaide, the American Bar Foundation, and the Max Planck Institute in Freiburg.

Colleagues at these institutions and at others where we have presented seminar papers have given us a host of useful criticisms and pointers. The same is true of legion contacts elsewhere. Whether or not they agree with central or any other parts of our argument, particular thanks are due to Patricia Apps, Ian Ayres, Valerie Braithwaite, John Byrne, Jack Coffee, Graeme Coss, Donald Cressey, Michael Detmold, John Donohue, Bernard Dunne, Paul Finn, David Fraser, Gilbert Geis, Bob Goodin, Peter Grabosky, Robert Gruner, George Hay, Jenny Hill, Michael Hill, QC, Barbara Huber, Michael Levi, Greg McCarry, Nikos Passas, Philip Pettit, Wojcieck Sadurski, Susan Shapiro, Peter Siegelman, Andrew Stewart, Tom Tyler, Diane Vaughan and our anonymous reviewers.

We also owe a great debt to hundreds of corporate executives and business regulators who have given freely of their time to discuss issues of corporate crime and accountability in which they have been involved. This book draws heavily on their contributions to several empirical projects on business regulation which have been conducted over the past decade and a half.

Heidi, Stephen, Megan and Adrian Fisse have been kind enough to assist us by providing a good deal of word-processing, computing and other support in preparing the manuscript.

Finally, we thank Robin Derricourt and Phillipa McGuinness of Cambridge University Press and Kaye Quittner, freelance editor, for their good natured and quiet efficiency at all times.

Brent Fisse
University of Sydney

John Braithwaite
Australian National University

Abbreviations

BCCI	Bank of Credit and Commerce International
CIA	Central Intelligence Agency (US)
CML	Colonial Mutual Life Assurance Society Ltd
DEA	Drug Enforcement Agency (US)
DPP	Director of Public Prosecutions
EC	European Community
FBI	Federal Bureau of Investigation (US)
FDA	Food and Drug Administration (US)
HBLRs	Harm-Based Liability Rules
HBLR(P)s	Penal Harm-Based Liability Rules
NSW	New South Wales (Australia)
SEC	Securities and Exchange Commission (US)
SOPs	standard operating procedures
UK	United Kingdom
US	United States

Abbreviations in Footnotes and Bibliography

ABA	American Bar Association
AC	Appeal Cases
AGPS	Australian Government Publishing Service
ALR	Australian Law Reports
ATPR	Australian Trade Practices Reporter
BNA	Bureau of National Affairs
CLR	Commonwealth Law Reports
CMLR	Common Market Law Reports
FLR	Federal Law Reports
FTC	Federal Trade Commission (US)
NJ	New Jersey
NSWLR	New South Wales Law Reports
NY	New York
NYT	*New York Times*
NZ	New Zealand
NZLR	New Zealand Law Reports
SMH	*Sydney Morning Herald*
UK	United Kingdom
US	United States
USC	US Code
VR	Victorian Reports
WSJ	*Wall Street Journal*
WSJE	*Wall Street Journal Europe*

1 Crime, Responsibility and Corporate Society

Contemporary Problems of Accountability for Corporate Crime

Two major problems of accountability confront modern industrialised societies in their attempts to control wrongdoing committed by larger scale organisations.[1] First, there is an undermining of individual accountability at the level of public enforcement measures, with corporations rather than individual personnel typically being the prime target of prosecution.[2] Prosecutors are able to take the short-cut of proceeding against corporations rather than against their more elusive personnel and so individual accountability is frequently displaced by corporate liability, which now serves as a rough-and-ready catch-all device.[3] Second, where corporations are sanctioned for offences, in theory they are supposed to react by using their internal disciplinary systems to sheet home individual accountability,[4] but the law now makes little or no attempt to ensure that such a reaction occurs.[5] The impact of

---

[1] Our central concern is the position in relation to large-scale business enterprises and governmental entities. Much of the analysis is also relevant to other kinds of organisations, including accounting and law firms; see, e.g., Schneyer, 'Professional Discipline for Law Firms'.

[2] On corporate criminal liability see generally Leigh, *The Criminal Liability of Corporations in English Law;* Brickey, *Corporate Criminal Liability;* Coffee, 'No Soul to Damn No Body to Kick'; Fisse, 'Reconstructing Corporate Criminal Law'; 'Developments in the Law—Corporate Crime'. As to individual criminal liability for conduct performed on behalf of corporations, see generally Brickey, *Corporate Criminal Liability,* ch. 5; Braithwaite, *Corporate Crime in the Pharmaceutical Industry,* 318–28; Leigh, 'The Criminal Liability of Corporations and Other Groups', 274–83; Goodwin, 'Individual Liability of Agents for Corporate Crimes...'; Spiegelhoff, 'Limits on Individual Accountability for Corporate Crimes'; McVisk, 'Toward a Rational Theory of Criminal Liability for the Corporate Executive'.

[3] There is, however, the possibility of individual responsibility being enforced through civil action. See further Ming, 'The Recovery of Losses Occasioned by Corporate Crime'; Coffee, 'Beyond the Shut-Eyed Sentry'; Pennington, *Directors' Personal Liability,* ch. 8.

[4] See Elzinga and Breit, *The Antitrust Penalties,* 132–8; Posner, 'An Economic Theory of the Criminal Law', 1227–9; Kraakman, 'Corporate Liability Strategies and the Costs of Legal Controls'.

[5] See Coffee, 'Corporate Crime and Punishment', 458–60. As to the legal control over the internal affairs of corporations, see generally Shearing and Stenning, *Private Policing;* Henry, *Private Justice;* Honoré, 'Groups, Laws, and Obedience'; Kirkpatrick, 'The Adequacy of Internal Corporate Controls'.

enforcement can easily stop with a corporate pay-out of a fine or monetary penalty, not because of any socially justified departure from the traditional value of individual accountability, but rather because that is the cheapest or most self-protective course for a corporate defendant to adopt.

The central aims of this book are twofold: to examine the extent to which existing theories help to resolve the problems of non-prosecution of individuals and non-assurance of internal corporate accountability; and to advance a more responsive program for achieving accountability for corporate crime.

In discussing these issues we do not try to address the problem, formidable as it is, of responsibility for corporate crime in the context of fraud and other offences by confidence tricksters or scam merchants who abuse a position of control over their own tightly held company or who make use of a corporation as a tool for implementing their own criminal objectives.[6] The main concern in that setting is not the balance to be struck between corporate and individual responsibility, but the difficulty of taking timely and effective action against the individuals concerned.

Non-prosecution of individuals

The problem of non-prosecution of individual representatives of companies for offences committed on their behalf has become increasingly visible.[7]

The problem of non-prosecution of individual persons implicated in corporate crime was highlighted by the Hutton affair[8] in the United States (US). E. F. Hutton and Co., a brokerage firm, engaged in a widespread fraudulent scheme in which its bank accounts were overdrawn by up to $US270 million a day without triggering debits for interest; approximately 400 banks were defrauded of $US8 million. E. F. Hutton and Co. pleaded guilty to 2,000

---

[6] As described in, e.g., Copetas, *Metal Men*; Stewart, *Den of Thieves*; Pizzo, Fricker and Muolo, *Inside Job*; Freiberg, 'Abuse of the Corporate Form'. Consider also takeover power-plays, as graphically illustrated by Burrough and Helyar, *Barbarians at the Gate*.

[7] See Grabosky and Braithwaite, *Of Manners Gentle*, 189; Cohen et al., 'Organizations as Defendants in Federal Court'; US, National Commission on Reform of Federal Criminal Laws, 1 Working Papers, 180; Green, Moore and Wasserstein, *The Closed Enterprise System*, 167; Clinard and Yeager, *Corporate Crime*, ch. 12; Geis, 'The Heavy Electrical Equipment Antitrust Cases of 1961'; Smith, *Corporations in Crisis*, chs 5–6; Watkins, 'Electrical Equipment Antitrust Cases'; Mills, 'Perspectives on Corporate Crime and the Evasive Individual'; Fisse, 'Criminal Law and Consumer Protection', 183; Spiegelhoff, 'Limitations on Individual Accountability for Corporate Crimes'; Alexander, 'Crime in the Suites'; 'White-Collar Crime Booming Again', *NYT*, 9 June 1985, S. 3, 1, 6; 'Bhopal Disaster Spurs Debate over Usefulness of Criminal Sanctions in Industrial Accidents', *WSJ*, 7 Jan. 1985, 18; Safire, 'On Sutton and Hutton'.

There are of course numerous cases where individual officers and employees have been held criminally liable. See, e.g., *Guthrie v Robertson* (1986) ATPR 40–744; 'Anthony Bryant and Directors Fined $96,000', *SMH*, 15 April 1987, 38; Tundermann, 'Personal Liability for Corporate Directors, Officers, Employees and Controlling Shareholders under State and Federal Environmental Laws'. For the notable Film Recovery Systems case, see *Los Angeles Times*, 15 Sept. 1985, 1; *NYT*, 15 June 1985, 1.

[8] See US, HR, Committee on the Judiciary, Subcommittee on Crime, *E. F. Hutton Mail and Wire Fraud Case;* Carpenter and Feloni, *The Fall of the House of Hutton*; Safire, 'On Sutton and Hutton'.

felony counts of mail and wire fraud and, under the plea agreement, agreed to pay a $US2.75 million fine and to reimburse the banks. No individuals were prosecuted despite the admission of the Justice Department that two Hutton executives were responsible for the fraud 'in a criminal sense'.[9] The explanation given by the US Assistant Attorney General was this:

> In assessing the manner in which this case ought to be handled, our prosecutors started from the proposition that individuals ought to be held personally responsible for their criminal misconduct. This is our normal policy from which we deviate only when faced with a compelling reason to make an exception. Pursuing in court in this case the known individual authors of the swindle would have had some merit, but not at the expense of foregoing the opportunity to dictate the key terms of and seize without delay this extraordinary settlement. To prosecute the individuals would have required us to drop the settlement in favor of a protracted court fight that would have taken years to complete. That was the choice.[10]

This explanation was severely criticised by the Subcommittee on Crime of the House of Representatives Committee on the Judiciary.[11] In the opinion of the Subcommittee:

> The Department has, in prosecuting other cases, shown great tenacity and willingness to ignore cost considerations and significant adverse odds. Yet in Hutton, the prosecutors seemed overwhelmed by the fact that discovery would be time-consuming, ... that the case would be complex, and that it might take months to try. ... The Hutton plea contributed to a decrease in public confidence in the fairness of the criminal justice system—a pervasive feeling that defendants with enough money and resources can 'buy' their way out of trouble.[12]

There have been other conspicuous compromises of individual accountability in the US.[13] One of the more glaring was the deal made in 1981 to settle the McDonnell Douglas bribery affair concerning sales to Pakistani Airlines.[14]

---

[9] *Time*, 10 June 1985, 53; *NYT*, 13 Sept. 1985, 1. In Hong Kong's $US21 billion counterpart to the E. F. Hutton scam, the targets of prosecution were six individual conspirators, and the financial institutions involved; see *WSJE*, 11 Oct. 1985, 11. Consider, by contrast, the refusal of the US Justice Department in the early 1970s to accept a plea of guilty by Abbott Laboratories in exchange for the dropping of charges against five of the company's executives; see Braithwaite, *Corporate Crime in the Pharmaceutical Industry*, 117.

[10] US, HR, Committee on the Judiciary, Subcommittee on Crime, *E. F. Hutton Mail and Wire Fraud Case*, Hearings, Pt. 1, 99th Congress, 1st Sess., 1985, 643–4.

[11] US, HR, Committee on the Judiciary, Subcommittee on Crime, *E. F. Hutton Mail and Wire Fraud Case*, Report, 99th Congress, 2nd Sess., 1986, 159–62.

[12] Ibid., 161.

[13] The E. F. Hutton case is hardly an isolated episode in US enforcement practice. See US National Commission on Reform of Federal Criminal Laws, 1 Working Papers, 180 (referring to widespread compromise of individual responsibility in plea agreements); Kraakman, 'Corporate Liability Strategies and the Costs of Legal Controls', 857–98, 858–9 (discussing 'iron law' of tort and criminal liability that '[l]iability risks, if unchannelled, ordinarily attach to the legal entity (the corporation) rather than to its officers, employees, or agents'); Green, Moore and Wasserstein, *The Closed Enterprise System*, 167 (Antitrust Division preference for indicting corporations); Orland, 'Reflections on Corporate Crime', 513; Fisse and Braithwaite, *The Impact of Publicity on Corporate Offenders*, 45, ch. 14; *United States v FMC Corporation*, Criminal No. 80–91, US District Court, ED Pa., 1980.

[14] See generally Fisse and Braithwaite, *The Impact of Publicity on Corporate Offenders*, ch. 14.

Fraud and conspiracy charges against four top McDonnell Douglas Corp executives were dropped in return for a guilty plea by the company to charges of fraud and making false statements. Under the plea agreement, McDonnell Douglas incurred a fine of $US55,000 and agreed to pay $US1.2 million in civil damages. This agreement was entered into at a meeting between the US Assistant Attorney General and representatives of the company. The prosecutors in the case (who had not been invited to the meeting and who subsequently resigned from the Justice Department) were of the view that the liability of the four executives had been 'bought off' by the settlement.[15]

Contrary to the orthodox line of prosecutors that their priority is to proceed against individuals and with corporations only secondary targets,[16] the statistics reveal a significant incidence of cases where individuals have not been prosecuted or, in the event of prosecution, have not been held liable.[17] In Clinard and Yeager's study of the incidence of corporate crime among large companies in the US in the late 1970s, it was found that in only 1.5 per cent of all enforcement actions was a corporate officer held liable.[18] Moreover, in addition to the E. F. Hutton case and other well-known instances of failure to proceed against individuals, any corporate crime-watcher's pile of newspaper clippings will contain numerous reports of cases where enforcement is directed at corporate entities rather than against their personnel.[19]

[15] Ibid., 163.
[16] Fine, 'The Philosophy of Enforcement'; Ayers, *The Processing and Prosecution of White Collar Crime by the States' Attorney Generals*, 61–2; BNA, 'White-Collar Crime: A Survey of Law', 369–70, n. 1719; Groening, *The Modern Corporate Manager*, 71, 239–40. Jail sentences are usually regarded as being far more effective as a deterrent than fines against corporations. See, e.g., Baker, 'To Indict or Not to Indict', 414. But see Elzinga and Breit, *The Antitrust Penalties*, ch. 3.
[17] See Cohen et al., 'Organizations as Defendants in Federal Court' (in 49 per cent of 1122 cases involving organisational convictions there was no individual co-defendant, and in 24 per cent of the cases there was a single individual co-defendant); Cohen, 'Corporate Crime and Punishment'; Cohen, 'Environmental Crime and Punishment'; American Bar Association, Final Report, *Collateral Consequences of Convictions of Organizations*, 87 (in 60 per cent of 73 cases surveyed some individual within the corporation was charged as well); Clinard and Yeager, *Corporate Crime*, 272; Whiting, 'Antitrust and the Corporate Executive', 986; Lewis, 'A Proposal to Restructure Sanctions under the Occupational Safety and Health Act', 1449–50; Dershowitz, 'Increasing Community Control over Corporate Crime', 291–3; Schrager and Short, 'Toward a Sociology of Organizational Crime' 410; Goff and Reasons, *Corporate Crime in Canada*, 94–5; Grabosky and Braithwaite, *Of Manners Gentle*.
[18] Clinard and Yeager, *Corporate Crime*, 272.
[19] See, e.g., *WSJE*, 29 Oct. 1985, 2 (plea agreement with Rockwell International Corporation *re* defence contract overcharging); *Asian Wall Street Journal*, 8 Jan. 1985, 5 (charge of involuntary manslaughter under Michigan law against General Dynamics but not corporate officials); 'The Complex Case of the US vs. Southland: To What Extent are Companies Liable for Their Employees' Crimes?', *Business Week*, 21 Nov. 1983, 108–11 (prosecution of Southland questioned given involvement of powerful top officials in offences alleged against company); *Financial Review*, 29 Aug. 1985, 27 (prosecution of Eli Lilly and Co. alone); *WSJ*, 30 March 1984, 15 (charges against officials of Hartz Mountain Corp. dropped when company pleaded guilty); *WSJE*, 10 Oct. 1985, 13 (US SEC proceedings against Kidder Peabody and its director of operations for allegedly misusing $US145 million in customer securities); 'Safety Agency Seeks Record Fine Against USX for Job Violations', *NYT*, 2 Nov. 1989, A10; 'Rockwell Pleads Guilty to Waste Dumping, Blasts US', *Los Angeles Times*, 27 March 1992, A14.

Non-prosecution of corporate executives is also prevalent in many other countries. In Canada, the pattern of enforcement under the Competition Act 1986 has been heavily oriented toward corporate defendants,[20] although Criminal Code offences are usually enforced against individuals.[21] Corporations are the targets of antitrust law enforcement in the European Community (EC).[22] In England, the conventional wisdom is that corporate criminal liability is of little practical significance as compared with individual criminal liability,[23] but there have been numerous cases in which companies alone have been prosecuted.[24] Moreover, the reputation of the English criminal justice system for holding individuals to account was blackened by the so-called Oilgate scandal surrounding the failure of the authorities to prosecute any of the persons responsible for the planned and persistent evasion by British Petroleum and Shell Oil of the British embargo on exporting oil to Southern Rhodesia.[25]

Systematic data are available from Australia where a study was made of the enforcement policies of 96 major business regulatory agencies.[26] Top management of each agency was asked if it had 'a policy or philosophy on whether it is better to prosecute the company itself as opposed to those individuals who are responsible within the company'. Twenty agencies said that they preferred to target the individuals responsible; for 41 the preferred target was the corporation;[27] five said they consistently tried to proceed against both

---

[20] See Goff and Reasons, *Corporate Crime in Canada*, 117–19; Stanbury, 'Public Policy Toward Individuals Involved in Competition Law Offences in Canada'.

[21] Canada, Law Reform Commission, Working Paper 16, *Criminal Responsibility for Group Action*, 33.

[22] See, e.g., 'EC Commission Sets Fines on Shippers in Africa Cartel', *WSJ*, 2 April 1992, 3; *Musique Diffusion Francaise SA, C. Melchers & Co., Pioneer Electronic (Europe) NV and Pioneer High Fidelity (GB) Limited v E. C. Commission* [1983] 3 CMLR 221; *ECS/AKSO* [1986] 3 CMLR 273; *Fanuc Ltd. and Siemens AG* [1988] 4 CMLR 945; *Eurofix Limited and Bauco (UK) Limited v Hilti AG* [1989] 4 CMLR 677; *Melkunie Holland BV* [1989] 4 CMLR 853; *Re the Welded Steel Mesh Cartel* [1991] 4 CMLR 13.

[23] See Williams, *Criminal Law*, 865; Hill, 'Recent Developments in Corporate Criminal Law in England'.

[24] See, e.g., *Tesco Supermarkets Ltd. v Nattrass* [1972] AC 153; *Alphacell Ltd. v Woodward* [1972] AC 824; *R v St. Margarets Trust Ltd.* [1958] 1 WLR 522; Carson, 'White-Collar Crime and the Enforcement of Factory Legislation'.

[25] See Bailey, *The Oilgate Scandal*; Bingham and Gray, *Report on the Supply of Petroleum and Petroleum Products to Rhodesia*; Box, *Power, Crime, and Mystification*, 46. For a sympathetic account of the decision of the DPP and Attorney General not to prosecute anyone, see Edwards, *The Attorney General, Politics and the Public Interest*, 325–34, which seems to turn British justice on its head. If Edwards' position is accepted, companies and their officers can expect not to be prosecuted provided that they operate via complicated organisational structures (preferably with the dirty work done through foreign subsidiaries), and procure several ministers or high-ranking members of the public service to condone their behaviour. For law officers of the Crown, the message seems to be that the more pervasive and intricate the deviance and corruption, and hence the more difficult the task of investigation and trial, the more justifiable the exercise of the discretion not to prosecute. Compare *Financial Times*, 11 Nov. 1985, 2 (magistrates in Palermo charge 475 Mafia suspects).

[26] See Grabosky and Braithwaite, *Of Manners Gentle*.

[27] For example, the Australian Tax Office. For a spokesman's description of the Office's policy and practice, B. Conwell, as quoted in Freiberg, 'Enforcement Discretion and Taxation Offences', 86–7.

the corporation and personnel concerned; and 30 had no policy or philosophy on the matter. The 20 agencies with a preference for individual liability were mostly in the areas of mine safety (where legislation often focuses liability on managers and supervisors)[28] and in maritime safety and maritime oil pollution regulation (where there is a tradition of viewing the ship's captain as the preferred target).[29] Thirty-eight of the 96 agencies had not proceeded against an individual during the previous three years (1981–84).

De facto immunity from individual criminal liability for corporate crime is also prevalent in Continental jurisdictions. In Germany, where the principle of individual responsibility for crime is so firmly entrenched that corporations are not subject to criminal liability,[30] the difficulty of prosecuting corporate officials is well recognised.[31] This has come about partly as a result of the Flick bribery case.[32] Representatives of Flick were alleged to have engaged in an extensive campaign of political bribery but, despite much protest in the media, only one person from the company was prosecuted. Memories go back to the Thalidomide prosecution in 1965, when nine executives of Chemie Grünenthal were indicted for involuntary manslaughter; after long delays in the trial process, the prosecution was eventually abandoned when the company paid $US31 million in civil compensation.[33] Today in Germany, administrative sanctions have become a mainstay of corporate regulation, especially in antitrust and environmental protection[34] and, where administrative sanctions are used, the usual targets are corporations, not individuals. The same dependence on administrative sanctions is apparent in EC enforcement, where total reliance is placed on corporate liability.[35] A stronger commitment to individual responsibility for organisational wrongdoing was often claimed of the old communist jurisdictions,[36] but it is unclear whether this was more

---

[28] See Coal Mines Regulation Act 1982 (NSW), ss. 160–2.
[29] See, e.g., Taylor, 'Criminal Liabilities of Ships' Masters'; Taylor, 'The Criminal Liability of Ships' Masters'; Warbrick and Sullivan, 'Ship Routeing Schemes and the Criminal Liability of the Master'.
[30] See Jescheck, *Lehrbuch des Strafrechts* 180–2.
[31] Muller, *Die Stellung der juristischen Person im Ordnungswidrigkeitenrecht*. In antitrust enforcement, the priority is to impose liability on individuals but the practice almost invariably is to impose liability on corporations.
[32] See generally Jung and Krause, *Die Stamokap-Republik der Flicks*; Horster-Philipps, *Im Schatten des Grossen Geldes*; Kilz and Preuss, *Flick: Die Gekaufte Republik*.
[33] See Knightley et al., *Suffer the Children;* Sjostrom and Nilsson, *Thalidomide and the Power of the Drug Companies*.
[34] See, e.g., Tiedemann, 'Antitrust Law and Criminal Law Policy in Western Europe'.
[35] See Kerse, *EEC Antitrust Procedure*; 'EC Commission Sets Fines on Shippers in Africa Cartel', *WSJ*, 2 April 1992, 3.
[36] In East Germany, for instance, administrative sanctions were used against state economic enterprises and individuals, with the emphasis on the latter. This was primarily because of the value attached to individual accountability, coupled with the relative ease of locating responsibility in a tightly structured environment where lines of accountability were clearly drawn. There was also a reluctance to use monetary penalties against state enterprises because of the risk of inflicting overspills on workers: Professor Erich Buchholz, Institute of Criminal Law and Criminology, Humboldt University, Berlin, personal communication, 30 Oct. 1985. See further Conklin, *'Illegal But Not Criminal'*, 121–2.

the official line than a reflection of practice.[37] In environmental enforcement, some Eastern European countries made extensive use of administrative penalties imposed on the enterprise.[38]

At some level of abstraction government agencies often assert a policy to proceed against individuals as a matter of priority, but such policies are generally a mystification. The frequent non-prosecution of corporate officers in practice is our concern, together with the implications of adopting a policy that is more honoured in the breach than in the observance. We do not suggest that prosecutors have no justification for targeting corporations rather than individuals. On the contrary, there are many reasons, theoretical as well as practical, why there is often little or no choice but to focus on corporate defendants.[39]

There are of course numerous instances where corporate officers have been prosecuted, often successfully.[40] One notable US example is the widely publicised prosecution and conviction for murder of three executives of an Illinois company, Film Recovery Systems, whose operations had resulted in the cyanide poisoning of a worker.[41] In this case, however, the company was a small concern and it was much easier for the prosecution to obtain incriminating evidence against the top managers than is typically the position where a large- or medium-sized corporation is involved. Another well-known English example is that of Ernest Saunders, the managing director of Guinness plc, who was convicted and sentenced to jail for offences relating to the manipulation of Guinness share prices to thwart a takeover by the Distillers Group. The main actors in this skulduggery were easy to identify; as in most cases of defensive measures against takeovers, relatively few people were in a position to call the shots.[42]

Compare these cases with Union Carbide's Bhopal disaster in India in 1984:[43] investigating exactly what happened at all relevant points down the

---

[37] For instance, in the former state of Yugoslavia it has been said that, often 'no one is responsible' for violations committed on behalf of economic enterprises: Professor Ljabo Baucon, Law School, University of Ljubljana, personal communication, 3 Oct. 1985. See also Schelling, 'Command and Control', 84–5.

[38] Sand, 'The Socialist Response'; Johnson and Brown, *Cleaning Up Europe's Waters*; Anderson et al., *Environmental Incentives*, 49.

[39] See, e.g., US House of Representatives, *White-Collar Crime* (testimony of Robert Fiske).

[40] See, e.g., Ermann and Lundman, *Corporate Deviance* (1st edn), 44 (Equity Funding prosecutions); Goldberg, 'Corporate Officer Liability for Federal Environmental Statute Violations'; Cohen, 'Environmental Crime and Punishment'; Schneider, 'Criminal Enforcement of Federal Water Pollution Laws in an Era of Deregulation', 667; *WSJE*, 13 Nov. 1985, 13 (charges against employees of Bindley Western); *Washington Post*, 3 Dec. 1985, 1 (General Dynamics Corp and four present or former executives indicted *re* defence contract fraud); 'Keating is Sentenced to 10 Years for Defrauding S. & L. Customers', *NYT*, 11 April 1992, 1.

[41] *Los Angeles Times*, 15 Sept. 1985, 1; *NYT*, 15 June 1985, 1. The convictions were quashed on appeal and a new trial ordered: *Illinois v O'Neill, Film Recovery Systems, Inc. and others* (1990) 55 NE 2d 1090.

[42] See further Hobson, *The Pride of Lucifer*.

[43] See, e.g., Muchlinski, 'The Bhopal Case'; Baxi, *Mass Disasters and Multinational Liability;* 'Evidence from Bhopal', *Multinational Monitor*, July 3, 1985, 1–7; *SMH*, 1 April 1985, 6.

company's lines of accountability for production plant safety would require a sizeable task force of investigators, and even then the location of individual responsibility would not necessarily be clear.[44] The same is true in many other contexts, some of the more obvious of which include the operations of the Bank of Credit and Commerce International (BCCI),[45] the savings and loan scandal in the US,[46] the deceptive practices of numerous government contractors in the US defence industry,[47] the Zeebrugge ferry disaster,[48] and the insurance-selling scam perpetrated by insurance companies against Australian Aboriginal people in North Queensland.[49]

Non-assurance of internal accountability within corporations

The second major problem of accountability for corporate crime is non-assurance that sanctions against corporations will result in due allocation of responsibility as a matter of internal disciplinary control.

In theory, the type of sanction usually deployed against corporations—the fine or monetary penalty—is supposed to pressure corporate defendants into taking internal disciplinary action.[50] An initial difficulty in some countries, including England, Australia and Canada, is that corporate criminal liability depends on the 'directing mind' principle,[51] which in practice means that large corporations are virtually insulated from criminal liability for serious offences.[52] This was in fact what happened in the Zeebrugge ferry case,[53] where the prosecution in England failed largely because of the insuperable obstacle of establishing that a directing mind had been criminally negligent. Putting aside that obstacle, however, there is no guarantee that monetary punishment will trigger any form of internal accountability.[54] This is a dark side

---

[44] See, e.g., *WSJE*, 8 Nov. 1985, 13 (claim by Jackson Browning, Union Carbide's vice-president in charge of health, safety and environmental affairs, that the disaster was caused by a reaction set off when 120–240 gallons of water were introduced into a storage tank by people whose identity is unknown, and that 'We have all but ruled out anything but a deliberate act'); *Financial Times*, 11 Nov. 1985, 3 (accusations that the disaster was caused by a cyanide gas leak). See generally 'Bhopal Disaster Spurs Debate over Usefulness of Criminal Sanctions in Industrial Accidents', *WSJ*, 7 Jan. 1985, 18; Walter and Richards, 'Corporate Counsel's Role in Risk Minimization'.
[45] See Chapter 7 in this book.
[46] See Mayer, *The Greatest Ever Bank Robbery*; Adams, *The Big Fix*.
[47] See Shirk, Greenberg and Dawson, 'Truth or Consequences'.
[48] See Chapter 7 in this book.
[49] See Chapter 7 in this book.
[50] See generally Posner, *Antitrust Law*, 225–8; Fisse, 'The Social Policy of Corporate Criminal Responsibility', 382–6; Stone, 'The Place of Enterprise Liability in the Control of Corporate Conduct', 29.
[51] *Tesco Supermarkets Ltd v Nattrass* [1972] AC 153.
[52] See Fisse, *Howard's Criminal Law*, 600–4.
[53] See *R v Stanley and others*, CCC No 900160, 19 Oct 1990; *R v HM Coroner for East Kent, ex parte Spooner* (1989) 88 Cr App R 10. Compare Bergman, 'Recklessness in the Boardroom'.
[54] See Coffee, 'Corporate Crime and Punishment', 458–60.

of corporate self-regulation about which little is known by outsiders.[55] A high degree of trust has been reposed in corporations to maintain internal discipline.[56] It is readily apparent, however, that companies have strong incentives not to undertake extensive disciplinary action. In particular, a disciplinary program may be disruptive,[57] embarrassing for those exercising managerial control,[58] encouraging for whistle-blowers,[59] or hazardous in the event of civil litigation against the company or its officers. Sometimes these incentives may be veiled by the claim that the problem has been sufficiently investigated and resolved by public enforcement action.[60] These factors have been discussed in the literature, but the law has failed to provide adequate means for ensuring that corporate defendants are sentenced in a manner directly geared to achieving internal accountability.[61]

The classic illustration of the ease with which corporate defendants can pay a fine and walk away from internal disciplinary action was the reaction of the Westinghouse Corporation upon being convicted and sentenced for its role in the US heavy electrical equipment price-fixing conspiracies of 1959–61.[62] Westinghouse decided against disciplinary action, partly on the ground of a watered-down version of the defence which failed in the

---

[55] For one empirical study see American Bar Association, Final Report, *Collateral Consequences of Convictions of Organizations*, 107–8 (according to the unverified responses of companies convicted and sentenced for federal offences over a two-year period, 41 per cent had since replaced senior management, 29 per cent had replaced middle management, 16 per cent had improved their peer review process, and 10 per cent had fired everyone responsible). See also Fisse and Braithwaite, *The Impact of Publicity on Corporate Offenders*, 60–1, 121, 154–5, 166–7, 172, 192–4, 209, 224, 234. Occasionally the responses become well known: see US, HR, Committee on the Judiciary, Subcommittee on Crime, *E. F. Hutton Mail and Wire Fraud Case*, Report, 99th Congress, 2nd Sess., 1986, 156–8. This report berated E. F. Hutton for failing to respond adequately to the extensive fraud committed on its behalf; ibid., 150–5, 159.

[56] See further Shapiro, 'Policing Trust'.

[57] Consider, e.g., the internal disciplinary inquiry described in McCloy, *The Great Oil Spill*.

[58] See, e.g., *Nation*, 18 Feb. 1961, 129 (editorial criticism of General Electric's top management after the company undertook disciplinary action against employees involved in the electrical equipment conspiracies).

[59] Coffee, 'Corporate Crime and Punishment', 459; Braithwaite, *Corporate Crime in the Pharmaceutical Industry*, 402.

[60] See Coffee, 'Corporate Crime and Punishment', 458–9. Such a claim was made by Westinghouse when it refused to take disciplinary action in the wake of the American electrical equipment price-fixing conspiracy prosecutions.

[61] Internal discipline is however one of a number of factors a court may take into account when determining sentence. See *Trade Practices Commission v Stihl Chain Saws* (Aust.) *Pty. Ltd.* (1978) ATPR 40-091; *Trade Practices Commission v Dunlop Australia Ltd.* (1980) ATPR 40-167; Freiberg, 'Monetary Penalties under the Trade Practices Act 1974 (Cth)', 13; 18 USC s. 3572(a)(4) (which provides that, when imposing a fine on a corporation, a court is to consider 'any measures taken by the organization to discipline its employees or agents responsible for the offense or to insure against a recurrence of such offense'); Coffee and Whitbread, 'The Convicted Corporation'.

[62] See Walton and Cleveland, *Corporations on Trial*, 103. The other companies involved, with the exception of General Electric, also refrained from internal disciplinary action. See Herling, *The Great Price Conspiracy*, 311.

Nuremberg trials: 'anybody involved was acting not for personal gain, but in what he thought was the best interests of the company'.[63] By contrast, the internal discipline by General Electric in response to the the heavy electrical equipment conspiracies was relatively severe.[64] All persons implicated in violations of corporate antitrust policy were disciplined by substantial demotion long before any of them were convicted. Those who were later convicted were asked to resign because 'the Board of Directors determined that the damaging and relentless publicity attendant upon their sentencing rendered it both in their interest and the company's that they pursue their careers elsewhere'.[65]

Another prominent example was the refusal of American Airlines to blame publicly any individuals within the company when it incurred civil penalties of $US1.5 million for violations of Federal Aviation Administration aircraft maintenance requirements. One of the violations had been committed by flying an 'unairworthy' plane from which an engine had fallen when struck by a piece of ice from an unrepaired leaky toilet.[66] A spokesman for the company said that no one had been fired as a result and indeed no one could be identified as accountable for the maintenance breakdowns because 'management systems' had been involved.[67] As Colman McCarthy observed, the buck stopped with the corporation:

> Under this general absolution, we are asked to believe that no living, breathing humans were responsible for designing and maintaining the planes. Nor was it the failure of any live human employees to fix the leaky toilet that caused the engine to fly off over New Mexico. That was a 'design malfunction.'
> This playing down of individual accountability is in line with the comparative puniness of the fine. The FAA [Federal Aviation Administration] has collected $1.5 million from a company that had operating revenues of $5.3 billion in 1984 and record profits of $234 million for the first half of 1985. Not a dime came out of the paychecks of the invisible managers.[68]

Efforts were made by American Airlines to revise its maintenance procedures and to expand its maintenance team,[69] but a maintenance system without accountability for non-compliance is unjustifiably dangerous, particularly in so cost-sensitive a business as running an airline. Thus, C. O. Miller, a former director of the transportation board's aviation safety bureau, questioned the strength of American's resolve to run a tight airship:

> There's nothing wrong with trying to save money, but if cost-cutting is the only message that comes through to your employees, then you're going to have people cut corners and have the kind of things that happened at American.[70]

[63] Ibid.
[64] Ibid., 96–101; Fisse and Braithwaite, *The Impact of Publicity on Corporate Offenders*, 192–3.
[65] US Senate, *Administered Prices* 17671–2.
[66] McCarthy, 'American: It's a Flying Shame', *WSJE*, 7 Nov. 1985, 1.
[67] McCarthy, 'American: It's a Flying Shame'.
[68] Ibid.
[69] *WSJE*, 7 Nov. 1985, 20.
[70] Ibid.

Non-assurance of internal accountability within corporations is hardly a uniquely American legal phenomenon. A telling Australian illustration is *Trade Practices Commission v Pye Industries Sales Pty. Ltd.*,[71] a decision of the Australian Federal Court. Pye was found to have committed resale price maintenance in violation of the Australian Trade Practices Act, and the court adjourned the matter for sentence. At the sentencing hearing the court was able to conclude that, at the time of violation, 'there was an almost total lack of supervision or interest by the board of directors in the conduct of their management and executives in relation to resale price maintenance'. However, the court was uninformed as to the nature of the company's disciplinary and other responses to the violation;[72] the company itself had not come forward with relevant evidence, and the evidence that had emerged from the trial related to the issue of whether a violation had been committed. The court, after describing the violation as 'ruthless', and yet having made no finding as to the adequacy or otherwise of the company's disciplinary reactions, imposed a penalty of $A120,000.

The extent to which corporations fail to insist on accountability in response to being fined is now impossible to say. Empirical research in this area has been limited[73] and some companies refuse to divulge what has or has not been done to punish insiders.[74] This dark side of corporate self-regulation usually becomes visible only if a company is forced out into the open by public pressure[75] or by threats from enforcement agencies.[76] Thus, the E. F. Hutton scandal led the company to make an independent internal investigation, which was conducted by Griffin Bell, a former US Attorney General. The subsequent report found 15 individuals accountable, and recommended fines of between $US25,000 and $US50,000 for six branch managers, as well as periods of probation. Hutton adopted the report and released it publicly, thereby prompting two top officials to resign.[77]

Sporadic attempts have been made by the law to enter the black box of corporations by means of non-monetary sanctions aimed directly at achieving effective internal accountability.[78] Mandatory injunctions have been used for this purpose from time to time, most notably by the US Securities and

---

[71] ATPR 40–089 (1978).
[72] A consideration plainly relevant to sentence: see references *supra* n. 61.
[73] See, e.g., Fisse and Braithwaite, *The Impact of Publicity on Corporate Offenders*, 60–1, 121, 154–5, 166–7, 172, 192–4, 209, 224, 234.
[74] For example, ibid., 166–7.
[75] See, e.g., 'Lloyd's Expels 2 Members for Reinsurance Payments', *WSJE*, 13 Nov. 1985, 9; 'Lloyd's Unravels Deals which Siphoned Millions of Pounds', *Financial Times*, 13 Nov. 1985, 10.
[76] Inducing internal accountability by threat was partly the strategy adopted by the US SEC in its Voluntary Disclosure Program in the bribery crisis of the mid-1970s. However, that program did not require publication of full details of internal accountability for bribery payments but merely generic disclosure of the amount and purpose of questionable payments. See US, SEC, *Report of the Securities and Exchange Commission on Questionable and Illegal Foreign Payments*, 6–7; Herlihy and Levine, 'Corporate Crisis, 584–94. See generally Wolff, 'Voluntary Disclosure Programs'.
[77] See *NYT*, 6 Sept. 1985, 1.
[78] See C. D. Stone, *Where the Law Ends*, 189, 192, 205–6.

Exchange Commission (SEC) in its campaign against bribery in the mid-1970s.[79] A number of corporations were required to establish special review committees for the purposes of conducting investigations and initiating appropriate internal action. The most celebrated example is that of the Gulf Oil Corporation, a special review committee of which prepared a 298-page report detailing the misuse of $US12 million for payment to US and foreign officials, and the role played by various Gulf Oil officials.[80]

Why Accountability for Corporate Crime is Important

These problems of accountability are hardly pin-pricks;[81] they sap the social control of corporate crime. Individual accountability has long been regarded as indispensable to social control, at least in Western societies,[82] but today is more the exception than the rule in the context of offences committed on behalf of larger-scale organisations.[83] Given the gravity with which corporate crime is increasingly perceived,[84] this is a remarkable state of affairs and one which awaits responsive solutions.[85]

The danger of 'headlessness'[86] in systems of collective social accountability has repeatedly been stressed. Recollect John Stuart Mill's advice, as given in *Considerations on Representative Government:*

---

[79] See Herlihy and Levine, 'Corporate Crisis'; Coffee, 'Beyond the Shut-Eyed Sentry', 1115-17.
[80] McCloy, *The Great Oil Spill.*
[81] Compare with Bierce, *The Devil's Dictionary* (1958), where 'corporation' is defined as 'an ingenious device for obtaining individual profit without individual responsibility' and 'responsibility' as 'a detachable burden easily shifted to the shoulders of God, Fate, Fortune, Luck or one's neighbour'.
[82] See further French, *Individual and Collective Responsibility*; Allport, *Institutional Behavior*, 219–39; Fauconnet, *La Responsibilité*; Sunga, *Individual Responsibility in International Law for Serious Human Rights Violations*; Lewis, *Uncertain Judgment*, 185–9; Komarow, 'Individual Responsibility under International Law'; Hessler, 'Command Responsibility for War Crimes'; Iseman, 'The Criminal Responsibility of Corporate Officials for Pollution of the Environment'. But see Clark, *The Japanese Company*, 130 ('in the West decisionmaking is presented as individualistic until adversity proves it collective').
[83] This is not to deny the growing frequency of prosecutions of individuals in the context of fraudulent activities performed under corporate cover.
[84] See further Grabosky, Braithwaite and Wilson, 'The Myth of Community Tolerance Toward White-Collar Crime'; Cullen, Maakestad, and Cavender, *Corporate Crime under Attack*, chs 1–2; Cullen, Link and Polanzi, 'The Seriousness of Crime Revisited; Kramer, 'Corporate Criminality'; Koprowicz, 'Corporate Criminal Liability for Workplace Hazards'. See generally Coleman, *The Asymmetric Society.*
[85] See Australia, Senate Standing Committee on Constitutional Affairs, *The Social and Fiduciary Duties and Obligations of Company Directors* (1989), Recommendation 21 (calling for a review of the mix of individual and corporate liability). The issue is not addressed, in e.g., Australia, Commonwealth Director of Public Prosecutions, *Prosecution Policy of the Commonwealth* (1990). Compare with Canada, Law Reform Commission, Working Paper 16, *Criminal Responsibility for Group Action* (1976), 33–5.
[86] Geyelin, 'Under Reagan, a Dismaying Trend to "Headlessness" '. See also Day and Klein, *Accountabilities*; Kafka, *The Castle*; Lewis, 'The Non-Moral Notion of Collective Responsibility'.

As a general rule, every executive function, whether superior or subordinate, should be the appointed duty of some given individual. It should be apparent to all the world, who did everything, and through whose default anything was left undone. Responsibility is null, when nobody knows who is responsible. Nor, even when real, can it be divided without being weakened. To maintain it at its highest, there must be one person who receives the whole praise of what is well done, the whole blame of what is ill.[87]

Mill's concern has often been echoed by politicians, not only in the context of ministerial or administrative responsibility, but also in relation to criminal liability. In a message to Congress on 20 January 1914, President Wilson severely criticised the failure of the Sherman Act 1890 to strike at what he took to be the real villains behind antitrust offences:

We ought to see to it, and the judgement of practical and sagacious men of affairs everywhere would applaud us if we do see to it, that penalties and punishments should fall not upon the business itself, to its confusion and interruption, but upon the individuals who use the instrumentalities of business to do things which public policy and sound business practice condemn. Every act of business is done at the command or upon the initiative of some ascertainable person or group of persons. These should be held individually responsible, and the punishment should fall upon them, not upon the business organization of which they make illegal use.[88]

When the Supreme Court in *United States v Park* (1975)[89] imposed a demanding standard of care and supervision upon corporate executives under the Food, Drug and Cosmetic Act 1938, some commentators saw this as the coming of a much-needed new deal in personal accountability:

The just allocation of fault is an essential ingredient in building a credible, healthy society. The growth of giant corporations with their multiple layers of bureaucratic responsibility has significantly complicated the critical process of fixing blame. The faceless quality of contemporary bureaucracies has had an important, though largely unexplored, impact on law enforcement. Fixing responsibility on a single manager or a small group of managers has received only passing attention from law makers and law enforcers.[90]

More recently, the E. F. Hutton scandal provoked many reaffirmations of the value of individual responsibility. In the opinion of Senator Howard M. Metzenbaum, the non-prosecution of any Hutton executives meant that 'something has gone awry' at the Department of Justice. 'What kind of a department is this?' he asked. 'If you wear a white collar you don't get prosecuted.'[91] More philosophical was the reaction of Thomas Donaldson, a leading writer on business ethics:

---

[87] At 393–4.
[88] 51 Congressional Record 9074 (1914).
[89] 421 US 685 (1975).
[90] McAdams and Tower, 'Personal Accountability in the Corporate Sector', 67.
[91] *NYT*, 13 Sept. 1985, 11.

What we're seeing, as corporations get larger and larger, is a breakdown in the lines of accountability. We've created some superstructures in business that are wildly complex, and we haven't tamed them yet.[92]

Perennial as the hope of individual accountability has been, the law has turned a blind eye to reality.[93] The way in which legal liability is structured today often confers a de facto immunity on corporate managers, who are typically shielded by a corporate entity which takes the rap. This is a fundamental difficulty of the deepest social significance.[94]

If the corporate form is used to obscure and deflect responsibility, whether intentionally or unintentionally, the growth of corporate activities in industrialised societies poses an acute risk of escalating breakdown of social control. This breakdown is already patent in domains like tax compliance[95] and toxic waste regulation.[96] Buck-passing is increasingly fostered not only by a burgeoning corporate birthrate (measured by new certificates of incorporation)[97] but also by tendencies for the majority of the population to work in corporations of increasing size and complexity.[98] A corporate society finds it easier to hide its skeletons in closets, and in a big corporation the closets are more numerous and more obscure.

Unless corrected, this danger is bound to increase because, as Christopher Stone has pointed out, there is a growing tendency in modern society for things to be done by and through corporations:

> When something goes wrong, whether a toxic spill or a swindle, chances are good that a corporation will be implicated ... the design of social institutions, once focused almost exclusively on how to deal with individual persons acting on their own account, has to be reconsidered in the light of a society in which bureaucratic organizations have come to dominate the landscape, and when persons are accounted for, if at all, not simply as individuals but as officeholders.[99]

---

[92] Alexander, 'Crime in the Suites', 53. See also Donaldson, *Corporations and Morality*, ch. 6.

[93] Compare Temby, 'Some Observations on Accountability, Prosecution Discretions and Corporate Crime', Paper presented to The Commercial Law Association of Australia, Sydney, 28 October 1986 (buck-passing through corporate liability not mentioned).

[94] Compare Lareau, *American Samurai*, 57–8 (contending that individuals in corporate systems are not responsible for most of the problems).

[95] Australia, Draft White Paper, *Reform of the Australian Taxation System*; Cooper, 'The Taming of the Shrewd'; Freiberg, 'Abuse of the Corporate Form'.

[96] Block and Scarpitti, *Poisoning for Profit*.

[97] C. D. Stone, 'Corporate Regulation'.

[98] One might well ask why, if the corporate birthrate increases rapidly while the human birthrate remains stable, does not the average person work in smaller companies? While merger activity among the largest companies has steadily increased the proportion of the population employed by mega-corporations, there has at the same time been a proliferation of tiny companies with just a few directors, many of them empty shells at the bottom of the range. These are widely used as vehicles for corporate crime to protect individuals from liability.

[99] C. D. Stone, 'Corporate Regulation'. See also Wells, 'The Decline and Rise of English Murder'.

Toward Accountability for Corporate Crime

The analytical thrust of this book is straightforward. We take the three pre-dominant theoretical domains of thought about allocation of responsibility for corporate crime and critically assess the worth of what they have to say. Those domains of thought are individualism, as discussed in Chapter 2, and two more collectivist traditions—law and economics (Chapter 3) and organisation theory (Chapter 4). From these diverse and promiscuous sources we extract a range of desiderata for the allocation of responsibility for corporate crime.[100] These desiderata are set out in Chapter 5 together with the Accountability Model that we construct to satisfy them. In Chapter 6, we provide a more detailed account of the Accountability Model and how it is responsive to the desiderata outlined in Chapter 5. Ultimately, in Chapter 7, we take a number of current fiascos which have posed real problems of accountability for corporate crime and indicate how they might conceivably have been resolved under the Accountability Model.

The theme of this book is the antithesis of orthodox cynicism. The quintessential cynic derives inspiration from Ambrose Bierce's definition of the corporation as 'an ingenious device for the maximisation of profit and the minimisation of responsibility'.[101] Our inspiration lies not in Bierce's barb but in the possibility that corporations can be harnessed as useful workhorses for assuring responsibility. The central theme we defend is that all who are responsible should be held responsible and that this ideal is attainable only if legal systems recognise corporate systems of justice and fully utilise their power.

We are led to this theme by two key observations: corporations have the capacity but not the will to deliver clearly defined accountability for law-breaking; courts of law, obversely, may have the will but not the capacity. Hence, the solution may lie in bringing together the capacity of the firm's private justice system—to identify who was truly responsible—with the will of the public justice system to demand accountability that is just rather than expedient.

To achieve this, the law should hold an axe over the head of a corporation that has committed the *actus reus* of a criminal offence. This may be almost literally an axe that ultimately can deliver the sanction of corporate capital punishment—liquidation, withdrawal of the licence or charter of the firm to operate. The private justice system of the firm is then put to work under the shadow of that axe. The axe would not fall if the private justice system of the corporation does what it is capable of doing—a self-investigation that fully identifies the responsible corporate policies, technologies, management systems, and decisionmakers and that comes up with a plan of remedial action,

---

[100] This approach is more instructive, we believe, than one which proceeds from simplistic or elliptical legal or political constructs of the corporation; compare the very limited explanatory or suggestive power of the three ideal types elaborated in Romano, 'Metapolitics and Corporate Law Reform'.

[101] Bierce, *The Devil's Dictionary*.

disciplinary action and compensation to victims that can satisfy the court. Should, however, the corporation cheat on its responsibility to make its private justice system work justly—by offering up a scapegoat, for example— then the axe would fall. These are the bare bones of the Accountability Model; the impatient or incredulous can turn immediately to Chapters 5 and 6, where flesh is put on these bones.

Clearly, this proposal involves a substantial restructuring of the law rather than minor tinkering. Is the enterprise utopian?[102] It would be if we thought that across-the-board implementation in one fell swoop was the reform objective. Instead, as discussed in Chapter 7, our objective is to persuade open-minded regulators, judges and defence lawyers to experiment with the model. In Australia, there are now regulators at the national antitrust and consumer protection agency (the Trade Practices Commission), prominent trade practices defence lawyers, and members of the Society of Consumer Affairs Professionals in Business who are committed to experimenting with the kind of reform advocated in this book. To date, their entrepreneurship has been supported by the judges involved in cases such as the Colonial Mutual Life Assurance Society (CML) settlement (see Chapter 7) and by the Attorney General of Australia. The Australian Chamber of Commerce and Industry has not warmly embraced the approach adopted by the Trade Practices Commission in the CML and similar cases, but it has expressed cautious tolerance of the continued practical implementation and development of the model. Praxis derived from the Accountability Model is thus feasible and indeed has emerged, at least embryonically.

---

[102] Consider the lessons revealed by, e.g., Yeager, *The Limits of Law*.

2 Individualism

Individualism as a Strategy for Allocating Responsibility for Corporate Crime

For the dogged individualist,[1] the solution to problems of accountability for corporate crime is simple: we should abandon reliance on corporate criminal liability and rely instead on individual liability. Individual criminal liability, it is claimed, can do the job of corporate criminal liability; if corporate criminal liability is abolished, prosecutors will be forced to proceed against individual officers and employees. Moreover, if corporate liability for crime were abolished, and if guilty corporate personnel were held criminally liable, there would be no need to worry about the problem of non-assurance of internal accountability which now arises where corporations are subjected to monetary sanctions. Individualism thus proposes radical surgery—amputating the corporate leg of criminal liability—as the cure for the present ills of non-accountability for corporate crime.

Many commentators have advocated that criminal liability be confined to individual persons. The early development of corporate criminal liability encountered an adverse reception from some quarters,[2] and the later history of the subject has seen the publication of numerous sceptical tracts, including Leonard Leigh's treatise, *The Criminal Liability of Corporations in English Law* (1969).[3] In recent times, the support mounted for an exclusively individualistic platform of criminal liability has intensified. In an extensive critique, Eliezer Lederman has contended that recognition of corporate criminal liability challenges 'the ideological and normative basis of criminal law and its

---

[1] Hardly a rare species. See generally Lukes, *Individualism*; Bellah et al., *Habits of the Heart*, ch. 6; Josephson, *The Robber Barons*.

[2] See, e.g., Collier, 'Impolicy of Modern Decision and Statute Making Corporations Indictable'; Francis, 'Criminal Responsibility of a Corporation', 305. Compare Leon Duguit's individualistic attack on the concept of state responsibility: Duguit, *Law in the Modern State*, 203–7.

[3] See also Mueller, '*Mens Rea* and the Corporation'; Caroline, 'Corporate Criminality and the Courts'; Kadish, 'Some Observations on the Use of Criminal Sanctions in Enforcing Economic Regulations'; Byam, 'The Economic Inefficiency of Corporate Criminal Liability'.

mode of expression and operation'.[4] A related theme has been pursued by Donald Cressey with the claim that the concept of corporate crime is a fiction, the uncritical use of which has saddled criminologists 'with the impossible task of finding the cause of crimes committed by fictitious persons'.[5] Some have even gone so far as to omit the subject of corporate liability from the agenda, one example being George Fletcher's *Rethinking Criminal Law* (1979), a leading doctrinal work which echoes the preoccupation with individual criminal liability once found in Continental thought.[6]

Four prime assumptions underlie individualism, old and new.[7] The first is a philosophical position, namely methodological individualism. Methodological individualism holds that only individuals act, that only individuals are responsible, and that corporate action or corporate responsibility is no more than the sum of its individual parts.[8] Second, individualism supposes that the theory of deterrent punishment implies the need for, or the sufficiency of, individual liability. Third, it is assumed that retribution postulates the punishment of individual persons, but not corporate entities. Fourth, the supposition is that individuals are best safeguarded against injustice by focusing on individual criminal responsibility and the substantive or procedural constraints that govern the imposition of criminal responsibility. The questionable validity of these four assumptions is examined below.

---

[4] Lederman, 'Criminal Law, Perpetrator and Corporation', 296.
[5] Cressey, 'The Poverty of Theory in Corporate Crime Research', 32. See also Alschuler, 'Ancient Law and the Punishment of Corporations'; Geis and DiMento, 'Is it Sound Policy to Prosecute Corporations?'
[6] See, e.g., Jescheck, *Lehrbuch des Strafrechts*, 180–2. Attention increasingly is paid to corporate liability; see Fauconnet, *La Responsibilité*, 339–41; Facolta Di Giurisprudenza Universita Degli Studi Di Messina, *La Responsabilita Penale Delle Persone Giuridiche in Diritto Comunitario*; Kruse, *Erhvervslivets Kriminalitet*, 385–90; Leigh, 'The Criminal Liability of Corporations and Other Groups: A Comparative View'; Lahti, 'Finland National Report', 261–2.
[7] See generally Lukes, *Individualism*; Dewey, *Individualism Old and New*. Other possible assumptions can be identified, including the false supposition that criminal liability can realistically be viewed in isolation from civil and hence enterprise liability; see further Fisse, 'The Social Policy of Corporate Criminal Responsibility', 397–405; Braithwaite, 'Challenging Just Deserts', 752. Another undercurrent is the emphasis in company law on the rights and duties of individual managers and shareholders; see further Wishart, 'A Conceptual Analysis of the Control of Companies'; C. D. Stone, 'The Place of Enterprise Liability in the Control of Corporate Conduct'.
[8] See generally O'Neill, *Modes of Individualism and Collectivism*; Brodbeck, *Readings in the Philosophy of the Social Sciences*, 254–303; Lukes, *Individualism*, ch. 17; Charles and Lennon, *Reductionism and Anti-Reductionism*; French, *Individual and Collective Responsibility*; May, *The Morality of Groups*; Curtler, *Shame, Responsibility and the Corporation*; Rorty, *The Identities of Persons*; Cohen, 'Criminal Actors, Natural Persons and Collectivities'; Luban, Strudler and Wasserman, 'Deeds Without Doers'. It is of course possible to take a position which rejects methodological individualism and yet which for other reasons posits moral responsibility as an exclusively individualistic construct; see, e.g., Dan-Cohen, *Rights, Persons, and Organizations*, chs 2–3; Hallis, *Corporate Personality*, 127–33.

Methodological Individualism, Corporate Action and Corporate Responsibility

Influential as methodological individualism has been as a philosophical force in the way people think about corporate crime and, indeed, about collectivities generally,[9] it is unable to account adequately for the corporateness of corporate action and corporate responsibility.

Methodological individualism and corporate action

Consider the position taken by F. A. Hayek, a leading advocate of methodological individualism:

> There is no other way toward an understanding of social phenomena but through our understanding of individual actions directed toward other people and guided by their expected behaviour.[10]

Methodological individualism as advocated by Hayek amounts to an ontology that only individuals are real in the social world, while social phenomena like corporations are abstractions which cannot be directly observed.[11] This ontology is spurious. The notion that individuals are real, observable, flesh and blood, while corporations are legal fictions, is false. Plainly, many features of corporations are observable (their assets, factories, decisionmaking procedures), while many features of individuals are not (for example, personality, intention, unconscious mind).[12] Both individuals and corporations are defined by a mix of observable and abstracted characteristics.

Clifford Geertz contends that 'the Western conception of the person as a bounded, unique, more or less integrated emotional and cognitive universe, a dynamic centre of awareness, emotion, judgement, and action organised into a distinctive whole ... is a rather peculiar idea within the context of the world's cultures'.[13] Reflecting upon his anthropological fieldwork, Geertz cites Balinese culture, wherein it is dramatis personae, not actors, that endure or indeed exist:

> Physically men come and go, mere incidents in a happenstance history, of no genuine importance even to themselves. But the masks they wear, the stage they occupy, the parts they play, and, most important, the spectacle they mount remain, and comprise not the facade but the substance of things, not least the self.

---

[9] Consider the individualistic position sometimes maintained in the context of reparation for disadvantaged groups. See, e.g., Sher, 'Groups and Justice'. Compare Ezorsky, 'On 'Groups and Justice'; Bittker, *The Case for Black Reparations*, ch. 8; Garet, 'Communality and Existence'. We are indebted to Wojcieck Sadurski, of the University of Sydney, Faculty of Law, for drawing our attention to this facet.

[10] Hayek, *Individualism and the Economic Order*, 6.

[11] This ontology contrasts starkly with that which sees corporations as the prime creative power in society.

[12] Compare McDonald, 'The Personless Paradigm', 225–6 (discussing the distinctively collective 'expressive character' of organisations).

[13] Geertz, *Local Knowledge*, 59. Individualism stems in part from the myth that constitutional and other associational arrangements are not natural: it is an entirely natural need for human beings to form groups, etc. See further Adler, *Ten Philosophical Mistakes*, ch. 9.

Shakespeare's old-trouper view of the vanity of action in the face of mortality—all the world's a stage and we are but poor players, content to strut our hour, and so on—makes no sense here. There is no make-believe; of course players perish, but the play does not, and it is the latter, the performed rather than the performer that really matters.[14]

The merging of the individual person with the land in Australian Aboriginal cultures, where a particular rock can be part of an ancestor or part of oneself, provides another example at odds with the conception of bounded unitary individualism. Even within the Western cultural tradition it is difficult to accept that individuals, unlike corporations, are characterised by a bounded unitary consciousness. As Hindess has pointed out, decisions made by individuals as well as those made by corporations have a diffuse grounding; they represent the product of 'diverse and sometimes conflicting objectives, forms of calculation, and means of action'.[15]

The polar opposite to methodological individualism is the methodological holism of the early European sociologists, notably Emile Durkheim.[16] For Durkheim, 'the individual finds himself in the presence of a force [society] which is superior to him and before which he bows'.[17] From this perspective, the collective will of society is not the product of the individual consciousness of members of society.[18] Quite the reverse: the individual is the product of evolutionary social forces.

Both the crude methodological individualism of Hayek and the crude methodological holism of Durkheim are unpersuasive. It is just as constricting to see the sailor as the navy writ small as it is to see the navy as the sailor writ large.[19] It is true to say that the activity of the navy is constituted by the action of individual sailors. But it is also true that the existence of a sailor is constituted by the existence of the navy. Take away the institutional framework of

---

[14] Geertz, *Local Knowledge*, 62. Another illustration (ibid., 60–1) is the central distinction between 'inside' and 'outside' in the Javanese sense of what a person is: '*Batin*, the "inside" word, does not refer to a separate seat of encapsulated spirituality detached or detachable from the body, or indeed to a bounded unit at all, but to the emotional life of human beings generally. It consists of the fuzzy, shifting flow of subjective feeling perceived directly in all its phenomenological immediacy, but considered to be at its roots, at least, identical across all individuals, whose individuality it thus effaces. And similarly, *lair*, the "outside" word, has nothing to do with the body as an object, even an experienced object. Rather, it refers to that part of human life which, in our culture, strict behaviorists limit themselves to studying—external actions, movements, postures, speech—again conceived as in its essence invariant from one individual to the next. These two sets of phenomena—inward feelings and outward actions—are then regarded not as functions of one another but as independent realms of being to be put in order independently.'

[15] Hindess, 'Classes, Collectivities and Corporate Actors'.

[16] For an extensive critique of early sociological theories of collectivism see Hallis, *Corporate Personality*, 106–34.

[17] Durkheim, *The Rules of Sociological Method*, 123.

[18] Durkheim, *De la Division du Travail*.

[19] Compare *Fontana Dictionary of Modern Thought*, Bullock and Stallybrass (eds), 387: 'It can be argued that the whole dispute [over methodological individualism] is as futile as a dispute between engineers as to whether what is important in a building or mechanism is its structure or the materials or components used. Clearly both are important, but in different ways.'

the navy—ships, captains, rules of war, other sailors—and the notion of an individual sailor makes no sense.[20] Institutions are constituted by individuals and individuals are socially constituted by institutions. To conceive of corporations as no more than sums of the isolated efforts of individuals would be as silly as conceiving the possibility of language without the interactive processes of individuals talking to one another and passing structures of syntax from one generation to another.[21]

Equally, a sociological determinism that grants no intentionality to individuals, that sees them as wholly shaped by macro-sociological forces, is absurd. Sociological functionalism, as championed by Durkheim, indulges this absurdity. Mesmerised by the achievements of evolutionary theory in biology, the functionalists failed to recognise that human beings are capable of reflecting upon causal laws and engaging in purposive social action which does not conform to those laws or, indeed, which is intended to defeat them.[22] We may readily agree with Durkheim that each kind of community is a thought world which penetrates and moulds the minds of its members, but that is not to deny the capacity of individuals to exercise their autonomy to resist and reshape thought worlds.

All wholes are made up of parts; reductionism can be a near-infinite regress. Psychological reductionists can argue that the behaviour of organisations can only be understood by analysing the behaviour of individual members of the organisation. Biological reductionists can argue that the behaviour of individuals can only be understood by the behaviour of parts of the body—firing synapses in the brain, hormonal changes, movement of a hand across a page. Chemical reductionists might argue that these body parts can only be understood as movements of molecules. At all of these levels of analysis, reductionism is blinkered because the whole is always more than the sum of the individual parts; in each case there is a need to build upon reductionism to study how the parts interact to form wholes.

In the case of organisations, individuals may be the most important parts, but there are other parts, as is evident from factories with manifest routines operating to some extent independently of the biological agents who flick the switches. Organisations are systems ('socio-technical' systems, as they have sometimes been described),[23] not just aggregations of individuals. More

---

[20] Compare with Compte's view that a society is 'no more decomposable into individuals than a geometric surface is into lines, or a line into points': Compte, II *Systeme de Politique Positive*, 181, quoted in Lukes, *Individualism*, 111.

[21] For Giddens, this exemplifies 'the duality of structure'. For further explanation of this term, see Giddens, *Central Problems in Social Theory*, 5; see also Giddens, *The Constitution of Society*. Giddens takes issue with Popper's methodological individualism, correctly in our view: see Popper, II *The Open Society and Its Enemies*, 98. Giddens argues persuasively, in our view, in *Central Problems in Social Theory*, 95, that Popper's claim only seems a truism if we understand 'individual' to mean something like 'human organism'.

[22] For example, an investor may sell in anticipation of reduced profits and thereby defeat a causal law that reduced profits will be followed by a fall in share price. As Carr said, 'One reason why history so rarely repeats itself is that the dramatis personae in the second performance have prior knowledge of the *denouement*': Carr, *A History of Soviet Russia*, 88.

[23] Emery, *Systems Thinking*. Compare with Teubner, 'Enterprise Corporatism', 139–40 (a cyclically linked and self-referential social action system).

crucially, however, organisations consist of sets of expectations about how different kinds of problems should be resolved. These expectations are a residue of the individual expectations of many past and present members of the organisation. But they are also a product of the *interplay* among individuals' expectations which distinguish shared meanings from individuals' views. The interaction between individual and shared expectations, on the one hand, and the organisation's environment, on the other, constantly reproduces shared expectations. In other words, an organisation has a culture which is transmitted from one generation of organisational role incumbents to the next. Indeed, the entire personnel of an organisation may change without reshaping the corporate culture; this may be so even if the new incumbents have personalities quite different from those of the old.

The products of organisations are more than the sum of the products of individual actions; while each member of the board of directors can 'vote' for a declaration of dividend, only the board as a collectivity is empowered to declare a dividend. The collective action is thus qualitatively different from the human actions which, in part, constitute it. 'Groupthink'[24] and the group polarisation or risky-shift phenomena also illustrate how collective expectations can be quite different from the sum of individual expectations. A number of psychological studies suggest that group decisionmaking can make members of the group willing to accept stupid ideas or hazardous risks[25] that they would reject if making the same decision alone. More fundamentally, social norms and values are properties of group formation and are irreducible to the properties possessed by individual members of the social group. In Turner's words:

> The most prototypical ... position is not the sum or mean of ingroup responses, nor an individual property of the member holding it, but is a higher order, category property, reflecting the views of all members and, indeed, the similarities and differences between them and in relation to others. The prototypical member's persuasiveness, perceived competence, leadership, the perceived validity of their information, etc., are mediated by and based on his or her membership of the group as a 'whole'. The prototypical position is a product of social relations in interaction with the psychological processes (of categorization, comparison, etc.,) which represent them. It is accepted throughout that action as group members is psychologically different from action in terms of one's personal self because it represents action in terms of a social categorization of self and others at a higher level of abstraction.[26]

Donald Cressey underpins his questioning of the concept of corporate criminal liability by suggesting that organisations do not think, decide and act;

---

[24] Janis, *Victims of Groupthink*; Steiner, 'Heuristic Models of Groupthink'; Stubbing, *The Defense Game*.
[25] See Janis and Mann, *Decision Making*, 423, where, however, it is also pointed out that there are some studies suggesting that an initially dominant risk-aversive viewpoint within a group may shift an individual away from risk.
[26] Turner, *Rediscovering the Social Group*, 88.

these are all things done by individuals. So we are told that it is a crass anthropomorphism to say that the White House decided upon a course of action, or that the US declared war. Instead we should say that the President decided and that the President and a majority of members of Congress decided to go to war. If saying that 'the White House decided' connotes that 'the White House' would decide in the same way as an individual person, then we are certainly engaging in anthropomorphism. Yet people who decode such messages understand that organisations emit decisions just as individuals do, but that they reach these decisions in rather different ways. They fully accept that 'the White House decided' is a simplification given that many actors typically have a say in such decisions. Nevertheless, it is probably less of a simplification than the statement 'the President has decided'. Indeed it may be fanciful to individualise a collective product. The President may never have turned his mind to the decision; he may have done no more than waive his power to veto it; or he may have delegated the decision totally.

Similarly, it makes more sense to say that the US has declared war than to say that the President and a majority of Congress have decided to do so. A declaration of war commits many more individuals and physical resources to purposive social action than the individuals who voted for it; it commits the US as a whole to war, and many individuals outside the Congress participate or acquiesce in the making of that commitment:

> A man does not have to agree with his government's acts to see himself embodied in them any more than he has to approve of his own acts to acknowledge that he has, alas, performed them. It is a question of immediacy, of experiencing what the state 'does' as proceeding naturally from a familiar and intelligible 'we'.[27]

The temptation to reduce such decisions to the actions of individuals is widespread, as in the suggestion, once common, that wars be settled by a fist-fight or duel between the protagonist heads of state.

The expression 'the White House decided' is a social construction; as a matter of social construction, the same organisational output might be expressed as 'the President decided' or 'the Administration decided' or 'the United States decided' or 'the President gave in to the decision of the Congress'. Equally, the concept of 'deciding' is a social construct (what amounts to 'deciding' for some is 'muddling through' or perhaps even 'ducking a decision' for others). To talk of individual decisions as real and of collective decisions as fictions, as Cressey does, is to obscure the inevitability of social construction at any level of analysis.

In many circumstances, the social construction 'the White House decided' will be a workable one for analytic purposes. This does not mean that we should treat this as the only accurate description of what happened any more than we should accept 'the President decided' as a real description of what happened. Indeed, in the social control of corporate crime, much depends on how those involved with a crime socially construct the responsible

---

[27] Geertz, *The Interpretation of Cultures*, 317.

individuals or collectivity. The key to unlocking the control of corporate crime is granting credibility to multiple social constructions of responsibility and investigating the processes of generating and invoking these social constructions; as Geertz has explained, '[h]opping back and forth between the whole conceived through the parts that actualize it and the parts conceived through the whole that motivates them, we seek to turn them, by a sort of intellectual perpetual motion, into explications of one another'.[28]

Social theory and legal theory are thus forced to stake out positions between individualism and holism. The task is to explore how wholes are created out of purposive individual action, and how individual action is constituted and constrained by the structural realities of wholes.[29] This exploration extends to how responsibility for action in the context of collectivities is socially constructed by those involved as well as by outsiders. Moral responsibility can be meaningfully allocated when conventions for allocating responsibility are shared by insiders and understood by outsiders. Metaphysics about the distinctive, unitary, irreducible agency of individuals tend to obstruct analysis, as do metaphysics about the special features of corporateness.[30] As elaborated in the following section, the moral responsibility of corporations for their actions relates essentially to social process and not to elusive attributes of personhood. As Surber has indicated, the issue is 'more a matter of what we consider moral responsibility to be, rather than what sort of metaphysical entities corporations may turn out to be'.[31] If responsibility is conceived as a metaphysical concept, then the intrinsic features of responsible entities assume special importance. But if responsibility is taken to be a functional concept of social action, then nothing necessarily hinges on the intrinsic characteristics of different social entities: the question is the extent to which holding them responsible will prevent corporate crime or otherwise achieve desired effects.[32]

Methodological individualism and corporate responsibility

Corporations are often regarded as blameworthy but, according to the logic of methodological individualism, such blameworthiness reduces to blameworthiness on the part of individual representatives or to causal responsibility (as opposed to moral responsibility) on the part of a corporation.[33] This

---

[28] Ibid., 69, where Geertz also comments on the 'familiar trajectory' of 'the hermeneutic circle'.

[29] See further Coleman, *Individual Interests and Collective Action*, 266.

[30] Walt, Laufer and Schlegel in 'Corporations, Persons and Corporate Criminal Liability' suggest that the issue is whether successful predictive or explanatory theories make ineliminable reference to corporations.

[31] Surber, 'Individual and Corporate Responsibility', 81. For an analysis of state crimes consistent with this conception of corporate responsibility, see S. Cohen, 'Human Rights and Crimes of the State'.

[32] Goodin, 'Apportioning Responsibility'; Goodin, 'Responsibilities'; Pettit and Goodin, 'The Possibility of Special Duties'.

[33] See Wolf, 'The Legal and Moral Responsibility of Organizations', 275–6. As to the concept of responsibility, see further Shaver, *The Attribution of Blame;* H. L. A. Hart, *Punishment and Responsibility*, 210–15.

reductionism is difficult to accept. The fact is that organisations are blamed in their capacity as organisations for causing harm or taking risks in circumstances where they are expected to have acted otherwise. We often react to corporate offenders not merely as impersonal harm-producing forces but as responsible, blameworthy entities.[34] When people blame corporations, they are not merely channelling aggression against the ox that gored.[35] Nor are they pointing the finger only at individuals behind the corporate mantle. They are condemning the fact that the organisation either implemented a policy of non-compliance or failed to exercise its collective capacity to avoid the offence for which blame attaches.

Many instances of corporate blameworthiness have been documented, especially in the context of disasters.[36] A patent illustration is the finding of the Royal Commission which investigated the crash of an Air New Zealand DC 10 near Mount Erebus, Antarctica, in 1979.[37] According to the Commission, the crash resulted primarily from the failure of the flight operations centre at company headquarters to communicate the correct navigational co-ordinates to the flight crew.[38] The Commission did not engage in any ritualistic slaying of the equipment involved; no radio transmitter or word-processor was ceremoniously disembowelled. Nor was the Commission prepared to blame the personnel in the flight operations centre. Rather, condemnation was directed at 'the incompetent administrative airline procedures

---

[34] See further French, *Collective and Corporate Responsibility*; French, 'Types of Collectivities and Blame', 166; Lucas, *The Principles of Politics*, 281; Donaldson, *Corporations and Morality*; Dworkin, *Law's Empire*, 168–75; S. Cohen, 'Human Rights and Crimes of the State'. But see Dan-Cohen, *Rights, Persons, and Organizations*, chs 2–3 (corporations analysed not as moral agents but as 'intelligent machines'); Velasquez, 'Why Corporations Are Not Morally Responsible for Anything They Do'. Compare the analysis advanced in Stoljar, *Groups and Entities*, ch. 12, that the outstanding feature of corporateness is a common shared fund, and the attempt, ibid. ch. 11, to explain corporate criminal liability in terms of pecuniary liability from a common fund. In our view, the use of the criminal law against corporate entities cannot realistically be explained merely in terms of compensation or the extraction of a tax or penalty; account must be taken of the criminal law's capacity for expressing the unwantedness of certain forms of behaviour. See Nozick, *Anarchy, State and Utopia*, 67; Drane and Neal, 'On Moral Justifications for the Tort/Crime Distinction'. Compare also the position taken in Hallis, *Corporate Personality*, xxxvii, that '[philosophical as opposed to legal] personality can exist only in the individual human being with his single centre of self-consciousness and will'. In our view, the moral responsibility or blameworthiness of corporate entities is a complex issue which is most unlikely to be resolved by resort to the question-begging notion of philosophical 'personality'. As explained in Surber, 'Individual and Corporate Responsibility'; and Goodin, 'Apportioning Responsibility', the starting point is not the attributes of moral personality but the attribution of responsibility and blame.

[35] Compare Florman, *Blaming Technology*; Hyde, 'The Prosecution and Punishment of Animals and Lifeless Things in the Middle Ages and Modern Times'; Finkelstein, 'The Goring Ox'.

[36] In addition to the Mount Erebus case discussed here, see Great Britain, *Report of the Public Inquiry into the Accident at the Hixon Level Crossing*; Victoria, *Royal Commission into the Failure of the West Gate Bridge*; Great Britain, *Report of the Tribunal to Inquire into the Disaster at Aberfan*; 'DOT is Criticised over Marchioness', *Financial Times*, 16 August 1991, 7 (Department of Transport report finding that no individual was to blame for the disaster).

[37] NZ, *Report of the Royal Commission to Inquire into the Crash on Mount Erebus, Antarctica of a DC10 Aircraft Operated by Air New Zealand.*

[38] Ibid., para. 392.

which made the mistake possible'.[39] Air New Zealand, viewed as a collectivity, had failed in this respect to live up to the navigational standards expected of an international airline.

Nonetheless, it may be replied that the phenomenon of corporate blameworthiness is a phantom. It is often said that a corporation cannot possess a guilty state of mind. If this is so, then how can a corporation be blameworthy?[40]

Although it is often said that corporations cannot possess an intention, this is true only in the obvious sense that a corporate entity lacks the capacity to entertain a cerebral mental state. Corporations exhibit their own special kind of intentionality, namely corporate policy.[41] As Peter French has pointed out, the concept of corporate policy does not express merely the intentionality of a company's directors, officers or employees, but projects the idea of a distinctively corporate strategy:[42]

> It will be objected that a corporation's policies reflect only the current goals of its directors. But that is certainly not logically necessary nor is it in practice true for most large corporations. Usually, of course, the original incorporators will have organized to further their individual interests and/or to meet goals which they shared. [But] even in infancy the melding of disparate interests and purposes gives rise to a corporate long range point of view that is distinct from the intents and purposes of the collection of incorporators viewed individually.[43]

Blameworthiness requires essentially two conditions: first, the ability of the actor to make decisions;[44] second, the inexcusable failure of the actor to perform an assigned task.[45] Herbert Simon has defined a formal organisation as a

---

[39] Ibid., para. 393.
[40] See Duguit, *Law in the Modern State*, 203–7; See also 'Developments in the Law—Corporate Crime', 1241.
[41] See further French, *Collective and Corporate Responsibility*, ch. 3; Nonet, 'The Legitimation of Purposive Decisions'; Kreimer, 'Reading the Mind of the School Board'; Fisse, 'The Attribution of Criminal Liability to Corporations'; Tigar, 'It Does the Crime But Not the Time', 234. Compare the concept of 'collective knowledge' as adopted in *United States v. Bank of New England* (1987) 821 F. 2d 844 at 855. In 'Developments in the Law—Corporate Crime', 1241, it is contended that *mens rea* 'has no meaning when applied to a corporate defendant, since an organization possesses no mental state'. This proposition is based on the false and silly assumption that one should be looking for a humanoid mental state.
[42] French, *Collective and Corporate Responsibility*, 45–6; French, 'The Corporation as a Moral Person', 214. Compare the argument in Wolff, 'On the Nature of Legal Persons', 501, that '[w]hat is known as collective will is in reality the result of mutually influenced individual wills'.
[43] See also Mitchell, 'A Theory of Corporate Will'.
[44] In the case of corporate actors, French, *Collective and Corporate Responsibility*, ch. 4, identifies 'corporate internal decision structures' consisting of (1) organisational responsibility structures (e.g., flowcharts of the organisational power structure), and (2) corporate decision recognition rules (usually embedded in corporate policy).
[45] The focus is not on the attributes of moral personhood as such (consider the problematic status of Tokugawa in Milan, *The Cybernetic Samurai*) but on the performance of entities in carrying out their prescribed roles. See Surber, 'Individual and Corporate Responsibility'; Goodin, 'Apportioning Responsibility'. Contrast the positions discussed in Hallis, *Corporate Personality*, 137–65; Wolff, 'On the Nature of Legal Persons', 499–505; Goodpaster, 'The Concept of Corporate Responsibility'; Velasquez, 'Why Corporations Are Not Morally

'decision-making structure'.[46] Under this definition, a formal organisation has one of the requirements for blameworthiness that a mob, for example, does not have.[47] We routinely hold organisations responsible for a decision when and because that decision instantiates an organisational policy and instantiates an organisational decisionmaking process which the organisation has chosen for itself. A decision made by a rogue individual in defiance of corporate policy (including unwritten corporate policy), to undermine corporate goals, or in flagrant disregard of corporate decisionmaking rules, is not a decision for which the organisation is morally responsible.[48]

This is not to say, however, that we cannot hold the organisation responsible if the intention of individuals is other than to promote corporate goals and policies. It may be that two individuals, A and B, hold the key to a particular corporate decision. A decides what to support because of a bribe; A's intention is to collect the bribe rather than to advance corporate goals. B decides to support the same course of action out of a sense of loyalty to A, who is an important ally and mentor; B's intention is formed from a consideration of bureaucratic politics rather than corporate goals.[49] Even though the key individuals do not personally intend to further corporate policy by the decision, it may be that they cannot secure the acquiescence of the rest of the organisation with the decision unless they can advance credible reasons as to why the decision will advance corporate policy. If the reasons given are accepted and acted on within the corporate decisionmaking process, then we can hold the corporation responsible irrespective of any games played by individual actors among themselves. It is not just that corporate intention (the instantiation of corporate policy in a decision) is more than the sum of individual intentions; it may have little to do with individual intentions.

Blameworthiness also requires an inexcusable failure to perform an assigned task. Any culture confers certain kinds of responsibilities on certain kinds of actors. Parents have responsibilities not to neglect their children. Doctors bear special responsibilities in the giving of medical advice. Just as parents and doctors can be held to different and higher standards of responsibility by virtue of role or capacity, so it is possible for corporations to be held to different and higher standards of responsibility than individuals because of their role or capacity as organisations.[50]

Responsible for Anything They Do'. For an extensive review of the implications of different constructs of corporateness see Morgan, *Images of Organization*. Legal theories of the corporation are canvassed in Millon, 'Theories of the Corporation'. On corporate rights see Coleman, *Individual Interests and Collective Action*, chs 14–16; Dan-Cohen, *Rights, Persons, and Organizations*, chs 4–5, 8; Hallis, *Corporate Personality*; Scott and Hart, *Organizational Values in America*; McDonald, 'The Personless Paradigm'; McDonald, 'Collective Rights and Tyranny'; Stone, 'A Comment on "Criminal Responsibility in Government" ', 250–1.

[46] Simon, *Administrative Behavior*.

[47] See French, *Collective and Corporate Responsibility*, ch. 2. But see Manning, 'The Random Collectivity as a Moral Agent'.

[48] As to the limits of corporate criminal liability in such instances see *Canadian Dredge & Dock Co. Ltd. v The Queen* (1985) 19 CCC (3d) 1.

[49] Compare Aoki, *The Co-Operative Game Theory of the Firm*.

[50] This perspective is consistent with the model of task-responsibility (as opposed to blame-responsibility) developed in Goodin, 'Apportioning Responsibility'.

Pamela Bucy's interesting recent contribution to the literature argues that the basis of corporate criminal responsibility should be the Aristotelian notion of the 'ethos' of the corporation—whether this was a corporation with an ethos that encouraged the criminal conduct at issue.[51] This involves an admirable broadening of French's notion of corporate policy to include matters such as compliance education endeavours, compensation and indemnification practices.[52] The virtue of Bucy's reformulation of corporate criminal responsibility is that it rewards (as a defence) 'those corporations that make efforts to educate and motivate their employees to follow the letter and spirit of the law'.[53] This is also the direction in which Jay Sigler and Joseph Murphy seek to take us in *Interactive Corporate Compliance*.[54] Sigler and Murphy go further than Bucy (too far, in our view)[55] by advocating effective immunity to corporate criminal liability for firms that implement corporate compliance systems beyond a certain standard. A corporation with a criminally irresponsible ethos might implement the corporate compliance systems that meet the minimum standards for effective immunity from criminal liability under the Sigler and Murphy proposal. The difficulty with the Bucy proposal, however, is that, as a general requirement, it may be impractical to expect the state to marshal all the evidence needed to prove that a corporate defendant had a criminal ethos.[56]

It is not a legal fiction for the law to hold corporations responsible for their decisions; in all cultures it is common for citizens to do so. When the law adopts these cultural notions of corporate responsibility, it does more than reflect the culture; it deepens and shapes the notions of corporate responsibility already present in the culture. The law can clarify the content of what we expect corporations to be responsible for. Thus, the law can require large chemical companies to be responsible for an inventory of all hazardous chemicals on their premises, a responsibility not imposed on individual householders. More fundamentally, the law is not only presented with the cultural fact that a corporation can be blamed; the law, more than any other institution in the society, is constantly implicated in reproducing that cultural fact. Thus, the Roman law tradition of treating corporate persons as fictions and the

---

[51] Bucy, 'Corporate Ethos'. See also Australian Standing Committee of Attorneys-General, Criminal Law Officers Committee, *Model Criminal Code, Discussion Draft, Chapter 2, General Principles of Criminal Responsibility*, cll 501.3.1, 501.3.2 (concept of corporate culture adopted as one means of reflecting the fundamental principle of corporate blameworthiness).
[52] French, *Collective and Corporate Responsibility*, 45–6.
[53] Bucy, 'Corporate Ethos', 1100.
[54] Sigler and Murphy, *Interactive Corporate Compliance*. See also Sigler and Murphy, *Corporate Lawbreaking and Interactive Compliance*.
[55] Braithwaite, Book Review of 'Interactive Corporate Compliance'.
[56] Compare the Accountability Model discussed in Chapters 5 and 6. Under this model egregious cases can be prosecuted on the basis of the evidence initially available. However, there is also a pyramid of enforcement which is designed to induce corporations to disclose the circumstances in which an alleged offence occurred. The evidence thereby disclosed can be used to assess not only whether the corporation is reactively at fault but also whether there was fault at the time when the *actus reus* of the offence was committed.

Germanic realist theory that law cannot create its subjects (or that corporations are pre-existing sociological persons), both overlook the recursive
nature of the relationship between law and culture.[57]

Corporations are held responsible for the outcomes of their policies and
decisionmaking procedures partly because organisations have the capacity to
change their policies and procedures.[58] Thomas Donaldson has pointed out
that, like corporations, a computer conducting a search and a cat waiting to
pounce on a mouse are making decisions and are even doing so intentionally.[59] We grant moral agency to the corporation and yet not to the cat or the
computer for two reasons, according to Donaldson.[60] First, the corporation,
like the individual human being and unlike the cat, can give moral reasons for
its decisionmaking.[61] Second, the corporation has the capacity to change its
goals and policies and to change the decisionmaking processes directed at
those goals and policies.

If an anthropomorphised notion of corporate, feline, or digital intention is
not necessarily at the heart of the responsibility of actors, then it becomes relevant to move beyond corporate responsibility for policy decisions to the
sphere of negligence. In practice, the predominant form of corporate fault is
more likely to be corporate negligence than corporate intention. Companies
usually are at pains not to display any posture of inattention to legal requirements; on the contrary, compliance policies are *de rigueur* in companies
which have given any thought to legal risk minimisation.[62]

Corporate negligence is prevalent where communication breakdowns
occur, or where organisations suffer from collective oversight. Does corporate
negligence in such a context amount merely to negligence on the part of individuals? It may be possible to explain the *causes* of corporate wrongdoing in
terms of particular contributions of managers and employees, but the attribution of *fault* is another matter.[63] Corporate negligence does not necessarily
reduce to individual negligence. A corporation may have a greater capacity to
avoid the commission of an offence and it may be for this reason that a finding of corporate but not individual negligence may be justified. We may be

---

[57] For a discussion of these Roman and German legal traditions see Hallis, *Corporate
Personality*, xix–xx, xxxviii–xl, 137–65; M. Wolff, 'On the Nature of Legal Persons'; French,
Collective and Corporate Responsibility, 35–7.

[58] On corporate choice see generally Warner, *Organizational Choice and Constraint*; Bower,
When Markets Quake.

[59] T. Donaldson, *Corporations and Morality*, 22.

[60] Ibid., 30–1.

[61] Is 'understanding' as opposed to intention or knowledge distinctively human? Not if one
accepts Derrida's analysis that words have no inherent meaning and that linguistic meaning is
fundamentally indeterminate because the contexts which fix meaning are never stable. On this
analysis, context is everything, including the corporate contexts in which words such as
'knowledge', 'intention', 'negligence', and 'understanding' are used. See Derrida, *Limited
Inc*.

[62] See, e.g., Arkin, I *Business Crime*, 6A–7; Sciamanda, 'Preventive Law Leads to Corporate
Goal of Zero Litigation, Zero Legal Violations'; Bruns, 'Corporate Preventive Law Programs'.

[63] See further Shaver, *The Attribution of Blame*, ch. 5.

reluctant to pass judgement on the top executives of Union Carbide for the Bhopal disaster (perhaps because of failures of communication within the organisation about safety problems abroad), but higher standards of care are expected of such a company given its collective might and resources.[64] Thus, where a corporate system is blamed for criminogenic group pressures, that blame is directed not at individual actors but rather toward an institutional set-up from which the standards of organisational performance expected are higher than those expected of any personnel.[65] As Donaldson has observed in the context of corporate intelligence:

> Corporations can and should have access to practical and theoretical knowledge which dwarfs that of individuals. When Westinghouse Inc. manufactures machinery for use in nuclear power generating plants, it should use its massive resources to consider tens of thousands of possible consequences and be able to weigh their likelihood accurately. Which human errors might occur? How are they to be handled? How might espionage occur? How should human systems interface with mechanised ones? ... Good intentions for Westinghouse are not adequate. Westinghouse must have, in addition to good intentions, superhuman intelligence.[66]

Corporations, it may thus be argued, can be blamed for intentional or negligent conduct. Michael McDonald has gone further by arguing that organisations are paradigm moral agents:

> Not only does the organization have all the capacities that are standardly taken to ground autonomy—vis., capacities for intelligent agency—but it also has them to a degree no human can. Thus, for example, a large corporation has available and can make use of far more information than one individual can. Moreover, the corporation is in principle 'immortal' and so better able to bear responsibility for its deeds than humans, whose sin dies with them ...[67]

Granted, corporations lack human feelings and emotions, but this hardly disqualifies them from possessing the quality of autonomy.[68] On the contrary, the

---

[64] See Walter and Richards, 'Corporate Counsel's Role in Risk Minimization'; Hans and Ermann, 'Responses to Corporate versus Individual Wrongdoing'; Hans and Lofquist, 'Jurors' Judgments of Business Liability in Tort Cases'; Hans, 'Attitudes Toward Corporate Responsibility'. For legal models or reform proposals which explicitly recognise the concept of corporate negligence, see Ozone Protection Act 1989 (Cth), s. 65; Australia, The Law Reform Commission, Report No. 60, 1 *Customs and Excise*, Customs and Excise Bill (1992), cl 28; Australia, Standing Committee of Attorneys-General, Criminal Law Officers Committee, *Model Criminal Code, Discussion Draft, Chapter 2, General Principles of Criminal Responsibility*, cl. 501; New South Wales, Independent Commission against Corruption, *Report on Unauthorised Release of Government Information,* ch. 9; Fisse, 'The Attribution of Criminal Liability to Corporations'; Field and Jörg, 'Corporate Liability and Manslaughter'.
[65] See Cooper, 'Responsibility and the "System"'.
[66] T. Donaldson, *Corporations and Morality*, 125. See further Etzioni, *The Moral Dimension*, ch. 11. For a cyberpunk interpretation see Gibson, *Burning Chrome*, 129.
[67] McDonald, 'The Personless Paradigm', 219–20.
[68] Compare the assertion in Wolf, 'The Legal and Moral Responsibility of Organizations' 279, that a necessary condition of moral agency is the possession of the emotional capacity to be moved by moral concerns (i.e., organisations are not moral agents because they lack souls).

lack of emotions and feelings promote rather than hinder considered rational choice and in this respect the corporation may indeed be a paradigm responsible actor.[69]

There are other difficulties with the view that corporate responsibility amounts to merely an aggregation of individual responsibility. Repeatedly in organisational life, individual actors contribute to collective decisionmaking processes without being conscious of the totality of that process—each individual actor is a part of a whole which no one of them fully comprehends.[70] Indeed, even that part which an individual contributes may be unconscious. Consider the predicament of the campaigner for clearer writing who is concerned at how children learn excessive use of the passive voice when they should use the active voice. Our activist wants to allocate blame for the way that children leave school with ingrained habits of passive voice overuse. Empirically, he or she may find that in general neither students nor teachers have a conscious understanding of what it means to use the passive versus active voice. Unconsciously, they understand how to choose between them— more precisely, they have 'practical consciousness' but not 'discursive consciousness' of the choice.[71] The lack of intentional individual action in making these choices makes the blaming of teachers or students problematic. Yet it might be quite reasonable for blame to be directed at the English Curriculum Branch of the Education Department. Conscious awareness of the distinction between the active and passive voice is widespread throughout the Branch because it is, after all, the job of the Branch to attend to such matters, and to raise the consciousness of teachers and students. It may thus make sense to lay collective blame for social action produced unintentionally, even unconsciously, by all the individual actors. Apart from the justice our campaigner may perceive in blaming the English Curriculum Branch rather than the students or teachers, he or she might conclude that change is more likely to be effected by collective blame. This raises the issue of collective action and deterrent efficacy, as discussed in the next section.

Deterrence, Corporate Conduct and Responsibility

Individualism depends not only on the philosophical foundation of methodological individualism but also on certain assumptions about deterrence and retribution, the two pole stars in the galaxy of theories of punishment. The assumptions made about deterrence are essentially these:
(1) only human agents are capable of responding to the deterrent threat of punishment;
(2) in the absence of any cogent theory of corporate action there is no warrant for punishing corporate entities;

---

[69] We are indebted here to the analysis in McDonald, 'The Personless Paradigm', 219–20. Compare Ladd, 'Morality and the Ideal of Rationality in Formal Organizations' (where it is urged that corporations are goal-oriented to the point of not being moral agents).
[70] Consider, e.g., Demb and Neubauer, *The Corporate Board*.
[71] See Giddens, *Central Problems in Social Theory*; Giddens, *The Constitution of Society*.

(3) corporations are not wrongdoers to be punished but entities to be reformed;
(4) deterrence of corporate crime can be sufficiently achieved by punishing the individual persons responsible; and
(5) it is impossible to punish a corporation in an effective manner.

Are these assumptions sound?

Deterrence and choice

Criminal liability, it is often said, presupposes human choice, a premise from which the conclusion has been drawn by Lederman that criminal liability should be exclusively individual:[72]

> Penal law, being a prescriptive branch of law, purports to direct the behaviour of individuals in accordance with society's interests and values. A prerequisite for the achievement of this goal is transmitting the criminal law dictates to an addressee capable of grasping the message, namely the human consciousness. ... [T]he justification for punishing violators rests mainly on the assumption that it will deter future conscious violation by the transgressor and others. ... This cohesive link within criminal law, between the commanding authority and the conscious individual who alone is susceptible to guidance, is threatened when confronted with the imputation of criminal liability to corporations, which by their very nature lack any consciousness.

To similar effect, Cressey has asserted that 'even depicting the horrors of hellfire and damnation which await evil persons ... can have no influence on fictitious persons who do not have the psychological make-up of real ones'.[73]

This line of argument is based on a *non sequitur*. Even if one accepts the methodological individualist's position that corporate choice reduces to the choice of individual persons, it does not follow that deterrent punishment should be directed exclusively at individual persons. Punishment directed at a corporate entity typically seeks to deter a wide range of individual associates from engaging in conduct directly or indirectly connected with the commission of an offence. Individual persons who are directly implicated in offences may be difficult or impossible to prosecute successfully, and those who influence the commission of offences indirectly may fall outside the scope of liability for complicity or other ancillary heads of criminal liability.[74] The punishment of collectivities with a view to inducing compliance with the law by human agents is thus consistent with a deterrent hypothesis based on the human calculation of costs versus benefits; the threat of corporate punishment

---

[72] Lederman, 'Criminal Law, Perpetrator and Corporation', 296.
[73] Cressey, 'The Poverty of Theory in Corporate Crime Research', 35.
[74] See the heading 'Deterrence and the limits of individual liability' below.

can be a substitute for the threat of individual punishment when the legal system is unable to impose punishment directly on the personnel responsible.[75]

Account must also be taken of the logic of collective choice. Collective choice does not reduce simply to individual preferences, as Mancur Olson, Kenneth Arrow, and others have shown.[76] Accordingly, a deterrence hypothesis that focuses exclusively on the preferences of individual associates of an organisation is not fully rational. Where collectivities act in accordance with a rational actor model,[77] prevention of offences committed on behalf of a collectivity requires that collective incentives to engage in the commission of offences be countered by collective punishment costs sufficient to influence a law-abiding collective choice. The profit or enhancement of power that a company may stand to gain from the commission of an offence is countered by the threat of punishing the corporate entity; potential collective benefit is negatived by potential collective cost.[78] Compare this with collective deterrence in the domain of foreign policy. Following Cressey,[79] we could adopt the view that individuals decide to go to war, nations do not. Instead of threatening nuclear or commercial retaliation against a nation should it invade another, we could threaten to find out who were the political actors who lobbied for the invasion and to send assassination squads after them. This policy option is not usually commended[80] largely because of an enduring belief in the virtue of rapid replacement of slain kings. If collective deterrence is a fiction, it is a fiction on which strategic analysts in the US and other great powers have based the future of the world.[81]

It is quite possible to deter by damaging collective interests even when individual members of an organisation are not personally affected. In an earlier study of 17 adverse publicity crises experienced by large organisations, we concluded that adverse publicity surrounding allegations of corporate crime was an effective deterrent, but not mainly because of fear of the financial consequences of the publicity.[82] Companies value a good reputation for its own sake, as do universities, sporting clubs and government agencies. Individuals who take on positions of power within such organisations, even if they as individuals do not personally feel any deterrent effects of shaming

---

[75] See, e.g., Hawkins, *Environment and Enforcement*, 146.
[76] Olson, *The Logic of Collective Action*; Arrow, *Social Choice and Individual Values*. See also Schelling, *Micromotives and Macrobehavior*.
[77] A rational actor model of corporate conduct is of course a simplification and misleading if viewed as an exclusive guide to policy: see Kriesberg, 'Decisionmaking Models and the Control of Corporate Crime'; Byrne and Hoffmann, 'Efficient Corporate Harm'; Kagan and Scholz, 'The 'Criminology of the Corporation' and Regulatory Enforcement Strategies'.
[78] See, e.g., *United States v Bank of New England* (1987) 821 F. 2d 844. From a deterrence angle one can understand why the court viewed the corporation as exercising collective rationality.
[79] Cressey, 'The Poverty of Theory in Corporate Crime Research'.
[80] There are examples of attempts at direct individual deterrence in foreign policy, but spectacularly successful instances do not spring to mind. Take the US bombing raid on Tripoli: Colonel Gaddafi's home was targeted and his daughter killed as a result of the attack.
[81] See, e.g., Schelling, *The Strategy of Conflict*; Schelling, 'The Strategy of Inflicting Costs'.
[82] Fisse and Braithwaite, *The Impact of Publicity on Corporate Offenders*.

directed at their organisation, may find that they confront role expectations to protect and enhance the repute of the organisation. For example, an academic might be indifferent to the reputation of his or her university, and indeed might do more to snipe at the incompetence of the administration than to defend it publicly. But, if appointed as dean of a faculty, the academic confronts new role expectations to protect the university's reputation. The academic may do this diligently, not because of the views brought to the job as an individual member of the university community, but because he or she knows what the position requires, and wants to be good at the task. Thus, in organisations where individuals are stung very little by collective deterrents, deterrence can still work if those in power are paid good salaries on the understanding that they will do what is necessary to preserve the reputation of the organisation or to protect it from whatever other kind of collective adversity is threatened.

Deterrence and theories of corporate action

It is sometimes suggested that insufficient is known about corporate behaviour to justify the punishment of corporations or the design of sanctions against companies. For instance, Cressey[83] has maintained that it is not possible to account for corporate conduct in terms of biological or psychological characteristics, and hence that it is impossible to develop a theory of crime causation for corporate crime: '[b]ecause corporations cannot intend actions, none of their so-called criminal behavior can be explained'.[84]

This objection carries theoretical caution to an extreme.[85] If the objection is accepted, then even individual criminal liability for corporate malfeasance should be held in abeyance until a watertight theory of corporate action is found: if we lack an adequate theory of corporate action, we also lack an adequate theory of human action within corporations. In Chapter 4, we indeed show that the prospects for a theory of corporate action with general explanatory power that can guide the design of corporate criminal law are dim. There are many models which have limited explanatory power in limited contexts, and in most contexts there are multiple models which share some explanatory power.

---

[83] See, e.g., Cressey, 'The Poverty of Theory in Corporate Crime Research'.

[84] Ibid., 48. Cressey's focus is on the importance of managerial fraud; the conclusion of his paper neglects the structural considerations which often allow such fraud to occur in larger organisations. In a complex case such as the E. F. Hutton banking fraud, discussed in Chapter 1, the corporate conditions which gave rise to pervasive fraud almost certainly require corporate as well as individual liability to achieve a potent deterrent response.

[85] Consider the rich and constructive response to theoretical diversity in Morgan, *Images of Organization*. Recollect Holmes: 'Every year if not every day we have to wager our salvation upon some prophecy based upon imperfect knowledge' (*Abrams v United States* (1919) 250 US 616). Compare Vaughan, *Controlling Unlawful Organizational Behavior*, 105–12 (evolutionary program of reduction of transactional complexity urged rather than program calculated to exploit the potential deterrent capacity of non-monetary sanctions against corporations). For a critique of atheoretical incrementalism see Goodin, *Political Theory and Public Policy*, ch. 2.

What policy guidance can the lawmaker derive from such an analysis? Usually it would be impossible or impractical to pin-point which model most closely corresponds to the realities of decisionmaking within a particular corporation, and hence their different implications are of limited practical significance. The prime need is for sanctions capable of reflecting the implications of all the different models. Take, as one example, the punitive injunction, as discussed below.[86] Injunctive sanctions could be directed at individual actors within an organisation, regardless of what decisionmaking pattern predominates. Additionally, punitive injunctions against corporate offenders would be consistent with the model which views the corporation as a value-maximising rational actor. In other words, corporate as well as individual sanctioning effects could be achieved simultaneously by means of the one versatile sanction.

Although there may be no general theory of corporate action useful for criminal justice policy, we can at least devise multi-purpose sanctions like the punitive injunction and thereby hedge our theoretical bets.

Deterrence and corporate reform

The view has been advanced that punishment relates to individual wrongdoing whereas reform is the appropriate method of preventive control for corporations. A bold expression of this viewpoint is Owen Fiss's rejection of the concept of wrongdoing in the context of governmental bureaucracies:

> The concept of wrongdoer is highly individualistic. It presupposes personal qualities: the capacity to have an intention and to choose. Paradigmatically, a wrongdoer is one who intentionally inflicts harm in violation of an established norm. In the structural context, there may be individual wrongdoers, the police officer who hits the citizen, the principal who turns away the black child at the schoolhouse door, the prison guard who abuses the inmate; they are not, however, the target of the suit. The focus is on a social condition, not incidents of wrongdoing, and also on the bureaucratic dynamics that produce that condition. In a sense, a structural suit is an in rem proceeding where the res is the state bureaucracy. The costs and burdens of reformation are placed on the organization, not because it has 'done wrong', in either a literal or metaphorical sense, for it has neither an intention nor a will, but because reform is needed to remove a threat to constitutional values posed by the operation of the organization.[87]

This reconstruction lacks substance. First, as explained earlier, organisations are capable of manifesting intent in the form of corporate policy.[88] Second, the blameworthiness of organisational behaviour can be assessed by reference to patterns of behaviour and systems of control; corporate offences are now

---

[86] See the section 'Deterrence and sanctions against corporations' below.
[87] Fiss, 'The Supreme Court 1978 Term—Foreword: The Forms of Justice', 22–3.
[88] See the section 'Methodological individualism and corporate responsibility' above.

typically defined in a way which focuses upon incidents of wrongdoing, but that focus could well be changed[89] and indeed there are already some offences which in effect proscribe certain unwanted patterns of corporate behaviour (for example, unlawful manipulation of the stock market).[90] Third, organisations are often held blameworthy by the community which in consequence demands corporate reform; the ordinary reaction of people to avoidable corporate disasters is that the company involved can reform and that the event occurred because the company inexcusably failed to achieve the minimum standards expected of an organisation in that position.[91]

No one would disagree that civil rather than criminal process is typically the less drastic and more effective avenue for achieving compliance with the law through organisational change.[92] The point is that, contrary to individualistic preconceptions, the corporate condition does not preclude corporations from being labelled and punished as wrongdoers. Moreover, there is no reason to suppose that corporations must be sanctioned negatively (for example, fines, dissolution, temporary bans on activity) as opposed to positively in a manner geared to organisational reform. Indeed, where institutional reform by a corporation is necessary, the blameworthiness of a corporate defendant might well justify the use of a punitive injunction to insist on institutional reforms which, by reason of the element of punishment, are more exacting than those warranted by way of merely remedial injunctive relief.[93]

Deterrence and the limits of individual liability

The more acute deterrent angle of individualism is the claim that deterrence of corporate crime can be sufficiently achieved by punishing the individual persons responsible for offences. This claim, which is difficult to square with the development of corporate criminal liability at common law or the use of monetary penalties against companies under statute,[94] underestimates the

---

[89] See Braithwaite, *Corporate Crime in the Pharmaceutical Industry*, 309–10.
[90] See Securities Industry (NSW) Code, ss. 123–4.
[91] Consider, e.g., the pungent response in newspapers to the English Channel ferry disaster, especially the finding of an official inquiry that the ferry company, Thomson Thoresen, was comprehensively 'infected with the disease of sloppiness'; see UK, Department of Transport, *mv Herald of Free Enterprise*, para. 14.1; 'The Zeebrugge Disaster—Crime or Negligence' (1987) 137 *New Law Journal,* 959; 'Ferry Verdict Clears Way for Prosecutions: Manslaughter Charges to be Considered by DPP', *The Times,* 9 Oct. 1987, 1; Young, 'Where Does the Buck Stop?'
[92] See Hawkins, *Environment and Enforcement*, chs 6–10; Grabosky and Braithwaite, *Of Manners Gentle*, 190–4; Braithwaite, *To Punish or Persuade*, ch. 5; Ayers and Frank, 'Deciding to Prosecute White-Collar Crime'.
[93] For example, in a context such as the English Channel ferry disaster, the corporation concerned might be required to research, design, and implement bow-door safety devices and checking systems which improve upon state-of-the-art technology or compliance methods.
[94] See Brickey, *Corporate Criminal Liability*, ch. 2; Elzinga and Breit, *The Antitrust Penalties*. Proposals for codification of the criminal law in England and Canada echo the common law in its recognition of corporate criminal liability as a general principle: Great Britain, Law Reform Commission, *Report No. 143, Codification of the Criminal Law*, 94–7; Canada, Law Reform Commission, *Recodifying Criminal Law*, 22–4.

difficulties of enforcing individual liability as a general prescription.[95] These difficulties include enforcement overload; opacity of internal lines of corporate accountability; expendability of individuals within organisations; corporate separation of those responsible for the commission of past offences from those responsible for the prevention of future offences; and corporate safe-harbouring of individual suspects.[96]

Attention has repeatedly been drawn to the time-consuming nature of corporate crime investigations.[97] As two US federal prosecutors summed up the position:

> [E]conomic crimes are far more complex than most other federal offenses. The events in issue usually have occurred at a far more remote time and over a far more extensive period. The 'proof' consists not merely of relatively few items of real evidence but a large roomful of often obscure documents. In order to try the case effectively, the Assistant United States Attorney must sometimes master the intricacies of a sophisticated business venture. Furthermore, in the course of doing so, he, or the agents with whom he works, often must resolve a threshold question that has already been determined in most other cases: Was there a crime in the first place?[98]

If anything, this understates the difficulties which arise. Prosecutors are confronted with what amounts to a network of complexities: tortuous legislation, intricate accounting practices, convoluted organisational accountability, amnesia among witnesses, and jurisdictional complications.

A graphic example of the labour-intensiveness of corporate crime investigation emerged from the work of the special review committee which investigated questionable payments made by McDonnell Douglas to sell planes outside the US from 1969 to 1978.[99] The head of the committee conducted interviews over an eighteen-month period, and toted up 3,250 hours of billable time. Added to that effort, 15,000 hours were expended by his law firm, and Price Waterhouse logged a further 43,000 hours. These efforts were just a preliminary to the subsequent Department of Justice investigation.

It is also notorious that enforcement staff are thin across the ground.[100] This

[95] See generally C. D. Stone, 'The Place of Enterprise Liability ...', 30–1; Clinard and Yeager, *Corporate Crime*, ch. 12.
[96] Other considerations include the vigour and resources with which prosecutions of corporate officers are typically defended. See further Mann, *Defending White-Collar Crime*. For an instructive review of the difficulties encountered in the reckless homicide prosecution against the Ford Motor Company in the Pinto case see Cullen, Maakestad, and Cavender, *Corporate Crime under Attack*, chs 5–6.
[97] See, e.g., Bureau of National Affairs, *White-Collar Justice*, 3–4; Ogren, 'The Ineffectiveness of the Criminal Sanction in Fraud and Corruption Cases'.
[98] Wilson and Matz, 'Obtaining Evidence for Federal Economic Crime Prosecutions', 651. As one US Federal investigator reflected: 'When you walk into a US Attorney's office with three tons of records, you know you have just lost his attention' (Inspector General of the Department of Defense, J. H. Sherick, as quoted in Loomis, 'White-Collar Crime').
[99] 'McDonnell Investigator: Interviews for 1 1/2 Years', *NYT*, 31 July 1980, D2.
[100] See, e.g., Australia, Trade Practices Commission, *Annual Report 1980–1981*, ch. 1; Bequai, *White Collar Crime*, 148–50; Box, *Power, Crime, and Mystification*, 45–6; 'Swamped SEC is Forced to Retreat in Enforcement of Securities Laws', *WSJ*, 27 Dec. 1985, 11.

issue was aired at some length in 1978 during hearings conducted by the US Senate Subcommittee on Crime under the chairmanship of Senator Conyers. Concerned about the adequacy of the Justice Department's initiatives against white-collar crime, Senator Conyers put this question:

> The Department of Defense has 4,000 investigators and 6,000 auditors, and as we know, some planes do not fly and some ships still do not float. Let us face it, we are talking about only 6 per-cent of the Department of Justice's resources going into this incredibly complex legal prosecutorial effort against white-collar crime that is international in dimension. Can you give me some assurances that you can even just keep track of the files and the cases as they come in, much less follow them through to any conclusion? We seem to be enormously outnumbered.[101]

Individualism also presumes that accountability within companies can be readily determined. However, organisations have a well-developed capacity for obscuring internal accountability if confronted by outsiders.[102] Regulatory agencies, prosecutors and courts find it difficult or even impossible to unravel lines of accountability after the event because of the incentives personnel have to protect each other with a cover-up. As one of the authors concluded from an earlier study:

> [C]ompanies have two kinds of records: those designed to allocate guilt (for internal purposes), and those for obscuring guilt (for presentation to the outside world). When companies want clearly defined accountability they can generally get it. Diffused accountability is not always inherent in organizational complexity; it is in considerable measure the result of a desire to protect individuals within the organization by presenting a confused picture to the outside world. One might say that courts should be able to pierce this conspiracy of confusion. Without sympathetic witnesses from within the corporation who are willing to help, this is difficult. In the pharmaceutical industry, at least, the indictment of senior executives for corporate crimes has almost invariably been followed by their acquittal, even when the corporation is convicted.[103]

Outside investigators face many handicaps in getting to the truth. They have a rather limited capacity to arrive unannounced or to inspect a workplace without arousing suspicion. Outsiders can rarely match the technical knowledge insiders have of unique production or documentation processes. Internal investigators' specialised knowledge of their employer's product lines make them more effective probers than outsiders who are more likely to be generalists. Their greater technical capacity to spot problems is enhanced by a greater social capacity to do so. Inside compliance personnel are more likely than outsiders to know where problems of illegality have occurred previously, and

---

[101] US, HR, Committee on the Judiciary, Subcommittee on Crime, *White-Collar Crime*, Hearings, 95th Cong., 2nd Sess., 1978, 100.
[102] The Challenger disaster is one spectacular instance. See McDonnell, *Challenger: A Major Malfunction*; Vaughan, 'Autonomy, Interdependence and Social Control'.
[103] Braithwaite, *Corporate Crime in the Pharmaceutical Industry*, 324.

to be able to detect cover-ups.[104] This is rather like the difference between the capacity of government inspectors and that of internal compliance staff in the pharmaceutical industry to get answers:

> Our instructions to officers when dealing with FDA inspectors is to only answer the questions asked, not to provide any extra information, not to volunteer anything, and not to answer any questions outside your area of competence. On the other hand we [the corporate compliance staff] can ask anyone anything and expect an answer. They are told that we are part of the same family, and unlike the government, we are working for the same final objectives.[105]

The response of the present law to the difficulties of enforcement overload and opacity of organisational lines of accountability is to extend criminal liability to corporate entities in the hope of spurring companies to undertake internal disciplinary action and impose individual accountability as a matter of private policing. Monetary sanctions provide no guarantee that a corporate defendant will in fact take disciplinary action, although in theory they are supposed to provide sufficient pressure to achieve that aim.[106]

Another factor which tends to limit the deterrent efficacy of individual criminal liability for corporate crime is the expendability of individuals within organisations.[107] It is a truism that bureaucracies have greater staying power than their human functionaries; as Kenneth Boulding put it, the corporation 'marches on its elephantine way almost indifferent to its succession of riders'.[108] The risk thus arises of rogue corporations exploiting their capacity to toss off a succession of individual riders and, if necessary, to indemnify them in some way.[109] The continuing relevance of the risk of personnel expendability is evident from the reported reaction in England of Sir Jeffrey Stirling, Chairman of Peninsular and Oriental Steam Navigation Company, to the Zeebrugge ferry disaster: 'Responsibility lies squarely with those on board who had professional responsibility to ensure that the ship sailed safely'.[110] This assignment of responsibility contrasts starkly with the finding of an

[104] Consider the difficulty of unravelling accountability in cases such as *Brown v Riverstone Meat Co. Pty. Ltd.* (1985) ATPR 40–576 (the company was prosecuted on 24 counts; no employees were prosecuted). Consider also the problem of pinpointing all the individuals implicated in the widespread securities trading violations committed by banks in India; see 'India Scandal Growing', *SMH*, 4 June 1992, 40; 'ANZ Admits Indian Breach', *SMH*, 31 Oct. 1992, 38.

[105] Braithwaite, *Corporate Crime in the Pharmaceutical Industry*, 137.

[106] See the section 'Deterrence and sanctions against corporations' below.

[107] C. D. Stone, *Where the Law Ends*: 66; Clinard and Yeager, *Corporate Crime*, 298; Elzinga and Breit, *The Antitrust Penalties*, 38–40.

[108] Boulding, *The Organizational Revolution*, 139. See also Coleman, *The Asymmetric Society*, 26–7 ('The irrelevance of persons').

[109] See generally C. D. Stone, *Where the Law Ends*, 64–6; C. D. Stone, 'The Place of Enterprise Liability ...', 45–56; Ramsay, 'Liability of Directors for Breach of Duty and the Scope of Indemnification and Insurance'; Kraakman, 'Corporate Liability Strategies...', 861–2; Note, 'Indemnification of the Corporate Official for Fines and Expenses Arising from Criminal Antitrust Litigation'.

[110] As scathingly reported in Young, 'Where Does the Buck Stop?'; compare the reply of Stirling, *Guardian Weekly*, 25 Oct. 1987, 2.

official inquiry that the management of the ferry company, Townsend Car Ferries Limited (a subsidiary of P&O), had been jointly at fault in failing to ensure adequate standard operating procedures on board the ferry:

> All concerned in management, from the members of the Board of Directors down to the junior superintendents, were guilty of fault in that all must be regarded as sharing responsibility for the failure of management. From top to bottom the body corporate was infected with the disease of sloppiness.[111]

In such a case, corporate liability provides a broad-spectrum antidote which proceedings against employees would not necessarily achieve.

Consider also the extreme tactic adopted by some companies of setting up internal lines of accountability so as to have a 'vice-president responsible for going to jail'.[112] By offering an attractive sacrifice, the hope is that prosecutors will feel sufficiently satisfied with their efforts to refrain from pressing charges against the corporation or members of its managerial elite. Corporate criminal liability hardly avoids this risk of scapegoating but alleviates it by imposing responsibility on the corporate ruler.

The deterrent efficacy of individual criminal liability for corporate crime is further limited by the organisational divorce of responsibility for past offences from responsibility for future compliance. Deterrence of unlawful behaviour on behalf of organisations depends not merely upon threat-induced abstinence from illegality but upon threat-induced catalysis of preventive controls.[113] The personnel held responsible for a past offence, however, are not necessarily in a position to institute effective preventive action within an organisation. They may be moved elsewhere by the organisation (perhaps to some corporate Siberia, such as secondment to a university) or deprived of the power or status necessary to mount a preventive campaign.[114] Accordingly, there is reason to doubt the wisdom of a deterrent strategy which focuses merely upon individuals responsible for the commission of offences in the past. By contrast, corporate liability provides an incentive for the management of the day to undertake responsive organisational change whatever the proximity or remoteness of that management's connection with the events giving rise to prosecution.

Nor should it be forgotten that corporations are sometimes willing and able to provide individual suspects with a safe harbour. Suspected personnel may lie beyond the reach of extraterritorial process, or, where within reach, may nonetheless be hard to bring to justice.[115] An officer of an interstate or

---

[111] UK, Department of Transport, *mv Herald of Free Enterprise*, para. 14.1.
[112] Braithwaite, *Corporate Crime in the Pharmaceutical Industry*, 308.
[113] See Fisse, 'Reconstructing Corporate Criminal Law', 1159–60.
[114] Jail is the most obvious possibility. However, some exceptional entrepreneurs have been known to run their businesses successfully from behind bars. See, e.g., Horster-Philipps, *Im Schatten des Grossen Geldes*, 80–3 (Friedrich Flick launched his post–Second World War commercial empire from Landsberg jail while doing time as a convicted war criminal; meetings with key managers posing as legal advisers were held during visiting hours).
[115] See generally American Law Institute, *Model Penal Code, Tentative Draft No. 4* (1955), 150–1; Canada, Law Reform Commission, *Criminal Responsibility for Group Action*, 30; Fisse, 'The Social Policy of Corporate Criminal Responsibility', 380–2.

transnational company may authorise or instigate an offence without setting foot within the local jurisdiction or, after committing an offence locally on behalf of a corporation, may be transferred to an interstate or overseas branch or affiliate. In the former case, the officer's conduct may be immune because no act has been committed against local law, or it may not be covered by extradition arrangements. If the offence is extraditable, and if the offender can be extradited, the costs and resources involved in pursuing proceedings are too great to be incurred very often. If the offence is triable summarily, the officer usually may be prosecuted and tried *in absentia*, but it is not always possible to obtain enough evidence to secure a conviction or to enforce a sentence effectively. Where these impediments arise and a local corporation can be held liable for the relevant conduct, corporate liability provides a convenient alternative. By holding the local corporation liable, internal discipline may be stimulated abroad as well as locally; in effect, the corporation can be used as a medium for the international administration of the criminal law.[116]

Deterrence and sanctions against corporations

The individualist belief that it is impossible to punish corporations effectively[117] rests on the ground that corporations can be punished only by means of a fine or monetary penalty.[118] It is then pointed out that monetary sanctions are unlikely to make a deterrent impact on managers unless imposed at so high a level as to have unacceptable spillover effects on shareholders, workers, consumers and perhaps even the general economy.[119] However, it seems short-sighted to suppose that more suitable forms of sanction cannot be devised.[120]

Corporate entities cannot be sent to jail in any realistic sense,[121] and the sanction now almost always used—the fine or monetary penalty—tends to be

---

[116] Compare Timberg, 'The Corporation as a Technique of International Administration'.

[117] See, e.g., Lederman, 'Criminal Law, Perpetrator and Corporation'; Doig, Phillips and Manson, 'Deterring Illegal Behavior by Officials of Complex Organizations'.

[118] See, e.g., 'Developments in the Law—Corporate Crime', 1365–8; Posner, 'An Economic Theory of the Criminal Law', 1228–9; Byam, 'The Economic Inefficiency of Corporate Criminal Liability'.

[119] Compare Coffee, 'No Soul to Damn No Body to Kick', 400–5.

[120] See Australia, The Law Reform Commission, *Sentencing Penalties*, paras. 283–307; Cullen and Dubeck, 'The Myth of Corporate Immunity to Deterrence'; Braithwaite and Geis, 'On Theory and Action for Corporate Crime Control'; Coffee, 'No Soul to Damn No Body to Kick'; Geraghty, 'Structural Crime and Institutional Rehabilitation'; Yoder, 'Criminal Sanctions for Corporate Illegality'; Fisse, 'Reconstructing Corporate Criminal Law', 1221–43; Moore, 'Taming the Giant Corporation?'

[121] Corporations may, however, be subjected to dissolution or other forms of incapacitation but the overspill effects of negative sanctions of this nature are unacceptable except in dire cases calling for corporate capital punishment; see Chapter 5. See further Yoder, 'Criminal Sanctions for Corporate Illegality', 54–5; Braithwaite and Geis, 'On Theory and Action for Corporate Crime Control', 308–9; Fisse, 'Responsibility, Prevention and Corporate Crime'; Bosly, 'Responsibilité et Sanctions en Matière de Criminalité des Affairs'; Screvens, 'Les Sanctions Applicables aux Personnes Morales dans les Etats des Communautes Européenes'; Delatte, 'La Question de la Responsibilité Penale des Personnes Morales en Droit Belge', 210.

treated as a relatively minor cost of doing business.[122] There are, however, a number of other possibilities to be considered. These include equity fines (stock dilution), probation and punitive injunctions, adverse publicity, and community service.[123]

One promising possibility is corporate probation,[124] as now reflected in the US Sentencing Commission's *Guidelines for Organizational Defendants*, and as recommended in the following American Bar Association's *Standards for Criminal Justice*:

> Continuing judicial oversight. Although courts lack the competence or capacity to manage organizations, the preventive goals of the criminal law can in special cases justify a limited period of judicial monitoring of the activities of a convicted organization. Such oversight is best implemented through the use of recognized reporting, record keeping, and auditing controls designed to increase internal accountability—for example, audit committees, improved staff systems for the board of directors, or the use of special counsel—but it should not extend to judicial review of the legitimate 'business judgment' decisions of the organization's management or its stockholders or delay such decisions. Use of such a special remedy should also be limited by the following principles:
> (A) As a precondition, the court should find either (1) that the criminal behavior was serious, repetitive, and facilitated by inadequate internal accounting or monitoring controls or (2) that a clear and present danger exists to the public health or safety;
> (B) The duration of such oversight should not exceed the five- and two-year limits specified in standard 18.2.3 for probation conditions generally; and
> (C) Judicial oversight should not be misused as a means for the disguised imposition of penalties or affirmative duties in excess of those authorized by the legislature.[125]

A more stringent form of sanction[126] is the punitive injunction, a penal variant

---

[122] See, e.g., (1987) 1(3) *Corporate Crime Reporter* 10.
[123] See, e.g., Australia, The Law Reform Commission, *Sentencing Penalties*, paras. 283–307.
[124] See ABA, 3 *Standards for Criminal Justice*, 18.162–3, 18.179–84 ; Gruner, 'To Let the Punishment Fit the Organization'; C. D. Stone, 'A Slap on the Wrist for the Kepone Mob'; Geraghty, 'Structural Crime and Institutional Rehabilitation'; Solomon and Nowak, 'Managerial Restructuring'; Coffee, Gruner, and Stone, 'Standards for Organizational Probation'; Miester, 'Criminal Liability for Corporations that Kill'; Lofquist, 'Organizational Probation and the US Sentencing Commission'. In Australia, corporate probation can be ordered in theory (as under Crimes Act 1914 (Cth.), s. 19B; *see John C. Morish Pty. Ltd. v Luckman* (1977) 30 FLR 89; *Sheen v George Cornish Pty. Ltd.* (1978) 34 FLR 466; *Lanham v Brambles-Ruys Pty. Ltd.* (1984) 55 ALR 138), but has very rarely been used in practice.
[125] *ABA*, 3 *Standards for Criminal Justice*, 18.2.8(a)(v). For a discussion of the US Sentencing Commission's approach, see Lofquist, 'Organizational Probation and the US Sentencing Commission'.
[126] The limitations imposed under ABA Standard 18.2.8(a)(v)(A)(2), and (C) make the sentence of continuing judicial supervision remedial in nature and hence much akin to the civil injunctions which the SEC and other agencies have used to make corporations improve their compliance systems. In our view, this does not go far enough. Probation and continuing judicial oversight are rather benign sanctions. Certainly probation has usually been regarded as a soft sentencing option because it is more in the nature of a rehabilitative remedy than a deterrent or retributive punishment. Serious cases, it may be argued, call for a more potent sanction (e.g., a punitive injunction, as discussed below) which can impose deterrent punishment as well as spur internal compliance.

of the civil mandatory injunction.[127] A punitive injunction could be used not only to require a corporate defendant to revamp its internal controls but also to do so in some punitively demanding way. Instead of requiring a defendant merely to remedy the situation by introducing state-of-the-art preventive equipment or procedures, it would be possible to insist on the development of innovative techniques. The punitive injunction could thus serve as both punishment and super-remedy.

Although the idea of corporate probation and punitive mandatory injunctions may seem novel, the oddity is that the criminal law has developed such options so little. As John Coffee has observed, 'It is a curious paradox that the civil law is better equipped at present than the criminal law to authorise [disciplinary or structural] intervention. Corporate probation could fill this gap and at last, offer a punishment that fits the corporation'.[128]

As has been elaborated elsewhere,[129] probationary conditions or punitive injunctions offer a means of overcoming the worst limitations of fines or monetary penalties against corporations. One potential advantage is that the deterrent impact of these sanctions would rest largely on internal disciplinary sanctions and detraction from corporate or managerial power; these are impacts which, unless carried to extremes, can be borne by corporations without sending them into financial ruin. Another advantage would be to provide a specific means for achieving individual accountability for corporate offences: unlike fines or monetary penalties, probationary conditions or punitive injunctions could be used as a means of requiring corporate defendants to report in detail on the disciplinary action taken in response to being found liable.[130] The problem of overspills on relatively helpless or innocent persons might also be greatly reduced. The dominant impact of probation or punitive injunctions would be interference with managerial power and prestige, not exaction of cash or dilution of the value of shares. Accordingly, the loss inflicted would flow mainly to managers rather than to shareholders, workers or consumers. Moreover, instead of making an indiscriminate attack on all managers,[131] it would be possible to target particular managers or classes of manager under the terms of the probationary or injunctive order imposed.

The main question surrounding the prospect of probationary directives and punitive injunctions is whether they could be used without subjecting corporations to inefficient and excessively intrusive governmental intervention. Two answers may be given here. First, we tolerate the high social costs of imprisonment because of the view that fines of sufficient deterrent or retributive weight typically cannot be paid by individual offenders.[132] Because we

---

[127] See further Fisse, 'Reconstructing Corporate Criminal Law', ll56–7, ll64–5, l223–4. Compare with Fiss, *The Civil Rights Injunction*.
[128] Coffee, 'No Soul to Damn No Body to Kick', 459.
[129] Fisse and Braithwaite, 'Sanctions against Corporations'.
[130] Supervision and monitoring then becomes essential, one solution being to rely on special court-appointed masters or monitors. See further ABA, 3 *Standards for Criminal Justice*, l8.l62–3, l8.l82–3; Brakel, 'Special Masters in Institutional Litigation'.
[131] Compare the suggestion in Pepinsky, *Crime and Conflict*, 139, that fines against companies be paid by their personnel. Note also the implications for shareholders of the pass-through fines proposed in Kennedy, 'Criminal Sentences for Corporations'.
[132] Posner, *Economic Analysis of Law*, l68–9.

tolerate these costs, then the administrative and other costs associated with corporate probation or punitive injunctions may be defended on a similar ground. The options available are either to maintain a crime control system based on cash fines, which cannot be expected to work very well, or to resort to an alternative means of control which, although regrettably more costly, is more likely to be effective. Second, probation or punitive injunctions could be controlled in such a way as to avoid corporations being subjected to any overbearing regime of state control. For one thing, the customary sentencing practice of imposing severe sanctions only for serious offences is unlikely to be abandoned. For another, sentencing criteria could and should be devised so as to maximise freedom of enterprise in compliance systems.[133] One possibility would be to stipulate in the empowering legislation that, wherever practicable, corporate defendants be given the opportunity to indicate before sentence what disciplinary or other steps they propose to take in response to their conviction.

Retribution and Allocation of Responsibility for Corporate Crime

A further set of assumptions, derived from retributive thinking, underpins individualism. These assumptions are threefold:
(1) retributive theories of punishment presuppose individual as opposed to corporate responsibility;
(2) retributive punishment is preconditioned on fault, and there is no ethically defensible or workable concept of corporate fault; and
(3) punishment in its application to corporations violates the retributive principle of just desert.
These assumptions, it will be argued, rest on quicksand.

A threshold difficulty is the questionable status of retributive theories of criminal justice. It has been argued that retributive theories of criminal justice are fundamentally flawed because they fail to provide any coherent answer to the problem of how to reduce crime in modern society.[134] It is unnecessary here to enter into that debate. It is sufficient to point out that the field of retribution is not obviously bounded by individualism. There are flags of corporate retributivism.

Retribution, responsibility and desert

The conventional wisdom is that retributive theories of punishment dictate individual as opposed to corporate responsibility. Sceptical inquiry, however, reveals that retribution is not inherently tied to the requital of individual desert; the notion of desert may be corporate or individual.

Let us take retributivism as a collection of theories of punishment which have in common the belief that punishment of criminals should be what they

---

[133] Fisse, 'Criminal Law and Consumer Protection', 194–9.
[134] Braithwaite and Pettit, *Not Just Deserts*.

deserve rather than what is necessary as a matter of utility.[135] For the retributivist, it can be right to punish in proportion to the culpability of the offender even if no good comes of doing so. There are many versions of retribution; perhaps the most popular today is the conception of punishment in proportion to desert as a measured way of expressing the community's degree of reprobation for a wrongdoer.[136]

We have already argued that reprobative feelings are directed at corporations as well as at individuals, and that corporations are appropriate subjects of blame and responsibility. Hence, if one is willing to concede the validity of the reprobative interpretation of retribution, a parallel view of retribution is applicable to corporations.

The classic interpretation of retribution was vindication or social amends for the evil done, the core idea being justice as fairness.[137] When one moral agent breaks the law while all other moral agents bear the burdens of self-restraint, fairness requires the imposition of an offsetting burden on the lawbreaker.[138] This offsetting burden is punishment. If we accept that corporations are moral agents[139] and that organisations bear burdens of self-restraint in complying with the law, then this form of retribution applies to corporate as well as to individual persons. Applying it in a coherent and useful way is another matter, however, whether for corporations or individuals. Retribution as a balancing of benefits and burdens is based on the notion of restoring an equitable distribution of the burdens of self-restraint. However, the burdens of self-restraint are so various as to make equality of distribution fanciful. Individual males face a burden of restraining themselves from rape that females do not. A chemical company faces burdens of environmental compliance that an individual or a finance company does not confront; for General Motors, refraining from stealing a loaf of bread is no burden whereas a slum-dweller may be exposed to hunger pangs. The notion of punishment as restoring an 'equilibrium' or 'balance' of benefits and burdens thus seems incoherent for both individual and corporate wrongdoers. We will not attempt to settle this debate here. Our only point is that the retributive theory in question is not exclusively individualistic in application but could be extended to corporate entities.

At heart, most concerns about punishing corporations expressed by retributivists reduce to the assumption that because corporations are inanimate they do not deserve to be blamed or punished. Here the retributivist confronts exactly the same dilemma as deterrence theorists and other consequentialists. Do corporations qualify as responsible agents? We hope that we have convinced the reader that they do. Moreover, in some respects corporations may

[135] See generally Singer, *Just Deserts*; Murphy, *Retribution, Justice and Therapy*; Grupp, *Theories of Punishment*, 13–114; Ezorsky, *Philosophical Perspectives on Punishment*, 102–34.

[136] See von Hirsch, *Past or Future Crimes*.

[137] See Kant, *The Metaphysical Elements of Justice*, 99–107.

[138] See further Falls, 'Retribution, Reciprocity, and Respect for Persons'; Finnis, 'The Restoration of Retribution'; Sadurski, *Giving Desert Its Due*.

[139] See the section 'Methodological individualism and corporate responsibility' above.

be better endowed than individuals to be the subject of responsibility. Corporations, it may be argued, have a number of advantages when it comes to rational decisionmaking, including access to a pool of intelligence and the resources to acquire a superior knowledge of legal and other obligations. Indeed, it can even happen that while the corporation deserves to be blamed for a corporate crime, no individuals deserve blame. For example, a corporation may be culpable for sloppy standard operating procedures (SOPs) that provide inadequate assurances of product safety. These SOPs may have been written by a committee, the members of which are now employed elsewhere, retired or dead. Or the SOPs may have been collectively written by a committee dominated by executives of a parent company that once owned this company. These circumstances will be unusual, however. Mostly, there will be both individuals and a corporation that are available to be blamed and deserving of blame. In these latter circumstances, the positive retributivist prescription is clear that all who deserve blame should be blamed.[140] Generally, however, positive retributivists have ducked the implication of their theory that 'all who are blameworthy, no matter how many, should be punished in proportion to their blame'.[141] In later chapters, we argue the weaker position that all who are blameworthy should at least be held responsible, though not necessarily subjected to formal punishment by the state. To this extent, positive retributivists should applaud our practical policy prescription as headed in the direction of an improvement over present selective punishment practices, even if it does not go far enough in their terms by failing to insist on formal punishment proportionate to blameworthiness. While we advance a consequentialist rationale for seeking to hold all responsible who are responsible, positive retributivists must approve this principle on retributive grounds. Positive retributivists should view it as a necessary but not a sufficient condition for securing justice.[142]

Defining corporate fault

Is it possible to devise an ethically defensible and workable concept of corporate fault?[143] This is a difficult task, but given that corporate blameworthiness

---

[140] This is not true of negative retributivists. It is only true for full and positive retributivists. Negative retributivists support only 1 and 3 of the following constraints; positive retributivists support 2 and 4; full retributivists support all four: (1) no one other than a person found guilty of a crime may be punished for it; (2) anyone found guilty of a crime must be punished for it; (3) punishment must not be more than of a degree commensurate with the nature of the crime and the culpability of the criminal; (4) punishment must not be less than of a degree commensurate with the nature of the crime and the culpability of the criminal. See Braithwaite and Pettit, *Not Just Deserts*, 34–5; Mackie, 'Morality and the Retributive Emotions'.

[141] Braithwaite, 'Challenging Just Deserts', 725. A retributivist who has refused to duck this issue is Schlegel, *Just Deserts for Corporate Criminals*.

[142] While positivist retributivists must agree with the principle that all who are responsible should be held responsible, they may also disagree with the methods we will advance for securing this objective. Some retributivists may believe that holding a person responsible by any mechanism short of formal determination of guilt by a criminal court is unjust.

[143] See further Fisse, 'Reconstructing Corporate Criminal Law', 1183–213.

is a well-known phenomenon,[144] there is reason to believe that a workable concept can be constructed.[145]

The general principle at common law is that corporate criminal liability requires personal corporate fault, a principle endorsed in England by the House of Lords in *Tesco Supermarkets v Nattrass*.[146] This principle is highly unsatisfactory, mainly because it fails to reflect corporate blameworthiness.[147] To prove fault on the part of one managerial representative of a company is not to show that the company was at fault as a company but merely that one representative was at fault; the *Tesco* principle does not reflect personal fault but amounts to vicarious liability for the fault of a restricted range of representatives exercising corporate functions. This compromised form of vicarious liability is doubly unsatisfactory because the compromise is struck in a way that makes it difficult to establish corporate criminal liability against large companies. Offences committed on behalf of large concerns are often visible only at the level of middle management whereas the *Tesco* principle requires proof of fault on the part of a top-level manager. By contrast, fault on the part of a top-level manager is much easier to prove in the context of small companies. Yet that is the context where there is usually little need to impose corporate criminal liability in addition to or in lieu of individual criminal liability. This inability to reflect the demands of enforcement in the context of large companies has led to the abandonment of the *Tesco* principle under the Australian Trade Practices Act,[148] an approach consistent with the general common law principle under US federal law that a company is liable for the conduct and fault of any employee acting on its behalf.[149]

One possible solution is to focus more on a company's reactions to having committed the *actus reus* of an offence.[150] Corporate liability for wrongdoing traditionally has depended on proof of responsibility for causally relevant acts or omissions at or before the time the wrongdoing is manifested.[151] It is difficult to see why the law should focus exclusively on that timeframe. Even with individual offenders, community sentiments of reactive fault can run quite deep. Consider the hit-run driver: it is not so much the hitting but the running after the event that provokes condemnation.

---

[144] For the philosophical backdrop, see French, *Collective and Corporate Responsibility*.

[145] In any event, as Stone has pointed out, corporate moral blameworthiness is not necessarily an essential condition for imposing corporate criminal liability: C. D. Stone, 'A Comment on "Criminal Responsibility in Government"', 243.

[146] [1972] AC 153. See also *Universal Telecasters (Qld) Ltd. v Guthrie* (1978) 32 FLR 361; *Nordik Industries Ltd. v Regional Controller of Inland Revenue* [1976] 1 NZLR 194; *Canadian Dredge & Dock Co. Ltd. v The Queen* (1985) 19 CCC (3d) 1.

[147] For a criticism of this and other weaknesses of the *Tesco* principle see Fisse, 'Consumer Protection and Corporate Criminal Responsibility', 113.

[148] Trade Practices Act 1974 (Cth.), s. 84. See further Australia, *The Trade Practices Act*, 28–9.

[149] *United States v Illinois Cent. R.R.* (1937) 303 US 239; *Standard Oil Co. v United States* (1962) 307 F.2d 120. See further Brickey, *Corporate Criminal Liability* 3.04; 'Developments in the Law—Corporate Crime', 1247–57. See also *R. v Australasian Films Ltd.* (1921) 29 CLR 195.

[150] See Fisse, 'Reconstructing Corporate Criminal Law', 1183–213; French, *Collective and Corporate Responsibility*, ch. 11.

[151] See generally Fisse, *Howard's Criminal Law*, 13–16.

Corporate blameworthiness can be judged within a reactive timeframe, a timeframe which generates the concept of reactive corporate fault.[152] Reactive corporate fault may be broadly defined as unreasonable corporate failure to devise and undertake satisfactory preventive or corrective measures in response to the commission of the *actus reus* of an offence by personnel acting on behalf of the organisation. This concept reflects three commonplace factors:

(1) the strength of communal attitudes of resentment toward corporations that stonewall or otherwise fail to react diligently when their attention is drawn to the harmful or excessively risky nature of their operations;[153]

(2) the inevitability in large- or medium-size organisations of management by exception, whereby compliance is treated as a routine matter to be delegated to inferiors and handled by them unless a significant problem arises;[154] and

(3) the extensive reliance on civil modes of enforcement in corporate regulation and the typical perception among enforcement agencies that criminal prosecutions against companies usually are warranted only where civil enforcement has failed.[155]

The concept of reactive fault offers a way of attributing intentionality to a corporation in a manner both workable and corporate in orientation.[156] Corporations can and do act intentionally in so far as they enact and implement corporate policies.[157] Frequently, however, a boilerplate compliance policy will be in place,[158] and it is rare to find a company displaying a criminal policy, at least not a written one, at or before the time of commission of the *actus reus* of an offence. The position is different if the timeframe of inquiry is extended so as to cover what a defendant has done in response to the commission of the *actus reus* of an offence. What matters then is not a corporation's general policies of compliance, but what it specifically proposes to do to implement a program of internal discipline, structural reform, or compensation.[159] This reorientation allows blameworthy corporate intentionality to be flushed out more easily than is possible when the inquiry is confined to corporate policy at or before the time of the *actus reus*.

---

[152] See Fisse, 'Reconstructing Corporate Criminal Law', 1201–13.

[153] See, e.g., Black, 'The Erebus Inquiry', 189–90; 'Forewarnings of Fatal Flaws', *Time*, 25 June 1975, 58 (Firestone 500 tyre scandal); *Corporate Crime Reporter*, 3 April 1989, 15 (Ashland Oil case).

[154] See generally Bittel, *Management by Exception;* Mintzberg, *The Structuring of Organizations*, ch. 21.

[155] See, e.g., Hawkins, *Environment and Enforcement*.

[156] See Fisse, 'Reconstructing Corporate Criminal Law', 1183–92.

[157] See the section 'Methodological individualism and corporate responsibility' above.

[158] Fisse, 'Reconstructing Corporate Criminal Law', 1191–2. Typically, corporations take the elementary precaution of installing compliance policies and procedures sufficient to show the absence of such *mens rea*. The classic example is General Electric's Policy Directive 20.5, as more honoured in breach than observance during the electrical equipment conspiracies. See Fisse and Braithwaite, *The Impact of Publicity on Corporate Offenders*, ch. 16.

[159] Fisse, 'Reconstructing Corporate Criminal Law', 1205.

Consider the Firestone 500 tyre scandal in the US, which arose in 1979 from the failure of this large corporation to cease marketing or to recall a radial tyre which proved to be unsafe in use.[160] It was impossible to find any palpable flaw in Firestone's general compliance policies, and no manager could fairly be blamed for putting the tyre on the market. However, it was relatively easy to show that the company had impliedly adopted a reactive policy of not promptly implementing a recall program in response to the overwhelming evidence that the tyre was unsafe. Provided that a company in such a situation is placed fully on notice that it is expected to react by creating and implementing a convincing and responsive program of preventive or remedial action, failure to comply within a specified reasonable time would usually[161] manifest a corporate policy of non-compliance, or at least negligence as a collectivity in failing to achieve compliance.[162] Under this approach, a company could be held liable where, having committed the *actus reus* of an offence,[163] it displays a reactive policy of non-compliance with the requirements imposed by the court before which a finding of liability for the *actus reus* is made.[164] Such an approach is consistent with French's injunction to reject the abstraction of moral persons into 'mere ahistorical decision-makers' and to treat them instead as 'historical, unique entities, actors with memories, pasts and projects'.[165]

Retribution and desert in distribution

A further plank of individualism is the alleged injustice of punishing a corporate entity given that the impact will be transmitted to morally unresponsible associates. How can the distribution of punishment to innocent personnel, shareholders or consumers be reconciled with a desert-based position that moral responsibility requires personal fault?

[160] US, HR, Committee of the Judiciary, Subcommittee on Crime, *Corporate Crime*, 3.
[161] In some cases failure to comply might arise from the conduct of external parties or the occurrence of natural events.
[162] Such an approach is also capable of exposing blameworthy personnel, especially if particular managers are named in advance as being individually accountable for initiating and supervising compliance by the company. See further Coleman, *The Asymmetric Society*, 102–4; Geraghty, 'Structural Crime and Institutional Rehabilitation', 372; Fisse, 'Responsibility, Prevention and Corporate Crime', 272. However, it would be unwise to rely exclusively on individual liability. One reason for targeting a corporate defendant in compliance-oriented enforcement is that it may be impossible, impractical or unfair to impose individual criminal liability in the event of non-compliance by a corporation with its side of the deal. It is also apparent that when compliance is the prime goal, enforcement seeks to harness the corporate elephant rather than temporary individual riders: *Hartford-Empire Co. v United States* (1945) 323 US, 386, 433–4. See further Whiting, 'Antitrust and the Corporate Executive', 951–7.
[163] Via any employee acting on its behalf, and not in the *Tesco Supermarkets v Nattrass* sense of 'personal' corporate liability.
[164] For more detailed proposals as to the legal structure of reactive corporate fault see Fisse, 'Reconstructing Corporate Criminal Law', 1201–6.
[165] French, 'Commentary' (1983) 2 *Business and Professional Ethics Journal*, 89, 91.

A corporation itself may be regarded as a blameworthy moral agent, and if punishment is inflicted upon a corporation which has displayed corporate fault, the indirect infliction of suffering upon innocent associates falls into a similar category as the suffering experienced by the family of a person convicted and sentenced to punishment. This is a problem to be addressed but does not preclude the punishment of companies for several reasons. First, cost-bearing associates are not themselves subject to the stigma of conviction and criminal punishment—they are not convicts but corporate distributees.[166] Second, employees and stockholders accede to a distributional scheme in which profits and losses from corporate activities are distributed on the basis of position in the company or type of investment rather than degree of deserved praise or blame. Participants in the scheme are estopped from denying that the flow-through of corporate losses is just, because they have opted for entitlements subject to corporate risk, not 'just deserts'.[167] Third, and above all, not to punish an enterprise at fault would be to allow corporations to accumulate and distribute to associates a pool of resources which does not reflect the social cost of production. Justice as fairness requires, as a minimum, that the cost of corporate offences be internalised by the enterprise. Where an offence has been committed through the fault of an enterprise, punishment may prevent the cost of that offence from being externalised and thereby imposed on other innocent parties.[168]

Safeguarding Individual Interests

A fourth postulate of individualism is that individuals are best safeguarded against injustice by focusing on individual criminal responsibility and the substantive or procedural constraints that govern the imposition of criminal responsibility. There is some force in this way of looking at individual criminal responsibility, which has often been portrayed as a refined form of liability that has displaced the crudity and injustice of vicarious or collective forms of liability. However, there are major flaws in what individualism has to offer. Four are addressed in the following sections:
(1) individualism's failure to consider the likelihood that abolition of corporate liability would result in the oppressive imposition of individual liability;

---

[166] Lederman, 'Criminal Law, Perpetrator and Corporation', 322, does not answer this point.
[167] We disagree with Lederman, 'Criminal Law, Perpetrator and Corporation', 321. First, if shareholders opt for a system of entitlements as opposed to one based on just deserts, it is irrelevant that they fail to foresee particular incidents affecting the pool of resources in which they are entitled to share. Second, given the incidence of serious corporate crime over the past decade and earlier, naive would be the investor who believes that his or her chosen company is immune to involvement in major offences.
[168] In Lederman, 'Criminal Law, Perpetrator and Corporation', 332–4, it is argued that illegal profits should be removed not by corporate criminal liability but by civil action. This misses the point that blameworthy corporate offences represent a social cost of production which justice as fairness requires to be internalised irrespective of whether such offences result in financial profit.

(2) individualism's neglect of procedural justice within internal corporate justice systems;

(3) individualism's inattention to structural inequality; and

(4) the tendency of both target-driven and objective-driven strategies for enforcement against individuals to scapegoat while missing the major offenders and the deepest problems.

Substantive protection of individuals

Individualism neglects the important role of corporate criminal responsibility in providing a safety valve which avoids the need to impose harsh forms of liability on individual managers or employees. Corporations provide convenient surrogates in situations where it is harsh to impose individual criminal liability, whether by reason of corporate pressures, oppressive rules of criminal liability or resort to exemplary punishment.[169] Corporate criminal liability can be economical of distress by avoiding the socially bruising experience of conviction and punishment in a significant range of cases where individual criminal liability might otherwise be imposed.[170] From the standpoint of retributive theory, the punishment of corporations may preserve the distributive principle of desert by avoiding the imposition of undeserved or disproportionate forms of criminal liability on individual personnel.

This point is often neglected by the supporters of individualism. Dennis Thompson, for instance, has suggested that liability be imposed on managers for failure to take reasonable care in supervision and that negligence-based liability is justifiable in the context of organisational harm-causing:

> The degree of care demanded by a standard of conduct traditionally has been set in proportion to the apparent risk; arguably, that risk may be higher in organisations. The magnitude and persistence of the harm from even a single act of negligence in a large organisation is usually greater than from the acts of individuals on their own. The greater risk comes from not only the effects of size but also from those of function. In the common law of official nonfeasance, for example, public officials whose duties include the 'public peace, health or safety' may be criminally liable for negligence for which other officials would not be indictable at all. Because of the tendency of organisational negligence to produce greater harm, we may be justified in attaching more serious penalties to less serious departures from

---

[169] As in the case of 'show-case' prosecutions where the aim is to make a general deterrent or educative impression (e.g., the Sharp microwave advertising prosecution, discussed in Fisse and Braithwaite, *The Impact of Publicity on Corporate Offenders*, ch. 10), where the offence imposes strict responsibility (e.g., *Darwin Bakery Pty. Ltd. v Sully* (1981) 36 ALR 371; *Majury v Sunbeam Corporation Ltd.* [1974] 1 NSWLR 659; *Allen v United Carpet Mills Pty. Ltd.* [1989] VR 323; *Alphacell Ltd. v Woodward* [1972] AC 824), or where the scope of a prohibition is being expansively interpreted (*United States v United States Gypsum Co.*(1978) 438 US 422, 440–1).

[170] Compare McCormack, 'The Tightening White Collar'.

standards. Although the departure may be ordinary, the potential harm may be gross.[171]

Although the gravity of much harm of organisational origin is undeniable, Thompson's proposal for stricter standards of individual liability is fraught with the risk of injustice.[172] As Christopher Stone has remarked:[173]

> [T]o move the law in this direction is, at least by degrees, to loosen the criminal law's moral tethers. Negligence is shadowy. Vicariousness is plastic (who, after all, will appear, after the fact, to have been in 'a responsible position?'). Neither squares well with fair notice, intent, or real blameworthiness.[174]

Indeed, a vicious irony of Thompson's approach is that in seeking to impose stricter standards of individual liability it departs from the liberal values traditionally manifest in individualism.[175] Where stricter standards need to be imposed, a more obvious approach is to rely on corporate liability and thereby to minimise the need to sacrifice liberal protections for individuals. Who would disagree with the liberal premise that the rights of individuals are more fragile and less easily defended by their beneficiaries than are the rights accorded to collectivities?[176]

Procedural justice in internal disciplinary systems

Individualism focuses on procedural protections in the criminal justice system at the expense of the less visible but nonetheless real risks of injustice within corporate internal disciplinary systems. If criminal liability were to be confined to individual criminal liability, it would hardly follow that the risk of injustice could be controlled by the protections available within the criminal

---

[171] D. F. Thompson, 'Criminal Responsibility in Government', 208–9. This approach has been adopted under the California Penal Code, s. 387. Bolder still are proposals for holding corporate officers strictly responsible for offences committed by subordinates. See, e.g., Pepinsky, *Crime and Conflict*, 139; Stretton, *Capitalism, Socialism and the Environment*, 127–8. Strict liability has been imposed in the US in some statutory contexts under the *Park* doctrine: see *US v Park* (1975) 421 US 658. For a defence of strict liability, based partly on an optimistic view of the exercise of prosecutorial discretion, see Brickey, 'Criminal Liability of Corporate Officers for Strict Liability Offenses'. For more critical analyses see Spiegelhoff, 'Limits on Individual Accountability for Corporate Crimes'; Hare, 'Reluctant Soldiers'.
[172] Which is not to deny that such an approach may be unworkable as well; see Conard, 'A Behavioral Analysis of Directors' Liability for Negligence'.
[173] See further Watkins, 'Electrical Equipment Antitrust Cases'; Duke, 'Conspiracy, Complicity, Corporations, and the Federal Code Reform'; Grippando, 'Caught in the Non-Act'; Kahan, 'Criminal Liability under the Food, Drug, and Cosmetic Act'; Goodwin, 'Individual Liability of Agents for Corporate Crimes under the Proposed Federal Criminal Code'; Kruse, 'Criminal Liability for Negligence of Business Leaders'; Gelb, 'Director Due Care Liability'.
[174] C. D. Stone, 'A Comment on "Criminal Responsibility in Government"', 246.
[175] An irony highlighted by the trial of General Yamashita: see *In re Yamashita* (1945) 327 US 1; Reel, *The Case of General Yamashita*.
[176] See Dan-Cohen, *Rights, Persons, and Organizations*, ch. 4.

justice system. Thus, the effect of holding a director criminally responsible for failure to exercise reasonable care and due diligence in the management of a company could easily extend to internal disciplinary action against the subordinates whose conduct has triggered the director's criminal liability. Indeed, it may be hypothesised that the tougher the resort to individual liability for corporate crime, the higher the pressure to take consequential disciplinary action against other personnel involved. The most obvious course of action for directors under concerted personal attack is deflection of blame by launching a disciplinary assault on others.

The fundamental underlying failure of individualism lies in its failure to recognise the existence of private systems of justice within corporations. As Clifford Shearing and Phillip Stenning have explained:

> What [the liberal frame of individualism] does is construct and juxtapose two ideal entities: the state and the individual. The category 'individual' has taken on a residual character in that if a political legal entity is not part of the state it is then conceived of as an individual. This analytic strategy has made possible the political–legal sleight of hand through which corporations are treated, for certain important purposes, as 'individuals' even though they are empirically very different from flesh and blood individuals and, indeed, very often are more similar to states. Although this piece of conjuring has maintained the liberal frame it has not been useful in facilitating an understanding of critical aspects of private policing. Most important, it has obscured the similarity between the state and large corporations as political–legal entities. The latter's stature as authorities with the resources and power to rival the influence of the state *and* with jurisdiction over substantial territories and communities has not been adequately explored. This has been particularly detrimental to our understanding of the role of corporations in defining and maintaining social order.[177]

Ironically, individualism has tended to inhibit our understanding of individual responsibility: it has concealed rather than revealed the capacity of corporate liability to achieve individual accountability at the level of internal discipline.[178]

Inequality

Individualism also has disturbingly inegalitarian implications.[179] If scarce enforcement resources are taken away from the imposition of corporate liability and reallocated to the pursuit of individual defendants, what is likely to occur?

Resources would be invested in the costly, resource-intensive task of chasing individuals instead of easing the problem by proceeding against corporations, particularly where it is difficult to mount effective prosecutions against

---

[177] *Private Policing*, 14.
[178] See further Chapters 3–5 in this book.
[179] See generally Braithwaite, 'Paradoxes of Class Bias in Criminal Justice'.

individuals. It is not difficult for powerful actors to structure their affairs so that all of the pressures to break the law surface at lower levels of their organisation, or in another subordinate organisation. The American executive of a drug company who wants to sell products to Middle Eastern governments hires an agent to do the negotiation. The agent is paid an enormous fee, which is sufficient to cover bribes to government officials. The drug company, which would not dream of putting pressure on its own scientists to compromise their standards of integrity, will give the toxicological testing of a new drug to an outside laboratory known for its sloppy standards. The contract laboratory maintains its popularity with the pharmaceutical giant by telling it what it wants to hear about the safety of the drug, even if it involves fudging data. The reputable chemical corporation can contract out to a disposal company, which, being controlled by organised crime, is not particularly fussy about environmental laws. A classic illustration of the passing of blame downward in the class structure is in mining. A common strategy of mine owners is to put workers on piece rates based on the amount of coal or asbestos extracted in a given day. Such a strategy often produces the situation of miners wanting to go into workings that are unsafe, or even doing so against the counsel of management.

Even if there were enough enforcement resources to implement a crime control strategy of individualism, it would not follow that those resources should be used exclusively in the pursuit of individual criminal liability. The potential gain would be a minimal increase in the numbers of individuals brought to justice at the expense of losing the indirect but multiple sanctioning effects of corporate liability. Granted, the odds might be altered by reducing the substantive and procedural protections now enjoyed by defendants in the criminal process (for example, by departing from subjective fault requirements,[180] or by generally inverting the persuasive burden of proof),[181] but this would be a drastic step and one rarely taken seriously. A more commendable approach is to adopt a mixed strategy, retaining corporate as well as individual liability, and improving the capacity of corporate liability to achieve accountability at the level of internal discipline.

Target-driven v objective-driven enforcement

Individualism receives much support from US prosecutors and commentators who believe that the only way to genuinely deter corporate crime is to put the individuals responsible behind bars. As an outgrowth of this belief, some American prosecutors have a score-card mentality, measuring their own performance against how many big players they can put in prison. This individual target-driven model can be contrasted with an objective-driven model, which is more predominant among Australian and, we suspect, most British

---

[180] Compare Proceeds of Crime Act 1987 (Cth.), ss. 81, 82, 85.
[181] Compare Taxation Administration Act 1953 (Cth.), s. 8Y.

Commonwealth enforcement agencies. We will see that both approaches are susceptible to enforcement failure and convenient scapegoating of individuals.

Under the objective-driven model, objectives are set for a major investigation, then criminal targets are set for individuals whose conviction would assist the accomplishment of those objectives.[182] Under the target-driven model, as soon as the investigator gets promising evidence against any major target, he or she goes after that target. When the evidence becomes strong with that target, it is deal time, and item number one on the prosecutor's deal-making agenda is to extract information from the suspect on bigger and better targets. So the investigator is led from target to target instead of from objective to target. We see this clearly with the series of major insider trading cases on Wall Street in the mid to late 1980s. First, Dennis Levine gave in and then helped the government to lay charges against other members of his ring—investment bankers from Shearson Lehman; Lazard Freres; Goldman, Sachs; and a lawyer from Wachtell Lipton.[183] Ultimately, Ivan Boesky was caught in the net. 'Boesky, to the surprise of few on the street, had offered up Martin Siegel ... Siegel, in turn, had offered up Robert Freeman, head of the arbitrage department at the impeccable Goldman, Sachs; Richard Wigton, head of arbitrage at Kidder, Peabody; and Timothy Tabor, former head of arbitrage at Merrill Lynch'.[184] After dramatic Wall Street arrests of these suspects, with handcuffs slapped publicly on them, their indictments were finally dropped. However, the trail ultimately led to the conviction of the junk-bond king, Michael Milken.

This was a case where the target-driven strategy led ultimately to a netting of a truly major shark and many lesser sharks. More typically, however, the strategy is side-tracked away from the major sharks and settles for a sequence of medium-sized sharks. So clear was this perception of the way the world worked at Drexel Burnham Lambert that when Dennis Levine was accused by the US SEC of making $12.6 million in illegal profits through insider trading in 54 stocks, the following joke did the rounds at Drexel: 'Did you hear why Mike [Milken] fired Dennis [Levine]?' quips the Drexel investment banker. 'Because anybody who had to do fifty-four trades to make twelve million dollars couldn't be any good.'[185]

It seems harsh to criticise US corporate law enforcers for following a target-driven strategy because at least this strategy has delivered a much more impressive record of individual convictions than British Commonwealth enforcers can boast as a result of their objective-driven investigations. A fair

---

[182] This is a fair description of the conceptual framework of enforcement of the Australian Trade Practices Commission, where one of the authors is a part-time Commissioner. For a more detailed description of the model by a consultant to the Australian Securities Commission responsible for the major 'Rothwell's' investigation, see Warnick, 'The Investigation of Fraud'.

[183] Bruck, *The Predators' Ball*, 254.

[184] Ibid., 328.

[185] Ibid., 254.

juxtaposition of the failures of the two strategies is provided by the BCCI case. After its collapse, this internationalised bank, which operated principally out of London, was characterised by the Governor of the Bank of England as a criminal culture up to the top of its structure.[186] The Bank of England was the most important among many regulatory authorities that had failed to take credible enforcement action against the bank until it was too late. The objective-driven investigation that the Bank of England had underway for a long time before the collapse was an utter failure.[187] The Governor of the Bank of England was aware of allegations of extensive money laundering, but rested content with the convictions of two junior employees in the UK who had been involved. The Bank of England was satisfied that 'there was no evidence that a senior level of management was implicated'.[188]

US regulators also failed to incapacitate a criminal organisation that would seem to have been involved in fraud, tax evasion, and drug and terrorist money laundering on an unprecedented scale. Yet the failure of the entrepreneurial target-driven US enforcement system was not so total. A target-driven sting operation in 1988 led to the jailing of five BCCI officers in connection with Florida drug money laundering and the conviction of one of BCCI's main units.[189] One might say that while the British were happy to settle for blaming two junior scapegoats as they sat on their hands, at least the Americans did put five slightly more senior scapegoats in jail. But law-enforcers in neither nation got to the bottom of the systemic operation of an off-books bank within a bank, immune from the supervision of any regulatory authority, and run at the behest of senior management, until after the bank began to collapse. The question we must ask is whether there is a more effective process for determining the systemic significance of such individual convictions secured by the target-driven American process. Is there a better investigative process than the Bank of England model, driven by such preoccupation with the objective of keeping a bank solvent that the agency is all too willing to accept top management assurances that any wrongdoing is the fault of a couple of junior scapegoats?

Scapegoating vilified individuals is endemic in legal systems.[190] It may involve a corporate–state conspiracy to send whistle-blowers to jail to punish them for whistle-blowing.[191] More commonly, it involves corporate account-

[186] WSJE, 24 July 1991, 9.
[187] 'Bingham Finds the Old Lady Seriously Wanting', Guardian Weekly, 1 Nov. 1992, 4.
[188] Financial Times, 24 July 1991, 6.
[189] WSJ, 8 July 1991, A3.
[190] Examples persist notwithstanding such dramatic antidotes as the film 'Breaker Morant'. A recent instance is the blood contamination scandal in France, leading to the prosecution and conviction of three doctors but not the bureaucrats and politicians who fostered the disaster; see 'Doctors Gaoled over Aids-Infected Blood', Guardian Weekly, 1 Nov. 1992, 13; 'French "Exported HIV in Blood"', Guardian Weekly, 8 Nov. 1992, 13.
[191] A notorious case of this sort was the Swiss government's jailing of Hoffman La Roche whistle-blower, Stanley Adams; see Adams, Roche Versus Adams. In his current nursing-home project, Braithwaite is studying a case in which criminal charges were laid against a large corporation and some senior executives for neglect of residents. The charges were laid after advice from a whistle-blower. A prosecutor has alleged to Braithwaite that, after large

ability policies to deflect criminal responsibility away from chief executives and other top management.[192] Equally importantly, however, individual criminal scapegoating involves deflecting non-criminal responsibility for systemic problems away from actors outside the corporation. When indicted (Australian) National Safety Council fraudster John Friedrich shot himself before his trial, many Australians, including these authors, responded sympathetically to the front-page coverage given to the minister officiating at his funeral:

> Does no responsibility rest with banks, which approved the loans, with government officials and ministers … with auditors to whom the community entrusted responsibility for examining the accounts of public bodies? If no responsibility rests there, then why not? If some does rest there, why is the focus so much on one person?[193]

The answer to this question is that successful prosecution in the criminal process often involves a simplification and distortion of responsibility. It induces targeting. That means getting all of the responsible actors who are not targets to co-operate with the illusion that blameworthiness resides totally with the chosen target. Of course they are delighted to co-operate in passing all of their responsibility on to the unfortunate target. Those who are most directly responsible are those who are most willing to obfuscate and lie so as to place blame squarely on the shoulders of a scapegoat. Hence, the criminal process can offer up a spurious individualisation of responsibility on the head of not the most responsible target, but the most defenceless target.

Conclusion: The Need for Strategies That Transcend Individualism

Under the strategy of individualism, the response to the present problems of non-accountability for corporate crime is to abolish corporate criminal liability and thereby apply pressure on enforcement agencies to prosecute individual personnel. This strategy is unconvincing because, at the most fundamental levels of inquiry, individualism persistently fails to capture the corporate significance of the corporate operations over which the law seeks to exercise control. The philosophical platform of methodological individualism is as lop-sided as its opposite, methodological holism. The logic and practical imperatives of deterrence do not preclude corporate responsibility but, on the contrary, impel it. Retributive theories of punishment are more compatible with corporate criminal liability than the individualist's intuitions about retribution would have one believe. Yet ultimately retributivism is unhelpful in trying to resolve the key problems of accountability: non-enforcement of individual accountability in the criminal law, and non-enforcement of individual

---

political contributions by the defendant corporation, charges were dropped against the corporation and its executives and laid against the whistle-blower.

[192] The heavy electrical equipment price-fixing conspiracies provide perhaps the most celebrated example about which this kind of allegation has been most persistently made. See the references cited in Fisse and Braithwaite, *The Impact of Publicity on Corporate Offenders*, ch. 16.

[193] *Canberra Times*, 2 Aug. 1991, 1.

accountability within corporations that are subjected to sanctions. Individualism is also an enforcement strategy prone to threaten the very protections of individuals against injustice that liberal individualists most cherish. It fails to recognise, much less to exploit, the internal disciplinary systems that have become an essential feature of modern corporate existence.

3   Enterprise Liability

Enterprise Liability and Economic Analysis of Law

Individualism contrasts sharply with enterprise liability, which is the strategy of relying primarily or even exclusively on corporate liability. Enterprise liability is supported by a number of economically oriented studies of individual and corporate liability for offences, monetary penalties, and regulatory taxes. Economic analysis has become a major current in legal thinking, especially in North America, and has been influential in many areas of corporate regulation. This is readily understandable given that an economic regime of controls holds the promise of low cost and a limited degree of government intervention. The purpose of this chapter is to review the major contributions that are relevant to our inquiry, and to examine the extent to which they help to resolve the problems identified in Chapter 1.

Five major contributions in the literature are taken as the basis of discussion. The first is the pioneering, although now somewhat dated, analysis of monetary penalties by Kenneth Elzinga and William Breit in 1976.[1] Second, there is Reinier Kraakman's leading article, 'Corporate Liability Strategies and the Costs of Legal Controls', published in 1984.[2] The third is Christopher Stone's earlier study, 'The Place of Enterprise Liability in the Control of Corporate Conduct'.[3] Fourth is the influential report of the Pearce Commission on environmental protection;[4] this is an exemplar of the control of corporate harm-causing by taxes on outputs of harm. Finally, we consider the recent paper by Mitchell Polinsky and Steven Shavell, 'Should Employees be Subject to Fines and Imprisonment Given the Existence of Corporate Liability?'

There are dangers in confining attention to these particular strands of economic thought.[5] One is the risk of overlooking points in what is now an extensive and diverse body of literature on economic analysis of law;[6] there

---

[1] Elzinga and Breit, *The Antitrust Penalties*.
[2] (1984) 93 *Yale Law Journal*, 857.
[3] (1980) 90 *Yale Law Journal*, 1.
[4] Pearce, Markandya and Barbier, *Blueprint for a Green Economy*.
[5] There are deeper philosophical issues beyond the dangers mentioned. See Loasby, *Choice, Complexity and Ignorance;* Shackle, *Epistemics and Economics*; Shackle, *Imagination and the Nature of Choice*; Sen, *On Ethics & Economics*; Sagoff, 'At the Shrine of Our Lady of Fatima or Why Political Questions Are Not All Economic'.

are probably as many theories or sub-theories of corporate regulation as there are lawyer-economists. Another patent danger is failure to grasp all the nuances of micro-economic theory. Sophisticated micro-economic theories of the firm proliferate and it seems unwise to assume that their legal implications have been fully extracted.[7]

While recognising these dangers, we see no present alternative but to focus on those economic contributions that have tackled the allocation of responsibility for corporate crime. In general, theories of the firm, mainstream or leading edge, do not address the problems of responsibility with which we are concerned. The micro-economic literature on the behaviour of the firm centres on such issues as competition, maximum corporate growth under uncertainty, and efficient forms of organisation.[8] For these reasons we have limited our discussion to the law and economics literature that does explore the optimal allocation of individual and corporate responsibility for offences, monetary penalties, and regulatory taxes. Incomplete as those explorations may be, they provide a useful starting point for identifying problems which may be generic to the economic approach. When the strengths and weaknesses of existing law and economic models are understood, then perhaps we may see the emergence of economic models that are more responsive to the issues with which we are concerned.[9]

The discussion below first outlines the five different approaches to enterprise liability mentioned above. Then follows a critical examination of three central underlying assumptions:

(1) economic modelling is critical to the prediction of corporate behaviour;
(2) deterrence is best analysed in terms of financial incentives;
(3) a regime of enterprise liability will promote rather than detract from the interests of individuals.

Enterprise Liability: Five Approaches

Elzinga and Breit: The Antitrust Penalties

Elzinga and Breit's *The Antitrust Penalties* is an early attempt to analyse the deterrence of corporate crime from a law and economics standpoint.[10] It is a

---

[6] See Posner, 'An Economic Theory of the Criminal Law'; Shavell, 'Criminal Law and the Optimal Use of Nonmonetary Sanctions as a Deterrent'; Klevorick, 'On the Economic Theory of Crime'; Coffee, 'Corporate Crime and Punishment'; Cooter and Ulen, *Law and Economics*, ch. 11; Hovenkamp, 'Antitrust's Protected Classes'; Ellis, 'Fairness and Efficiency in the Law of Punitive Damages'; Sykes, 'The Economics of Vicarious Liability'; Chapman and Trebilcock, 'Punitive Damages: Divergence in Search of a Rationale'; Haddock, McChesney and Spiegel, 'An Ordinary Economic Rationale for Extraordinary Legal Sanctions'.

[7] For useful overviews of theories of the firm see Ricketts, *The Economics of Business Enterprise*; Sawyer, *Theories of the Firm*; O. Hart, 'An Economist's Perspective on the Theory of the Firm'.

[8] See Marris and Wood, *The Corporate Economy*.

[9] Consider, e.g., Sen, *On Ethics & Economics*; Etzioni, *The Moral Dimension*; Ellickson, 'Bringing Culture and Human Frailty to Rational Actors'. For an example of economic analysis aimed at recognising and informing rather than trying to dictate or pre-ordain political choice, see Stiglitz, 'Approaches to the Economics of Discrimination'.

widely cited work, and a seminal contribution, even if it has now been over-taken by agency theories of the firm and other modern currents of economic thought. Although the analysis is presented in the particular context of antitrust offences, the approach is of general relevance to the control of cor-porate crime.

The thesis advanced by Elzinga and Breit is that antitrust behaviour is unlikely to be controlled effectively if reliance is placed on imprisonment or, in relation to corporate defendants, low fines, treble damages, or dissolution. The optimal strategy, it is argued, is to abolish the present multi-pronged approach and to subject corporate offenders to fines assessed at the rate of 25 per cent of the firm's pre-tax profits for every year of anticompetitive activ-ity.[11] The approach thus targets corporations and contrasts sharply with the strategy of individualism discussed in the previous chapter.

Elzinga and Breit explicitly address the problem of non-prosecution of individual managers, a problem which, as we have seen in Chapter 1, is a central issue of corporate crime control. In their view, the threat of imprison-ment is largely a fiction because typically it cannot be carried out:

> [I]n cases involving large corporations it is difficult for a court to pinpoint guilt above the level of those who overtly carry out the antitrust violations. It is not sur-prising, therefore, that the businessmen who have been sentenced to serve time in jail are typically the chief officers of small closely held corporations or low-level and relatively minor officials of large companies. For this reason the jail penalty has not served as an effective deterrent to monopolistic practices.[12]

The responsive solution, according to Elzinga and Breit, is to impose finan-cial penalties on the corporation and thereby influence the behaviour of controlling shareholders and management. Fines against corporations are seen as a more efficient sanction than imprisonment of individuals, mainly because of the relatively high costs of imprisonment as a means of deterrence:

> [T]here is some marginal rate of substitution between financial penalties and *any* other penalty, including jail, which means that the jail penalty, like any other penalty, can always be collapsed into its monetary equivalent. Thus the ineffi-ciency of the jail penalty can be easily seen. For any given period of time spent in

---

[10] Optimal financial penalties were advocated in the earlier work of Becker, 'Crime and Punishment'. The more recent contributions include Parker, 'Criminal Sentencing Policy for Organizations'; Wray, 'Corporate Probation under the New Organizational Sentencing Guidelines'; Posner, 'An Economic Theory of the Criminal Law'.

[11] Elzinga and Breit, *The Antitrust Penalties*, 134–5. Considerable difficulty can arise in deter-mining what exactly constitutes the 'firm' in such a context; see Collins, 'Ascription of Legal Responsibility to Groups in Complex Patterns of Economic Integration'. Basing the fine on the firm's profits in all lines of business is also highly problematic: see Hay, 'Review of Elzinga and Breit, *The Antitrust Penalties*', 439.

[12] Elzinga and Breit, *The Antitrust Penalties*, 38.

jail, there is some fine capable of securing the same deterrent effect. However, since the size of the fine can be changed without the expenditure of additional resources, while increased use of incarceration always involves greater costs to society, incarceration is an inferior penalty. Whenever any penalty can give the same amount of deterrence at the cost, or additional deterrence for the same cost, that option is economically superior.[13]

What do Elzinga and Breit have to say about the further major problem of lack of insistence on individual accountability within corporations subjected to monetary penalties? The position taken is that the law should concentrate on the expected utility function of crime and try to provide a disincentive sufficient to make the expected utility of crime less than the expected utility of compliance with the law. This means that the law should focus not on the function of accountability in corporate crime control, but on the financial incentives under which entrepreneurs operate. Thus, where a corporation has been fined under the incentive scheme prescribed, the law signals that the utility to be expected from committing the offence is less than that from compliance. Although the assumption is that fines imposed on the firm will be borne by individual entrepreneurs, the aim of entrepreneurial cost-bearing is not to enforce personal accountability but to reinforce the scheme of financial disincentives. The theory does not require that any attempt be made to impose accountability by pin-pointing particular managers or shareholders and holding them responsible.

Kraakman: 'Corporate Liability Strategies ...'

Reinier Kraakman has advanced a sophisticated account of the optimal conditions for allocating corporate and individual liability.[14] Unlike the relatively simple rational actor model provided by Elzinga and Breit, Kraakman's analysis explores the particular circumstances in which monetary penalties imposed on the corporation are likely or unlikely to be an efficient means of controlling corporate behaviour. The exploration is intensive and wide-ranging, and does much to refine what is meant by efficiency in the allocation of liability for corporate crime.

The key issue for Kraakman is whether the benefit of fewer offences can be purchased more cheaply by means of enterprise liability than by imposing liability on managers as well as on the corporation. His argument is that corporate liability alone is usually more efficient and that individual liability is needed only where corporate liability is inefficient. In his view, corporate liability is not enough in three main kinds of situation:

---

[13] Ibid., 123.
[14] For other agency-based analyses see M. A. Cohen, 'Environmental Crime and Punishment'; Haddock, McChesney and Spiegel, 'An Ordinary Economic Rationale for Extraordinary Legal Sanctions'; Macey, 'Agency Theory and the Criminal Liability of Corporations'.

(1) asset insufficiency;
(2) sanction insufficiency; and
(3) enforcement insufficiency.
Having identified these problems, Kraakman pursues the implications they hold for the optimal allocation of individual and corporate liability.

Kraakman's starting point is the 'iron law' of tortious and criminal liability for delicts that liability risks, if left unchannelled, attach to the corporation rather than its officers or employees. Managers routinely shift their risk of liability through insurance, indemnification, or by delegating risky functions to subordinates. Although this risk-shifting seems to undermine the provision made in law for individual liability, it is explicable on efficiency grounds.

If managers are exposed to personal risk, they will demand insurance or indemnification. The risk premium is high given that they are undiversified risk-bearers who face loss of all their personal assets from one ruinous legal action. By contrast, if they are able to shift the risk through insurance or indemnification, the cost to the firm will be lower because shareholders and insurers are diversified risk bearers who are able to spread the cost on an average basis over numerous firms. Another relevant consideration of efficiency is the complexity and hence cost of administering a scheme that accurately compensates managers for their job-related risks of incurring personal liability. As Kraakman points out:

> [E]ven the most elaborate compensation schemes may not overcome a risk-averse manager's temptation to 'cheat' shareholders by surreptitiously choosing business strategies that are less profitable to the firm but less risky for its managers.[15]

Given these costs, Kraakman takes the view that personal liability is generally inefficient because it does not offer a sufficient deterrent gain to offset the burden that would be imposed on firms under a regime of absolute personal liability. The reasoning is as follows:

> Even if contract and market controls do not fully align managerial interests with those of the corporation, enterprise liability holds out the same promise as personal liability prodding corporate officers into following socially desirable policies. Hefty damage awards or fines will reduce a firm's earnings—and therefore managerial rewards—at least as much as routine business losses of a comparable magnitude, and probably even more. In addition, unlike managerial self-dealing, typical corporate offenses such as antitrust violations, tax evasion, or hazardous waste dumping are undertaken to benefit the corporation rather than to benefit its managers directly. Except on occasions, managers stand to gain only when the firm itself stands to gain.[16]

Enterprise liability is seen as deficient, however, where the aggregate costs of using corporate liability alone exceed the costs of imposing the risk of liability upon agents as well as firms. The first and most obvious situation where

[15] Kraakman, 'Corporate Liability Strategies...', 865.
[16] Ibid., 866.

this may occur is 'asset insufficiency',[17] by which is meant a firm's lack of sufficient assets to pay the price imposed by law for a violation. Managerial liability plays a back-up role here, the theory being that managerial risk-shifting through indemnification or insurance will force the firm and its shareholders to internalise the expected liability costs that undercapitalisation would otherwise impose on victims.[18] At present that role is limited by the ease with which managers can insulate themselves from liability by delegating risky functions to minions. The solution advocated by Kraakman is a strict rule of personal civil liability for managerial failure to supervise corporate activities, at least in areas where asset insufficiency is a significant problem.[19] This expanded legal duty of managerial supervision would leave managers to select the optimal strategy for covering risk from among insurance, self-insurance, and risk reduction through control of the firm's activities.[20]

A second area of difficulty is 'sanction insufficiency' in the sense that the legal system cannot charge enterprises a price high enough to deter adequately illegal corporate behaviour. Sanctions imposed on the enterprise may be insufficient given two prime factors: the greater deterrent capability of a dual system of enterprise liability and unshiftable personal criminal liability; and the limits that restrict the size of the sanctions that can be imposed on corporations.

Personal criminal liability is difficult for managers to offset by means of compensation or indemnity, and provides an additional deterrent pressure point. Moreover, the size of corporate sanctions is constrained by a number of factors. One is the ability of the corporate offender to pay.[21] Another is the desire to avoid unwanted spill-over effects. Above all, there is the deterrence trap: a fine high enough to reflect the returns from a corporate crime and the chance of conviction (a million dollar return would need to be multiplied by 100 if the chance of being punished was one in a hundred), a fine so high as to deplete the liquidity of the corporation to such an extent that innocent creditors, consumers and workers may suffer. Unshiftable personal criminal liability is unjustified, however, if the costs of adding this arm of liability exceed the benefits; the total costs of legal control must be assessed. The relevant benefits include the use that enforcement agencies can make of individual criminal liability to induce managers to provide evidence of corporate offences. The relevant costs include those of compensating managerial risk-bearing, overcommitment to risk avoidance, and over-deterrence of managerial agents.

Ideally, individual criminal liability should be used only after weighing its costs against the alternative of increasing sanctions on the firm alone. A 'serviceable proxy' for making this calculation is the general rule allowing indemnification where a manager has acted in good faith and without reason to believe that his or her conduct is criminal:

[17] Ibid., 868–76.
[18] Ibid., 870.
[19] Ibid., 872–6.
[20] Ibid., 874.
[21] See Siliciano, 'Corporate Behavior and the Social Efficiency of Tort Law'.

The rule is formulated this way not because ignorant managers are helpless to prevent firm delicts—liability provides an incentive to become informed—but because it radically circumscribes the risk of liability triggered by personal legal mistake. Such a rule minimizes the risk-bearing and agency costs of innocent firms because it assures that their managers will rarely blunder into absolute penalties without prior notice.[22]

A third problem area identified by Kraakman is 'enforcement insufficiency', where the combination of enterprise liability and individual criminal liability is not enough to achieve sufficient compliance at an acceptable cost. Here the question is whether 'gatekeepers'—conscripted deputies—should be used to plug the enforcement gap.[23] Gatekeeper liability enlists the support of outside directors, bankers, accountants, lawyers, underwriters and other external participants in the firm when the firm's internal monitors have failed. Liability may be civil or criminal, and individual or corporate. The economic rationale behind imposing liability on gatekeepers is worth quoting at length:

Each has or might have low-cost access to information about firm delicts. Contractually or informally, each already performs a private monitoring service on behalf of the capital markets. But most important, each is an *outsider* with a career and assets beyond the firm. At the very least, these potential gatekeepers face incentives that differ systematically from those of inside managers; in the usual case, they are likely to have less to gain and more to lose from firm delicts than inside managers. Indeed, gatekeeper liability can jeopardize not only the personal interests of individual lawyers and accountants, but also the larger interests and reputations of their respective firms or even of their entire professions.[24]

Gatekeeper liability adds a significant dimension to the allocation of liability for corporate conduct:

[W]henever potential offenders must employ incorruptible outsiders to gain legitimacy or expertise or to meet a legal requirement, gatekeeper liability will thwart a class of offenses that are unreachable through enterprise-level or managerial sanctions. Of course, firms will also pay for the risk of additional liability in the familiar ways. If outside gatekeepers cannot shift their liability risks, they will charge high risk premiums. In addition, they will have a powerful incentive to lobby for the overinvestment of firm resources in monitoring for offenses and against profitable but risky innocent conduct. In the extreme, they may even withdraw their services entirely from small or risky firms.[25]

As Kraakman points out, however, the cost-effectiveness or otherwise of gatekeeper liability depends on several critical factors, including the duties imposed on the gatekeeper, the area of expertise, and the extent to which gatekeeper liability is shiftable.

Kraakman's analysis thus departs substantially from that of Elzinga and

[22] Kraakman, 'Corporate Liability Strategies...', 887–8.
[23] For a detailed analysis of this concept see Kraakman, 'Gatekeepers'.
[24] Kraakman, 'Corporate Liability Strategies...', 891.
[25] Ibid., 891–2.

Breit and casts a different light upon the problems tackled in this book. Kraakman does not see the non-prosecution of individuals for corporate crime as a problem. It is more a superficial paradox that can readily be explained. Enterprise liability is usually the most cost-effective solution. For some cases or for some offences, enterprise liability needs to be supplemented by individual criminal liability. Specific criteria are not spelt out, but one rule of thumb when applying the general criterion of cost-effectiveness is that managers are appropriate targets where they have acted in bad faith or with reason to believe that their conduct is criminal.

Kraakman also addresses the problem that arises where enterprise liability fails to produce adequate internal monitoring. This problem is tackled in terms of the incentives needed for managers to monitor and supervise activities within the firm rather than in terms of the value of individual accountability within organisations. Where breakdowns in internal monitoring and supervision occur, the solution suggested is that gatekeepers be induced to perform the role of monitoring and supervision. The mode of inducement is liability for the firm's delicts.

Stone: 'The Place of Enterprise Liability ...'

Christopher Stone's major essay in 1980[26] provides another systematic account of enterprise liability as a means of controlling corporate illegality. Although Stone's main focus[27] is the balance to be struck between non-interventionist and interventionist methods of controlling corporate behaviour, he also deals specifically with the question of allocation of corporate and individual liability.

Stone contrasts the non-interventionist approach of Harm-Based Liability Rules (HBLRs) or Penal Harm-Based Liability Rules (HBLR(P)s) with the interventionist approach of standards which impose constraints on managerial autonomy over product and process variables, administrative arrangements, product and service performance, and disclosure of information. In the context of HBLRs or HBLR(P)s, Stone rejects the strategy of individualism on three grounds. First, it is a mistake to suppose that enterprise liability is the antithesis of individual liability: individuals may well be sanctioned by the enterprise as a matter of internal control.[28] Second, it is typically less costly to identify and convict the enterprise responsible than to go further and impose responsibility on the agents of the enterprise.[29] Third, responsibility is often diffused within an organisation and the source of wrongdoing may easily lie in bureaucratic shortcomings (for example, defective organisational procedures) than in intentional non-compliance by particular individuals.

---

[26] C. D. Stone, 'The Place of Enterprise Liability...'.
[27] Compare the interventionist theme of C. D. Stone's earlier work, *Where the Law Ends*.
[28] C. D. Stone, 'The Place of Enterprise Liability', 28–9.
[29] Ibid., 29. Compare Coffee, 'Corporate Crime and Punishment', 463 (enterprise liability may be more cost-effective because corporations are more likely to settle than individuals, especially individuals who face the possibility of being sentenced to jail).

Stone does not, however, reject individual liability. Rather, individual liability is seen as necessary to take up 'some of the slack' where enterprise liability is deficient.[30] Enterprise liability is inadequate, in his view, where the agent's conduct is 'so egregious as to demand a penalty, such as imprisonment, that is beyond the power of the enterprise to mete out'.[31] In the case of offences carrying a fine, Stone contends that agent liability is warranted where the law has a retributive or denunciatory role that requires 'the ceremonial trappings of public prosecution for symbolic and educative purposes'.[32] Moreover, individual liability for fines may often be useful to deal with situations where enterprise liability does not lead to effective internal discipline:

> The enterprise's own notions of what constitutes blameworthy conduct may be too lenient to suit the collective preferences of society. In addition, we may suspect the integrity of the enterprise's internal sanctioning process, which is, after all, largely in the hands of high-level managers who have their own welfare to protect. The managers may tend either to find a scapegoat or to accord light treatment to a true culprit in exchange for his not implicating them.[33]

The exact balance to be struck, however, is unclear because it is impossible to say what precise mix is optimal:

> To make a comparison of the responsiveness of unwanted conduct to increments in enterprise-targeted and agent-targeted enforcement programs, we would have to place the penalties in a broader context. What burdens do the respective penalties impose on agent and on enterprise, considering all the direct and indirect, monetary and non-monetary implications? What does each party stand to gain if the conduct is not deterred? What are their respective risk preferences, and their respective capacities to modify the unwanted outcomes? There is simply no way to answer these questions in the abstract, or even, with a high degree of confidence, in any concrete situation.[34]

Stone concludes, however, by suggesting that the balance struck is unlikely to matter where the conduct is not blameworthy and hence where the agent may readily be compensated or indemnified against personal loss. In such a context, the ultimate allocation of liability depends not on the decision at trial but on the market forces that govern compensation for managerial risk or indemnification for managerial liability.

Parallel considerations apply to the allocation of liability for breach of standards, except in one critical respect. In Stone's view, standards enhance the opportunity to achieve a higher level of individual accountability:

> Agents can often avoid stiff penalties [for HBLR(P)s] because of the difficulty of establishing individual accountability, both moral and legal, in a giant, complex

---

[30] C. D. Stone, 'The Place of Enterprise Liability…', 28.
[31] Ibid., 30.
[32] Ibid., 30. However, private sanctioning can be symbolic and educative, as is often the position in Japan.
[33] Ibid., 30.
[34] Ibid., 35.

institution. ... But when we require bureaucratic standards that make certain features of the agent's performance mandatory and visible to all, accountability can be improved in two ways. First, we can attach individual liability to non-performance of the required tasks. With lines of responsibility clarified, the costs of identifying and prosecuting violators will decline, and the penalty that the non-performing agent can realistically expect will be brought into line with the ideal level. Second, we should not forget that the control of organizational behavior depends importantly, perhaps ultimately, upon how people feel about themselves and their jobs. Clarifying what is expected of a person may make the agent *feel* responsible and may be effective in modifying his performance, quite aside from the threat of suit. Both the legal and the social-psychological effects should translate into a lower incidence of violation, and the social costs may well prove moderate.[35]

A second and separate major issue examined by Stone is the extent to which agent liability for penalties may be undermined as a result of indemnification by the enterprise. While conceding that it is difficult in practice to discover or combat the indemnification of agents by corporations, Stone recommends that some attempt should be made given the serious dangers at stake. The relevant dangers are specified as follows:

> Indemnification and its surrogates have the power not only to undo the law's judgments against executives who have been caught; they also lend themselves to undermining prosecutorial efforts against others. In cases of corporate wrongdoing, the successful prosecution of top management often requires the testimony of lower- and middle-level managers; yet the willingness of those managers to turn state's evidence may be eroded by the promise that the company will take care of them, provided they demonstrate their loyalties. Indeed, the value of a prosecutor's grant of immunity is surely debased if the corporation, through indemnification, can dole out something resembling an immunity on its own.[36]

Given these concerns, Stone advocates the introduction of specific rules against indemnification of fines or penalties,[37] complemented by court prohibitions on direct or indirect indemnification of their judgments.[38]

Finally, Stone criticises the way in which limited liability can be used to insulate shareholders against the burden of fines, penalties or damages. In his opinion, the non-liability of a shareholder for the undischarged debts of the corporation nullifies the goal of deterrence:

> those who stand behind an enterprise can disregard in their calculations any levels of penalty beyond the firm's ability to pay. ... [the law benefits] a select group of social actors, thwarting with one hand the control strategies that it is legislating with the other.[39]

Accordingly, two recommendations are made. First, the corporate veil should be pierced so as to allow recovery against shareholders, not as joint and

---

[35] Ibid., 44–5.
[36] Ibid., 55.
[37] Ibid., 55–6.
[38] Ibid., 56.
[39] Ibid., 68.

severally liable partners, but in proportion to the extent of their equity interest in the corporation.[40] Second, where a company is unable to pay a penalty, prosecutors should intensify action against responsible corporate agents, and place more reliance on jail.

Stone's commentary thus represents a further variation on the theme of cost-effective allocation of liability for corporate crime. Like Kraakman, Stone rejects both individualism and enterprise liability as corporate crime control strategies and commends a mix of agent and enterprise liability. However, the mix proposed by Stone attaches more importance to individual criminal liability. It also recognises the potential of standards to achieve a higher level of individual responsibility without running into the costs and other difficulties that arise where attempts are made to impose individual liability under HBLRs. Another significant difference is that Stone rejects a *laissez faire* approach to indemnification and limited liability and proposes certain correctives to guard against abuse. He advocates that indemnification be banned and that shareholders be held proportionately liable to pay for harm inflicted by their corporation.

Stone deals expressly with the problem of inadequate internal discipline that may arise in the wake of enterprise liability. Unlike Kraakman, Stone acknowledges the value of individual accountability within organisations. This leads him to suggest that managers be prosecuted where internal discipline is unlikely to work, and that individual accountability be enhanced by subjecting managers to standards which impose particular duties upon them.

Pearce Report: Enterprise taxes on harm

Another important direction in law and economics thought is non-fault-based enterprise liability in the form of taxes or charges to reflect the externalities of corporate action.[41] This approach has been advocated in a variety of regulatory contexts, notably environmental protection and occupational health and safety.[42] It has been supported by numerous commentators, most prominently by David Pearce and others in *Blueprint for a Green Economy* (1989), known

---

[40] Ibid., 74. Parent–subsidiary relationships can be manipulated to reduce or avoid the impact of corporate sanctions; see, e.g., *Waters-Pierce Co. v Texas* (1900) 177 US 28; (1909) 212 US 86 (Standard Oil structured its exposure to legal liability through the use of subsidiaries).

[41] See generally Staaf and Tannian, *Externalities*.

[42] Ackerman and Hassler, 'Beyond the New Deal'; Ackerman and Hassler, *Clean Air, Dirty Coal*; Gaines and Westin, *Taxation for Environmental Protection*; Andenaes, *Punishment and Deterrence*; Ashford, *Crisis in the Workplace*; Bequai, *Organized Crime*; Bernstein, *Regulating Business by Independent Commission*; Gunningham, *Pollution, Social Interests and the Law*; Irwin and Liroff, *Economic Disincentives for Pollution Control*; Johnson and Brown, *Cleaning Up Europe's Waters*; Kriegler, *Working for the Company*; Mendeloff, *Regulating Safety*; Mitnick, *The Political Economy of Regulation*; Packer, *The Limits of the Criminal Sanction*; Page and O'Brien, *Bitter Wages*; President's Commission on Coal, Staff Findings; 'Ex-Owner Says Mob Took Over Chemicals Firm', *NYT*, 24 Nov. 1980; Reiman, *The Rich Get Richer and the Poor Get Prison*; Rose-Ackerman, 'Effluent Charges'; Sand, 'The Socialist Response'; Scott, *Muscle and Blood*; Settle, *The Welfare Economics of Occupational Safety and Health Standards*; Stewart, 'Regulation, Innovation, and Administrative Law'; Sutton and Wild, 'Corporate Crime and Social Structure'.

as the 'Pearce Report'.[43] In this section, we examine what the Pearce Report conception of taxes and charges entails for the allocation of individual and corporate liability.

A key proposal of the Pearce Report is that market-based incentives be used to protect the environment and that the pollution charges or taxes be used to regulate environmental harm. Under this approach a charge is set on the product so as to raise the cost of production. The charge is set so as to bear some relationship to the value of the environmental elements used in production. For any product which imposes pollution damage, the product produced should be priced according to the following basic equation:

$$P = MC + MEC = MSC$$

where P is the price, MC the marginal cost, MEC the marginal external cost, and MSC the marginal social cost. The underlying idea is that the state should promote the control of corporate harm by incorporating environmental externalities into the operation of market forces rather than by using costly court-adjudicated forms of liability.

Pollution taxes or charges are claimed by the Pearce Report to be more effective than the criminal law, civil penalties, or other command and control strategies:

> The basic reason why charges are likely to be better than 'command and control' techniques is that charges enable a polluter to choose how to adjust to the environmental quality standard. Polluters with high costs of abating pollution will prefer to pay the charge. Polluters with low costs of abatement will prefer to install abatement equipment. By making abatement something that 'low cost' polluters do rather than 'high cost' ones, charges tend to cut down the total costs of compliance. … A tax adjusts market prices to reflect the use of environmental services which are otherwise erroneously treated as being free. Command and control policies adopt a regulatory stance which ignores the efficiencies of the market mechanism.[44]

The implications for the allocation of individual and corporate liability seem plain, although they are not discussed in the Pearce Report. Taxes or charges are borne by the producer of the relevant product. Where, as is typically the case, the producer is a corporation, it follows that liability is corporate. Individual liability does not figure in the pricing equation for corporate producers. However, individual civil liability could become relevant in the event of the inability of a corporate producer to pay its pollution taxes. Since no question of individual criminal liability arises, there is no problem of criminal prosecutions being biased towards corporations.

What of the individual accountability of managers and other key personnel within corporate producers? This issue dissolves under the Pearce model. The hypothesis is that, by giving corporations an appropriate financial incentive to

[43] See also Pearce and Turner, *Economics of Natural Resources and the Environment*.
[44] 161–2.

contain pollution, individual managers and other agents will automatically step into line. Like the approach taken by Elzinga and Breit, the analysis of the Pearce model is thus based essentially on a unitary rational actor model of corporate decisionmaking.

Polinsky and Shavell: Deducting individual liability from enterprise liability

Mitchell Polinsky and Steven Shavell's paper, 'Should Employees be Subject to Fines and Imprisonment Given the Existence of Corporate Liability?',[45] pursues the question whether, from the perspective of the economic theory of deterrence, it is socially desirable to impose public sanctions on employees when corporations themselves face liability. The argument is that such sanctions may be beneficial. The magnitude of fines and imprisonment may exceed the highest sanctions that a firm can impose on its employees and the threat of public sanctions is therefore often likely to induce employees to exercise greater levels of care than they otherwise would. To the extent that employees face public sanctions, the firm's liability should be reduced accordingly. If the firm's liability is not reduced by the amount of the costs imposed upon employees who are fined or jailed, then the price of the firm's product would exceed the social cost of production. Polinsky and Shavell also contend that criminal sanctions on employees should be imposed only if the employees are negligent, whereas the firm should be strictly liable for harms occasioned by its activities.

If firms are made strictly liable for their harms, they will want to reduce their liability payments and hence will design rewards and punishments for their employees that will lead those employees to reduce the risk of causing harm. The prices of firms' products will also reflect the cost of the harms that result from production of those products.

However, a firm may not be able to induce its employees to take enough care because its ability to discipline them may be limited. Polinsky and Shavell take the view that the effect of dismissal is limited by 'the presence of alternative opportunities for employees' and by the limited assets that employees may have available for recovery by the firm. Thus, the highest penalty that a firm can impose on an employee may be much less than the harm his or her actions may cause. The employee's incentive to reduce the risk will then be too small.

The state can impose a financial penalty on an employee in excess of what a firm can impose because 'the state can more easily collect criminal fines than private parties can obtain civil judgments'. When employees face the risk of fines, they will have an incentive to demand higher compensation from firms. This will lead firms to pay fines in the form of higher wages. On this analysis, the level of liability that is optimal to impose on a firm is the harm

[45] See also Segerson and Tietenberg, 'Defining Efficient Sanctions'; M. A. Cohen, 'Environmental Crime and Punishment'.

caused less the fine paid by the employee. The sum of the employee's fine and the firm's liability should equal the harm.

It is in a firm's interest for its employees to be subject to fines where the firm is limited in its ability to discipline employees. Although the firm will have to pay higher wages to compensate employees for the risk of paying fines, fines lead employees to take more care, and the resulting reduction in the cost of the harms occasioned by the firm's production is said to outweigh the increased wages.

The threat of fines may not be enough to induce employees to take socially optimal levels of care. The state is limited in the fines that it can extract because it cannot obtain more from an employee than his or her present and future assets. Non-monetary sanctions are therefore necessary, and imprisonment may justifiably be used if the social cost is 'sufficiently low'. Where imprisonment is used, the optimal level of liability on the firm will be the harm plus the social cost of imprisonment less the private disutility of imprisonment (and any fines that are imposed).

In short, Polinsky and Shavell maintain that, as under the present law, there should be individual as well as corporate criminal liability. Unlike the position taken by Elzinga and Breit or Pearce, they do not see enterprise liability as displacing the need for individual liability. Unlike Kraakman and Stone, they do not seek to delimit the range of situations where enterprise liability breaks down and where individual liability is efficient. Rather, the main burden of Polinsky and Shavell's argument is that where individual liability is imposed the costs thereby imposed should be deducted from the liability of the firm.[46]

Economic Rational Actors, Financial Incentives, and Corporate Behaviour

A basic assumption typically underlying law and economics analyses of responsibility for corporate crime is that economic models are critical to the prediction of corporate behaviour.[47] Without denying the worth of modelling, the models produced to date seem simplistic and other worldly. One model of corporate action, as followed in Elzinga and Breit's *The Antitrust Penalties*, Pearce and others' *Blueprint for a Green Economy* and Polinsky and Shavell's paper, is that of the corporation as a unitary rational actor. Another model is the agency theory of the firm, as reflected in the contribution of Kraakman and which is also implicit at times in the analyses of Stone and

---

[46] Polinsky and Shavell do not address the utility of using corporate liability as a lever to facilitate individual criminal liability. On the contrary, the implication of their analysis appears to be that proceedings against employees need first to be finalised before the costs imposed on them can be deducted from the costs imposed on the firm. Why not proceed against the corporation first and then discount fines against the corporation according to the number of individual suspects against whom the corporation provides evidence leading to conviction?

[47] This is not to suggest a monolithic view of economics: there are many differences in approach to the use of models and to the importance attached to empirical testing of models.

Polinsky and Shavell. While some useful insights emerge from these models, they are unrealistic in many respects.

The rational actor model

The rational actor model depicts human entities as rational agents who seek to maximise their self-preferences.[48] In some economic accounts of corporate behaviour, the rational actor model is extended to the firm, with the firm serving as a surrogate maximiser of the preferences of its human investors or managers. Thus, Elzinga and Breit treat the corporation as a rational unitary actor that seeks to maximise the interests of the firm in a manner that simultaneously maximises the interests of its backers. The same conception of corporate rational actors underlies the Pearce proposal that corporate polluters be required to pay taxes or charges that reflect the social cost of the pollutants they discharge. It is also implicit in Polinsky and Shavell's constant reference to the behaviour of 'the firm'.

The rational actor model may hold true of corporate behaviour in some cases, and where this is so the implication is that financial penalties should be applied to the corporation and not to individual associates: if the same deterrent effect can be achieved by one corporate penalty as by multiple individual penalties then plainly the former is more efficient.[49] As explained below, however, the rational actor model is one among many conceivable models of corporate behaviour and in practice usually it is impossible to tell which model predominates in any specific explanatory context within a corporation.[50] The extent to which reliance should be placed on the rational actor model as a guide to the allocation of individual and corporate liability thus depends on the extent to which one is prepared to discount such uncertainty. This raises the issue of management of uncertainty, which we address in the context of deterrent efficacy.

The rational actor model is consistent with corporate criminal and civil liability. Unlike individualism, the rational actor conception of enterprise liability rejects the view that corporations have no mind. Rather, it allows recognition of corporate intentionality (in the sense of corporate policy) and corporate negligence (in the sense of a failure to exercise the care expected of a corporation in the same position). However, the corporation is depicted as a unitary rational decisionmaker, which is unrealistic given the bureaucratic complexities of organisational behaviour. The rational actor model echoes Stanley Jevons' nineteenth-century 'economic man'.[51] As John Byrne and Steven Hoffman have observed, this model is hopelessly anachronistic:

---

[48] The meaning of 'rational' action is a matter of perennial debate in the social sciences. See Benn and Mortimore, *Rationality and the Social Sciences*; Etzioni, *The Moral Dimension*; Sen, *On Ethics & Economics*; Coleman, *Foundations of Social Theory*; Wilson, *Rationality*.

[49] For an instructive study in the context of insurance risk adjustment, see Heimer, *Reactive Risk and Rational Action*.

[50] See Kagan and Scholz, 'The "Criminology of the Corporation" and Regulatory Enforcement Strategies'.

[51] Jevons, *The Theory of Political Economy*.

> [It] was constructed to stand for the thought patterns and behavior of an individual, not the twentieth-century corporation composed of many individuals, many products, many decisions, many values, and many goals.[52]

The lack of realism in the single unitary conception of the firm became apparent as early as 1932 when Berle and Means showed that owners of large corporations had relinquished control to the managers they needed to employ.[53] That study revealed that the interests of owners and managers, far from being in harmony, conflicted because the maximisation of company profits was not necessarily in the best personal interests of managers. Although the Berle and Means thesis has not gone unchallenged, the relationship between corporate ownership and corporate control is complex and depends on many variables.[54] These variables include the extent to which the stock market discounts the shares of corporations whose managers behave opportunistically,[55] and the extent to which investors are able to use effective controls to monitor the conduct of managers.[56] In short, shareholders and their managers have their own utility functions, and these functions may differ substantially.[57]

Another questionable assumption is that the rational actor will seek to maximise the value obtainable from its production. An alternative view, for which there is much support, is that corporate decisionmaking is suboptimal.[58] Given the difficulties associated with making accurate decisions, managers opt for what they regard as a satisfactory as opposed to optimal level of achievement. It may be that 'satisficing' is merely a constrained form of rational value maximising behaviour rather than a qualitatively different kind of human action,[59] but even if this is so, it becomes impossible to prescribe an efficient level of deterrence. If the level is pitched at rational optimisers, then the amount will be inefficient in relation to sub-optimisers. If the level is pitched in relation to sub-optimisers, then the amount will be incorrect for the deterrence of rational optimisers.

A more fundamental although less obvious weakness of the rational actor model is that it portrays corporations as entities akin to human decisionmakers rather than as communities or collective systems.[60] More complex models could conceivably be constructed to reflect the utility functions of individuals within corporations but such a step is a far cry from the simplistic models presented by Elzinga and Breit, Pearce, and Polinsky and Shavell.

---

[52] Byrne and Hoffmann, 'Efficient Corporate Harm'.
[53] Berle and Means, *The Modern Corporation and Private Property*. See also Herman, *Corporate Control, Corporate Power*. Note Apps and Rees, 'Taxation and the Household', where it is argued that a household utility function blocks out critical individual social welfare functions.
[54] For an unfolding of the complexity in the context of takeovers, see Coffee, 'Shareholders Versus Managers'.
[55] Jensen and Meckling, 'Theory of the Firm'.
[56] Williamson, 'The Modern Corporation'.
[57] See Coffee, 'Corporate Crime and Punishment', 460–1.
[58] Simon, *Models of Man*, 204–5, 241–56.
[59] Alchian, 'The Basis of Some Recent Advances in the Theory of Management of the Firm', 39–40.
[60] See Shearing and Stenning, *Private Policing*, 14. See also Frug, 'The City as a Legal Concept'; Horwitz, 'The History of the Public/Private Distinction'; Tombs, 'Corporate Crime and "Post Modern" Organizations'.

The agency theory of the firm

The agency theory of the firm depicts the corporation as a nexus or web of contracts between the owners of the enterprise and the agents they employ to run the enterprise. There are many variants of this theory, including Jensen and Meckling's widely cited version. On their analysis,

> The private corporation or firm is simply one form of legal fiction which serves as a nexus for contracting relationships and which is also characterized by the existence of divisible residual claims on the assets and cash flows of the organization which can generally be sold without permission of other contracting individuals. While this definition of the firm has little substantive content, emphasizing the essential contractual nature of firms and other organizations focuses attention on a crucial set of questions. ...
>
> Viewed this way, it makes little sense to try to distinguish those things that are 'inside' the firm from those that are 'outside' of it. There is in a very real sense only a multitude of complex relationships (i.e., contracts) between the legal fiction (the firm) and the owners of ... inputs and the consumers of output.[61]

It is this image of the corporation that animates Kraakman's analysis.[62]

The agency theory of the firm, as explored in detail by Kraakman, yields five main presumptions about the nature of action and responsibility in the context of corporate crime. The first is that corporate action decomposes to the actions of individuals who contract among themselves to optimise their own preferences. The second is that managers enter into arrangements to shift the risk of personal liability. Third, the interests of managers and those of owners are not necessarily aligned and indeed may often conflict. Fourth, the firm is not a single decisionmaking unit but a legal tool that can be used to internalise the social cost of offences in a manner that impacts upon individual actors. Fifth, individual actors are responsible for internalised social costs on a contractual basis; responsibility does not necessarily depend on blameworthiness for particular acts or omissions, nor is it based on their office or position within the organisation.

These conceptions take a more realistic view of the role of individuals within organisations than is apparent from the rational actor model. They also explode the assumption that corporate action and corporate responsibility are mirror images of individual action and individual responsibility. Even so, however, the picture they paint of corporate action is distorted.[63]

The first observation to be made is that the agency theory of the firm, at least as presented by Jensen and Meckling, is rooted in methodological

---

[61] Jensen and Meckling, 'Theory of the Firm'. See also Williamson, 'Corporate Governance'. For instructive criticial overviews see Bratton, 'The New Economic Theory of the Firm'; Mitnick, 'The Theory of Agency and Organizational Analysis'.

[62] Kraakman, 'Corporate Liability Strategies...', 862.

[63] We do not pursue here the range of problems which principal (P) and agency (A) models pose from the standpoint of economic theory (e.g., different probability beliefs on the part of P and A; collusion among agents); see generally Rees, 'The Theory of Principal and Agent', 46–90. It may also be questioned whether the agency theory of the firm necessarily provides a sound guide for efficient corporate management structures; see, e.g., Donaldson and Davis, 'Stewardship Theory or Agency Theory'.

individualism, and hence fails to account for the reality of corporate action
and corporate responsibility as phenomena that cannot be explained simply in
terms of the performance of individual actors. At this point, the agency theory
of the firm is vulnerable to the same fundamental objections as individualism
and we need not repeat the critique provided in Chapter 2. Suffice it to say
that the corporation is not merely a legal fiction, as Jensen and Meckling
would have us believe, but an empirically observable actor that decides and
behaves in ways of its own.

The agency theory of the firm is also unrealistic because it takes an excessively contractarian view of corporate behaviour.[64] As Robert Clark has
pointed out, the conception that corporate managers are agents of investors
materially departs from the position in law:

> (1) corporate officers like the president and treasurer are agents of the corporation
> itself; (2) the board of directors is the ultimate decision-making body of the corpo-
> ration (and in a sense is the group most appropriately identified 'the corporation');
> (3) directors are not agents of the corporation but are sui generis; (4) neither offi-
> cers nor directors are agents of the stockholders; but (5) both officers and directors
> are 'fiduciaries' with respect to the corporation and its stockholders.[65]

For Clark, a contractual approach obscures analysis of the obligations actually
at work within organisations. As he explains, corporate officers are subject to
a raft of statutory, common law and equitable duties and there is no evidence
to suggest that these reflect historical contractual patterns or even some hypo-
thetical original contractual position.[66] Clark also questions the accuracy of
assumptions made about the contractual preferences of corporate officers. In
his argument, contractual reasoning about corporate behaviour is indeterminate, prone to manipulation, and subject to facile optimism about the optimal-
ity of existing institutions or rules.[67] Accepting that managers are economic
rather than legal agents, the construct of a nexus of contracts is much too one-
dimensional. While modern corporations can be usefully understood for some
purposes as a nexus of contracts, sole reliance on this model would give us an
impoverished understanding of organisational life.

Beyond the criticisms made by Clark, it is also apparent that a contractarian perspective tells us much less about the actual workings of corporations
than research in the sociological tradition. Instead of making assumptions
about individual preferences, and instead of assuming that contractual arrangements are the prime guide to life for managers, sociological inquiry explores
how individuals actually behave within organisations, how organisations
work, and how the concepts of individual and corporate responsibility are
constructed internally and by outsiders. Moreover, at the theoretical level,

---

[64] See further Bratton, 'The "Nexus of Contracts" Corporation'.
[65] Clark, 'Agency Costs Versus Fiduciary Duties'. See also Brudney, 'Corporate Governance,
Agency Costs, and the Rhetoric of Contracts'.
[66] See also DeMott, 'Beyond Metaphor'.
[67] Clark, 'Agency Costs Versus Fiduciary Duties', 68–71. See also Shapiro, 'The Social Control
of Impersonal Trust', 632–4.

sociological contributions provide a far richer vision of the corporation.[68] A prime example is Gareth Morgan's *Images of Organization*, a work which, as we shall see in Chapter 4, canvasses a wide range of metaphors that help us to understand the nature of action and responsibility in modern corporate society. From this vantage point, the agency theory of the firm seems tunnel-visioned: the contractual metaphor is merely one among many relevant and useful metaphors.

Another conspicuous limitation of the agency theory of the firm is the failure to account for the status of corporations as miniature legal systems with rule-enforcement regimes of their own. Like the rational actor model, the agency theory of the firm presupposes a state–individual polity and neglects the pluralistic view of corporations as systems of government.[69] Modern corporations are much more than a nexus of contracts. While it is true that the construct of implicit contracts can be used to explain command and control within organisations and even the workings of the state in society,[70] it suffers from a major failure of realism. The agency theory of the firm adheres to the liberal doctrine that corporations (including the state) are conduits or ciphers for maximising the interests of their human members. The state is given extensive power to define and preserve the peace because the peace is a matter of 'public' concern and needs to be 'publicly' maintained.[71] Private corporations are not seen as communities with social control mechanisms of their own; they are artificial legal entities or useful machines.[72]

By contrast, pluralistic models of social organisation focus on the institutional arrangements that govern the human condition. Corporations (including the state) are seen as centres of power with goals, procedures and practices that serve the interests of their constituency.[73] Within a pluralistic framework, private corporations are communities with social control mechanisms of their own; they are self-governing groups. As self-governing groups, private corporations have extensive power to define and preserve their own peace, the role of the state being to police or regulate spheres of activity beyond the interest or competence of private governments. It might perhaps be possible to construct agency theories of the firm which take account of this pluralistic framework, but the models would be vastly more complicated than those reviewed in this chapter.

Ultimately therefore, both the rational corporate actor model and the agency theory of the firm provide an elliptical view of corporate action. The

---

[68] See, e.g., Mouzelis, *Organisation and Bureaucracy*; Emmet, *Rules, Roles and Relations*, ch. 9; Shapiro, 'The Social Control of Impersonal Trust'; Tombs, 'Corporate Crime and "Post Modern" Organizations'. Transdisciplinary studies may be richer again; see, e.g., Rudge, *Order and Disorder in Organizations*.

[69] See generally McConnell, *Private Power and American Democracy*.

[70] Hart and Holmstrom, 'The Theory of Contracts'.

[71] Shearing and Stenning, *Private Policing*, 11–12.

[72] See Dan-Cohen, *Rights, Persons, and Organizations*.

[73] Shearing and Stenning, *Private Policing*, 13–14; Dan-Cohen, *Rights, Persons, and Organizations*, ch. 8. Taken to an extreme, as under fascist interpretations, the state is idealised as a transcendent, superior being.

rational corporate actor model does recognise the concept of corporate responsibility, but only by analogy to the position of individuals. The agency theory of the firm does not regard corporations as responsible agents, but rather as useful tools for internalising the social costs of production. With these basic features in mind, we turn to a second assumption that governs much of the thinking in law and economics about corporate and individual responsibility for crime—the goal of deterrence is best analysed in terms of financial incentives.

Deterrence and Efficiency

The law and economics contributions we are examining proceed on the footing that financial incentives are of paramount importance in working out an effective deterrent strategy.[74] This assumption is open to serious question on a range of grounds.

Valuing individual responsibility

The first and most fundamental problem is the focus on financial incentives to the virtual exclusion of a coherent notion of responsibility. A limited or even non-existent value is attached to individual responsibility. Under the approach taken by Elzinga and Breit, and Pearce and others, the economic calculus of financial cost displaces individual responsibility because fines or charges imposed on the enterprise in themselves provide the incentive required for compliance.[75] Kraakman, by contrast, is at pains to explore the position of individual actors within the firm, but ultimately this leads him to suggest a narrow arena for individual liability: individual criminal liability is appropriate in an exceptional range of cases, as where the manager acted in bad faith or had reason to believe that his conduct was criminal; individual civil liability for gatekeepers may sometimes be desirable to induce a sufficient level of monitoring. Stone accords individual criminal liability a wider role than Kraakman, but individual liability is still treated as exceptional. Moreover, Stone sees the opportunity to enhance individual accountability as an important feature in the context of standards, but is unclear as to the value of individual responsibility in the more typical context of HBLRs. Polinsky and Shavell regard individual criminal liability as generally warranted within an overall framework of incentives wherein companies pay no more and no less that what is needed to internalise the social costs of their production.[76] All of these approaches seem odd given the importance traditionally attached to

---

[74] For a critique of this fundamental postulate in neoclassical economics see Etzioni, *The Moral Dimension*.

[75] See also Posner, 'An Economic Theory of the Criminal Law', 1228. Compare Coffee, 'Corporate Crime and Punishment', 458–9.

[76] See also Cohen, 'Environmental Crime and Punishment'.

individual accountability in Western societies. It is therefore worth looking more closely at the value of individual accountability and why account should be taken of it in working out effective deterrent strategies.

One of the main reasons for valuing individual responsibility is to guard against the danger that persons to blame within an organisation will rationalise their behaviour or deflect blame to others.[77] Another main reason is that the step of holding individuals responsible is in itself a major component of deterrence as orthodoxly understood.

The process of imposing individual criminal responsibility is complex and goes far beyond the impact of the penalty ultimately imposed. As Malcolm Feeley found in his classic study of the operation of criminal justice systems, the process of arrest and trial had more serious consequences for defendants than the sentence imposed.[78] From the standpoint of labelling theory, a criminal trial can be depicted as a status degradation ceremony, the impact of which is enormous even in the absence of punishment.[79] Moreover, at trial the conduct of the accused is exposed to close scrutiny and is the focal point of what is often a sustained examination.

The imposition of individual accountability within corporate internal discipline systems is less formal and usually invisible to the general public, but again it is misleading to discount the deterrent impact. Breaches of company rules may jeopardise opportunities for promotion or even retention of one's job. Being upbraided by a superior may be a trying experience. Discomfort may result from being made to feel disloyal or untrustworthy. Above all, there is the risk of being shamed before one's peers. Shaming has a personalised conscience-building and educative role that is lacking in purely legalistic regimes of punishment. Furthermore, shaming within corporations may involve the repeated day-to-day attentions of a group of associates. By contrast, a financially oriented regime of enterprise liability is not geared to achieving such effects: a financial disincentive is imposed on the enterprise and the loss is passed on to shareholders and any other persons to whom the cost may be transmitted without anyone necessarily experiencing a sense of personal responsibility. This exemplifies the tendency of economic analysis to abstract itself from non-market but nonetheless essential features of social life. As Robert Heilbroner has observed in the general context of socialisation, 'the market exerts its social pressure with a minimum of face to face contact and without any explicit show of force. The economy surfaces from its social surroundings as a "disembedded" process, an independent and autonomous realm of activity'.[80]

---

[77] See, e.g., Mill, *Considerations on Representative Government*, 393–4.
[78] Feeley, *The Process is the Punishment*.
[79] In Braithwaite, *Crime, Shame and Reintegration*, it is argued that the effect of such ceremonies will be positive if the shaming is integrative, but can be negative where the shaming is stigmatising.
[80] Heilbroner, *Behind the Veil of Economics*, 20. See also Bell, 'Models and Reality in Economic Discourse'; Shapiro, 'The Social Control of Impersonal Trust'; van der Haas, *The Enterprise in Transition*, ch. 19; Mintzberg, *Mintzberg on Management*, ch. 15.

Individual accountability within corporate systems of justice

It may be that the deterrent value of individual criminal liability is often out-weighed by the costs of attaining it. As we have indicated in Chapter 2, there are many situations where the pursuit of individual criminal liability is likely to be a very costly exercise. If one accepts that position, however, it hardly follows that enterprise liability for financial penalties is the only alternative. Another option is to require the enterprise to impose individual accountability at the level of its internal discipline system. As the Law Reform Commission of Canada has observed, corporate liability is potentially an efficient dispenser of individual accountability:

> In a society moving increasingly toward group action it may become impractical, in terms of allocation of resources, to deal with systems through their components. In many cases it would appear more sensible to transfer to the corporation the responsibility of policing itself, forcing it to take steps to ensure that the harm does not materialize through the conduct of people within the organization. Rather than having the state monitor the activities of each person within the corporation, which is costly and raises practical enforcement difficulties, it may be more efficient to force the corporation to do this, especially if sanctions imposed on the corporation can be translated into effective action at the individual level.[81]

Such a possibility is rarely addressed in the law and economics literature. This is hardly surprising in the context of taxes and charges because they avoid the need to apply sanctions upon those responsible for violating a legal command. However, it is remarkable that the command and control strategies advanced by Elzinga and Breit and by Kraakman do not pursue the relative economy of forcing corporate offenders to bring about individual accountability as a matter of internal disciplinary control. Elzinga and Breit discuss the sanction of corporate dissolution, but not the far less drastic option of compelling a corporation to activate its internal discipline system. Kraakman, unlike Elzinga and Breit, explicitly recognises the impact of enterprise sanctions on managers within the organisation, but does not consider how they might be held accountable where individual criminal liability would not be cost-effective. He does discuss the potential for improving internal controls by imposing civil liability on gatekeepers, but the gatekeeper concept is a secondary or even tangential approach. Stone explicitly mentions the internal disciplinary effects that enterprise liability may bring about,[82] but in this particular work he does not pursue the capacity of corporations to secure individual accountability within their systems of private justice. It is in other, non-economistic contributions that Stone has explored that question.[83] Polinsky and Shavell address the effect of internal disciplinary action against employees, but within a very narrow and, it seems, a sociologically uninformed framework of reference. On their analysis, the only relevant type of internal disciplinary action is

---

[81] Canada, Law Reform Commission, *Criminal Responsibility for Group Action*, 31.
[82] C. D. Stone, 'The Place of Enterprise Liability...', 29.
[83] See, e.g., C. D. Stone, *Where the Law Ends*, ch. 17.

recovery of damages from employees, a conception that leads to the conclusion that individual criminal liability is necessary in cases where, as is often the position, firms are unable to recover from employees the full costs of harms caused within the scope of their employment. This conception of internal justice systems neglects the significance of dismissal, shame, relocation, delay in promotion and other sanctions, the non-monetary effects of which may be more important than monetary loss.[84]

These failures to explore the deterrent potential of internal discipline systems may partly flow from an assumption that corporations are merely tools for achieving the interests of individuals in society. From that perspective, corporations do not have justice systems. By contrast, if corporations are constructed as polities with justice systems of their own,[85] then it becomes obvious that an inquiry into relative deterrent efficiency must deal with the possibility of using those systems to secure individual accountability. In other words, once corporations are seen as politico-legal systems rather than as economic tools or artificial legal entities in a competitive free-market environment, it is spurious to confine an analysis of efficient deterrence to what happens in the public system of justice. The analysis must embrace the private as well as the public worlds of policing in the modern state.[86]

Non-monetary deterrent or preventive effects

Apart from stunting the value of individual responsibility and taking an elliptical view of corporate internal discipline systems, economic analysis stresses financial incentives and tends to pay scant attention to the non-monetary effects of some forms of sanction.[87]

The pricing paradigm makes profit and loss the engine of corporate deterrence. However, in bureaucratic practice, if not in standard economic theory, corporations serve many non-monetary goals. The more important non-financial considerations, as specified by Robert Gordon, are sevenfold: the urge for power, the desire for prestige, the creative urge, the need to identify with a group, the desire for security, the urge for adventure, and the desire to serve others.[88] This is hardly to dispute the axiom that survival in the corporate

---

[84] Polinsky and Shavell refer to the opportunities that employees may have for other employment if they are dismissed, but their account underrates the adverse and unwanted effects that may nonetheless result. Most distinguished academics have many alternative employment opportunities, but presumably few would feel neutral about being dismissed from Stanford or Harvard. The same goes for executives in major companies.

[85] See further Lakoff and Rich, *Private Government*; Shearing and Stenning, *Private Policing*; Henry, *Private Justice*; Latham, 'The Body Politic of the Corporation', 11.

[86] See further Stewart, 'Organizational Jurisprudence', 378–9, 387–8. Some writers have addressed the role of institutional investors in exerting disciplinary pressures on managers. This is is only one dimension of private justice systems and, in any event, its operation depends on the vicissitudes of shareholder reactions. See further Coffee, 'Liquidity Versus Control'; Monks and Minow, *Power and Accountability*.

[87] See further the framework advanced in Freiberg, 'Reconceptualizing Sanctions'.

[88] Gordon, *Business Leadership in the Large Corporation*, 305. See also van der Haas, *The Enterprise in Transition*, ch. 17.

sector ultimately depends on profitability. Nor is it denied that emphasis on profits has been accentuated within many companies by the pressure to maximise their wealth to minimise the chance of becoming an attractive takeover target. Non-financial values are nonetheless sufficiently important to warrant the use of deterrent models that reflect them. This can be seen by reconsidering John Kenneth Galbraith's observation that '[i]n the American business code nothing is so iniquitous as government interference in the *internal* affairs of the corporation'.[89] Monetary sanctions do not bear down upon sensitivity to governmental interference, whereas other forms of sanction do. As several commentators have pointed out, corporate probation is one vehicle for reaching this part of the corporate underbelly, as by requiring a corporate offender to indicate to the sentencing court what exactly it proposes to do to discipline the personnel implicated in the offence.[90]

It may also be argued that, even if profit were the sole preoccupation of corporate decisionmaking, the law might well change the playing field. One well-known difficulty is the deterrence trap—the inability of corporations, especially highly leveraged corporations, to pay fines of the amount needed to reflect the gravity of the offence and the low risk of detection and conviction. Another factor is the attention-grabbing capability of non-monetary sanctions. Sanctions that have non-financial impacts may transcend the commercial banality of money and hence be more likely to command the attention of managers. They are also more difficult for managers to deflect to consumers and shareholders because the main burden of probation and other non-monetary sanctions is typically borne by management. At least this is so when these sanctions are well designed and intelligently applied. Moreover, non-financial sanctions introduce different forms of risk into decisionmaking and hence play upon the fear of uncertainty that typically pervades business.

Considerations such as these have prompted the suggestion that corporate offenders be subject to punitive injunctions.[91] The punitive injunction is a sentence intended for serious offences and would require a corporate defendant to revamp its internal controls in some punitively demanding way:

> The animating idea is to intervene in the organizational processes of a corporate offender in some punitively demanding way that reflects the aims of corporate criminal law. The most obvious organizational processes worth subjecting to punitive intervention are policies and procedures relating to internal discipline and

[89] Galbraith *The New Industrial State*, 77. See further Silk and Vogel, *Ethics and Profits*, ch. 6.
[90] Australia, Law Reform Commission, *Sentencing Penalties*, Discussion Paper No. 30, paras. 283–307; South Australia, Criminal Law and Penal Methods Reform Committee, Fourth Report, *The Substantive Criminal Law*, 357–64; American Bar Association, 3 *Standards for Criminal Justice*, 18.160–185; Geraghty, 'Structural Crime and Institutional Rehabilitation'; Coffee, 'No Soul to Damn No Body to Kick'; Coffee and Whitbread, 'The Convicted Corporation'; Gruner, 'To Let the Punishment Fit the Organization'; Lofquist, 'Organizational Probation and the US Sentencing Commission'.
[91] Fisse, 'The Punitive Injunction as a Sanction against Corporations'. Compare the extreme and magical reductionist claim that the effects of interventionist sanctions of this kind ultimately reduce simply to monetary loss: Parker, 'Criminal Sentencing Policy for Organizations', 571; Wray, 'Corporate Probation under the New Organizational Sentencing Guidelines', 2032.

compliance with the law. Instead of requiring a corporate offender merely to take reasonable precautions by way of internal discipline or compliance programming it is possible to punish a defendant by requiring extra steps to be taken. In more concrete terms, it could well be a mandatory condition of a punitive injunction that the defendant undertake a program with three punitive essences:[92] first, a task force involving a range of senior and middle managers; secondly, an intensive internal disciplinary program; and thirdly, a comprehensive and rigorous review and revision of accountability mechanisms and compliance precautions relating to the type of offense for which the defendant has been convicted.[93]

A sanction such as the punitive injunction is thus intended to change the medium of deterrence and thereby reduce the chance that managers have to treat punishment for offences as merely a financial cost which can readily be transmitted to others. Moreover, the deterrence trap is avoided by providing a sanction that can be used forcefully against highly leveraged corporations that are unable to pay a fine commensurate with the severity of their offences. The more serious the offence and the less the ability of the company to pay a high fine, then the greater the justification for imposing stringent monitoring of the company's future activities. The more serious the offence and the less adequate the financial sanction that can be exacted from the company, then the greater the justification for imposing intrusive monitoring controls on the company.

One reason why punitive injunctions and other potentially hard-hitting non-monetary sanctions have not figured in economic analyses of corporate crime control to date[94] is that corporations are not seen as responsible, blameworthy agents, but as tools for maximising the self-preferences of individuals. The design of sanctions against corporations is fundamentally affected by the designer's conception of corporate responsibility and blameworthiness. If one takes the view that corporations are merely useful machines or vehicles for maximising the interests of individuals, it is difficult to see the point of trying to create a corporate sanction of comparable potency to imprisonment. From this angle, the task of design is not to create a sanction capable of reflecting the seriousness of the offence and the blameworthiness of the offender. Instead, the task is to adjust the throttle on the corporate engine so as to produce greater or lesser resources for distribution to the persons using the machine to maximise their own interests. By contrast, if corporations are taken to be blameworthy responsible actors, there is a need to devise sanctions that can express corporate blameworthiness and impose punishment in a way that impresses upon corporate defendants the fact of their responsibility.

---

[92] There are other possibilities, including insistence on facilitation of restitution in ways that would not be required as a matter of remedy.

[93] Fisse, 'The Punitive Injunction as a Sanction against Corporations'.

[94] But note that, unlike Elzinga and Breit, Kraakman, Pearce, or Polinsky and Shavell, C. D. Stone does qualify the economic calculus by proposing that interventionist strategies, including the use of probation, be used where HBLRs are insufficient: 'The Place of Enterprise Liability', 36–45.

Another major question is whether economic deterrence sufficiently reflects the way in which the criminal law prohibits unwanted types of conduct. Economic analyses typically collapse the distinction between civil and criminal liability because all forms of liability are reduced to the monetary cost of harms. From this standpoint, fines, monetary penalties and taxes are functionally the same because they all express the price to be paid for non-compliance. Superficially plausible as this approach may be, however, it attaches insufficient weight to the prohibited or unwanted nature of offences. Punishment in the criminal law is not merely a form of penalty or tax. In Joel Feinberg's words,

> punishment is a conventional device for the expression of attitudes of resentment and indignation, and of judgments of disapproval and reprobation, on the part either of the punishing authority ... or of those 'in whose name' the punishment is inflicted. Punishment, in short, has a *symbolic significance* largely missing from other kinds of penalties.[95]

To this it should be added that the focus of condemnation is the unwantedness of the harm caused, coupled with the blameworthiness of the actor in causing that harm.

The element of unwantedness in criminally proscribed harm is apparent from the way that offences typically are regarded. Offences are not merely commodities to be bought or sold, but socially unwanted invasions of protected interests.[96] Those invasions are unwanted even if we know that, in the event of being harmed, we will receive full compensation. Thus, no amount of money can make up for harm caused by offences of the kind illustrated by the Kepone case (1976), where the Allied Chemical Corporation dispersed toxic pesticide wastes into the James River and Chesapeake Bay in the US. If a serious offence is punished merely by means of a fine, the connotation is not so much disapproval as crime for sale. Accordingly, one reason for imposing criminal liability in such a case is to subject the defendant and the offending conduct to emphatic public disapproval. As Coffee has observed:[97]

> A world of difference does and should exist between taxing a disfavored behavior and criminalizing it. We tax cigarettes, but outlaw drugs. Both are disincentives, but the criminal sanction carries a unique moral stigma. That stigma should not be overused, but, when properly used, it is society's most powerful force for influencing behavior and defining its operative moral code. ... The message needs to be clearly communicated that there is no price that, when paid, entitles you to engage in the prohibited behavior.[98]

---

[95] Feinberg, *Doing the Deserving*, 98.

[96] This is apparent in many contexts; see, e.g., Shirk, Greenberg, and Dawson, 'Truth or Consequences'.

[97] Note that Coffee uses stigma to refer to shame in general; contrast Braithwaite, *Crime, Shame, and Reintegration*, 102–3, where stigma is defined as a (less productive) sub-set of shame.

[98] Statement to US, Sentencing Commission, Hearing, New York, 11 Oct. 1988. See also Gibbons, 'The Utility of Economic Analysis of Crime'. For an empirical study indicating that people are guided more by normative attitudes and social values than by rational self-interest, see Tyler, *Why People Obey the Law*. Compare M. A. Cohen, 'Environmental Crime and Punishment', 1105–6.

Whether or not offences are reduced to prices materially affects perceptions of the way in which individual and corporate liability should be allocated. If offences are treated as purchasable commodities, there is an initial bias toward civil liability: an economic regime of cost internalisation requires no more than the use of civil process, and to use the criminal process to impose merely a system of economic penalties or civil remedies would be inefficient in the extreme.[99] In turn, civil liability creates a bias toward corporate liability: the concern is to secure payment and, as a general rule, enterprise liability is more expedient than individual liability as a vehicle for recovering damages or monetary penalties. In contrast, if offences are treated as non-purchasable, allocating liability for them is not a matter of expedient recovery of damages or penalties sufficient to reflect the financial cost of offences. The focus is more on preventing unwanted conduct and on finding a balance of individual and corporate responsibility sufficient to impress the need for compliance on people and their organisations. There is an incentive structure here, but it is not merely a financial one. Weight is attached to the imposition of responsibility because the blameworthiness of the relevant actors—individual or corporate—is an integral part of the unwantedness of the criminally proscribed behaviour.

Another important factor that is missing in a financial regime of deterrence is the role played by negotiation and bargaining as a means of getting compliance with the law. Empirical studies have suggested that enforcement agencies often rely on persuasion more than on punishment, not just because persuasion is less costly, but rather because it is believed to be more effective.[100] Theoretical inquiries have also been conducted into the best mix of persuasion and punishment. John Scholz has argued that, from a game-theoretic standpoint, the optimal strategy across a range of plausible pay-offs in the regulatory game is 'tit-for-tat', with punishment being held back so long as the corporation co-operates with the enforcement agency in working toward compliance.[101] Ayres and Braithwaite have advanced a strategy that revolves around an 'enforcement pyramid'—a set of enforcement options specified by the enforcement agency in ascending order of escalation.[102] The options in the enforcement pyramid range from informal advice and warnings at the base of the pyramid to criminal liability with severe sanctions at the apex. Ayres and Braithwaite suggest that the taller the enforcement pyramid, the more the levels of possible escalation, and then the greater the pressure that can be exerted to motivate 'voluntary' compliance at the base of the pyramid.[103] From this perspective, compliance depends more on a dynamic enforcement game than on an economically optimal scaling of penalties. The

[99] See Posner, 'An Economic Theory of the Criminal Law', 1228–9; Byam, 'The Economic Inefficiency of Corporate Criminal Liability'.
[100] See, e.g., more than 30 studies cited in Hawkins, *Environment and Enforcement*, 3. See also the study of 96 Australian agencies by Grabosky and Braithwaite, *Of Manners Gentle*.
[101] Scholz, 'Deterrence, Cooperation and the Ecology of Regulatory Enforcement'; Scholz, 'Voluntary Compliance and Regulatory Enforcement'.
[102] Ayres and Braithwaite, *Responsive Regulation*.
[103] Ibid., ch. 2.

reasoning in support of this approach need not be detailed here. The point of present concern is that the implications for the allocation of individual and corporate liability are quite different from those yielded by the hypothesis that effective deterrence depends on pricing crime at an optimal rate.

If compliance is taken to be a dynamic enforcement game, then the focus is on getting commitment from corporations and their personnel to comply with the law. The process is partly one of instilling and maintaining a sense of responsibility on the part of corporations as corporations and on the part of key personnel within the organisation. By contrast, an optimal scale of penalties is not concerned with the value of responsibility as a mechanism of social control, but with the value of financial incentives as a regulator of harm-causing. A related point is that on-the-job enforcement bargaining and negotiation can be more educative than an away-from-the-scene system of cost-internalisation. This is a significant limitation of taxes as a means of controlling corporate behaviour:

> [I]nspectors who directly monitor environmental and safety performance ... play an important educative role. They diffuse environmental and safety innovations by drawing management's attention to new technologies, policies, and standard operating procedures which the inspector has seen other companies successfully apply.[104]

The range and weight of the bargaining chips available to enforcers are critical from a compliance perspective. The bargaining chips in a tall enforcement pyramid would include both individual and corporate criminal liability: the threat of individual criminal liability might well be useful as a lever for obtaining evidence against the corporation, and vice versa. There would also be an escalating range of sanctions; in the case of corporations, the range would embrace not only fines but also probation, punitive injunctions and other non-monetary sanctions.[105] Part of the purpose served by the range of corporate sanctions would be to enable enforcers to persuade corporations to impose individual responsibility as a matter of internal discipline. In the event of a corporation not playing the game, corporate probation could then be used formally to coerce compliance. In the event of recalcitrance, the stakes could be raised by means of a punitive injunction. In comparison, a system of optimal financial penalties depends on relatively static assumptions about corporate responses to the threat of sanctions and no attempt is made to induce

---

[104] Braithwaite, 'The Limits of Economism in Controlling Harmful Corporate Conduct', 495.
[105] See US, Sentencing Commission, Preliminary Draft, *Sentencing Guidelines for Organizational Defendants*; US, Sentencing Commission, *Discussion Materials on Organizational Sanctions*; US, Sentencing Commission, 'Discussion Draft of Sentencing Guidelines and Policy Statements for Organizations'; Australia, Law Reform Commission, *Sentencing Penalties*, Discussion Paper No. 30, paras. 283–307; South Australia, Criminal Law and Penal Methods Reform Committee, Fourth Report, *The Substantive Criminal Law*, 357–64; American Bar Association, 3 *Standards for Criminal Justice*, 18.160–85; Geraghty, 'Structural Crime and Institutional Rehabilitation'; Coffee, 'No Soul to Damn No Body to Kick'; Coffee and Whitbread, 'The Convicted Corporation'; Gruner, 'To Let the Punishment Fit the Organization'; Lofquist, 'Organizational Probation and the US Sentencing Commission'.

corporations to take particular compliance measures, such as taking internal disciplinary action, against those responsible for an offence.

It may nonetheless be argued that a preventive strategy of negotiation and bargaining, backed by probation, punitive injunctions and other non-monetary sanctions, is relatively costly when compared with a scheme of financial disincentives. Negotiation and bargaining are labour intensive and sanctions like probation do impose the expense of supervision and monitoring. However, there are reasons to challenge any claim that monetary sanctions are necessarily the most efficient way of preventing corporate crime.

First, the strategy of relying on a regime of optimal monetary sanctions is highly risky and the projected gains from using such an approach must be discounted accordingly. One major risk is that the change-over from a system that stresses the value of responsibility and the unwanted nature of offences will tend to undermine deterrence and moral education. We have canvassed these limitations above. Another danger is that a system of optimal monetary deterrence does not provide the same safeguards as a system which has many different avenues of prevention. A typical feature of the present law in most jurisdictions is that there is a good deal of overlap and hence redundancy in the avenues of prevention provided. Individual and corporate criminal liability are available as options. Corporations as well as individuals are subject to probation as well as to fines and monetary penalties. Enforcement agencies use the offences and penalties provided to negotiate and bargain for compliance. Incapacitative sanctions, such as imprisonment and licence revocation, also come into play. This approach is costly if one believes that a one-weapon strategy of monetary sanctions will work, but there is an obvious danger in abandoning the multi-weapon safeguards of the present system.

It is worth stressing that a deterrent threat leaves corporations with the choice of complying or not complying and, no matter how sophisticated the computation of optimal monetary sanctions, there will be sub-optimising offenders who disregard the threat. As Coffee has observed:

> From a general deterrent perspective, the problem with 'pricing' the criminal behavior is that the 'price' is set in terms of the *mean* defendant's incentives (that is, the expected cost must equal the expected gain from the offense, after discounting that gain by the likelihood of apprehension). Even if we assume that it were possible to determine the precise expected gain and the precise probability of apprehension for that *mean* offender, a 'price' so determined would deter only that average offender (and also those offenders who perceived even less gain or a greater likelihood of apprehension). What happens to the offender who either perceives a greater expected gain or who estimates the odds of apprehension (accurately or inaccurately) as being more favorable to it? In short, if in real life there is a dispersion of potential offenders (some optimistic, some pessimistic; some more skilled at crime than others; some more risk averse than others), a pricing system that focuses only on the average offender will by definition under-deter the above-average offender. Similarly, it will not deter the less risk averse or the more optimistic offender. The point here is that, even within the four corners of deterrence theory, there is a need to employ substantial penalties that exceed the expected level necessary to deter the average potential offender.[106]

---

[106] Statement to US Sentencing Commission, Hearing, New York, 11 Oct. 1988.

Rather than providing a cushion by increasing the level of monetary penalties to a higher level, and rather than making do with an approach which by hypothesis is sub-optimal as to the range of potential offenders to whom it is directed, it is possible to diversify the available means of control. Thus, compliance-oriented negotiation and bargaining, backed by an array of non-monetary sanctions, widen the safety net and give the legal system greater flexibility. This multiplex approach is suggested by the general practice in policy analysis of using more than one instrument to deal with complex problems. Inevitably, some redundancy results and a multiplex system of legal control is more costly to run. However, there are major benefits. Redundancy (multiple concurrent avenues of control) has considerable value as a means of helping to ensure that the law keeps its promises. It also provides a useful method for managing uncertainty in many areas of law and government,[107] and may be indispensable in the context of sanctions against corporations where the actual impact of any given deterrent is unknown and unknowable.

Before discussing the significance of uncertainty, it should be stressed that control strategies that rely on non-financial techniques do not necessarily involve massive costs of supervision and monitoring. It is a mistake to think in terms of nationalisation of private enterprise, the bane of most Right-thinking entrepreneurs. A more realistic model in many contexts is enforced self-regulation, in the sense of internal controls designed and administered by corporations but with the state insisting that corporations have in place a system that promises to work and which meets certain basic conditions.[108] Such possibilities as corporate probation should be seen in this light.[109] Thus, the sentencing criteria that govern the use of corporate probation could and should be devised so as to maximise freedom of enterprise in compliance systems.[110] One possibility would be to stipulate in the empowering legislation that, wherever practicable, corporate defendants be given the opportunity to indicate before sentence what disciplinary or other steps they propose to take in response to their conviction.

Management of uncertainty

The strategy of relying on economically optimal financial penalties rests on the assumption that it is possible to assess costs and benefits in a realistic if

---

[107] See generally Bendor, *Parallel Systems*; Landau, 'Redundancy, Rationality, and the Problem of Duplication and Overlap'.
[108] See Braithwaite, 'Enforced Self-Regulation'. Compare Insider Trading and Securities Fraud Enforcement Act of 1988 (1988) 1304 CCH Federal Securities Law Reports 1, esp. 20–2; Gerber, 'Enforced Self-Regulation in the Infant Formula Industry'. There is now an extensive literature on corporate compliance systems; see Sigler and Murphy, *Interactive Corporate Compliance*; Braithwaite, 'Taking Responsibility Seriously: Corporate Compliance Systems'; Fisse, 'Corporate Compliance Programmes: The Trade Practices Act and Beyond'.
[109] See further Gruner, 'To Let the Punishment Fit the Organization'.
[110] Fisse, 'Criminal Law and Consumer Protection', 194–9.

not first-best manner.[111] Making the necessary calculations, however, is easier said than done.[112] This problem is recognised to some extent by Stone and Kraakman. However, it is glossed over by Elzinga and Breit, Pearce and others, and Polinsky and Shavell. It is worth at least outlining the difficulties that arise because they unfold a dimension of the question of responsibility that is missing in the law and economics literature. The missing dimension is the way in which responsibility serves as a useful device for managing the uncertainty that pervades corporate sanctioning. Imposing individual and corporate responsibility can well be seen as a practical step that can be taken to side-step the problems of trying to calculate optimal economic penalties.

Uncertainty immediately confronts the lawmaker who looks to the law and economics literature for guidance on the allocation of individual and corporate liability. There is a spectacular diversity of opinion. As we have seen, Elzinga and Breit advocate a regime of enterprise liability. The Pearce Report recommends a system of no-fault taxes borne by enterprises. Kraakman and Stone propose a mix of enterprise and individual liability, but advance different criteria for determining the mix. Polinsky and Shavell advocate concurrent corporate and individual liability, with corporations strictly liable and employees liable for negligence.[113] Others take different positions again. Dorsey Ellis contends that individual liability is optimal.[114] Alan Sykes prefers a rule of joint and several liability for principals and agents.[115] The Coase theorem suggests that, depending on the transaction costs, either corporate or individual criminal liability is capable of producing an efficient outcome.[116]

Apart from the far-ranging division of opinion among economic theorists themselves,[117] there are real difficulties in working out particular costs and benefits when applying the deterrence equation. An initial obstacle is putting a value on the impact of imposing or not imposing individual responsibility. What exactly is lost if we depend on a system of enterprise liability which does not involve the process of individual persons being held accountable for their particular contribution to an offence? It seems impossible to put a

---

[111] First-best solutions are often unrealistic; see further Lipsey and Lancaster, 'The General Theory of Second Best'.
[112] See Byrne and Hoffmann, 'Efficient Corporate Harm'. There have been few empirical studies of the actual effects of civil penalties. See, e.g., Altrogge and Shughart, 'The Regressive Nature of Civil Penalties' (FTC penalties were disproportionately high for small firms and thus redistributed wealth to large firms). The literature contains many diverse views as to the efficacy of financial penalties. See, e.g., Hopkins, *The Impact of Prosecutions under the Trade Practices Act*; Hurley, 'Section 76 of the Trade Practices Act'. As regards uncertainty and deterrence hypotheses, see Zimring and Hawkins, *Deterrence*, ch. 4; Braithwaite and Makkai, 'Testing an Expected Utility Model of Corporate Deterrence'.
[113] Polinsky and Shavell, 'Should Employees be Subject to Fines and Imprisonment Given the Existence of Corporate Liability?'
[114] Ellis, 'Fairness and Efficiency in the Law of Punitive Damages'.
[115] Sykes, 'The Economics of Vicarious Liability'.
[116] See further Romano, 'Theory of the Firm and Corporate Sentencing', 377; Cohen, 'Environmental Crime and Punishment', 1064–5.
[117] As recognised in Hart, 'An Economist's Perspective on the Theory of the Firm'. Compare the disingenuity of, e.g., Posner, 'An Economic Theory of the Criminal Law'.

monetary value on this kind of item. Likewise, how does one put a dollar value on holding corporations responsible as blameworthy actors rather than treating them merely as useful conduits for the internalisation of social costs? Moreover, what relative weighting is to be given to individual and corporate responsibility?[118]

Another layer of complexity is putting a price on many of the harms that are caused by offences. This is particularly evident in the context of offences causing injury or death. The technical and moral difficulties in estimating the value of a human life are well known. And, as Coffee has pointed out, there is a significant difference between tortious and criminal harm:

> Tort law has historically been keyed to the goal of compensation and has valued human life in terms of lost earnings. Of course, few of us would sell our lives so cheaply. Liability under the criminal law generally arises only for 'knowing' or 'reckless' violations—i.e. intentional misconduct. Thus, it seems inappropriate to apply the damages awarded for negligent behavior to intentional misbehavior; indeed, tort law would typically award punitive damages in such a case. Use of 'lost earnings' measures to establish the value of life (or bodily injury) exacerbates the problem of turning the criminal law into a pricing system. Carried to its reductio ad absurdum extreme, this approach would have created an incentive two decades ago for General Motors to pay the Mafia to assassinate Ralph Nader, because his life would have been valued only according to a mechanical actuarial calculation.[119]

Assuming that it is possible to attach realistic figures to the value of responsibility and the social cost of the harm flowing from offences, a further complication is the need to factor in the relevant probabilities. Under the model advanced by Elzinga and Breit, the rational corporate actor must calculate four probabilities: (1) the probability of detection and conviction; (2) the probability of being fined a particular amount; (3) the probability of gains or losses from the criminal conduct; and (4) the probability of foregone opportunities.[120] The information base required to assess these probabilities is massive and corporate decisionmakers might understandably 'satisfice' by making sloppy estimates or by following a rule of thumb, such as 'if in doubt, comply with the law'. Doubt has also been cast on the reality of using probability rules to predict conduct that is not repetitive and regular. These problems are compounded if the calculations are made on the basis of an agency theory of the firm because additional probabilities then have to be assessed, including the probability of managers being able or unable to shift risk, and the probability of different costs of risk-shifting.[121]

---

[118] Consider the crudity of the approach to fixing penalties against individuals and the corporation in, e.g., *TPC v Sony (Australia) Pty Ltd* (1990) ATPR 41–031.
[119] Statement to US Sentencing Commission, Hearing, New York, 11 Oct. 1988. Consider, e.g., the *Exxon Valdez* disaster: 'What Exxon Will be Leaving Behind', *NYT*, April 2 1989, s. 4, 7 ('[n]o amount of money will make Prince William Sound look as it did before the disaster').
[120] Byrne and Hoffmann, 'Efficient Corporate Harm', 115–16. For a rare example of due recognition of these problems in the law and economics literature, see Cass, 'Sentencing Corporations', 302.
[121] This is not to suggest that we endorse so limited a framework of inquiry. Compare, e.g., Hwang and Lin, *Group Decision Making under Multiple Criteria*.

Given the imponderables of cost-benefit analysis, it is not surprising to find that Elzinga and Breit ultimately modify their economic calculus and advance a rough-and-ready proposal that corporations be fined at the rate of 25 per cent of the firm's pre-tax profits for every year of anticompetitive activity.[122] The following explanation is given:

> The 25 percent figure is not sacrosanct, but it does represent our judgment of a penalty that would deter in an evenhanded fashion. Even a management relatively isolated from its firm's owners would feel the impact from a fine of this magnitude. The experience of lower stock prices, greater difficulties in attracting funds, and an increased probability of a takeover bid would be unpleasant consequences of such a fine. The figure of 25 percent would, on the other hand, not seem so high as to cause violators to go out of business, nor so onerous as to offend most persons' sense of equity. If experience with this percentage finds the antitrust authorities still uncovering frequent violations, Congress could increase it until anticompetitive behavior becomes rare.[123]

Rough-and-ready pragmatism of this kind sits uncomfortably with the postulate that deterrence is best analysed in terms of an economic calculus of financial cost.

Kraakman largely concedes the problem of uncertainty in applying the agency theory of the firm in practice, but does little to provide a solution. This limitation is particularly apparent in his discussion of gatekeeper liability. For Kraakman, gatekeeper liability is seen as a useful method for controlling corporate conduct where internal controls have broken down. This proposal has some appeal, but only if it is possible to decide readily when in fact internal controls have become inadequate. Kraakman does not define exactly what is meant by a breakdown in internal controls. Nor does he discuss the difficulties of measurement involved in deciding whether the internal control system has in fact broken down. The proposal thus seems nebulous and difficult to apply in practice; whether or not resort to gatekeeper liability would be efficient seems to be anyone's guess.

Polinsky and Shavell indicate that allowance needs to be made for the probability of a firm being found liable, but offer no guidance on how this probability is to be assessed in practice. They are also troubled by the difficulty firms may face in detecting the employees who have caused harm: the lower the risk of detection, the higher the sanction which needs to be imposed; and the higher the sanction which needs to be imposed, the less likely the adequacy of internal action to recover the costs from employees. In a world where the risks of corporate detection are usually unknown, this theoretical precept is of minimal practical relevance.

What lawmakers need is not so much an economic calculus of deterrence as practical methods for managing the uncertainty that plagues attempts to impose effective sanctions on corporations and their managers. One method for managing this uncertainty is the use of a range of overlapping and

---

[122] Elzinga and Breit, *The Antitrust Penalties*, 134–5. See the instructive critique in Hay, 'Review of Elzinga and Breit, *The Antitrust Penalties*', 436–44.
[123] Elzinga and Breit, *The Antitrust Penalties*, 134–5.

concurrent legal controls, as mentioned earlier. Redundancy (multi-weapon safeguards) of this kind can be useful where one control mechanism fails to work as hoped but does not in itself provide the feedback that lawmakers require if they are to revise the law in light of experience. The traditional case-by-case approach of the common law supplies some feedback, but the potential has not been fully realised. In the context of sanctions against corporations, the supply of feedback has been limited because the sanction typically used—the fine—tells us very little about the way it works in practice let alone about the nature of corporate decisionmaking and internal disciplinary systems. However, other types of sanction against corporations, notably probation, can provide much more useful feedback because, unlike fines, they are concerned with the supervision or monitoring of corporate behaviour.

A more fundamental way of managing the uncertainty surrounding the impact of sanctions against corporations and their personnel is apparent in the importance traditionally attached to the concept of responsibility. As explained earlier, the process of holding individuals responsible is an important component of the deterrent and educative program of the criminal law. The emphasis placed on responsibility reflects a 'rules of action'[124] approach that has been adopted to avoid the need to make difficult and unreliable probabilistic calculations about the effects of financial incentives.[125]

Two rules of action are involved. First, we should disapprove of certain types of actions (such as crimes) by recognising them as wrong. Second, we should hold responsible those who are blameworthy as wrongdoers. In legal as well as everyday decisionmaking, these rules of action may be more workable than case-by-case calculation of the uncertain range of costs and benefits that may attach to any given act. Simple rules of action have lower information and transaction costs, especially in domains where uncertainty or inestimability of benefit–cost are so great as frequently to cause major estimation errors. Simple rule-following may even result in better average returns in terms of benefit–cost. A little knowledge of benefit–cost under conditions of great uncertainty is a dangerous thing. We might well make better judgements by assuming that any knowledge we have is likely to be misleading if we accept it in isolation from all the other knowledge we lack. Put another way, we seek an alternative decisionmaking approach which is more forgiving of uncertainty about what we know. Further, we might take the view that courts are institutions that are well equipped to follow rules of action about assessing responsibility. But we might also consider them poorly equipped to measure the financial benefits and costs of particular decisions made by others, or indeed by themselves.

The highly questionable assumption that deterrence is best analysed in terms of financial incentives rather than in terms of responsibility, shame and

---

[124] See Russell, *Human Knowledge*, 416–7; Fisse, 'Probability and the Proudman v Dayman Defence of Reasonable Mistaken Belief', 496–505. On rules of thumb in economics, see Etzioni, *The Moral Dimension*, ch. 10.

[125] Rules of action are used for this purpose in the context of insurance risk adjustment; see Heimer, *Reactive Risk and Rational Action*. They are also prevalent as a way of handling information overload in organisations; see Reiss, 'The Institutionalization of Risk'.

other related deterrent effects has led Jules Coleman to contend that '[a] purely economic theory of crime can only impoverish rather than enrich our understanding of the nature of crime'.[126] While we agree that simplistic economic theories are a prescription for poor policy, we disagree with any suggestion that economic analysis of corporate crime is uninstructive. By exploring the underlying assumptions and over-reductionist tendencies of the economic models advanced to date, one is forced to identify the distinctive features of criminal liability and to explain exactly why those features may be worth preserving. This is particularly true of the concept of responsibility, both as an avenue of deterrence in its own right and as a device for avoiding the uncertainty of trying to assess an optimal level of penalty.

Safeguarding Individuals

A third assumption implicit in the law and economics analyses discussed in this chapter is that a regime of enterprise liability promotes rather than detracts from the interests of individuals. Enterprise liability does have the major advantage of avoiding the harsh impact which the criminal law may have on individuals. However, account must be taken of internal discipline systems, an arena where enterprise liability leaves individuals vulnerable to abuse. Another problem is the unequal application of individual criminal liability: enterprise liability deflects liability from managers, whereas street offenders typically have no enterprise to take the rap.

Enterprise liability seeks to control organisational conduct by imposing liability on the corporate entity rather than on individuals and, in the context of corporate criminal liability, reprobation and denunciation are directed against the corporate body rather than against individual personnel or shareholders.[127] The infliction of harm on individuals to deter offences is thus minimised and to this extent enterprise liability is a parsimonious weapon of social control. Little point is served by exposing individuals to the harshness of criminal liability if the same level of prevention can be achieved by less drastic means.[128]

Enterprise liability displaces individual liability wherever the social costs of production can be internalised without imposing individual criminal liability. The aim is not to protect individuals by using corporate liability as a surrogate for individual liability in cases where individuals would otherwise be exposed to strict responsibility or exemplary punishment. The aim is to exclude individual criminal liability on efficiency grounds, and this is so even in cases where liability and punishment would be consistent with retributive notions of just deserts.

[126] J. L. Coleman, 'Crime, Kickers, and Transaction Structures', 326.
[127] The latter are rarely identified; for an exception, see 'Putting a Face on Corporate Crime', *NYT*, 14 July 1989, B8 (attendance of senior corporate management in court required when corporate defendant sentenced).
[128] Indeed, in Braithwaite and Pettit, *Not Just Deserts*, it is argued that it is morally wrong to impose criminal liability when dominion can be protected by less drastic means.

This parsimonious feature of enterprise liability provides a welcome contrast to individualism, which lends itself to the extreme of luckless minions being prosecuted as scapegoats for corporate disasters. Such an extreme is illustrated by the fate of Robert Morgan, a train driver who was prosecuted for manslaughter after the Purley train crash in England in March 1989.[129] Morgan did in fact go through a red light, but this appears to have been the result of stressful working conditions. Imposing enterprise liability in such a case would reflect the organisational conditions which led to the disaster, and internal disciplinary action would be enough to hold the driver accountable and to reflect the degree of his responsibility. The driver may have been criminally negligent if judged from the standpoint of an unstressed person in his shoes, but to apply the standard in that way would be unrealistic because no account would be taken of the actual conditions in which the driver was employed to work.

The ability to spare bit players from the heavy hand of the criminal law is one of the most appealing features of enterprise liability and yet little is made of this advantage by Elzinga and Breit, Kraakman or Pearce and others. Elzinga and Breit focus on ways of achieving deterrence; their concern about individual criminal liability is that prison sentences are unlikely to be imposed with sufficient frequency to work as a deterrent.[130] Kraakman stresses the tendency of corporate officers to shift the risk of criminal liability through indemnification, but does not examine the extent to which the denunciatory impact of a criminal conviction can in fact be offset by compensation from the corporation, especially where a jail sentence is imposed.[131] Pearce and others extol the advantages of using taxes to internalise the social costs of corporate harm-causing, but do not examine the extent to which a regime of taxes would reduce the need to rely on individual criminal liability as a means of deterrence.

Stone, unlike the other writers mentioned above, treats this issue in some detail. For him, enterprise liability usually is warranted because of the difficulty in pin-pointing criminally responsible actors:

> [T]he bulk of harm-causing corporate conduct does not typically have, at its root, a particular agent so clearly 'to blame' that he or she merits either imprisonment or a monetary fine extracted in a public ceremony. A bribe, for example, can be traced to a particular hand and mind; not so a new car with flawed brakes. In a large organization, the division of bureaucratic functions makes it difficult to ascribe individual responsibility for the brake design even when we are using 'responsibility' in its moral sense. To establish the legal responsibility of an agent is even more costly and problematic, especially in criminal actions where the burden of proof and various due process constraints impede prosecution. Indeed, there may be circumstances in which we find it appropriate to judge that a wrongful act has occurred,

---

[129] See Bergman, 'Recklessness in the Boardroom', 1501.
[130] Elzinga and Breit, *The Antitrust Penalties*, 43.
[131] The contention that imprisonment can simply be converted into a monetary equivalent underestimates the obstacles that face jailed executives who seek monetary comfort: see Coffee, 'Corporate Crime and Punishment', 443–6.

but to ascribe it—both in morals and in law—to the corporation rather than to any agent. Such an attribution has appeal when, for example, the society wishes to denounce the conduct and rehabilitate the actor, but the source of the wrongdoing seems to lie in bureaucratic shortcomings—flaws in the organization's formal and informal authority structure, or in its information pathways—rather than in the deliberate act of any particular employee. In these circumstances, it may be more intelligible, and make better policy, to focus the sanction on the enterprise.[132]

Stone further observes that the difficulty in pin-pointing individual criminal actors cannot be resolved by creating more broadly defined offences or by imposing strict responsibility:

> Thus, although proposals recur to legislate severe penalties for conduct such as failure to supervise, it is far from clear that such reforms are either prudent or workable. To criminalize behavior that is essentially beyond the actor's control undermines the moral basis of the entire criminal justice system. Even at this high price, we are likely to realize only a marginal diminution in misconduct, for the more the conduct is unpremeditated, or is a joint product of many agents' acts over which the targeted agent has limited control, the more inelastic its 'supply' will be to changes in expected penalty levels. The likely results are a rate of conviction of those prosecuted, and a level of punishment of those convicted, that are far lower for the same offense than the enterprise would be likely to bear.[133]

Polinsky and Shavell see individual criminal liability as having an extensive and generally concurrent role alongside enterprise liability. Their analysis does not explore the harsh effects and the actual costs borne by individuals exposed to conviction and the other stigmatic processes of the criminal law. Nor is there any examination of the potential which internal disciplinary systems may have for minimising the need for reliance on individual criminal liability. Instead, the focus is on internalising the social costs of production and in providing theoretically neat and tidy proofs in support. The key human dimension—the severe harms inherent in the use of the criminal law to control individual behaviour—is radically discounted without justification.

Accepting that enterprise liability offers the advantage of minimising the need to resort to individual criminal liability, what does it do to protect the interests of individuals at the stage of internal allocation of costs? This question is not addressed by Elzinga and Breit, or by Pearce and others: their approach depends on a rational corporate actor model under which the interests of individuals are identical to those of their corporation. Kraakman proceeds from a different angle, namely the contractual arrangements that individuals arrive at under an agency theory of the firm; for Kraakman, it is up to individuals to protect their own interests by contracting for compensation commensurate with the risk of liability they bear. Stone also recognises the role of internal contractual arrangements, but unlike Kraakman explicitly links enterprise liability to the operation of internal disciplinary systems. This

---

[132] C. D. Stone, 'The Place of Enterprise Liability...', 31.
[133] Ibid., 32–3.

leads him to express concern about the danger of scapegoating within organisations, and to suggest that scapegoating be controlled by prosecuting the
managers who might otherwise engage in it. Polinsky and Shavell take a
different tack again, and show no apparent concern for what actually happens
within private justice systems. None of these various conceptions of enterprise liability fully addresses the issue of injustice at the level of internal disciplinary action.

The rational corporate actor model, as adopted by Elzinga and Breit and by
Pearce and others, neglects the operation of internal discipline systems by
omitting it from the deterrence equation. This omission ignores the basic
social fact that internal discipline systems are a typical feature of organisational life. As Shearing and Stenning have pointed out, we live in an age of
private policing and the most common private enforcement agency is the corporation.[134] Moreover, internal discipline is usually a key element stressed in
compliance manuals.[135] It is also a factor taken into account when sentencing
corporations.

The agency theory of the firm, as espoused by Kraakman, does help to
expose the way in which individuals within organisations bear or shift the risk
of liability. However, individual actors are conceived as free agents who can
rely upon contractual arrangements to protect their interests. This way of
looking at the interests of individuals within corporations is unrealistic
because it blocks out a number of the dangers that employees and managers
face.

First, the assumption that all individual actors are free contractors is
unwarranted. Power plays typify much organisational life, a point documented in a vast literature that includes Robert Michels' pioneering work on
oligarchies within political parties,[136] Melville Dalton's *Men Who Manage*
(1959), Anthony Downs' *Inside Bureaucracy* (1967), James Coleman's
Power and the Structure of Society (1974), David Ewing's *Freedom Inside
the Organisation* (1977), Alan Westin's and Stephan Salisbury's well-known
anthology, *Individual Rights in the Corporation* (1980), and Robert Jackall's
Moral Mazes (1988).

The reality of imbalances of power is reflected by the labour and corporate
laws that have evolved in most legal systems in response to widely practised
abuses by employers and corporate promoters and managers. If all participants in enterprises were in fact free agents on a level playing field, then law
in modern society would wear a completely different face. It thus seems
rather pointless to indulge the assumption that individual participants in corporate action are free and voluntary contracting agents. A more useful path of
inquiry is to examine the abuses of power that actually arise and to devise
responsive solutions.[137]

---

[134] Shearing and Stenning, *Private Policing*.
[135] See, e.g., BellSouth Corporation, *Antitrust Compliance Guidelines*, 39.
[136] Michels, *Political Parties*.
[137] See Dallas, 'Two Models of Corporate Governance'.

Second, the agency model of the firm focuses on the contractual underpinnings of cost-bearing and risk-shifting and neglects other ways in which control is exercised within organisations. In particular, no explicit account is taken of the role of internal discipline systems, which have been a prominent feature of corporate social structure at least since the East India Company transported British justice to India during the seventeenth and eighteenth centuries.[138] Internal discipline systems have a normative standard-setting function that transcends contractual arrangements. They reflect the fact that corporations are forms of government with private systems of justice. Once this is seen, it is apparent that the justice dispensed within organisations may vary in quality and fall much below what is expected and insisted upon in the public system of justice. It then becomes necessary to examine the standards of justice applied in internal discipline systems and, if necessary, to revise public legal controls in such a way as to safeguard individuals against private abuse. This dimension of the impact of corporations in society has been discussed by many commentators, including Richard Eells in *The Government of Corporations* (1962), Grant McConnell in *Private Power and American Democracy* (1966), and Stuart Henry in *Private Justice* (1983). Viewed from the political or sociological perspective provided by such works, the agency theory of the firm emerges as a prehistorical fiction. Individual actors are put in an original position in some nascent world where they are shielded from the actual forces of corporate existence. It is a romantic vision which distracts attention from the problem, which is to find ways of guarding against unjust internal discipline while harnessing the role that corporations play as relatively autonomous centres of power in pluralistic societies.

Stone avoids the romanticism of the agency theory of the firm and expressly draws attention to the problem of scapegoating within corporations. However, the solution he suggests—prosecuting the managers rather than allowing them to scapegoat others within the organisation—seems inadequate. The fact that managers are prosecuted would not provide an adequate safeguard against scapegoating. Being subjected to criminal prosecution could easily prompt managers to blame or discipline other employees in an attempt to deflect public criticism or to mitigate sentence. Stone does not stay to resolve the problem of finding a workable and effective method for protecting the interests of individuals who are exposed to the operation of internal discipline systems.

Another issue of concern is inequality. Enterprise liability reduces the extent to which managers and employees are subjected to criminal liability. As we have explained above, this can be seen as a positive feature of enterprise liability. A negative side, however, is that enterprise liability bestows on corporate personnel a protection that is not conferred upon street offenders, who rarely operate on behalf of any punishable corporate entity. The spectre is of managers being spared from jail for an offence comparable to that which

---

[138] See Timberg, 'The Corporation as a Technique of International Administration'.

would lead to jail in the case of a street offender. Even where there is no risk of jail, there is a disparity in treatment if managers are disciplined internally by a corporation and street offenders are convicted and denounced publicly as offenders. The law and economics analyses reviewed above do not squarely address the inequality potential of cost-minimising strategies of corporate crime control; Polinsky and Shavell advocate general reliance on individual as well as corporate liability, but equality is not explicitly factored into their analysis.

Differential application of the criminal law to managerial and non-managerial classes understandably excites attention and hostility in the community and cannot be dismissed lightly. Such inequality is inconsistent with the basic moral precept of equal application of laws. Moreover, it generates costs that need to be taken into account if one's frame of reference is economic. Those costs include the psychic injury or demoralisation that people are likely to experience if one class of offender is given a privileged status denied to other offenders whose conduct is no more blameworthy. As Coffee has observed, in mocking 'Ecospeak':

> [A]n externality may result when the criminal justice system fails to achieve equivalence among the severity of the various forms of sanctions it employs, or when it seeks only to set the punishment at a level sufficient to cancel out the expected gain without regard for the differing impact of the same punishment on different offenders.[139]

The assumption that the interests of individuals are adequately safeguarded under a regime of enterprise liability thus requires substantial qualification. Enterprise liability does offer the advantage of minimising the need to expose individuals to the often harsh and crucifying processes of the criminal justice system. However, enterprise liability neglects the risk of injustice at the level of corporate discipline or internal allocation of responsibility. Market-oriented arrangements for allocating costs are at a loss when it comes to computing the value of responsibility and the disvalue of abuses in the allocation of responsibility within internal discipline systems. Nor is sufficient account taken of the unequal application of individual criminal liability in a society where enterprise liability protects managers but gives street offenders no comparable shelter from criminal liability. If the interests of individuals are to be adequately safeguarded against abuses of internal disciplinary power, then some richer and more relevant analysis must be found.

Conclusion: The Central Issue of Responsibility

The law and economics commentaries reviewed above do not provide persuasive solutions to the fundamental issues of allocation of responsibility addressed in this book. None of the three main underlying assumptions stands

---

[139] Coffee, 'Corporate Crime and Punishment', 448–9.

up to scrutiny. First, the concepts of action and responsibility require a much fuller explanation and understanding. Second, there are reasons to deny that deterrence is best analysed in terms of a narrow economic calculus of financial incentives. Third, a regime of enterprise liability may expose corporate officers and employees to serious risks of injustice or abuse of power.

These are our reactions to what we perceive as limitations of the law and economics commentaries that we have dissected. More insights might have been expected, especially given the aura that law and economics analysis has acquired in the US. Why has the yield been so low? It is worth asking this question for the answer gives us an important clue about the direction that might best be taken if we are to solve the problems of passing the buck for corporate crime.

The law and economics analyses that we have considered all proceed on the footing that the allocation of liability is geared to the operation of financial incentives. The inquiry then becomes locked into comparisons of different regimes of financial incentives. Yet, as we have seen, uncertainty pervades the task of trying to make the necessary economic calculations.

An entirely different way of looking at the problems of passing the buck is to see them as legal and moral problems that need to be resolved on the basis of responsibility rather than merely on the ground of financial incentives. From the perspective of responsibility, the task is not to choose between different possible targets in terms of relative cost-effectiveness, but to try to uphold responsibility against all the actors who are responsible for a given offence. This approach may well involve imposing responsibility on corporate actors, subunits, subsidiary companies, managers, employees, gatekeepers, and government agencies. The animating idea is that all responsible actors should be held responsible wherever this is practicable.

Seen in this light, the law and economics analyses considered in this chapter emerge as dismal failures.[140] Elzinga and Breit pass the buck to shareholders, for it is they who would bear the monetary penalties imposed. Kraakman passes the buck sometimes to shareholders, sometimes to shareholders and managers, sometimes to managers, and sometimes to gatekeepers. Stone passes the buck to shareholders, or to shareholders and managers. For Pearce and others, the buck stops with shareholders. Polinsky and Shavell pass the buck to employees and then deduct it from the costs of production payable by the firm.

The challenge ahead is to devise an approach which, as a matter of law,[141] reflects the commonplace principle that everyone responsible in some way for an offence should be held responsible accordingly. At first glance this may

---

[140] Compare Hart, 'An Economist's Perspective on the Theory of the Firm', 1757 ('[m]ost formal models of the firm are extremely rudimentary, capable only of portraying hypothethical firms that bear little relation to the complex organizations we see in the world'); Siliciano, 'Corporate Behavior and the Social Efficiency of Tort Law' (experience indicates that tort law is far from efficient and that economic models have failed to reflect real-world complexities).

[141] Compare moral responsibility and the relative ease of imposing it: see Walsh, 'Pride, Shame and Responsibility'.

seem utopian, or utterly profligate in terms of cost. However, it would be premature to come to any such conclusion. It may well be possible to devise an approach that imposes responsibility at an acceptable cost across a comprehensive range of responsible actors and yet requires only a parsimonious level of punishment. This possibility leads us to examine in Chapter 4 the implications of theories of organisational behaviour. Do these hold the key to clarifying lines of accountability for corporate crime?

4 Organisation Theory Perspectives

Organisation Theory and Allocation of Responsibility

A good theory of organisational behaviour might supply some guidance as to who or what to hold responsible for organisational crime. If we understood how organisations decide to break the law or how they drift into breaking the law, we might be able to prescribe legal accountability principles which are consonant with organisational realities. It was this insight which led Kriesberg to the view that '[t]he basic problem is that the law is not founded on an understanding of the decisionmaking process that the law must shape in order to deter corporate lawbreaking.'[1]

In this chapter, we look at the implications for individual and corporate legal responsibility of a number of alternative conceptions of organisational structure and functioning. We then consider four alternative strategies for harmonising these conceptions of organisational structure and functioning with legal accountability principles for corporate crime. Four typologies of organisational life will be considered: one based on models of decisionmaking; one on the structuring of organisations; another on role-taking in organisations; and another on the ways organisations assign internal responsibility for wrongdoing. The first is based on Kriesberg's decisionmaking models in organisational life.[2]

First Cut: Kriesberg's Decisionmaking Models for Organisational Action

Simeon Kriesberg has produced an analysis of corporate decisionmaking based substantially upon Graham Allison's *Essence of Decision: Explaining*

---

[1] Kriesberg, 'Decisionmaking Models and the Control of Corporate Crime'. See also Hopkins, *The Impact of Prosecutions under the Trade Practices Act*; Baysinger, 'Organizational Theory and the Criminal Liability of Organizations'; Tombs, 'Corporate Crime and "Post Modern" Organizations'.

[2] Kriesberg, 'Decisionmaking Models...', 1091–29.

the Cuban Missile Crisis.[3] Three models of corporate decisionmaking are advanced. Model I, the Rational Actor Model, postulates that corporations are unitary rational decisionmakers. We have seen that neoclassical economics shares this view of the corporation as a unitary actor which seeks to maximise value. Model II, the Organisational Process Model, describes the corporation as 'a constellation of loosely allied decisionmaking units (for example, a marketing group, a manufacturing division, a research and development staff), each with primary responsibility for a narrow range of problems, the resolution of which is governed by standard operating procedures ('SOPs'), established by written or customary organisational rules'.[4] According to Model II, most organisational activity is to be understood simply as subunits following these regularised procedures. Model III, the Bureaucratic Politics Model, views corporate decisionmaking not in terms of rational process or set procedures, but rather as 'a bargaining game involving a hierarchy of players and a maze of formal and informal channels through which decisions are shaped and implemented.'[5] It is Model III which grants recognition to Burns' observation that there is a 'plurality of action systems' open to actors, who may define what they do in terms of their consequences for certain intra-corporate and extra-corporate political and status systems instead of the way they affect the rational attainment of organisational goals.[6]

Kriesberg has maintained that these three models, though not intended to be exhaustive, have varying implications for the design of corporate and individual criminal sanctions. Model I implies that sanctions imposed on the decisionmaking unit, the corporate entity, are relevant and efficacious if they relate to the particular values (such as profit, prestige and stability) which rational corporate actors seek to maximise.

Kriesberg sees Model II (the Organisational Process Model) as implying that liability be imposed on the individual personnel in a position to enact and supervise SOPs. However, we have already seen that the enacting of SOPs may be the collective product of a committee or even of the entire subunit.[7] Although Kriesberg does not consider the possibility, Model II might, in addition to individual managerial liability, imply liability for some intra-corporate collectivity such as a safety committee or an entire division.

Another alternative policy inference is that the Organisational Process Model shows the need for legal interventions which guarantee that defective SOPs will be remedied. Corporate probation (for example, where the court appoints a safety expert as a corporate probation officer to oversee the remediation of defective SOPs that led to a serious occupational health and safety offence) is a more rigorous way of assuring the court and the community that

[3] Allison, *Essence of Decision.*
[4] Kriesberg, 'Decisionmaking Models...', 1101.
[5] Ibid., 1103.
[6] Burns, 'On the Plurality of Social Systems'.
[7] See ch. 2, 21–2, 46.

irresponsible organisational processes will be fixed than is an act of faith that a collective or individual punishment will bring about organisational reform.[8] Even without installing an expert probation officer in the organisation, the court could impose a management restructuring order in an attempt to ensure remediation of the defective organisational processes.[9] There are, however, practical limits on how far this legal response can be taken: courts of law generally do not have the expertise to be competent management consultants.[10] They may come up with solutions which solve the legal non-compliance problem at great expense to productive efficiency. While there are occasions when the expense and time of the court finding and employing a relevant management or technical expert to act as a corporate probation officer is justified, most cases will not justify the risks and resources involved in such interventionism.

The Organisational Process Model thus has highly ambiguous implications for principles of legal responsibility: it can be read (as Kriesberg reads it) as implying individual managerial responsibility for those who enact and oversee SOPs, or collective responsibility on the group accountable for the criminogenic SOPs, or corporate responsibility to facilitate corporate probation or a management restructuring order.

Unlike Model II, the Bureaucratic Politics Model (Model III) conceives of key individuals as advocates who consciously attempt to influence decisions, rather than conceiving of individuals as constrained followers of preselected procedures. Thus, Model III is the one which most strongly implies individual liability. Players under Model III do not necessarily articulate their action to corporate goals but to a disparate variety of status and political concerns— personal empire-building, promotion, and revenge against the player who won the last game. To the extent that players orient their actions to organisational goals, they may be the goals of other organisations to which they also perceive themselves as owing allegiance (the union, the industry association, the ethics committee of a professional association).

A player in an organisation who advocates an illegal political contribution to a political party may perceive his or her action as oriented toward achieving the goals of the other organisation to which he or she belongs (the political party) rather than (or in addition to) the goals of the organisation which

---

[8] On corporate probation and management restructuring orders, see C. D. Stone, *Where the Law Ends*; Coffee, 'No Soul to Damn No Body to Kick; South Australia, Criminal Law and Penal Methods Reform Committee, Fourth Report, *The Substantive Criminal Law*; Geraghty, 'Structural Crime and Institutional Rehabilitation'; Fisse, 'Responsibility, Prevention and Corporate Crime'; Yoder, 'Criminal Sanctions for Corporate Illegality'; Solomon and Nowak, 'Managerial Restructuring'; Gruner, 'To Let the Punishment Fit the Organization'; Coffee, Gruner and Stone, 'Standards for Organizational Probation'.

[9] Solomon and Nowak, 'Managerial Restructuring'.

[10] See C. D. Stone, 'Corporate Regulation', 19: 'Whenever we on the outside displace managerial choice, we are meddling in a delicate process about which we ordinarily know considerably less than do the participants. The Interventionist "remedy" may cost society more than the harm it was seeking to avert.'

breaks the law. It follows that the individual players who advocate breaking the law, rather than the organisation which is the site for the offence, should be targeted for prosecution. And perhaps those individuals within the organisation who battled against the decision to break the law should be targeted for public expressions of praise.

The problem with the three models as alternative guides to law reform is that we will never reach the position of viewing one as right and the other two as wrong, or even one as more often right than the other two. Organisational life will continue to throw up cases where we can understand why the law was broken by conceiving of the corporation as a unitary rational actor; others where we can explain illegality by subunit compliance with defective or criminogenic SOPs; and still others where crime is the result of an internecine bureaucratic political struggle. Moreover, cases of all three types can occur at different times in the same organisation.

More problematic for drawing any policy lessons from the models is that we can often best understand why the organisation acted the way it did by considering interactions among the three models. In Allison's original development of the model on the Cuban missile crisis, he showed how the unitary interest of the US government in averting nuclear war clashed, for example, with the actions of its subunit, the US Navy, with its propensity to slavishly follow SOPs and to operate as a political player.[11] As a political player, the navy sought to exploit the crisis to show that its 'Hunter–Killer' Anti-Submarine Warfare Program, which was out of favour in some Washington circles, was effective.[12] When Defense Secretary McNamara challenged Admiral Anderson, Chief of Naval Operations, on the need for US ships to be sensitive to the political implications as well as to the military implications of how they managed the naval blockade of Cuba (for example, to avoid humiliating the Russians), there was an angry exchange in which Anderson picked up the Manual of Naval Regulations and said, 'It's all in there'.[13] McNamara was quick to point out that the logic of military SOPs did not apply to an exercise where the Navy was being used to communicate a political message rather than to inflict a military defeat. In other words, the ultimate outcome was partly explicable in terms of the successes and failures of the US government in asserting its unitary interest in averting the holocaust over the propensity of subunits to follow SOPs and to pursue other political agendas. Yet if all three models and interactions among them have some purchase on understanding even within the one case, then the only policy implication possible is that a strategy for controlling organisational decisionmaking must be capable of simultaneous accommodation of all three models. Kriesberg does not really show us the choice to be made, but more the need for an 'integrated Rational, Organisational and Bureaucratic Model'.[14]

---

[11] Allison, *Essence of Decision*.
[12] Ibid., 138.
[13] Ibid., 131–2.
[14] Fisse, 'Reconstructing Corporate Criminal Law'.

Second Cut: Mintzberg's Structuring of Organisations

Henry Mintzberg's *The Structuring of Organizations* has become an influential contribution to positivist organisation theory, providing one of the most detailed and elegant typologies of organisational structuring in the literature.[15] Could it be that Mintzberg's five types of organisations make for clear alternative implications on the types of legal responsibility which will control organisational crime? We will consider his five types in turn—Simple Structure, Machine Bureaucracy, Professional Bureaucracy, Divisionalised Form, and Adhocracy.

The Simple Structure

Organisations characterised by Simple Structure in fact have little structure at all. The division of labour is loose and little of its behaviour is formalised. Co-ordination is achieved by direct supervision from the top. The chief executive typically has a very wide span of control. Often everyone will report to him or her. To the extent that simple structure is achieved under the direct control of a single chief executive, individual chief executive officer liability for corporate illegality would seem the appropriate liability principle. If, on the other hand, the direct control is exercised by more than one top manager, then the particular top manager who exercised direction over the offence would be culpable.

The Machine Bureaucracy

The Machine Bureaucracy achieves co-ordination predominantly by standardisation of work processes. Organisations like post offices and airlines tend to have such structures, structures tuned to deal with routine work as integrated, regulated machines. It is Max Weber's vision of bureaucracy.[16] The 'technostructure' made up of the analysts who design the SOPs is the key part of a machine bureaucracy, according to Mintzberg. Accordingly, as with Kriesberg's Organisational Process Model, it would be the individual technocrats and the technostructure collectively which provide the obvious targets for criminal responsibility when these organisations run afoul of the law.

The Professional Bureaucracy

The Professional Bureaucracy achieves co-ordination by standardisation of skills. Accounting firms, general hospitals, universities, and social work

---

[15] Mintzberg, *The Structuring of Organizations*. See also, *Mintzberg on Management*.
[16] Gerth and Mills, *From Max Weber*, 196–266.

agencies are examples of organisations which rely on the skills and knowledge of their operating professionals to function. The key actors in these organisations are the operating professionals and these are therefore the obvious targets for liability when organisational wrongdoing occurs. If the hospital patient has the wrong leg amputated, the surgeon will be the first choice as a suspect.[17]

The Divisionalised Form

The Divisionalised Form is 'not so much an integrated organisation as a set of quasi-autonomous entities coupled together by a central administrative structure'.[18] Co-ordination is achieved by a performance control system. 'In general the headquarters allows the divisions close to full autonomy to make their own decisions, and then monitors the results of these decisions.'[19] This would seem to leave most power and responsibility in the hands of senior divisional management. Yet we know from empirical research on the pharmaceutical industry, for example, that the headquarters of divisionalised corporations can impose powerfully criminogenic performance pressures on their divisions: 'Don't bother us with how you achieve your sales quota or how you get the drug approved for marketing in your country, but get it done'.[20] When the distant collectivity of 'head office' in a divisionalised form imposes performance expectations which are difficult to meet without breaking the law, then the case for corporate liability is strong.

If, on the other hand, the division breaks the law in the absence of criminogenic pressures from the top, the division as a collectivity or certain individuals within it (which will depend on the decisionmaking structure of the division) should be called to account. For reasons which we will not go into here, Mintzberg argues that the Divisionalised Form works best with machine bureaucratic structures in its divisions and the Divisionalised Form drives its divisions toward machine bureaucratic form.[21] Where this is the case, the conclusions reached earlier about criminal liability in Machine Bureaucracies should apply within divisions.

The Adhocracy

Adhocracies are designed for innovation, as in a computer software company or a space agency. 'The Simple Structure can certainly innovate, but only in a relatively simple way. Both the Machine and Professional Bureaucracies are performance, not problem-solving, structures. They are designed to perfect

---

[17] See Bosk, *Forgive and Remember*.
[18] Mintzberg, *The Structuring of Organizations*, 380.
[19] Ibid., 382.
[20] Braithwaite, *Corporate Crime in the Pharmaceutical Industry*.
[21] Mintzberg, *The Structuring of Organizations*, 384–7.

standard programs, not to invent new ones.'[22] Adhocracy, a term coined by
Alvin Toffler,[23] is about fusing experts from different disciplines into
smoothly functioning ad hoc project teams. The structure is organic and informal, eschewing all forms of standardisation for co-ordination. In Hedberg and
others' terms, the structure is that of a 'tent' instead of a 'palace'.[24] The structure of a tent is temporary, movable and somewhat ambiguous. In adhocracies, precedents and policies are irrelevant and jurisdictional lines are blurred.

At first blush one is tempted to say that the multidisciplinary team is the
likely target for collective responsibility in an Adhocracy. But by the time an
offence for which the team was reponsible came to court, team members
would be dispersed among a new set of teams. Moreover, the practical difficulties of proving who was in the tent at the time of an offence is difficult in
organisations which establish flux and confused accountability for collective
endeavour as virtues:

> An organizational tent actually exploits benefits hidden within properties that
> designers have generally regarded as liabilities. Ambiguous authority structures,
> unclear objectives, and contradictory assignments of responsibility can legitimate
> controversies and challenge traditions ... Incoherence and indecision can foster
> exploration, self-evaluation and learning.[25]

Adhocracies have very little in the way of policies or SOPs; strategy is not so
much formulated consciously by identifiable managers but evolves implicitly
out of the day-to-day decisions generated by shifting matrices of innovators.
As Barnard argued decades ago, the distinction between policy and administration is a rather artificial one in all organisations;[26] in Adhocracies the distinction practically disappears altogether.

If there is little in the way of intentional policy, little standardisation of
procedure and no way of knowing who is responsible for what, one despairs
about the difficulties and justice of imposing any form of criminal liability
when corporate action runs afoul of the law. The pragmatic temptation is to
impose simple collective liability on the corporation in the face of the difficulty of ascertaining who and what set the criminal conduct in train. Yet the
justice of this is compromised by the fact that in an Adhocracy the head of the
organisation often has little idea what its hands are doing, and indeed the
head–hand metaphor is rather meaningless. The utility of corporate liability is
compromised because the board and top management has less capacity to
rehabilitate the organisation in response to a corporate sanction than does the
board of, say, a Machine Bureaucracy. The latter can call in the identifiably
responsible managers for a given area of compliance, pin-point the SOPs
which require sharpening, and issue directives for predictably effective
reform. The lack of standardisation and specialisation in the Adhocracy makes

[22] Ibid., 432.
[23] Toffler, *Future Shock*.
[24] Hedberg, Nystrom and Starbuck, 'Camping on Seesaws'.
[25] Ibid., 45.
[26] Barnard, *The Functions of the Executive*.

this predictability elusive for a top management which wishes to tighten up on compliance with the law.

Mintzberg shares with many futurologists the view that the Adhocracy is the type of organisation which is the wave of the future.[27] It is the form of structuring best adapted to innovative high-technology industries. If all this is right, then the problems of designing a coherent jurisprudence of corporate crime will become even more perplexing than today. At least in the past, the greater organisational complexity resulting from increased size has been tempered by the tendency for larger organisations to opt for greater standardization of policies, procedures and roles.[28] Accountability in the twenty-first century will be an acute problem if there is a trend to Adhocracy while the tendency for economic activity to become more concentrated in larger organisations which transcend jurisdictional boundaries continues. The problem of allocating responsibility for fraud in the development and safety testing of pharmaceuticals by transnational corporations (which tend to Adhocracy in their research divisions) is perhaps a window into the future.[29]

Overlaying Mintzberg with Kriesberg

At least until we struck the Adhocracy, we seemed to be doing swimmingly well in articulating how different types of individual and collective liability are implied by Mintzberg's different types of organisational structuring. When pondering the preferred target for liability in a Professional Bureaucracy it seemed so clear that if the wrong leg were amputated, the surgeon would be the obvious target. But if we do a second cut of the Professional Bureaucracy itself with Kriesberg's three models, this might not be so obvious. We might see that less fault lay with the surgeon than with defective hospital SOPs which mixed the file of Mr Smith, who needed a left leg amputation, with Mr Jones, who required a right leg amputation. Or we might see, through the lens of the Bureaucratic Politics Model, fault as lying with Dr No, an arch enemy of both the surgeon and the filing section, who sought revenge for a previous humiliation at the hands of the surgeon by scheduling him for 20 hours straight in the emergency operating theatre. Or, through the lens of the Rational Actor Model, our instinct to hold the surgeon rather than the hospital responsible may be tempered when we learn that this is a private hospital infamous for unnecessary surgery, for sacking young doctors who challenge the wisdom of proceeding with overservicing, and for forcing a recklessly speedy production line on to its operating theatres.

In short, Mintzberg's types, to the extent that they are empirically robust (a question we have not addressed), can provide no more than an indication of

---

[27] For example, Kanter, *The Change Masters*; Toffler, *Future Shock*.
[28] The series of Aston studies of organisational structuring clearly showed a positive correlation between the size of organisations and the degree of standardisation (SOPs), specialisation (division of labour) and formalisation (use of written communication and role definition): Pugh and Hinings, *Organizational Structure*.
[29] Braithwaite, *Corporate Crime in the Pharmaceutical Industry*, ch. 3.

the forms of liability which are more likely to be appropriate for different types of organisation. There is no prospect under it of an isomorphic relationship between type of reponsibility and type of structure. We are not faring well. Nevertheless, we will press on with another cut at the problem because the belief is persistent among scholars of corporate crime that if only we can get our organisation theory right, this will be the beacon which lights the way for law reform. Indeed, this has been our own belief in the past. So we will not be satisfied at just two cuts of the organisation theory cake, lest they are less compelling than neglected alternatives.

Third Cut: The Dramaturgical Model

> The dramaturgical model is based upon the idea that human actors improvise their performance within the often very broad limits set by the scripts their society makes available to them. The dramaturgical analogy alerts us to the fact that the social actor is both character and agent; his part may be written for him but it cannot be realized without his agency. Once the actor performs, agency and character are fused and become one.[30]

Iain Mangham, the author of this passage, has applied the dramaturgical notions of Irving Goffman to a variety of organisations—humans can fashion, follow and modify scripts as actor, playwright, director, author and critic. If a play amounts to an illegal act of pornography, who is to blame? It might be the greedy corporate producer who fires those who will not co-operate in producing plays that maximise profits by exploiting people. It might be the playwright who fashions the script, or the director who supervises its execution in a maximally pornographic way. And it might be the actor. The positivistic conceptions of organisation theory we have considered above construe the actor as a determined creature. In contrast, within the dramaturgical model 'the social actor is constrained by the scripts available to him, but in many, if not most, he has the possibility of choice, the potential to create or revise his scripts'.[31]

To varying degrees, actors are in a position to negotiate, to refuse or tone down the more pornographic features of the script. Actors exercise choice within structural constraints; their potential to create or revise scripts is often underestimated. Even in the most constrained situation, there is always the possibility of resigning.[32] It follows then that actors bear more responsibility than has been suggested for them under the earlier models.

The extent to which we move down in responsibility for crime from the corporate producer to the playwright, and from the director to the actor will depend both on the process for generating scripts and on how and where discretion exists for revising them. Here the crucial distinction is between a

---

[30] Mangham, *Interactions and Interventions in Organizations*.
[31] Ibid., 27.
[32] Granted that, for employees with dismal job prospects on the open market, resignation may not be a practical choice available to them.

top-down and a bottom-up decisionmaking structure. Some organisations are so bottom-up that there are no playwrights: the scripts are written in a process of negotiation between actors and directors. In these organisations, if the script is criminogenic and its execution criminal, responsibility lies with both the actor and the director.

In top-down organisations, in contrast, scripts are handed down to both directors and actors in immutable form. Here we would want to charge the playwright and producer. This is certainly so if the organisation is top-down with direct supervision of execution from the top, or top-down with delegation and systematic monitoring of execution. Top-down organisations with delegation and trust in the execution of the delegated expectations are more difficult cases, however, when the crime arises from a deviation from the approved script. Difficulty particularly arises when the producer is wilfully blind to a deviation from the script which will make money for him by cutting corners with the law.[33] Who is responsible turns on whether the tacit understanding among producer, director and actor is that the 'real' orders are to follow the script or to 'do whatever you have to do to get results'.

Similarly, there are critical variations in bottom-up organisations. Ideas for the script may come from below, but only in an advisory capacity, with the producer making the final decision. The buck may stop with the producer as an individual, or with the producer as a committee which decides upon a criminogenic script on the basis of unanimity, consensus or a bare majority vote. In the case of a majority vote it might not be just to hold all committee members responsible, but in the other two cases it may. With all cases, there is ambiguity over the responsibility of those below who were the originators of the criminogenic ideas. This ambiguity becomes more acute when those at the top do not positively decide to accept the idea, but where the decision-making process of the organisation is such that scripts coming from below routinely are enacted unless someone at a higher level seizes an opportunity to veto them. Here the constraints on the agency of those below are less profound, and the culpability of those at the top who lacked the wit to exercise a veto more doubtful.

So the allocation of responsibility among producers, directors and actors turns on a number of factors:

(1) How constrained actors are in exercising their choice to reject and revise scripts.
(2) How top-down versus bottom-up is the process by which scripts are generated.
(3) Whether the involvement of top management in scripts involves writing, approval or veto; whether their delegation involves direct supervision, monitoring, genuine trust or wilful blindness.

The dramaturgical model thus provides us with useful tools for analysing the level of the organisation at which responsibility should lie. But because it grants such a prominent place to human agency, because it humanistically

---

[33] On wilful blindness, see Wilson, 'The Doctrine of Wilful Blindness'.

denies that actors are totally determined by systems, it can give us no firm guidance on responsibility principles in advance of a knowledge of how particular individuals will exercise choice. It can instruct prosecutors on what questions to ask, but not legislators as to what level organisations should be held responsible in law in what circumstances.

The most interesting thing about the dramaturgical model is that it points us to potential targets for responsibility outside the organisation—the critic and the audience. The critic as responsible agent occurs when a company is given a nudge and a wink by a regulatory agency that a violation of the law will be tolerated and ignored. There are numerous instances in the regulatory literature of companies breaking the law in a good faith belief that this was acceptable because it was informally approved by the government.[34]

The audience as responsible agent arises when the violation is demanded by consumers—an audience at a seamy night club which throws objects on the stage when the script does not provide for the performer to take off his or her clothes. The best documented instances in the corporate crime literature are those where a superordinate organisation consumes the services of a subordinate organisation[35]—a transnational pharmaceutical company pressures a contract testing laboratory to produce results which show that its new product is safe;[36] an aerospace company imposes expectations on its independent sales agency that it should pay bribes to secure sales;[37] the chemical giant which pays below-market rates to a toxic waste disposal company which it knows to be run by organised crime.[38] In some of these cases, the 'audience' has a considerable hand in writing the script. This is not to say that the actors do not also remain responsible.

Fourth Cut: Braithwaite and Fisse's 'Varieties of Responsibility'

In an earlier study, we used fieldwork in Japanese corporations to identify four varieties of responsibility within business corporations: *noblesse oblige*, captain of the ship responsibility, nominated accountability, and fault-based individual responsibility.[39]

---

[34] In some cases, the law has responded to this by imposing liability on government regulators. The Kanazawa District Court has ordered under Japan's National Redress Law that the Japanese government bear one-third of the massive liability for the neurotoxic effects of the drug clioquinol for regulatory failure by the Pharmacy Affairs Bureau, and the manufacturers to bear the remaining two-thirds of the liability. Goldring and Maher have discussed two New Zealand product liability cases where the failure of government building and transport inspectors to do their job properly was found to be a basis for government liability: *Consumer Protection Law in Australia*.

[35] Braithwaite, 'Paradoxes of Class Bias in Criminological Research'.

[36] Braithwaite, *Corporate Crime in the Pharmaceutical Industry*, ch. 3; Schneider, 'Faking It'.

[37] Noonan, *Bribes*; Boulton, *The Grease Machine*.

[38] Block and Scarpitti, *Poisoning for Profit*.

[39] Braithwaite and Fisse, 'Varieties of Responsibility and Organizational Crime'.

Noblesse oblige

Noblesse oblige means the titular head of the organisation assuming strict individual responsibility for collective wrongdoing. In corporate life, the Japanese provide some of the most striking manifestations of *noblesse oblige*. The tradition has its roots in feudal times when the samurai were expected to satisfy higher standards of accountability and more exemplary self-control than common people.[40] Corporate *noblesse oblige* in Japan even today can impel managers to more than resignation: in extreme cases, only suicide may be perceived by traditionalists as restoring honour to the organisation.[41]

In a sense it is perverse that such onerous burdens are imposed on company presidents in Japan because Japanese presidents have somewhat less real power than their counterparts in other countries. Decisionmaking in Japanese corporations typically has been found to be bottom-up rather than top-down.[42] Relatively junior employees can be expected to generate many of the ideas about the direction the company should be taking and what it should do at critical decision points. Such ideas, however, should reflect *Jyoi-Katatsu*, the concept that the will and mind of the boss should be mirrored in the proposals of subordinates. These ideas then percolate up the organisation typically through the mechanism of the *ringi*—a written proposal circulated horizontally, then vertically, to as many as 30 officers who affix their name stamp to it. When the *ringi* finally arrives on the president's desk for endorsement, the merits of the proposal often will not be considered, the name stamps of many trusted executives being regarded as sufficient.

When the president automatically endorses so many decisions in this way, it seems unfair that he or she should be subject to strict responsibility in a way that Western chief executives, who often personally assume control over their corporation's activities, are not. But the point is that under Japanese bottom-up decisionmaking, it is not only hard to point justly the finger at the president, it is difficult to point justly the finger at anyone. As Doré has explained:

> The function of the system is to diffuse rather than to centralize responsibility. The superior, by affixing his seal, takes formal responsibility for the decision, though everyone knows that he cannot possibly acquaint himself with the details of every proposal to which he has to give approval in the course of a day. He may, when something goes wrong, 'take' responsibility (just as the head of the national railways will 'take' responsibility and resign when a ferry boat capsizes and drowns its passengers in a typhoon) but normally he would not be 'held' responsible. The need for ritual atonement by the titular head— resignation or grovelling apology— is seen not as a means of encouraging the others individually but of reawakening

---

[40] See Benedict, *The Chrysanthemum and the Sword*, 148.
[41] Chief executive suicide following scandal has also occurred in the US. The best-known case was the leap of the chairman of United Brands from the Pan Am building in New York following a bribery scandal in Honduras; see Jacoby, Nehemkis and Eells, *Bribery and Extortion in World Business*, 105–7. However, symbolic overtones of requital do not seem to loom large in such American suicides.
[42] See Clark, *The Japanese Company*; Gibney, *Japan*; Ouchi, *Theory Z*; Pascale and Athos, *The Art of Japanese Management*; but see Ohmae, 'Japanese Companies Are Run from the Top'.

throughout the organization a proper sense of commitment and a determination not to make mistakes. So it is missing the point to ask exactly where, up the hierarchical line through which the proposal has come, the real responsibility lies. It is diffused through the organization.[43]

Critics of Japanese imperialism in World War II have argued that the system of Imperial responsibility in which all decisions were in theory taken by the Emperor was in fact a 'system of general irresponsibility'.[44] But generalising this attack to corporate *noblesse oblige* would be a mistake because the Japanese do not see the function of presidential contrition being to punish the guilty, but rather to symbolise the importance to everyone of organisations not committing errors.

Under the *ringi* system usually no one can justly be held responsible. Yet consider the consequences of no-one 'taking' responsibility: the appearance would be created that corporate wrongdoing does not matter. However, if the function of taking responsibility becomes the symbolising of organisational wrongdoing, the titular head of the organisation can provide a dramatic symbolic sacrifice. But why should an individual person be sacrificed rather than the corporate ox that gored? For a collectivist culture, it is perverse that Japanese law does not direct more of the fire and brimstone of public shame at corporate entities rather than at individuals.[45]

While the efficacious moral educative effects of informal *noblesse oblige* cannot be denied, we must surely be wary of the criminal law formally enshrining this cultural reality. To hold an individual criminally responsible when there was not even evidence of negligence on his or her part would be an unacceptable departure from the fundamental principles of the criminal law. Thus, to hold the titular head of the organisation strictly responsible in criminal law would be to mirror a form of cultural adaptation of responsibility which would be unacceptable in the criminal law even in Japanese society. Corporate liability for the crime can be justly imposed by the state, and organisations imbued with the ethos of *noblesse oblige* will translate this quickly enough into assumptions of responsibility by the titular head.

Captain of the ship responsibility

There is also a widespread tradition within organisations of holding the captain of the ship strictly responsible. That is, the senior executive officer who is on location at the time of the act of organisational wrongdoing is held strictly accountable for it. Again, Japan provides clear illustrations, although traditions of mine manager responsibility in Commonwealth coal-mining companies also exemplify this form of responsibility.[46]

---

[43] Doré, *British Factory–Japanese Factory*, 228.
[44] Ibid., 229.
[45] Compare Fisse, 'The Social Policy of Corporate Criminal Responsibility', 378–9.
[46] See Braithwaite, *To Punish or Persuade*, 156–64.

If *noblesse oblige* is the principle of accountability for gross corporate wrongdoing which attracts media attention, the captain of the ship principle defines the day-to-day practice of accountability in many, though certainly not all, Japanese organisations. Japanese companies are generally divided into sections, and the section head assumes responsibility for the section's collective failures. Obviously, the president of a Japanese company is not blamed for minor corporate wrongs which may not attract media comment and do not so much as come to his notice, even after they have been punished by a regulatory agency. Rather, the head of the section concerned will generally take the blame.

The question of how far up the hierarchy blame will run for organisational wrongdoings of varying degrees of seriousness is an interesting one. The Japanese companies visited for our research all have informal rules to guide the social construction of the responsible collectivity within the organisation.[47] In the more traditional companies, the head of that collectivity would take most of the blame. At one company we were told that an 'innocent' boss who takes the rap will get much sympathy, while the 'guilty' junior, who may escape any formal sanction, will suffer loss of repute within the unit. As far as the corporation was concerned, it was the head of the section who lost a pay rise or suffered a black mark on file. By contrast, within the immediate work group, it was the person everyone knew to be immediately responsible who suffered informal sanctioning. Consequently, there was considerable social pressure on subordinates not to get their boss into trouble. In Japanese firms with traditions of lifetime employment, such work group pressures may have an inescapable quality which renders them very powerful.

Unfortunately, even in the West there are domains of business regulation where principles of organisational culture which hold the captain of the ship strictly responsible are effectively translated into criminal law. The literal case of captains of ocean-going ships is the best known.

The facts of *Hodge v Higgins* were straightforward and not in dispute. The Harcourt was a small coasting vessel of some 443 tons gross. On April 7, 1979 the vessel arrived off the River Humber with her usual complement of six crew. She had come from Holland and was bound for Gunness on the River Trent. The master radioed his agents and was told that there would be a delay of a few days as no berths were available. The vessel remained at anchor that day but the weather began to deteriorate and the master, Mr Hodge, was suffering from a bout of influenza. The next day therefore the Harcourt took on a pilot and proceeded up the Humber to the comparative shelter of Hull Roads. She was anchored in a safe anchorage away from the main navigation channel during the early afternoon of Sunday April 8. By this time the master's condition had worsened and he called for the mate and informed him of his intention to turn in and try and 'sweat it off'. The master gave the mate specific instructions for the anchor watch that was to be kept.

---

[47] The companies visited during our Japanese fieldwork were Mitsui and Co., Nippon Steel, Toyota Motor Sales, Sumitomo Corporation, IHI and Idemitsu Kosan. In addition, we have undertaken research within Australia on the Japanese corporation Sharp, and in the US on the Japanese pharmaceutical corporation Takeda.

He told the mate to be on watch personally at midnight when the vessel would swing with the tide. Finally he informed the mate that he, the master, should be called if any problem arose.

The mate kept watch during the afternoon and early evening and then handed over the watch to a deckhand. Both the mate and deckhand were very experienced seamen and well aware of what was required of them. However, at sunset the deckhand, when switching on the navigation lights, forgot to switch on the forward anchor light. This omission was noted by the river authorities ashore and efforts were made to contact the Harcourt by radio and other means. However, it was not until the mate came back on watch shortly before midnight that those on board Harcourt noticed that the light was not on. The mate switched the light on and admonished the deckhand for his omission.

The master remained unaware of what had happened until several days later when police went on board the vessel at Gunness. He confirmed that he had been on board at the time and that it was his responsibility to ensure that the proper lights were displayed. Captain Hodge pleaded not guilty to the prosecution brought against him under s. 27 but at Hull Stipendiary Magistrates' Court at June 18, 1979, he was found guilty. During that hearing he was asked if he, as a master, accepted that he was responsible for what went on board his ship and he confirmed that he did. Captain Hodge subsequently appealed the Magistrate's decision by way of a case stated. However, on July 15, 1980, the Divisional Court, consisting of the Lord Chief Justice, Lord Lane, and Mr Justice Comyn, dismissed the appeal. A subsequent application to the House of Lords for leave to appeal was also dismissed.[48]

In the literal captain of the ship context, it is interesting that the omnipotence of the captain is being undermined by the automation of controls and by the consequential dependence on systems engineers, electrical engineers and other members of the new maritime technocracy (one British company runs its ships by means of on-board committees). More fundamentally, owners and charterers are directing more and more of their ships' activities from onshore.[49] In the *Exxon Valdez* Alaskan oil spill in 1989, most fire was directed at onshore corporate actors, rather than at the captain of the ship.

Just as it is unacceptable to hold the titular head of an organisation criminally responsible in the absence even of negligence, it is also wrong to do this to the senior executive on site at the time of the offence. While the law in a case like that of Hodge might be seen as admirably responsive to the cultural traditions of decisionmaking responsibility at sea, it is also profoundly unjust to impose the stigma of individual criminality in these circumstances.

[48] Taylor, 'Criminal Liabilities of Ships' Masters'. But see the further discussion in Warbrick and Sullivan, 'Ship Routeing Schemes and the Criminal Liability of the Master'. Captain of the ship responsibility was not imposed in the *Marchioness* case where a verdict of not guilty on a charge of manslaughter was directed by the trial judge (*Financial Times*, 1 August 1991, 1). The offence charged required criminal negligence and there was insufficient evidence of that.

[49] See Perrow, *Normal Accidents*, 200.

Nominated accountability

Instead of imposing strict responsibility on the titular head of the organisation or the captain of the ship, it is possible to hold some other person strictly accountable on the basis of nominated responsibility. In the paradigm case, this is a person who has a special responsibility in the area of concern. For instance, the advertising manager may be nominated as the person strictly responsible for any false advertising which emanates from the firm, the quality control director of a pharmaceutical company as the person strictly responsible for the supply of impure drugs, and so on. There is a key difference between this kind of strict responsibility and that of *noblesse oblige*. Under the latter, responsibility is first defined on symbolic grounds and then the symbolic person is held strictly responsible. In comparison, for nominated accountability the responsible person is identified on a rational basis—presumptive fault—and then that person is held strictly responsible. To amplify, an environmental director may be nominated as responsible for environmental violations because he or she is the one person likely to be blameworthy for more violations than anyone else. If so, this person will subsequently be held responsible for violations for which he or she is not in fact to blame.

Nominated individual responsibility is difficult to find in Japan compared to the West where it is common in industries like pharmaceuticals and coal-mining.[50] The injustice of holding a middle manager strictly responsible for a certain type of offence within his or her span of direct control, having been put on notice of this responsibility before the event, is less than that with *noblesse oblige* or captain of the ship responsibility. Nevertheless, it is not difficult to imagine circumstances where the nominated manager has diligently implemented and monitored internal compliance systems to avert an offence, but an offence occurs because of the negligence or vindictiveness of a subordinate, or because of inadequate resources to do the job being provided by a superior.

Often within corporate cultures a collectivity is effectively nominated as accountable—the environmental affairs department is responsible for detecting and insisting upon appropriate remedies to all environmental offences detected, and if it fails to do so it may be sanctioned collectively, such as by undermining its independence and making it answerable to the regulatory affairs and law departments. In these circumstances, the criminal law might also seek to sanction collectively the environmental affairs department. For example, it may impose a community service order on the department as a collective obligation[51] or a corporate probation that monitors the rectification of the subunit procedures which led to the failure to meet its nominated responsibilities.[52]

---

[50] See Braithwaite, *Corporate Crime in the Pharmaceutical Industry*, 92–107; Braithwaite, *To Punish or Persuade*, 156–64.
[51] See Fisse, 'Community Service as a Sanction against Corporations'.
[52] See Gruner, 'To Let the Punishment Fit the Organization', 87–94.

Fault-based individual responsibility

More familiar to Western eyes is the imposition of individual responsibility on the basis of fault, whether in the form of intention, recklessness, or negligence. When a nuclear accident occurs in the West, the tradition is very much one of the corporation undertaking a witch-hunt to locate the person or persons (typically control-room operators) who 'didn't do their job'.[53] In the West, we tend to be attracted to fault-based responsibility for fear that any system of nominated responsibility will give those who are not nominated an incentive to cheat, given that they are immune from sanction until fault is established. Although fault-based individual responsibility is adopted in some Japanese corporations, traditions of collective decisionmaking very often rule it out.

Doré's study, *British Factory–Japanese Factory*, found that a major difference between the organisational cultures in English Electric and Hitachi lay in their approach to this kind of responsibility.[54] Whereas avoidance of strict responsibility and scapegoating was not of concern to the Japanese at Hitachi, fault was critical to the process of individual blaming at English Electric:

> The principle of the scapegoat which deals with the whole group's guilt is rejected in favour of justice—pinning the blame precisely on the individual who was at fault. 'When things go wrong I want to know why—in detail, and what is being done about it and who is OK and who is not,' to quote one top manager's circular.[55]

However, there are Japanese companies which have adopted Western ideas of fault-based individual responsibility.[56]

The way to implement a corporate cultural principle of fault-based individual responsibility is, of course, through the traditional jurisprudence of individualism. To the extent that fault-based individual responsibility genuinely is the accountability principle within the corporate culture under examination, traditional individualism will be both just and effective. However, many of the practical difficulties of detecting the culpable individual embedded in a complex organisation, as discussed in Chapter 2, will be formidable.

Beyond Positivist Organisation Theory

Overall, this fourth cut at conceptualising how organisations behave provides us with guidance every bit as ambiguous as the previous three should we wish to operationalise these varieties of corporate cultural responsibility into principles of legal responsibility. Whether we analyse organisations according to their decisionmaking processes (Kriesberg), their structuring (Mintzberg),

---

[53] See Perrow, *Normal Accidents*.
[54] Doré, *British Factory–Japanese Factory*.
[55] Ibid., 229.
[56] The examples we encountered in our fieldwork in Japan were that of Ishikawajima Harima Heavy Industries Company Ltd and, to a lesser extent, Mitsui and Co. Ltd.

their role-playing (Mangham), or their tendencies in allocating responsibility (Braithwaite and Fisse), the pursuit of an understanding of principles of corporate behaviour which can guide principles of legal responsibility for corporate behaviour has proved elusive.

Yet these were the ways of cutting organisational life which seemed to us most persuasively relevant to the jurisprudence of the organisation. We deliberated also upon the implications of cutting organisational life according to James Thompson's three types of technology (long-linked, mediating, and intensive),[57] Charles Perrow's distinction between routine and non-routine technology,[58] Christopher Hodgkinson's distinction between closed and open decisionmaking in organisations,[59] Andrew Van de Ven and André Delbecq's discerning of three structural modes based on task variability and task difficulty—systematised, service, and group;[60] Tom Burns and S. M. Stalker's distinction between mechanistic and organic management systems;[61] P. R. Lawrence and J. W. Lorsch's cutting of the cake on the basis of environmental uncertainty and the degree of differentiation and integration to ensure goal-directed behaviour thereby demanded;[62] Daniel Katz and Robert Kahn's 'genotypic' functions of organisations;[63] and Talcott Parsons' three levels of organisational responsibility and control—technical, managerial, and institutional.[64] All of these seemed even less fruitful as guides to law reform than the four cuts at the problem developed above.[65]

Some of these models not only posit such a diversity of organisation types that can give no clear guidance to the jurisprudence of the corporation, but also envisage enormous diversity within single organisations. For example, Lawrence and Lorsch's contingency approach implies that organisational styles may need to vary between subunits because of the radically different subenvironments they confront.[66] A production division may confront an environment of clear objectives, measurable evaluation and short-term time horizons, thereby rendering a machine bureaucratic type of organisation effective. The research division, on the other hand, may face ambiguous goals, long-term time horizons, and an environment whose mastery requires creativity and experimentation rather than routinisation.

Gareth Morgan's *Images of Organization*[67] is a masterly book about how to understand organisations using the kind of theoretical diversity we have

[57] Thompson, *Organizations in Action*.
[58] Perrow, 'A Framework for the Comparative Analysis of Organizations'.
[59] Hodgkinson, *Towards a Philosophy of Administration*.
[60] Van de Ven and Delbecq, 'A Task Contingent Model of Work Unit Structure'.
[61] Burns and Stalker, *The Management of Innovation*.
[62] Lawrence and Lorsch, *Developing Organizations*.
[63] Katz and Kahn, *The Social Psychology of Organization and Management*.
[64] Parsons, *Structure and Process in Modern Society*.
[65] Most of the foregoing suggestions were derived from the helpful listing of organisational typologies in Hrebiniak, *Complex Organizations*, 348–52.
[66] Lawrence and Lorsch, *Organization and Environment*; Lawrence and Lorsch, 'Differentiation and Integration in Complex Organizations'.
[67] Contrast Morgan's analysis with the limited stereotypes (e.g., the rational actor model) which organisations often project of themselves; see further Tombs, 'Corporate Crime and "Post Modern" Organizations'.

discovered here. While it is not a book about how to allocate responsibility for organisational action, it is helpful in comprehending what is involved in such an exercise. Morgan canvasses a number of images of organisations: the image of organisations as machines (Mintzberg's machine bureaucracy), as organisms (Lawrence and Lorsch's environmental contingency theory), as cultures (for example, the Japanese *noblesse oblige* type) and as political systems (Kriesberg's political actor model), as well as in several other ways not covered in the foregoing discussion. Some of these additional images of organisation are especially important to our enterprise because they show just how willing we must be to think in radically different and plural ways about organisations if we really want to understand what is happening within them. We will discuss a few of these below. But the important thing is Morgan's conclusion about how to handle all of this diversity. Faced with the ambiguous and paradoxical nature of organisational complexity, we should not think that what we must do is analyse which model fits where. Rather, we should treat the different models as metaphors which we use to unravel multiple patterns of significance and their interrelations. Morgan believes that the best intuitive readings made by managers occur when they are open to nuance, stemming from an appreciation that any organisational action can be many different things at once.

One of Morgan's evocative metaphors is of the organisation as a hologram. The interesting feature of the hologram is that if it is broken, any single piece can be used to reconstruct the whole image. Everything is enfolded in everything else. In the holographic organisation, all capacities required in the whole are enfolded in the parts. This enables subunits of the organisation to learn and self-organise. Morgan argues that building wholes into parts can be a conscious management strategy through creating redundancy, connectivity and simultaneous specialisation and generalisation. The upshot of wholes being built into parts is that subunits learn to learn and self-organise in response to changing environments. The holographic metaphor causes perplexing problems indeed for those who seek neat, clear models of who is responsible for what. Because the holographic organisation is about self-organisation, subunits might be held responsible for how they self-organise. Because holographic organisations build wholes into parts, the whole might also be held responsible. Hence the holographic metaphor directs us away from the conclusion that sometimes subunit actors are responsible and in other contexts corporate headquarters is responsible. In the perfectly holographic organisation, both will always bear responsibility. For such organisations, all strategies that force us to choose between individual and collective liabilities will be fatally flawed.

Morgan takes the principle of self-organisation a radical step further with the autopoietic image of the organisation. Autopoiesis is an approach to systems theory developed by the Chilean scientists Humberto Maturana and Francisco Varela. Their key proposition is that all living systems are organisationally closed systems of interaction that make reference only to themselves. The notion of living systems being open to the environment is a mistaken view of the organisation from the perspective of an outsider. Rather, living systems are only about producing themselves and self-renewing. They cannot engage in interactions that are not coded in the pattern of relations that define its organisation. The environment that is external from the viewpoint of the outside observer is coded as part of the system itself. The 'environment' is subordinated to the maintenance of a self-referential set of relations. Organisations enact their environment as projections of their own self-image. For example, a typewriter manufacturer that finds it is selling fewer typewriters redefines its image as a business machine manufacturer and enacts its market as the business machine or computer market rather than the typewriter market. Autopoiesis has been adapted to social and legal systems by Luhmann and Teubner.[68]

We do not take autopoiesis as seriously as these latter authors. That is, we do not view autopoiesis as a superior kind of socio-legal theory compared with some of the alternatives we discuss in this book. However, we do agree with Morgan that autopoiesis can be a useful metaphor for imagining how organisations work. To the extent that it is a revealing metaphor, it has a crucial implication for the effectiveness of the legal control of organisations:

> if systems are geared to maintaining their own identity, and if relations with the environment are internally determined, then systems can evolve and change only along with self-generated changes in identity.[69]

So, according to Morgan, 'if one really wants to understand one's environment, one must begin by understanding oneself, for one's understanding of the environment is always a projection of oneself'.[70] Equally, for those, like the judge or prosecutor, who want to effect change in an organisation from outside, they must learn to intervene in a way that helps organisations to come to grips with the law by understanding themselves. They must be enabled to internalise the law into self-referential systems that make the law count within the corporation's system of meaning. Put another way, the judge must learn what Gregory Bateson described as 'systemic wisdom'.[71] The judge must learn to frame interventions that steer the fabric of relations that define a system, rather than seek to mobilise external causes that will produce internal effects. Rather than seek to solve problems in a piecemeal way, the judge must consider that problems may be a normal consequence of the logic of the systems within which they are found. Only by catalysing a restructuring of the logic can the judge deal with the problems. The solution we advance in Chapter 6 is one that seeks to cultivate that systemic wisdom. It abandons thinking in terms of linear movement from causes to effects in favour of thinking in loops.

An additional way that Morgan suggests we must imagine organisations non-linearly is in terms of a dialectical metaphor. Interventions can heighten organisational contradictions that contain the seeds of the self-transformation

---

[68] See the essays in Teubner, *Dilemmas of Law in the Welfare State*; Teubner, *Autopoietic Law*.
[69] Morgan, *Images of Organization*, 239.
[70] Ibid., 243.
[71] Bateson, *Steps to an Ecology of Mind*.

of the organisation. For example, a court order requiring that work be done in a certain way to reduce pollution might be resented and resisted by employees who comply with the court order but find the time to do it by cutting other environmental protection activities, thereby leaving the environment worse off. Or they can resist to the point where they effectively demand a total transformation of the management structure; the extra control over them becomes the straw that breaks the camel's back, a quantitative change in control that causes a qualitative revolution in the organisation. When we have a dialectical imagination, we are sensitive to the possibility of phenomena being in tension with their opposites; we watch for contradictions. When we intervene in an organisation, we attempt 'to reframe the tensions and oppositions underlying the forces shaping the system',[72] thereby influencing their direction.

Morgan also sees organisations as instruments of domination. This is the metaphor of organisation as a process of domination where certain people impose their will on others. Or we can imagine organisations in a Foucaudian way as sets of disciplinary practices which regiment members—timeclocks, video surveillance, the speed of the production line itself—where those disciplinary practices have no particular author. That is, it is clear who is dominated and regimented, but it is not always clear which human actors are responsible for the domination. Thinking about organisations as instruments of domination will cause us to look for the scapegoating of junior employees as discussed in Chapter 2. It will also cause us to be sceptical about the justice of self-regulatory and private disciplinary systems, an issue we repeatedly return to in the next two chapters.

We have discussed so many different ways of seeing organisational action. How can all be useful? The answer is that in many situations most of them will not. Morgan suggests two steps to using a variety of metaphors to grasp the complex, ambiguous and paradoxical nature of organisational action. First, we should produce a diagnostic reading of the organisational action, applying many metaphors to reveal useful potential interpretations of it. Second, we should make a critical evaluation of these different interpretations and the possibilities for change they enable. Morgan argues, rightly we think, that to do this well, we do not have to be walking encyclopaedias of abstract concepts and masters of complex theories:

> We are simply encouraged to learn how to think about situations from different standpoints. We are invited to do what we do naturally, but to do so more consciously and broadly.[73]

Good managers and good judges are both sophisticated and well equipped by their practical experience to do the kind of intuitive theory-switching and frame-switching Morgan recommends:

> [T]he trick is to learn how to engage in a kind of conversation with the situation one is trying to understand. Rather than impose a viewpoint on a situation, one

[72] Morgan, *Images of Organization*, 266.
[73] Ibid., 336.

should allow the situation to reveal how it can be understood from other vantage points. In a way we can say that one should always be sensitive to the fact that a situation 'has its own opinion' in that it invites understanding through a frame of reference other than the one being applied.[74]

Our conclusion is not pessimistic about the usefulness of organisation theory for ensuring that the buck is not forever passed for corporate crime. What we have become pessimistic about is the possibility of settling on a simple model of organisational action from which we can derive clear principles of corporate criminal responsibility. Theorists that have done this, like Meir Dan-Cohen with his assumption that organisations are 'intelligent machines',[75] seem to us to lay the foundations for a crude and counterproductive organisational jurisprudence. We have seen that some areas of regulation are guided by a simple model of organisational behaviour—effluent charges systems of environmental regulation by a rational unitary actor model, maritime regulation in Australia and Britain by a captain of the ship model—and they are the worse for it.

The diversity of styles of organisational life is too great for this, whether we look at organisations through the prisms of decisionmaking process, structure, function, role diversity or accountability mechanisms. We find no single theory of how organisations make decisions to break the law, and how they hold actors accountable for them, of sufficient generality and explanatory power to be a practical guide to the design of a corporate criminal law appropriate to all types of organisations. It is not a matter of empirical evidence on organisations showing that the theories provide an overly simplified account of organisational diversity; the theories themselves posit a diversity which renders impossible a single model of legal responsibility consonant with organisational life.

Yet policy-makers have no choice but to do the best they can to write responsibility principles into the law which are maximally consonant with the way decisions are made in organisations. Friedman has expressed the premise which is the point of departure for this analysis:

> [A] law which goes against the grain, culturally speaking, will be hard to enforce and probably ineffective. Prohibition is the hackneyed example. But the converse is equally true. Laws that make use of the culture and draw on its strength can be tremendously effective. When a legal system contrives to cut with the grain, it multiplies its strength.[76]

A related premise is that not only will a law that goes with the grain of the corporate culture be more effective, it will be more just. When persons who are culturally defined as responsible by citizens are also legally defined as responsible by courts, the law is seen to be more just, and is more just.

---

[74] Ibid., 337.
[75] Dan-Cohen, *Rights, Persons, and Organizations*.
[76] Friedman, *The Legal System*.

The first step toward a concrete reform proposal to hold the buck for corporate crime is to explore more systematically responses to the problem of incompatibility between legal and organisational principles of responsibility. We consider in turn four solutions to the problem of disharmony between law and corporate cultures:

(1) making legal principles of responsibility conform to corporate principles of accountability;
(2) making corporate decisionmaking conform to legal principles of responsibility;
(3) making corporate and legal principles of responsibility conform to some ethical canon; or
(4) allowing corporations to propose their own principles of responsibility as the basis for a pluralist matching of legal principles and organisational cultures.

Making law conform to organisational structure

In the first part of this chapter, we demonstrated the difficulties of using a theoretically informed understanding of how organisations break the law to redesign legal responsibility. At least we can, perhaps, reform the law to better match the average tendencies in organisational culture. Thus, earlier we pointed out that Japanese corporate cultures tend to be more collectivist in their decisionmaking, while Western corporations tend to be relatively more top-down and individualist in their decisionmaking.[77] Yet Japanese law stresses individual responsibility for corporate crime,[78] while US law relies substantially on collective responsibility.[79] Overall, there would be a better match between law and culture if we imposed American legal principles of responsibility for organisational crime on Japanese society and Japanese legal principles of responsibility on American society. But in both cases a great residue of mismatching would occur because there are so many 'American-style' organisations in Japan and 'Japanese-style' organisations have become a vogue in the US.

---

[77] Braithwaite and Fisse, 'Varieties of Responsibility and Organizational Crime'.

[78] The Japanese Penal Code has no provision for corporate criminal responsibility, which can only be imposed as a matter of statutory exception (e.g., under the environmental pollution laws). The absence of a provision enabling criminal liability upon a corporation for unlawful homicide was the subject of much publicised judicial criticism in the Sennichi-Mae Building case (*Asahi News*, 16 May 1984, 1). We are grateful to Professor Koya Matsuo of the University of Tokyo Law School and Mr Akio Harada of the Japanese Ministry of Justice for assisting us in the above matters.

[79] Unlike the position in Japanese law, corporate criminal responsibility is both generally available and often imposed in the US. For one case where the collective knowledge of several employees was pieced together and held to be a sufficient mental element for the purpose of imposing corporate criminal responsibility, see *United States v Bank of New England* (1987) 821 F. 2d 844 at 855. See generally Fisse, 'Reconstructing Corporate Criminal Law', 1185–213.

One satisfactory route for bringing law into conformity with organisational structures would be to do it particularistically. Wherever a violation of law arose from the activities of an organisation, a judicial or administrative inquiry would be required to look into how accountability was defined within that particular organisation. For example, if consumers were killed because a pharmaceutical company distributed non-sterile products, the court or administrative body would look to company policies and procedures to see what person or what collectivity was defined as responsible for ensuring compliance. Thus, if the quality control director (an individual) was ascertained to be the person responsible for guaranteeing the sterility of drugs before they were let out of the plant, then he or she should be prosecuted. It sounds simple. But corporate statements of policy and organisation charts are often not to be believed.[80] There may be an informal social reality which is quite at odds with the proclaimed organisational structure. Everyone in the factory might understand that the quality control director did nothing without the approval of the plant manager, and everyone might know that the last quality control director who attempted to act independently was dismissed. If the plant manager had the real power, then he or she should be the prime target. The difficulty, however, is that courts will be given different views of the realities of power by actors looking at the power structure from different positions within the organisation. Moreover, it will often be a matter of defence tactics to try to get everyone off by putting out a smokescreen of diffused accountability to ensure that culpability beyond reasonable doubt cannot be proven against anyone.

Thus, the court or administrative authority, if it were to perform its task properly, would need to undertake a *de novo* sociological study of each organisation which came before it. However, the court would have a more demanding task than the average sociological researcher. The research would have to be completed in weeks rather than years if justice were to be swift. It would inevitably be conducted against a backdrop of defensiveness by informants who feared prosecution and wished to protect others and, in criminal cases, it would have to overcome the hurdle of proof beyond reasonable doubt. Not many of the small number of professionals who have experience in this kind of research would resign their positions to become court organisational sociologists.[81] If justice is to be swift, certain, and within the capacity of the taxpayers who support the criminal justice system, this approach suffers from dire problems.[82]

---

[80] See Gouldner, *Patterns of Industrial Bureaucracy.*

[81] Compare the expensive and time-consuming studies of organisations generally undertaken by academic sociologists (e.g., Vaughan, *Controlling Unlawful Organizational Behavior*; Bosk, *Forgive and Remember*; Selznick, *TVA and the Grass Roots*).

[82] Extensive presentence reports on corporate defendants are prepared from time to time in some jurisdictions: see, e.g., *United States v Olin Corporation* (1978) Criminal No. 78–30, slip op. D. Conn. 1 June, 1978. However, this practice is rare, at least in the US (interview with US Federal Probation Service, San Francisco, 18 Jan. 1984). Moreover, it must be wondered how effective probation officers are in penetrating the smokescreen which often surrounds accountability in large organisations.

Making organisational structure conform to law

On the face of it, making organisational structure conform to law may seem a silly alternative. Every social scientist knows it is easier to change law than to transform social structure. On the contrary, we would argue that the functionalist dominance in organisation theory, with its emphasis on equilibrium or homeostasis[83] has blinded social scientists to the reality that organisations change radically in those unusual situations when the law gives them no option but to change.[84] Conflict and adaptation are, after all, themes almost as recurrent in the organisational literature as stability.[85] Business organisations with immutable organisational structures are at risk of perishing in the natural selection process that is modern international trade. Companies unable to adjust to shifting consumer preferences, markets, and technological changes are frequently swallowed up by others that can. Of course, stability of identification and of fundamental values of excellence, quality of service and so on are also important to corporate survival.[86] But it is corporate structures— wherein old divisions are abolished and new staff functions added—which need to be most adaptable.

It should also be remembered that there are many instances where governmental intervention has brought about structural corporate reform.[87] Australian mine safety legislation provides one example where law has reshaped the course of corporate compliance by redefining managerial responsibilities. The Queensland Coal Mining Act 1925 and the NSW Coal Mines Regulation Act 1982 define a number of roles which must exist in the management structure of every coal mine in the state (for example manager, undermanager, deputy, shot-firer, surveyor) and sets down in some detail the obligations of persons who fill those roles. The management structure of all mines in Queensland and NSW conform to the requirements of the Acts; there has been no great problem in ensuring compliance with the government imposition of an organisational pattern.[88] Another illustration emerges from the Good Laboratory Practices Regulations, 1978, under the US Food, Drug and Cosmetic Act. These regulations require pharmaceutical companies engaged in the toxicological testing of drugs to have a Quality Assurance Unit and appoint a 'study director' with special responsibilities and powers in relation to each new drug being tested. Within six months of promulgation of the regulations a survey conducted by the Food and Drug Administration found a

---

[83] Selznick, 'Foundations of the Theory of Organizations'; Katz and Kahn, *The Social Psychology of Organizations*; Kaufman, *The Limits of Organizational Change*; Mintzberg, *The Structuring of Organizations*; Burrell and Morgan, *Sociological Paradigms and Organizational Analysis*.

[84] Compare C. D. Stone, 'The Place of Enterprise Liability...', 36–7, n. 142.

[85] Burrell and Morgan, *Sociological Paradigms and Organizational Analysis*; Burns and Stalker, *The Management of Innovation*; Bennis, *Beyond Bureaucracy*; Ginzberg and Reilly, *Effecting Change in Large Organizations*.

[86] Deal and Kennedy, *Corporate Cultures*.

[87] But see C. D. Stone, 'The Place of Enterprise Liability...', 39.

[88] Braithwaite, *To Punish or Persuade*.

99 per cent level of compliance with the appointment of study directors and a 79 per cent level of establishment of independent Quality Assurance Units.[89] The point could be laboured with some more obvious examples. For instance, how many companies ignore the requirements of the law that they have a board of directors and an outside auditor, or the requirements of the New York Stock Exchange that they have a board audit committee?

It is not difficult for the law to require companies to nominate a person as responsible for ensuring that certain procedures are complied with and that compliance reports are placed in the hands, of say, the captain of the ship. It is then made clear to everyone that both the nominated compliance officers and the captain of the ship will be held individually responsible should a violation occur. If responsibility is structured so as to insist upon the appointment of a compliance officer or unit with the expertise and time to achieve effective compliance, and if senior management are pin-pointed in advance as accountable for any violation, then fear of prosecution on the part of senior management is likely to ensure that the compliance officer or unit has the organisational power and capacity needed to do the job.[90] As we have seen, under the model of law conforming to organisational structure, management has an interest in creating a picture of confused accountability for wrongdoing. Where structure is made to conform to law, however, management has an interest in showing that it did everything possible to give full power to the compliance person to meet his or her statutory responsibilities. Making law conform to structure creates confusion; forcing organisational structure to conform to law makes for clarity of responsibilities. If the law puts people under the gun, especially when some of these people hold senior positions of influence, we can expect fear of conviction to bring about organisational change rapidly.

There are other provisions in the NSW Coal Mines Regulation Act which can add clarity to accountability. For example, any middle manager or employee who is given an instruction 'by or on behalf of the owner' may request confirmation in writing of the instruction from the higher management person who issued it, and such person must comply with the request. Hence, if a manager is under pressure from corporate headquarters to cut expenditure on safety, he or she may request confirmation of such a suggestion in writing to make it clear who is responsible for any deterioration in safety at the mine. Indeed, when an instruction is given to a manager or any other employee that the manager believes would impede safety or health, the manager is obliged to prevent execution of the instruction until it is confirmed in writing.[91] In other words, if senior executives compromise safety, the law imposes a duty to put their heads on the chopping block.

The main problem with an approach such as that adopted in Australian

---

[89] Cook, *Results of the Toxicology Laboratory Inspection Program.*

[90] Nonetheless, this power could conceivably be blocked in some possible situations where the costs of compliance with the law were enormous. Organisations can readily empower people for routine purposes while suspending that power in special situations.

[91] Coal Mines Regulation Act 1982 (NSW), s. 54(1).

coal mine safety law is that it stultifies managerial diversity.[92] Whatever view one has about the best way to manage a company, one must concede that it is helpful to look at the very different approaches adopted by other companies. The danger of a state-imposed management structure is that it will lag behind changes in technology, ownership patterns and other basic conditions of the industry and, through stereotyping and standardisation, inhibit managerial innovation.

As Christopher Stone has argued: 'Whenever we on the outside displace managerial choice, we are meddling in a delicate process about which we ordinarily know considerably less than do the participants. The Interventionist 'remedy' may cost society more than the harm it was seeking to avert'.[93]

Changing both law and organisational structure

Another possibility is to adopt a set of principles of responsibility which are consistent with some ethical canon. Public policy would then be asked to bend both law and organisational reality to this new position. Presumably for traditional Japanese philosophers the ethically preferred position would be one of collective responsibility overlaid with *noblesse oblige*, while Western traditionalists would seek to impose clearly defined individual responsibility based on fault.[94] The practical difficulty with this approach is that it combines the problems of bringing law into line with social structure with those of bringing social structure into line with law. Public policy which seeks to transform one major institution is challenge enough.

It should also be pointed out that danger lurks in any attempt to make law conform to traditional Western philosophical assumptions about individual and collective responsibility. Traditional Western moral notions of responsibility, it may well be argued, are not based on a critical let alone worldly-wise assessment,[95] but have been dominated by legalistic models of individualistic will.[96] Yet, as Walsh has explained, collective or vicarious responsibility may be more deeply rooted in the Western moral tradition than legalists assume:

> In law we seek to correct certain deviant members of society and for this purpose employ the principle that a man is answerable only for what in some degree issues from his will. To behave otherwise would be practically impossible, for though one can use a corporation in the person of its officials, one cannot bring a legal indictment against a whole family or a whole nation. It does not, however, follow that the legal notion of responsibility must be carried over entire into the moral sphere, and my contention is that it is not. The criminal who is caught brings punishment

---

[92] See C. D. Stone, 'The Place of Enterprise Liability...', 38; C. D. Stone, 'Corporate Regulation'; compare Mintzberg, *The Structuring of Organizations*, 438–67.

[93] C. D. Stone, 'Corporate Regulation', 19.

[94] Nemerson, 'Criminal Liability without Fault'; Lewis, 'The Non-Moral Notion of Collective Responsibility'.

[95] Mannheim, *Group Problems in Crime and Punishment*, 42–65; Seney, 'The Sibyl at Cumae', 844-53.

[96] See, e.g., Jacobs, *Criminal Responsibility*, 11–24.

upon himself, but he also brings shame and obloquy on his family and friends, who thus are saddled with the consequences of deeds they did not do themselves. There are persons today who say that this amounts to persecution of the innocent and would like, in consequence, to make radical alterations in our ways of dealing with offenders. I think that they ought to reflect on the function of law and morality before they proceed to any such conclusion. Law provides only a first line of defence against malefactors; it discourages anti-social conduct by the threat of definite penalties, which can, however, in most cases be paid off once and for all. Morals supplement law by bringing softer and subtler pressures to bear, pressures which affect a man not just in his personal capacity but also through his relatives, friends and associates, pressures which, again, are not always released when a prisoner completes his sentence or pays his fine. That things work out in this way may strike us as unfair; what I am concerned to stress now is only that this is how things are. The exercise of moral pressure in the way indicated is part of an elaborate system by which society tries to protect itself against undesirable forms of behaviour, and the man who proposes to sweep it away, or alter it radically, must tell us what he thinks could be put in its place. To insist on the principle of limited liability in morals as well as in law may have the unwelcome effect of destroying the possibility of stable society. But whether it does so or not, we should not make the change without being clearly aware of what it involves.[97]

Pluralistic matching of law and organisational structure

So far we have expressed a preference for forcing management structures to conform to the accountability requirements of law. However, as contended above, innovation in managerial design would be stultified under such an approach and state-imposed management structures might compromise efficiency. There is a solution to this problem. Companies could be allowed to define their own principles of accountability and register these with a regulatory agency such as the Securities and Exchange Commission (SEC) in the American context. For example, instead of an organisation simply notifying the US SEC of the name of its financial auditor, it might also be required to register the names of the persons who would be responsible for auditing compliance with environmental laws and the name of the senior manager to whom the environmental auditor's report would need to be delivered. The best strategy would be to require the company to register a detailed set of rules and principles defining accountability within the organisation. They could prescribe whatever mix of collective and individual responsibility suited the management style of the corporation. The writing and registering of the principles could come back to haunt the organisation and its personnel. No longer could the company claim after the event that, because of diffused accountability for a certain area of compliance, it was impossible to identify those responsible. The accountable person or group, having been publicly nominated before the event, would have been given notice that they would be put

---

[97] Walsh, 'Pride, Shame and Responsibility', 13; see also Moore, 'Legal Liability and Evolutionary Interpretation'; Boonin, 'Man and Society'; French, 'Types of Collectivities and Blame'; French, *Collective and Corporate Responsibility*.

on the spot should a violation occur. There would be no sociological investigation after the event into who should be blamed: a binding commitment as to responsibility would have been secured and agreed upon before the event.

If it is unrealistic to expect companies to lodge all-embracing principles of intra-corporate responsibility with an agency like the US SEC, there is, nevertheless, the possibility of regulatory agencies requiring a detailed prescription to be provided within their more limited ambit of concern. For example, environmental agencies might require lodgement of specific accountability plans to ensure nominated accountability for environmental offences. The management structure imposed by the NSW Coal Mines Regulation Act has been discussed along with the problem of stultification of innovation which this approach brings. In fact, in a 1982 revision of this legislation, some of the elements of a government-mandated management system were replaced by discretion for the company to design its own management structure. This was achieved by the device of making the mine manager responsible unless there was a written delegation of specified responsibilities to another person. An instrument of delegation, countersigned by the person to whom the new legal duties are delegated, must be sent to the district inspector.[98] A delegate may refuse to countersign an instrument of delegation and have the reasonableness of the delegation adjudicated by a court of law.[99] In explaining this change, the former Minister for Mineral Resources commented:

> It has for some time been apparent to my Department that the management structure provided for in the present Coal Mines Regulation Act does not permit the flexibility necessary in managing a modern coal mine through all stages of its development. Many instances have come to notice where the Act provides that a particular person shall perform some function yet in practice it is performed by some other person, often because it is more convenient to do so and indeed in some cases more logical. For this reason the Department, when it began the task of preparing the new legislation, decided that the legislation should, consistent with safety, give to the manager a wide discretion to draw up his own management structure having regard to his needs and the resources available to him.[100]

While this approach permits an array of accountability structures suitable for tiny mines at one extreme to mighty multinationals at the other, one problem is that companies are just as capable of naming scapegoats before the event as they are afterwards. Lines of accountability could be drawn, for example, in such a way that a 'vice-president responsible for going to jail', not the president, would suffer the consequences for any serious offence.

On the other hand, the public process of pin-pointing those accountable for achieving compliance would induce healthy soul searching as to where the company really did stand on principles of responsibility. Personnel at real risk of being subjected to criminal responsibility without having been given

---

[98] Coal Mines Regulation Act 1982 (NSW), s. 58.

[99] Ibid., s. 57.

[100] Ron Mulock, Address by the NSW Minister for Mineral Resources to the Colliery Managers' Association, University of NSW, 1981.

effective power to ensure compliance could be expected in some cases to: (1) successfully insist on being given that power (through pressure from their union or professional association or even by means of litigation); (2) take extra care to ensure compliance within the limits of their power; or (3) resign (a difficult option under the Japanese cultural tradition of lifetime employment and in many other cultural contexts). Because confrontation with employees set up unfairly as scapegoats would be a personnel relations disaster in a culture which disapproved of scapegoating, companies would be under pressure to be fair by bringing power and responsibility into alignment.

Pluralistic matching of law with the accountability principles of particular companies is an extension of a model of business regulation—the model of enforced self-regulation—which one of the authors has proposed elsewhere.[101] Under the enforced self-regulation model, governmental rules of corporate regulation are replaced by a requirement that companies write their own rules and submit them to a regulatory agency which ensures that they comply with minimum governmental standards. These privately written and publicly ratified rules are then treated in the same way as universalistic rules, so that the state is able to prosecute for their contravention. The suggestion now advanced is that individual companies be required not only to provide their own particularistic rules, but also to furnish particularistic principles of responsibility as an aid to public prosecution should violations subsequently occur.

The strengths and weaknesses of a particularistic approach to corporate crime control have been considered in detail elsewhere.[102] That discussion need not be repeated here. The general point to be stressed is that, from a quite different direction, we have reached the same impasse. Organisations are so different that any universalistic approach to controlling them will encounter difficulty. Inevitably, models of accountability, just like models of rule creation, are pushed toward particularism. There may be less injustice and better protection of the public by making private justice systems more explicit and giving them public recognition than by imposing universalistic laws upon organisational structures with which those laws are out of line. Certainly, there can be no universalistic solution to the fundamental problem of ensuring that the legal control of organisational crime is consonant with the diverse forms of organisational accountability in any modern society, even in the case of a society like Japan with its supposedly homogeneous organisational cultures.

In addition to the problem of scapegoating before the event, the main problem with the pluralistic matching option is the difficulty of achieving anything but partial coverage of the range of legal problems which bring corporations into conflict with the law. While one can imagine various regulatory agencies achieving more responsive law in their limited regulatory domain by adopting the pluralistic matching option, the problem will remain for areas of law covered by a regulatory agency which does not find this feasible and for areas of

---

[101] Braithwaite, 'Enforced Self-Regulation'.
[102] Ibid.

law where there is no regulatory agency which could act as the vehicle for rati-
fying corporate internal accountability rules.

Also, the approach might amount to an aggravating paperwork burden for
small businesses where formal statements of lines of responsibility would not
normally be prepared in the absence of government compulsion. However,
the smaller the business, the less the problems of cutting through the morass
of organisational complexity to identify responsible individuals; so there is a
strong case for regulatory agencies exempting small business from requirements to register internal accountability principles.[103] A more difficult problem to solve is with the larger companies that Mintzberg characterised as
Adhocracies.[104] These are organisations which achieve maximum scope for
innovation by making a virtue of free-floating responsibility and organisational flux. There are troubling concerns that requiring Adhocracies to set
their responsibility principles in concrete would stultify innovation, or that to
modify them frequently enough to keep up with the changing matrices of
responsibility would be a substantial and distracting paperwork burden.

Conclusion: The Need for Strategies Responsive to the Problems Posed by Organisation Theory

It seems such an obvious and uncontroversial aspiration to define legal principles of responsibility for corporate crime consistently with the way organisations actually make decisions. Yet we have seen that organisation theory
posits such diversity in the way organisations make decisions, in the way they
are structured, in their cultures, and in the way they define responsibility, that
positivist organisation theory can never give clear guidance to the law on this
question.

So we considered alternatives to the difficult task of making legal principles conform to the structural and procedural realities of organisational life.
One was to reverse direction by making corporate decisionmaking conform to
legally mandated principles of responsibility. Unfortunately, however, state-
imposed corporate accountability structures may render law enforceable at the
expense of compromising economic efficiency by straightjacketing management systems.

The alternative of changing both the structure of the law and the structure
of corporate decisionmaking to conform to a set of ethical principles of
responsibility was found to be unrealistic. It is a solution which combines all
the problems of the first two solutions.

The fourth solution seems the most promising—pluralistic matching of law
and organisational structure. However, there are limits in the coverage it can
afford. Where there is no regulatory agency with the staff resources to
approve particularistic accountability principles, the solution is unworkable.
For smaller organisations, it might cause an unreasonable paperwork burden.

---

[103] See the discussion of defaults in Ayres and Braithwaite, *Responsive Regulation*, 108.
[104] Mintzberg, *The Structuring of Organizations*, 431–67.

For Adhocracies, the very setting of responsibility principles in concrete could stop them from being ever-changing Adhocracies, and thus stultify innovation. Then there is the risk that companies will design accountability systems to ensure that illegal schemes flourish with minimal legal disruption. Just as scapegoating after the event is a problem, so can scapegoating before the event be a problem—oppressive advance nominations of 'vice-presidents responsible for going to jail'.

While we have failed to find a solution that is satisfactorily responsive to the realities of organisational life in this chapter, our deliberations at least indicate the problems which a satisfactory solution must solve. These problems are:

(1) How to achieve harmony with the varieties of structures, cultures, decisionmaking and accountability principles in large and small organisations.

(2) How to enable the law to respond with a nuanced appreciation of organisational actions that are many things at once. How can the law enable a diagnostic reading of organisational action using a variety of metaphors to reveal its complex, ambiguous and paradoxical nature?

(3) How to avoid the oppressive qualities of corporate disciplinary practices revealed when we apply Morgan's metaphor of the organisation as an instrument of domination. In particular, how do we deal with the most critical form this domination takes in the criminal domain—oppressive scapegoating?

(4) How to ensure that the law does not hamper economic efficiency by straightjacketing management systems into conformance with legal principles.

In the remainder of the book, we try to provide a more or less adequate solution which solves these problems, in addition to the problems identified in Chapters 2 and 3. The first task, performed in the next chapter, is to draw together all the desiderata that need to be satisfied if we are to find a persuasive solution to the problem of passing the buck for corporate crime.

5 Making the Buck Stop

Responsibility for Corporate Crime in Modern Society

Responsibility, as we saw in Chapter 2, is a device for achieving social control that does not depend on metaphysical or intrinsic qualities of 'moral persons' or human agents. Responsibility for corporate crime may thus be corporate as well as individual. Corporate responsibility may be based on corporate intentionality, in the sense of corporate policy, or corporate negligence, in the sense of an inexcusable failure to meet the standard of conduct expected of a corporation in the position of the defendant.

It was also shown in Chapter 2 that the theory of deterrent punishment is not confined to individual actors but is consistent with corporate criminal liability. Several reasons were given for this extension of deterrence theory:
(1) Deterrence does not imply that punishment must be directed at individual actors.
(2) Uncertainty as to the nature of corporate action does not have the policy implication that deterrent punishment should be limited to individual actors but is entirely consistent with sanctioning strategies that focus on corporate as well as individual actors.
(3) Deterrence and organisational reform are complementary rather than mutually exclusive means of controlling corporate conduct.
(4) The deterrent capacity of individual criminal liability is limited by various factors, namely: enforcement overload; opacity of internal lines of corporate accountability; expendability of individuals within organisations; corporate separation of those responsible for the commission of past offences from those responsible for the prevention of future offences; and corporate safe-harbouring of individual suspects.

Moreover, we argued in Chapter 2 that retribution is not necessarily inconsistent with corporate criminal liability; the more plausible retributive theories are capable of extension to corporate entities. The point has also been made repeatedly in the previous chapters that inequality in the application of the criminal law to white-collar offenders is unlikely to be relieved if scarce enforcement resources are channelled exclusively into the difficult and costly task of investigating and prosecuting offences by individuals. If the scales of justice are to be evened up, then less costly ways of delivering individual responsibility must be found. Furthermore, we have explained why it is that existing practices of individual enforcement for corporate crime stumble in the face of individual risk-shifting by insurance, indemnification, delegating risky functions to subordinates, and other practices which systematically shield strategic individuals from the burden of liability.

While Chapter 2 revealed the limits of individualistic liberal legalism, Chapter 3 unfolded the limits of the collectivist economism of enterprise liability. Chapter 4 then explored the limits of a variety of forms of sociological collectivism. The unifying problem running throughout Chapters 3 and 4 was the problem of uncertainty of enforcement impact. As avenues for informing the law, the doctrines of legal liberalism, economic analysis of law and organisation theory are all fraught with contingent and unpredictable effects for any program in which they might conceivably be put into practice.

In Chapter 3, we reached what we consider to be a watershed position, which is that the best device for managing uncertainty is the imposition of responsibility itself. While we can never get the information we need to calibrate optimal enforcement regimes, we can cope with this uncertainty by following this rule of action:

> *Seek to publicly identify all who are responsible and hold them responsible, whether the responsible actors are individuals, corporations, corporate subunits, gatekeepers, industry associations or regulatory agencies themselves.*

More economistically, this rule of action means that we should seek to maximise the sheeting home of responsibility for any given level of enforcement budget.

This strategy is hardly remarkable. An impressive body of psychological research indicates that it is exactly the approach taken by competent parents.[1] Only an incompetent parent would seek to regulate family life by calculating optimal penalties for different childhood transgressions. Practical, effective parents devote their scarce regulatory energies to ensuring that whenever wrongdoing occurs, a recognition of responsibility for it is brought home to the wrongdoers, and is seen to be sheeted home by all actors involved in the incident. Their objective is never to let wrongdoing slide, never to settle for 'nattering' at the naughty child, but to confront wrongdoing with a disapproval that communicates the seriousness of the degree of wrongdoing. The same applies to good managers in complex organisations: they are not managers who set optimal penalties; they are managers who focus their scarce resources on ensuring that those they are responsible for are always held responsible for their failures and successes. Put simply, our hypothesis is that the most efficient rule of action for parents and managers is also the most efficient rule of action for corporate law enforcers.

---

[1] See Baumrind, 'Current Patterns of Parental Authority'; Baumrind, 'Parental Disciplinary Practices and Social Competence in Children'; Patterson, *Coercive Family Process*.

Desiderata for the Just and Effective Enforcement of Responsibility for Corporate Crime

It is time to recapitulate by assembling the particular desiderata that have emerged for the allocation of responsibility for corporate crime. Twenty desiderata are listed below. After each of them we indicate the parts of our text that underpin the particular desideratum. Having listed the relevant desiderata in the present section, we consider some promising moves that have previously been taken toward developing models for the just and effective enforcement of responsibility for corporate crime. We use these as stepping stones toward our own model for the allocation of responsibility in corporate criminal enforcement. We then outline the key elements of our preferred model. Finally in this chapter, we illustrate how the model would operate in practice. Later, in Chapter 6, we evaluate our model precisely in terms of the desiderata summarised below.

The Desiderata

1

A strategy for allocating responsibility for corporate crime should reflect the received wisdom that individual responsibility is a pillar of social control in Western societies. The slide away from individual responsibility in our corporate law enforcement must be remedied. [pp. 2–8, 78–9]

2

A strategy for allocating responsibility for corporate crime should also accept that corporate action is not merely the sum of individual actions and that it can be just and effective to hold corporations responsible as corporations. [pp. 19–31, 44–7]

3

A strategy for allocating responsibility for corporate crime should seek to maximise the allocation of responsibility to all who are responsible, be they individuals, subunits of corporations, corporations, parent corporations, industry associations, gatekeepers such as accountants and indeed regulatory agencies themselves. [pp. 64–6, 92, 99]

4

The maximisation of the allocation of responsibility to all who are responsible should be pursued cost-efficiently, and in a way that does not place unrealistic burdens either on corporations or on the public purse. [pp. 37–41, 62, 69–72, 80]

5

The maximisation of the allocation of responsibility should be pursued justly in such a way as to safeguard the interests of individuals. Rights of suspects must be respected. Procedural justice must not be sacrificed on the altar of substantive justice. [pp. 50–3, 93–6]

6

Those who are responsible for equal wrongs should be treated equally. [pp. 53–7, 96–8]

7

A strategy for allocating individual responsibility should remedy the scapegoating that has been endemic when individual accountability for corporate wrongdoing has been pursued. [pp. 38–41, 55–7, 96–7, 129]

8

A strategy for sanctioning the responsible should minimise spillovers of the effects of sanctions onto actors who bear no responsibility for the wrongdoing. [pp. 49–50, 64]

9

A means must be devised to escape the deterrence trap—the situation where the only way to make it rational to comply with the law is to set penalties so high as to jeopardise the economic viability of corporations that are the lifeblood of the economy. [pp. 64, 82]

10

A strategy for sanctioning the responsible must recognise that actors are motivationally complex. Profit maximisation is an important motivation for many private corporate actors, but the maintenance of individual and corporate repute, dignity, self-image and the desire to be responsible citizens are also important in many contexts, as are various more idiosyncratic motivations. A good strategy will not be motivationally myopic. [pp. 33–4, 79–82]

11

A strategy for sanctioning the responsible should avoid myopia about which agents will dispense sanctions against those responsible with the greatest justice and effectiveness. Often, it will be enforcement agents of the state who will do the best job. Yet we should not privilege the state as the only law-enforcer that matters. In particular, corporate internal disciplinary systems must be taken seriously as legal orders with realised and unrealised potential for justice and effectiveness. [pp. 8–12, 77–81, 96–7]

12

Special care must be taken to ensure that the state does not cause private justice systems to become organised against the state justice system. The state should have enforcement policies that avert the formation of organised business cultures of resistance to regulatory law. [pp. 38–40]

13

A strategy for sanctioning the responsible should also avoid myopia about the aims of the criminal justice system. Narrowly focused utilitarianism or retributivism are prescriptions for disastrous corporate criminal enforcement policies. Criminal liability is not merely a matter of paying a price for crime, but has a prohibitory function which is reflected by the denunciatory emphasis of the criminal process. Nor should criminal liability be viewed simply as a matter of retribution. The harms protected against by corporate criminal law are too serious for us to indulge in retribution at the cost of increasing corporate harm-doing. [pp. 44–9, 84]

14

A strategy for allocating responsibility should be in harmony with the varieties of structures, cultures, decisionmaking and accountability principles in large and small organisations.
[pp. 117–18, 122–32]

15

A strategy for allocating responsibility should be capable of nuanced response to the likelihood that the same corporate action can be usefully understood in many different ways. Our mechanisms for allocating responsibility should not be so calibrated that the ambiguous and paradoxical nature of corporate action eludes us. In other words, we should be able to avoid the traps of narrowness of vision through institutions that are able to imagine corporate action in multiple ways. Our methodology for allocating responsibility should foster a dialogue that brings these multiple interpretations of responsibility into the open.
[pp. 77, 108–9, 119–23]

16

A strategy for allocating responsibility in a complex corporate world where the motivations of actors are multiple and where no single model of corporate action grasps the whole story should be based on redundancy. If the intervention fails for one reason, there should be other features of the intervention that might enable it to succeed. Redundancy should be built into interventions, while the inefficiencies of costly redundancies are avoided.
[pp. 73–6, 85–8, 91–2]

17

A strategy for allocating responsibility should ensure that the law does not straightjacket management systems into conformity with legal principles.
[pp. 126–7]

18

A strategy for allocating responsibility should operate with a conception of fault that is not time-bound, but copes with the dynamic nature of corporate action. [pp. 47–9]

19

A strategy for allocating responsibility should not be bound by a national jurisdiction; it should be capable of responding to the increasingly international nature of corporate action.
[pp. 40–1]

20

A strategy for allocating responsibility should be workable with public as well as private organisations.
[pp. 6–7, 13]

Developing a Model for the Allocation of Responsibility for Corporate Crime

A promising approach for achieving accountability for corporate crime would be to structure enforcement so as to activate and monitor the private justice systems of corporate defendants.[2] Already under the present law one aspiration of corporate criminal liability is to catalyse internal discipline, especially where organisational secrecy, numbers of suspects and other such considerations make it difficult or even impossible to rely on individual criminal liability.[3] Looking ahead, the challenge is not so much to expand the application of individual criminal liability[4] as it is to harness the policing power of corporations.

This direction was suggested in 1976 in a Working Paper prepared by the Canadian Law Commission,[5] but does not appear to have been taken further

---

[2] See Chapter 1, 15–16.
[3] See Chapter 2, 36–41.
[4] Compare Goodwin, 'Individual Liability of Agents for Corporate Crimes under the Proposed Federal Criminal Code'; Spiegelhoff, 'Limits on Individual Accountability for Corporate Crimes'; McVisk, 'Toward a Rational Theory of Criminal Liability for the Corporate Executive'.
[5] Canada, Law Reform Commission, Working Paper 16, *Criminal Responsibility for Group Action*, 31.

by the Commission. In 1977, the idea was developed by the Criminal Law and Penal Methods Reform Committee of South Australia, which recommended that internal discipline orders be introduced as a sanction against corporate defendants.[6] A similar approach was pursued by John Coffee in 1981 in an imaginative proposal for using probation or presentence reports as a vehicle for stimulating internal disciplinary action by corporate offenders.[7] This proposal is canvassed below.

Coffee's proposal

John Coffee took as his starting point the Gulf Oil Corporation report on bribery committed in the US and abroad by its personnel during the 1970s and earlier. The report was prepared by an outside counsel, John J. McCloy. The revelations in the McCloy study were sufficiently interesting to be picked up by the press and for the report to be republished as a paperback best-seller.[8] It brought about substantial internal reforms at Gulf and hastened the resignation of some senior officials named in it. Coffee was thus prompted to ask whether McCloy-style reports should become a routine part of corporate crime enforcement.

The mechanism favoured by Coffee was placing corporate defendants on probation, subject to a condition that they employ outside counsel to prepare a report which names key participants and outlines in readable form their *modus operandi*. Alternatively, the vehicle could be a presentence report:

> The suggestion, then, is that the presentence report on corporate offenders be prepared in considerable factual depth in the expectation that such studies will either find an audience in their own right or, more typically, provide the database for investigative journalism. This approach permits the government both to avoid the ethical dilemma of itself being a publicist, and to rely on the more effective public communication skills of the professional journalist. In a sense, this approach integrates public and private enforcement.[9]

The presentence report would be distributed to stockholders, and thereby in effect to the world.

Coffee concluded that adverse individual publicity in a McCloy-style report can deter culpable or negligent managers on three distinct levels:

[6] South Australia, Criminal Law and Penal Methods Reform Committee, Fourth Report, *The Substantive Criminal Law*, 361–2.
[7] Coffee, 'No Soul to Damn No Body to Kick'. Compare 18 USC s. 3572(a)(4) which provides that, when imposing a fine on a corporation, a court is to consider 'any measures taken by the organisation to discipline its employees or agents responsible for the offense or to insure against a recurrence of such offense'. See further Coffee and Whitbread, 'The Convicted Corporation'.
[8] McCloy, *The Great Oil Spill*.
[9] Coffee, 'No Soul to Damn No Body to Kick', 431.

First, the manager suffers a loss of public- and self-respect, which some research suggests is the most potent deterrent for the middle-class potential offender. Second, adverse publicity substantially reduces the official's chances for promotion within the firms. Competition for advancement is keen within almost all firms, and competitors of the culpable official can be relied upon to use such adverse publicity about their rival to their own advantage. SEC proxy disclosure requirements may pose a further barrier to such an official's advancement. Finally, disclosure of the identity of the culpable official also invites a derivative suit by which any costs visited on the firm can be shifted (at least in part) to the individual. Here again private enforcement is desirably integrated with public enforcement through the linking mechanism of disclosure.[10]

This approach is instructive because it exploits the capability that corporate justice systems have for delivering individual accountability. Instead of following the jurisprudential tradition of neglecting the existence of private legal systems within corporations,[11] Coffee revealed the potential for linking public law with internal corporate law in an expedient way designed to promote individual responsibility. However, Coffee's proposal is embryonic. Much fuller development is required if such an approach is to command acceptance. In our view, that development is best tackled by pinning down the desiderata that are relevant to the allocation of responsibility for corporate crime and by building a model that patently satisfies them. In the next section, we outline a model generated by our own attempt to struggle with the desiderata that have emerged from our analysis of the problem of passing the buck for corporate crime. We call this the 'Accountability Model'.

The Accountability Model

The Accountability Model we advocate is based most fundamentally on the rule of action that has already been spelt out:

> *Seek to publicly identify all who are responsible and hold them responsible, whether the responsible actors are individuals, corporations, corporate subunits, gatekeepers, industry associations or regulatory agencies themselves.*

This rule of action, which could readily be implemented by refining existing legislative and common law controls against corporate crime, suggests the need for a legal package containing the following essential elements:

(1) pyramidal enforcement whereby the legal response to non-compliance can be escalated progressively if necessary;
(2) guidelines which indicate the circumstances under which corporations and/or individuals are to be prosecuted for offences;

---

[10] Ibid., 433.
[11] See R. B. Stewart, 'Organizational Jurisprudence'.

(3) accountability agreements, orders and assurances under which disciplinary and other duties are to be performed by a corporate defendant and
relevant personnel;

(4) specification of the threshold requirements for accountability agreements,
orders or assurances;

(5) designation in advance of the individuals and collectivities primarily
responsible for ensuring responsibility with an accountability agreement,
order, or assurance;

(6) provision for supervising and monitoring of accountability agreements,
orders or assurances should such steps be required; and

(7) safeguards against scapegoating and other unjust practices by organisations subjected to accountability agreements, orders, or assurances.

1 Pyramidal enforcement

The basic regulatory framework of the Accountability Model is pyramidal
enforcement,[12] with informal methods of control at the base of the pyramid
and severe forms of criminal liability at the apex. One commendable pyramid
of enforcement, working up from the base, is this:

LEVEL 1
Persuasion, warnings, advice, and other informal methods of promoting
compliance.

LEVEL 2
Civil monetary penalties (corporate and individual).

LEVEL 3
Disciplinary or remedial investigation undertaken upon agreement with an
enforcement agency (accountability agreements) and court-approved assurance of an effective program of disciplinary or remedial action (accountability
assurances), coupled with publication of an accountability report.

LEVEL 4
Court-ordered disciplinary or remedial investigation (accountability orders) or
court-approved assurance of an effective program of disciplinary or remedial
action (accountability assurances), coupled with publication of an accountability report.

LEVEL 5
Criminal liability (individual and corporate), with community service, fines
and probation authorised for individual offenders, and adverse publicity
orders, community service, fines and probation for corporate offenders.

LEVEL 6
Escalated criminal liability (individual and corporate), with jail authorised for
individual offenders, and liquidation (corporate capital punishment), punitive
injunctions, and adverse publicity orders for corporate offenders.

---

[12] Braithwaite, *To Punish or Persuade*, 142–8; Ayres and Braithwaite, *Responsive Regulation*.

Figure 5.1: Pyramid of disciplinary and remedial interventions against corporate offenders

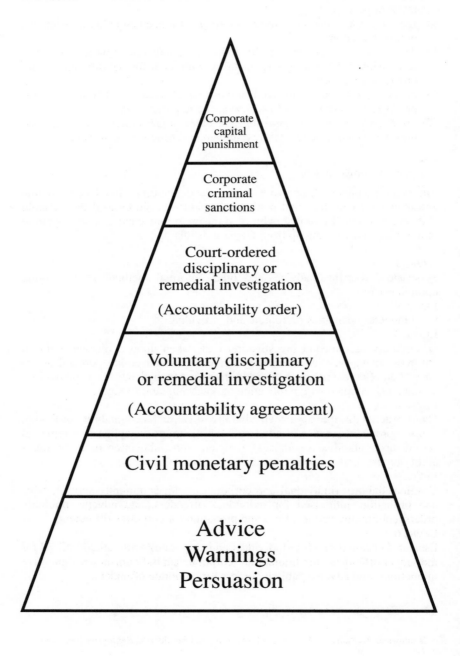

Figure 5.1 presents the corporate version of this pyramid. When regulatory persuasion and advice fail, warnings escalate to civil monetary penalties, to negotiation of voluntary accountability agreements, to accountability orders mandated by the courts to corporate criminal sanctions escalating from fines to community service to punitive injunctions and, if necessary, corporate capital punishment (for example, licence revocation).

The exact form of the pyramid may well vary from jurisdiction to jurisdiction, depending on such factors as the particular modes of regulation to which locals are accustomed, and the extent to which lawmakers are prepared to exercise their imagination. The options indicated above, however, are representative of those available in many jurisdictions. What matters for the purpose of the Accountability Model is not the infinitely various details into which one might be tempted to descend, but the strategy behind pyramidal enforcement and the implications which this strategy holds for the legal ordering of sanctions and remedies against corporate wrongdoing.

A central idea behind pyramidal enforcement is the game theoretic postulate that actors, individual or corporate, are most likely to comply if they know that enforcement is backed by sanctions which can be escalated in response to any given level of non-compliance, whether minor or egregious. The pyramid proposed is tall rather than squat, the theory being that the taller the enforcement pyramid, the more the levels of possible escalation, then the greater the pressure that can be exerted to motivate 'voluntary' compliance at the base of the pyramid.[13] Compliance is thus understood within a dynamic enforcement game where enforcers try to get commitment from corporations to comply with the law and can back up their negotiations with credible threats about the dangers faced by defendants if they choose to go down the path of non-compliance.

A key part of getting commitment from corporations to comply with the law is instilling and maintaining a sense of responsibility, corporate and individual, within the relevant organisation. To that end, the pyramid outlined is intended to give enforcers the leverage they need to persuade corporations to impose individual responsibility as a matter of internal discipline.

Where the violation is minor, the level of response warranted may be no more than a warning or a civil penalty. At the next possible tier, an enforcement agency may need to insist on a formalised accountability *agreement* under which the corporation and designated personnel would agree to undertake an internal disciplinary inquiry and, at a specified later date, to provide an *assurance*, to be approved by a court, that certain disciplinary action had been taken or was about to be taken.[14] In cases where the defendant is less trustworthy, application could be made to a court for an accountability order

[13] Ayres and Braithwaite, *Responsive Regulation,* 38–46.
[14] A variety of business regulatory statutes already empower regulatory agencies to enter into and enforce such agreements. See, e.g., *Fair Trading Act* (UK); *Trade Practices Act* (BC), s. 17. In Neilson's study of 90 formal trade penalties compliance agreements in three Canadian provinces, the use made of these tools was uneven and lacked a clear underlying strategy. See Neilson, 'Administrative Remedies'.

under which a corporate defendant and designated personnel would be required to make a disciplinary inquiry, to report back, and to give a satisfactory assurance about the disciplinary measures taken or planned. Note that the distinction between an agreement and an assurance is that an assurance is given to a court while an agreement is entered into with a regulatory agency only. The difference between an order and an assurance is that the order is mandated by the court whereas an assurance, like an agreement, is voluntarily given by the defendant organisation.

Accountability orders or assurances might also incorporate a variety of supervisory and monitoring mechanisms, depending on the severity of the offence and the compliance record of the defendant (see Section 6 below). For serious offences, including non-compliance with accountability agreements, orders or assurances, the corporation and individuals implicated in the offence would be subject to criminal liability. For very serious offences, including repeated non-compliance with accountability agreements, orders or assurances, the corporation and individuals implicated in the offence would be subject to criminal liability at an escalated level.

The range of sanctions in the pyramid for individuals is entirely conventional: jail, community service, probation, fines, civil penalties, damages, injunctions, reprimands and warnings. The range of sanctions for corporations, however, would need to be wider than the array of sentencing options that are currently available.[15] Thus, we envisage corporate capital punishment as the most severe form of sentence available against corporations. This suggestion, hardly novel,[16] is advanced not out of misguided vindictiveness but simply on the basis that a drastic form of punishment may occasionally be needed to deal with the most extreme forms of corporate intransigence. Another option, as canvassed in earlier chapters, is the punitive injunction, a hard-hitting and yet remedial form of punishment that would be appropriate in cases where liquidation would be unwarranted and yet where the record of non-compliance is such as to call for more than merely a probationary sentence or a fine. Another option again would be court-ordered adverse publicity, a sanction designed to play on corporate sensitivity about prestige. The less drastic options would include community service orders, probation, fines, civil monetary penalties, damages, injunctions, and informal browbeating and cajoling. This ground has been covered extensively in the literature and we see no point in reploughing the terrain.

The strategy of pyramidal enforcement is consistent with the more central

[15] See further US, Sentencing Commission, *Sentencing Guidelines for Organizational Defendants*; Australia, Law Reform Commission, *Sentencing Penalties*, Discussion Paper No. 30, paras. 283–307; South Australia, Criminal Law and Penal Methods Reform Committee, Fourth Report, *The Substantive Criminal Law*, 357–64; American Bar Association, 3 *Standards for Criminal Justice*, 18.160–85; Geraghty, 'Structural Crime and Institutional Rehabilitation'; Coffee, 'No Soul to Damn No Body to Kick'; Gruner, 'To Let the Punishment Fit the Organization'; Lofquist, 'Organizational Probation and the US Sentencing Commission'.

[16] As evident from the 'death penalty' for banks convicted of money laundering in the US: (1992) 4(1) *Money Laundering Alert*, 1.

desiderata which we have pinned down as critical to the just and effective allocation of responsibility for corporate crime.[17] Pyramidal enforcement gives practical expression to the importance of individual responsibility as a pillar of social control in Western societies (Desideratum 1): accountability agreements, orders, and assurances are vehicles for achieving individual responsibility at the level of internal corporate discipline systems, which are activated by threatening corporations and their officers with escalating sanctions should they fail to ensure that internal discipline takes place. Pyramidal enforcement also reflects the ideal that all who are responsible should be held responsible (Desideratum 3): by inducing internal disciplinary action, it is possible to sheet home responsibility across a much broader front than could ever be achieved by reliance on the criminal justice system alone. Cost-efficiency is a further feature of pyramidal enforcement. Emphasis is placed on stimulating self-regulatory mechanisms for achieving accountability: who would deny that internal investigative and sanctioning mechanisms are less costly to administer than the external criminal law method of dealing with corporate crime?

2 Prosecution guidelines for individual and corporate criminal liability

Consistently with Desideratum 3 (all who are responsible should be held responsible), both individual and corporate criminal liability have major roles under the Accountability Model proposed. That role is specified under published prosecution guidelines. A proposal on the content of these guidelines is discussed in Chapter 6 (Section 6). Here, we will confine ourselves to the function which prosecution guidelines serve under the Accountability Model.

The difficulty that arises in the context of individual criminal liability is deciding when to leave the sanctioning of guilty individual personnel to the private justice systems of organisations. Under the Accountability Model considerable reliance is placed on private justice systems to do the job, but there is a sphere within which individual responsibility is unlikely to be effective unless imposed by way of criminal liability. It is unclear in the abstract what that sphere should be and hence the need for clarification.

One possible approach would be to rely on internal discipline systems in all cases except those where a corporate defendant fails to provide a credible accountability report. Under this approach, an immunity from individual criminal liability would apply if the corporation complied with the accountability assurance or accountability order. We have not adopted that model, partly because of the dangers associated with guaranteed immunities, and partly because privately imposed sanctions may not be serious or public enough to reflect or signify the gravity of the worst forms of individual involvement in corporate crime.

[17] The strategy is also consistent with less central desiderata, including avoidance of the deterrence trap (D 9); heeding motivational complexity (D 10); minimising the risk of cultures of resistance (D 12); reflecting the aims of the criminal justice system (D 13); redundancy (D 16); and taking account of the dynamic nature of corporate behaviour (D 18).

We have followed the more flexible course of developing guidelines for the prosecution of individuals. As explained in Chapter 6, those guidelines deal with a range of cases where (1) private systems of justice break down, and (2) the gravity of the conduct is such as to warrant prosecution. Plainly enough, this focus on individual responsibility at the level of both private justice and criminal liability is impelled by Desideratum 1 (the need to prevent a slide away from individual responsibility in the context of corporate crime). A further underlying concern is Desideratum 6 (those who are responsible for equal wrongs should be treated equally). Our aim in this regard is to try to even up the scales by using corporate disciplinary systems to dispense individual accountability across a far broader range of corporate crime than is currently achieved and at the same time to foster individual criminal liability by reorienting enforcement priorities and by clearly spelling out the situations where individuals should be targeted for prosecution. Another salient feature is the emphasis thereby placed on treating serious corporate offences as serious and avoiding the impression that such offences are permissible provided that one is prepared to pay the price of a fine (see Desideratum 13: criminal liability is not merely a matter of paying a price for crime but has a prohibitory function which is reflected by the denunciatory emphasis of the criminal process).

Corporate criminal liability raises other considerations. Here the difficulty is not so much the adequacy or otherwise of private systems of justice[18] as differentiating between cases that call for civil liability and those that merit criminal liability.

Our solution again is to develop prosecution guidelines rather than to hazard legalistic rules. The approach taken is to pilot corporate liability through civil channels as the normal course and to lay out marker buoys for corporate criminal liability in cases where there is evidence of corporate blameworthiness. Corporate blameworthiness is a key factor in the guidelines, and here the Accountability Model plainly manifests Desideratum 2 (a strategy for allocating responsibility for corporate crime should accept that corporate action is not merely the sum of individual actions and that it can be just and effective to hold corporations responsible as corporations). The guidelines discussed in Chapter 6 reflect the concept of reactive corporate fault, by which is meant a deliberate or negligent corporate failure to comply with a reactive duty to mount an effective program of internal disciplinary action, institutional reform, or compensation. Thus, defendants who fail to comply with an accountability agreement, order or assurance would be prime targets for prosecution. The guidelines also provide for the prosecution of a corporation where the commission of the *actus reus* of the offence was a case where the conduct of the corporation prior to the offence was blameworthy.

---

[18] Although this problem can arise, as in the context of parental discipline of subsidiary corporations.

3 Accountability agreements, orders and assurances

A key element of the Accountability Model is the use made of accountability agreements, orders and assurances. Accountability agreements are akin to deeds of compliance, plea agreements, and consent decrees, but concentrate more specifically and emphatically on bringing relevant actors to account for a corporate offence. Accountability orders or assurances are related to mandatory injunctions or undertakings that are backed by liability for contempt of court; they are also comparable to conditions of corporate probation.[19] Like accountability agreements, they focus on achieving responsibility on the part of all responsible actors within the organisation of a corporate defendant.

This is not to suggest that enforcement agencies or courts should be preoccupied with internal discipline. On the contrary, accountability agreements, orders and assurances can and should also relate to other objectives, including the rectification of defective operating procedures or technologies that have contributed to violation of the law, and the provision of compensation or restitution to victims.[20] There may well be efficiencies in achieving a mixture of aims concurrently and the terms of accountability agreements, orders and assurances can and should be fashioned accordingly. Thus, where a violation of the law is proven for the purpose of obtaining an accountability order, it may often be efficient to use the same proceedings as a platform for awarding damages to persons who have suffered loss as a result of the violation.[21]

Accountability agreements or orders would require that designated persons undertake specified forms of investigative and disciplinary action within a particular time (for example, two months) and then report back to the court which has jurisdiction to enforce the agreement or order.[22] Accountability assurances would provide confirmation of what exactly had been done or, in cases where further action is needed, an undertaking about what is to be done. Those specified in the agreement, order or assurance as responsible for compliance would be under a duty to exercise due diligence and reasonable care to comply with the terms specified.

An accountability agreement or order would require a full investigation into the persons or units involved in the offence together with a report detailing the roles played by the various individuals or units and the exact nature of the disciplinary action taken or proposed against them.[23] The focus of the

---

[19] See further Gruner, 'To Let the Punishment Fit the Organization'.

[20] See further Fisse, 'Reconstructing Corporate Criminal Law', 1205.

[21] See 'Developments in the Law—Corporate Crime', 1311–65.

[22] This is our preferred model given the independence of a court and the power it has to safeguard the interests of employees, for example, and to intervene where improper deals have been negotiated between the enforcement agency and a defendant. A second best solution would be to allow informal deals, as happened in the US SEC voluntary disclosure campaign (see Wolff, 'Voluntary Disclosure Programs').

[23] Internal discipline systems may well be based on a pyramid of enforcement comparable to that recommended above for public systems of justice. The possible range of internal disciplinary sanctions is wide and includes punitive and non-punitive responses; see e.g., Campbell, Fleming and Grote, 'Discipline Without Punishment'. Existing practices may fall well short of a commendable approach; see, e.g., Stewart, 'Workplace Disciplinary Rules and Procedure'.

inquiry would not necessarily be confined to investigative or disciplinary action within the particular defendant's organisation, but could extend to related corporations or to other persons over which the defendant is in a position to exercise influence. It would also be open to a corporate defendant, when reporting upon the acts and events impugned, to document the conduct of other persons or entities whose conduct has contributed to the offence alleged (for example, lawyers who have given incorrect or misleading legal advice,[24] regulatory agencies which have condoned or promoted similar illegal conduct in the past).[25]

The task of conducting the investigative or disciplinary work specified in an agreement or order would be undertaken by the managers and staff of the defendant, with or without the assistance of outside experts such as lawyers or accountants. The report prepared would be filed with the court as a matter of public record. The investigative inquiry required would not be subject to legal professional privilege.[26] The privilege against self-incrimination would remain available to individual personnel, but those relying on this protection would be identified in the report.[27]

The idea of accountability agreements, orders and assurances is thus both straightforward and familiar. Consent orders and plea agreements are prime tools of corporate regulation in the modern world and recognise the necessity and inevitability of negotiated agreements between enforcement agencies and the corporations they police. Mandatory injunctions requiring corporate disciplinary action have also been used on numerous occasions by the US SEC,[28] a practice that heralds a parallel development in the context of corporate probation.[29] Undertakings to a court to comply with some requirement are typical in many regulatory settings, the underlying strategy being one of insistence upon self-regulation without excessive judicial interference in the internal affairs of organisations.

[24] As in *Bigelow v RKP Pictures* (1948) 78 F. Supp. 250, 259; *TPC v Commodore Business Machines Pty Ltd* (1990) ATPR 41-019.

[25] Naturally, however, one would not expect courts to give much weight to the blaming of actors outside the corporation unless a report was prepared by an independent outsider who had given these third parties full opportunity to rebut the allegations against them.

[26] *Osternak Industries, Inc.* (1979) 82 FRD 81; *SEC v Canadian Javelin Ltd.* (1978) 451 F. Supp. 594. Compare with *Diversified Industries Inc. v. Meredith* (1977) 572 F.2d 596, 610; *Upjohn v US* (1981) 449 US 383. See further Mann, *Defending White-Collar Crime*; Friedman, *Securities and Commodities Enforcement*, 56–61; Mathews, 'Internal Corporate Investigations'; Morvillo, 'Voluntary Corporate In-House Investigations'; Block and Barton, 'Internal Corporate Investigations'.

[27] The privilege is available to corporations in England *(Rio Tinto Zinc Corporation v Westinghouse Electric Corporation* [1978] AC 547), but not in the US *(Hale v. Henkel* (1906) 201 US 43). The High Court of Australia left the issue open in *Controlled Consultants Pty Ltd* (1984) 156 CLR 385, but in *Caltex Refining Co P/L v State Pollution Control Commission* (1991) 25 NSWLR 118 the NSW Court of Appeal held that the privilege applied to companies. Compare *N. M. Paterson and Sons Limited* (1980) CR (3d) 164. See further Dan-Cohen, *Rights, Persons, and Organizations*, 114–16; Fiebach, 'The Constitutional Rights of Associations to Assert the Privilege against Self-Incrimination'; Wylie, 'Corporations and the Non-Compellability Right in Criminal Proceedings'.

[28] See Coffee, 'Beyond the Shut-Eyed Sentry'; McCloy, *The Great Oil Spill*.

[29] See Gruner, 'To Let the Punishment Fit the Organization'.

As far as the drafting of accountability agreements, orders or assurances is concerned, a wealth of guidance is available from consent decrees, plea agreements, and injunctions in the past.[30] Readers may also wish to consult the growing literature on the design of probationary terms that require disciplinary action on the part of corporate offenders.[31]

Accountability agreements, orders and assurances respond to many of the desiderata elicited in this study. Accountability agreements, orders or assurances are designed specifically to activate and exploit private systems of justice within corporations and thereby to bring about responsibility on the part of all who are responsible for a corporate offence. They may thus be seen as direct projections of Desideratum 1 (individual responsibility is a pillar of social control in Western societies and should be upheld rather than allowed to wither away), Desideratum 3 (all who are responsible should be held responsible), Desideratum 4 (the maximisation of the allocation of responsibility to all who are responsible should be pursued cost-efficiently), and Desideratum 11 (corporate internal disciplinary systems must be taken seriously as legal orders with realised and unrealised potential for justice and effectiveness). Many other desiderata come into play as well.[32] The advantages of the Accountability Model in these respects are amplified in Chapter 6, where a systematic evaluation of the Model against each desideratum is provided.

4   Threshold requirements for accountability agreements, orders and assurances

Under the Accountability Model we visualise, the range of violations of law for which accountability agreements would be available would be all offences, and all civil violations that are subject to mandatory injunctive remedy or to a significant monetary penalty (say $10,000 or more). Accountability agreements would be negotiated in the context of a violation of law by or on behalf of a corporation where, in the view of the enforcement agency, it was in the public interest to take this route.

Accountability orders, on the other hand, would be available in the following situations:[33]

(1) where it is proved in civil proceedings that a relevant type of violation (see above) was committed by or on behalf of a corporation;

(2) where it is proved in criminal proceedings that an offence was committed by or on behalf of a corporation; or

---

[30] See, e.g., *US v Western Electric Company*, Civil Action No. 82–0192, Civil Enforcement Consent Order (2 Feb. 1989, US District Ct., Washington, DC).

[31] See especially Gruner, 'To Let the Punishment Fit the Organization'.

[32] Accountability agreements or orders can also be deployed and targeted in such a way as to avoid unwanted spillover effects and the deterrent trap (D 8 and 9); to achieve harmony with the varieties of structures, cultures, decisionmaking and accountability principles in large and small organisations (D 14); to foster a dialogue that brings multiple interpretations of responsibility into the open (D 15); to recognise the fact of motivational diversity within organisations (D 10 and 16); to avoid managerial straightjacketing (D 17); and to transcend national borders (D 19).

[33] Compare Fisse, 'Reconstructing Corporate Criminal Law', 1204–5, 1211–13.

(3) where it is proved in criminal proceedings that the *actus reus* of an offence was committed by or on behalf of a corporation.

Before imposing an accountability order, the court would be required to satisfy itself that the parties have had due opportunity to negotiate an accountability agreement. The corporate defendant would also be given the chance to indicate its preferred course of action, as by submitting a compliance plan outlining the disciplinary program that the company proposes to implement. Where a credible compliance plan is submitted, the relevant course would be for the court to accept an accountability *assurance* from the defendant rather than to adopt the more authoritarian stance of making an accountability *order*.

Accountability assurances would also apply where a corporate defendant reports back to a court about what exactly it has done to comply with an accountability agreement or order, or an accountability assurance given earlier. The threshold requirement in this context is that the defendant believes, on reasonable grounds, that it is in a position to certify that it has complied with the terms of the agreement or order.

Procedurally, it is envisaged that accountability orders or assurances would generally involve a two-stage process, with the threshold requirements of wrongdoing in issue at the first stage and the adequacy or otherwise of the accountability report in issue at the second. Where it is necessary at the second stage for a further order or assurance of future action to be given, there would be a third stage at which the issue of compliance with that further order or assurance would be reviewed.

The court before which an accountability report is brought pursuant to an accountability agreement would be empowered to review the adequacy of the terms of the agreement. Where the agreement is too lax, the court would have the power to insist that further action be taken by the defendant. The nature of the further action to be taken would be specified in an assurance given to the court by the defendant or, where the defendant was not prepared to enter into an assurance, in an accountability order made by the court.

The aim behind these suggested thresholds is to provide a broad platform for the operation of accountability agreements, orders and assurances. To take the thresholds applicable to accountability orders, threshold (1) above recognises the practical significance of civil modes of enforcement and would allow accountability orders to be made across a wide front of corporate regulation (compare this with the narrow threshold of criminal liability that governs Coffee's proposal for probationary internal discipline). Under threshold (3) an accountability order may be made upon proof of the *actus reus* of an offence as well as in cases where, as covered by threshold (2), it is possible for the prosecution to prove both the *actus reus* and the guilty mind required for criminal liability.

Clearly, this approach would enable many cases to be taken further rather than dropped for lack of evidence or prohibitive enforcement costs. It may well be easy to prove the *actus reus*, for instance, that pollution escaped from the factory of the defendant, and yet difficult to establish the element of fault required for criminal liability. Equally, however, many investigative headaches will remain problems under the Accountability Model. Thus, in the context of toxic waste dumping, it may be impossible in many instances to establish which of a number of possible firms was responsible.

Also, offences committed on behalf of government organisations are subject to accountability orders even where the organisation enjoys governmental immunity (it is sufficient that an offence, or the *actus reus* of an offence, was committed on behalf of such an organisation); this feature reflects Desideratum 20 (artificial distinctions between public and private sector organisations should be avoided) as well as Desideratum 3.

The use of accountability agreements or assurances rather than judicially imposed accountability orders is encouraged under the model proposed. This approach is based not only on expediency and the principle of least drastic means but also follows the postulate in Desideratum 12 that compliance is more likely to ensue if nurtured in a spirit of co-operation (enforcement policies should avert organised business cultures of resistance). Accountability orders would provide a back-up solution for cases where the usual informal process of negotiation and bargaining breaks down, or is inadequate given the intransigence or recidivism of the defendant. Where accountability orders are used, the same considerations of expediency, least drastic means and co-operative regulation would be relevant, so that the level of court direction of any specific internal affairs of the company would be kept to the minimum.

5   Primary responsibility for compliance with internal accountability
    agreements, orders or assurances

Another central feature of the Accountability Model is the capacity it has to promote responsibility by pin-pointing those who are primarily accountable for ensuring compliance with the terms of accountability agreements, orders or assurances. This feature plainly springs from several of the desiderata we have identified, especially Desideratum 1 (individual responsibility is a pillar of social control) and Desideratum 3 (all who are responsible should be held responsible).

Accountability agreements, orders or assurances can be used to promote the goal of compliance by designating the individuals who are expected to play a leading role in carrying out the disciplinary or remedial action required of a corporation. This approach has often been adopted in injunctions and consent decrees in the US in the past, but the practice is less apparent in other jurisdictions.[34] An accountability order should cast the burden of compliance

---

[34] For example, the Toshiba case, Australia, Trade Practices Commission, *Annual Report 1989–1990*, 40–1, criticised in Fisse, 'Recent Developments in Corporate Criminal Law and Corporate Liability to Monetary Penalties', 33–6. Instead of taking legal action against Toshiba (Australia) Pty Ltd for alleged resale price maintenance (RPM), the Commission negotiated a deed under which the company agreed to undertake a comprehensive three-year program of in-house training in the requirements of the Act. The deed set out strict performance criteria which the training must meet, and provided for Toshiba to meet the cost of the program and the Commission's costs in monitoring its effectiveness over three years. It required Toshiba to offer training to executives, relevant staff and agents. However, there was no specific requirement under the deed that Toshiba's top management be responsible for the

not merely on the company but also on a task force of specified officers and managers.[35]

There are several reasons for designating primary responsibility for compliance in this way. First, the time-frame allows the lines of accountability to be drawn proactively. Enforcement can be structured so that it is possible to know where the main culprits are located should the company fail to comply. The position is quite different where, as is typical under the present law, the enforcement of accountability for corporate crime depends on a reactive attempt to fathom who did what within the organisation. Second, the personnel designated in the terms of the agreement, order or assurance cannot remain faceless or shield behind the cloak of diffused accountability that so often confronts the outside observer of corporate behaviour. Thirdly, the basis of individual liability in the event of non-compliance is not limited to knowledge or other forms of subjective blameworthiness. Rather, those nominated as accountable are under a duty to exercise reasonable care and due diligence to ensure that there is compliance.

6 Supervision and monitoring

In the normal course, accountability agreements, orders or assurances would entrust the task of disciplinary investigation and sanctioning to the corporate defendant and the personnel charged with ensuring compliance. The strategy of the Accountability Model is to appeal in the first instance to the responsibility of a wrongdoer to voluntarily put things right, and to back up that appeal by providing an array of sanctions that can be escalated in the event of non-compliance (the pyramid of enforcement, as discussed in Section 1 above). The tectonic plates of trust and rational self-interest may buckle, however, and where this happens, or is likely to happen, provision needs to be made for more intrusive methods of controlling corporate behaviour. The dynamism of the Accountability Model is to shift our assumptions about corporate offenders from an assumption of trustworthiness, to an assumption of the corporation as a rational cheat which must be deterred, to an assumption that the corporation is an untrustworthy irrational resister to the law which must be incapacitated from further offending.

One conceivable solution where corporations are untrustworthy or resistant to appeals to self-interest is to put resources into the prosecution of the individuals responsible for the offence or for non-compliance with an

---

compliance initiatives required under the agreement. Under cl. 3(iii), responsibility must be nominated for the design and implementation of the compliance program. The person nominated need not be a senior manager and only one person need be specified. The Second Schedule, cl. 3(b), required the compliance program to extend to management, but that is not the same as nominating particular managers as responsible for ensuring that the compliance program is implemented and works effectively.

In the subsequent Solomons Carpets case (see Chapter 7), the Trade Practices Commission remedied a number of the deficiencies identified in this critique. See also the CML case (Chapter 7).

[35] Compare the task force approach often adopted by companies when faced with a crisis; see, e.g., Fisse and Braithwaite, *The Impact of Publicity on Corporate Offenders*, chs 5, 6.

accountability agreement, order or assurance. This will often be impractical, however, and in any event may not be the most efficient or least drastic solution. An alternative is to increase the pressure on a corporate defendant and its officers to undertake a proper disciplinary program. This can be done by supervising and monitoring the response within the organisation. Various possibilities exist. One method is to require an internal monitoring committee, with one or more outside directors,[36] to maintain a regular check and to report back to the court at specified intervals.[37] Another approach is to appoint an officer of the court, at the expense of the corporation, and to equip that officer with appropriate powers of investigation and supervision.[38] These and other techniques for ensuring institutional reform are not uncommon, and indeed may be traced back to the traditional concepts of corporate receivership and sequestration.[39]

7 Scapegoating

Scapegoating, whether by enforcement agencies when selecting targets for prosecution, or by corporations when taking internal disciplinary action, is a perennial problem in the allocation of responsibility for corporate crime. This problem is addressed under the Accountability Model in the following ways.

First, corporate liability is used as a lever to procure an accountability report which sets out internal responsibilities for a given offence. Enforcement agencies equipped with a report of this kind are in a stronger position than otherwise to assess who should or should not be prosecuted.

Second, under the Accountability Model safeguards are provided against scapegoating at the level of corporate internal discipline. The safeguards are essentially these:

(1) pyramidal enforcement where scapegoating or related forms or non-compliance with accountability agreements, orders or assurances result in sanctions which are escalated, if necessary, to a point far beyond the tolerance of rational corporate or managerial self-interest;
(2) judicial scrutiny of corporate action when accountability reports are submitted pursuant to accountability agreements, orders or assurances;
(3) empowerment of employees with a right to complain about scapegoating to a court and, where relevant, to an internal accountability monitoring committee of the corporate defendant;
(4) legal recognition of private systems of justice so as to foster participatory self-determination of issues such as the allocation of responsibility for offences committed on behalf of a corporation; and
(5) minimum procedural protections for individuals exposed to internal disciplinary proceedings.

---

[36] Ayres and Braithwaite, *Responsive Regulation*, ch. 3 (tripartism).
[37] As in, e.g., *US v Western Electric Company*, Civil Action No. 82–0192, Civil Enforcement Consent Order (2 Feb. 1989, US District Ct., Washington, DC).
[38] As under ABA, 3 *Standards for Criminal Justice*, 18.160.
[39] 'Developments in the Law—Injunctions', 1091–3.

There is no entirely satisfactory protection against scapegoating. The modest claim made for the Accountability Model, as explained in Chapter 6, is that it is more likely than other known models of corporate crime enforcement to provide protection where scapegoating the powerless by the powerful is a high risk. Empirical testing of this claim is warranted, a step fostered by the exploratory case studies in Chapter 7.

The Accountability Model Illustrated

The Accountability Model outlined above requires a good deal of further explanation and justification if it is to have any chance of successful implementation. Before embarking on that task in Chapter 6, it may be helpful to provide an illustration of the Accountability Model in practice.

Let us suppose that an illegal act of pollution, an injury through non-compliance with an occupational health and safety law, an antitrust offence, or an understatement of taxable income has occurred at one of the factories of the Sloppysops Corporation. The factory is in Texas, but it is the top management of Sloppysops in New York who are dragged into court. Sloppysops has had civil monetary penalties imposed for previous offences of this type and has not been a very co-operative company. The regulatory agency therefore decides to move up its enforcement pyramid, by-passing the voluntary accountability agreement option, taking the alleged offence to court with an eye to the accountability assurance or order option.

A civil enforcement action is taken against the company. The court finds, on the balance of probability, that the *actus reus* of the offence was perpetrated at the Texas factory, but stops short of inquiring into whether the offence was intentionally or negligently perpetrated, into whether any senior managers at Texas or New York knew of the offence or into who was responsible at any level.

Thus, what might otherwise involve a long criminal trial would initially be dealt with expediently in a civil proceeding; the evidence that a legally prohibited level of pollution was emitted from the Texas factory would be put to the court and the issue whether the *actus reus* had been committed would be determined by the court on the civil standard of proof with the enforcement agency bearing the persuasive burden of proof. Assuming that the *actus reus* was proven against Sloppysops, the judge would then invite the corporation to conduct an internal inquiry into the reasons for the failure of compliance. Should it wish to do so, and on the strength of its investigations and any suggestions made by the court, the company may choose to:

(1) prepare a report on the persons or entities responsible and file that report with the court;
(2) take disciplinary action against those responsible;
(3) voluntarily compensate those who were injured or suffered loss because of the offence; and
(4) commence a program of managerial reform, and revision of policies and procedures so as to guard effectively against repetition of the type of conduct proven against the company; and

(5) commence a program of compliance education within the firm and
    perhaps through the industry association as well.

The court will give Sloppysops a short time to decide whether it wishes to
accept the opportunity to undertake the inquiry and to make a submission on
how long the inquiry would take to complete. If the court is persuaded that the
company's proposed timeframe is genuine and realistic, then it will adjourn
until the agreed date when Sloppysops will bring forward the report on its
work. If the company does not take up the offer to provide an accountability
assurance, or proposes only a perfunctory investigation which does not satisfy
the court, then the enforcement agency will be invited to make a submission
on how long they need to prepare a case for an accountability order against
Sloppysops and/or individual officers within it, and a date will be set for the
resumption of the proceedings against the corporation.

The initial response of the court, though, is not to order the corporation to
conduct the inquiry. Nor is it suggested that the court should instruct the corporation on how to undertake the inquiry, though it might make suggestions
which the corporation would be foolish to ignore if it were keen to persuade
the court. Indeed, the judge might also invite the enforcement agency to make
suggestions, which the defendant would be equally free to take up or ignore.
The assumption underlying this voluntarism is that a self-investigation which
is compelled is less likely to incorporate the thoroughness and commitment to
satisfy the court than is an internal inquiry which is freely chosen, planned
and executed by the corporation. The other assumption is that corporations
will mostly find the offer of self-investigation an attractive one because, while
it will be expensive, the corporation in any case would be spending money on
inquiring internally into what went wrong, and the costs might well be less
than protracted litigation. More importantly, the corporation will usually take
up the offer to enhance its self-image as a responsible corporate citizen and to
present itself to the court, the regulatory authorities and the community as a
responsible self-regulating organisation. Also, the desire to avoid criminal liability by doing the job properly will be a factor, as will the desire to avoid a
poorly conceived court-imposed management restructuring order which might
reduce the productivity of the organisation. There may also be some less principled reasons for co-operating, such as the fear that an extended period of
governmental investigation may unearth other skeletons in the organisation,
or prompt employees to blow the whistle on other matters.

As it neared the completion of its investigation, a prudent Sloppysops
would tell the judge, the prosecutor and the regulatory authority what it had
done so far and whether they had any suggestions for other matters which
should be further pursued internally. On the day the hearing of the case
resumed, it would then be in a position to present an accountability report
which it believed to be acceptable to the court.

The court would review the corporation's accountability report. Depending
on the adequacy or otherwise of the action taken by the corporation, the court
would then:

(1) discharge the defendant; or
(2) ask for a further assurance that additional action be taken; or
(3) make an accountability order requiring further steps to be taken; or

(4) subject the corporation and the personnel specified in the assurance to liability for contempt of court.

A discharge would be appropriate where the accountability report persuasively showed that:

(1) the responsibility lay with a range of individuals and subunits within the Sloppysops organisation and that appropriate disciplinary action had been taken against all parties implicated;

(2) the defective operating procedures and technologies that had contributed to the commission of the *actus reus* of the offence had been reviewed and adequately revised; and

(3) the corporation had been exposed to the adverse publicity of a self-condemnatory report and had voluntarily borne the costs of compensating victims and/or the community.

Even in these circumstances, however, the court would normally order copies of the accountability report, and the court's findings in relation to it, to be sent to a long list of media outlets. This is predicated on the need to communicate an educative and deterrent message to other corporations, and on the empirical evidence that adverse publicity is the stuff of effective informal community control over corporate crime.[40]

If Sloppysops failed to hand up an accountability report or failed to comply with some term in the accountability assurance given to the court, the court could proceed to make an accountability order, with specific provision for supervision and monitoring by an officer of the court at the expense of the company. If breach of the assurance occurred, the corporation would also be liable to punishment for contempt of court. The range of punishments would include a punitive injunction directing that extraordinary action be taken by the company on an emergency basis, and an adverse publicity order requiring that the company's pigheadedness be exposed in the news media. The directors and managers charged in the assurance with responsibility for compliance would also be subject to liability for contempt. The range of sanctions for them would include community service, fines and probation.

In the event that Sloppysops failed to comply with the terms of the accountability order or punitive injunction, it would again be liable for contempt of court. On this occasion, however, the punishment would escalate. Thus, a more intrusive punitive injunction might well be appropriate. For instance, the board of directors could be required to dedicate itself to the task of compliance for a month and to report daily to an officer of the court on the progress being made. In an extreme case, Sloppysops would be sentenced to capital punishment by placing it in liquidation. The directors and staff members nominated in the accountability order or punitive injunction as the individuals responsible for ensuring compliance would also be subject to liability for contempt. Here too the sanctions would escalate, jail being one possibility.

Alternatively, Sloppysops might well provide an exemplary accountability report. Nonetheless, Sloppysops' initial conduct in committing the *actus reus*

---

[40] See Fisse and Braithwaite, *The Impact of Publicity on Corporate Offenders.*

of the offence could have been outrageous. In that case, it could be necessary for stronger deterrent or condemnatory steps to be taken by launching a criminal prosecution against the company and/or particular officers or personnel. The court would have the power to so recommend. In recommending prosecution, the court would be informed by the guidelines on corporate and individual criminal liability published by the prosecutor's office as well as by the information revealed in the accountability report or from questioning conducted during the civil accountability proceedings.

Sloppysops' encounter with the Accountability Model might ultimately lead to the conviction of both the company and its key officers or managers. Such an outcome would depend on whether all of these parties were sufficiently at fault to satisfy the prosecutor's guidelines. In the event of trial, the legal principles applicable would require corporate blameworthiness for corporate criminal liability, and individual blameworthiness for individual criminal liability. If convictions ensued, the pyramid of enforcement would provide an escalated range of sanctions for egregious offences, and a lower range of punishments for less serious offences. Thus, if the offence were monstrous then, assuming that Sloppysops was pervasively infected with the disease of sloppiness and utterly beyond redemption, the sanction would be liquidation. On the other hand, a lesser offence and a greater degree of corporate tractability could well result in a punitive injunction or a term of corporate probation.

To outline how the Accountability Model would work, however, is not to provide justifications for adopting it. To that task we now turn.

6 Assessing the Accountability Model

This chapter takes stock of the Accountability Model by reference to the various desiderata that influence attempts to achieve accountability for corporate crime. We do not contend that the Accountability Model in practice will meet all these desiderata in any case. Indeed, in any particular case trade-offs will have to be made between different desiderata using a framework such as Braithwaite's and Pettit's republican theory of criminal justice, as discussed in Section 5 below. Our contention is that the Accountability Model satisfies more of the desiderata more of the time than current practice or any alternative reform proposal of which we are aware.

We proceed desideratum by desideratum, beginning with the first, which upholds the importance of individual responsibility as a means of social control.

1 Individual Responsibility as a Pillar of Social Control

Desideratum
A strategy for allocating responsibility for corporate crime should reflect the received wisdom that individual responsibility is a pillar of social control in Western societies. The slide away from individual responsibility in our corporate law enforcement must be remedied.

The Accountability Model that we have suggested would be responsive to the problem of non-prosecution of corporate managers which is now pandemic in modern societies. Justice for individuals would be meted out by private justice systems monitored, as a safeguard against inaction or scapegoating, by the public justice system. This may be the most practicable way of imposing responsibility on those individuals who are primarily responsible.

Even though the sanctions available to private justice systems—fines, dismissals, demotions, and shame—may be less potent than some of those available in the public arena,[1] it seems better to have weaker sanctions hitting the

---

[1] But note Braithwaite's argument that shaming by intermediate groups such as corporations and families is a more important crime control weapon than sentences imposed by the state; Braithwaite, *Crime, Shame, and Reintegration*, 54–83.

right targets than stronger weapons pounding those who are easy prey or luckless bystanders. In any case, if one believes that shamings delivered by peer groups are more effective sanctions than formal punishments delivered by the state,[2] then private justice systems might even be seen as providing more potent sanctions.[3]

Using collective liability as a lever for bringing internal accountability out into the open would also be responsive to the second major problem of unaccountability with which this book is concerned—the inability of corporate sanctions, as presently deployed, to provide any real assurance of accountability at the level of internal corporate discipline. The approach suggested is geared to making the corporation itself responsible for investigating and reporting on internal discipline following an offence, and also to enforcing that responsibility. Unlike the inscrutability of fines against companies, a court order requiring internal discipline to be undertaken would expressly communicate the message that it is the responsibility of the corporation to ensure accountability. The strategy here is to rely on the good faith of corporations while at the same time to make it plain that lack of good faith will be severely punished.[4] When the law imposes obligations on corporations, most will feel obliged to comply; the model of the good corporate citizen is not merely an artefact displayed for public relations.[5] If, on the other hand, the law treats corporations as unworthy of any trust, then resentment is inevitable and non-compliance is likely to be a self-fulfilling prophecy.

To the extent that corporations have capacities both to identify clearly who is responsible for internal purposes, and to create a smokescreen of confused responsibility for external purposes, a strategy which compels the corporation rather than the court to do the internal sanctioning will have merit. To the extent that we change the incentives for the corporation from an interest in covering up to incentives to open up, crime control will be enhanced.

We are not advocating the abandonment of criminal prosecution of individuals responsible for corporate crime. In Section 6 (equal application of

---

[2] As Tittle concluded from his major empirical work on deterrence: 'to the extent that individuals are deterred from deviance by fear, the fear that is relevant is most likely to be that their deviance will evoke some respect or status loss among acquaintances or in the community as a whole' (Tittle, *Sanctions and Social Deviance*, 198). Beyond this study, the perceptual deterrence literature generally demonstrates a much stronger effect of informal sanctions on deviance than formal legal sanctions. See Akers et al., 'Social Learning and Deviant Behavior'; Anderson, Chiricos and Waldo, 'Formal and Informal Sanctions'; Kraut, 'Deterrent and Definitional Influences on Shoplifting'; Meier and Johnson, 'Deterrence as Social Control'; Jensen and Erickson, 'The Social Meaning of Sanctions'; Burkett and Jensen, 'Conventional Ties, Peer Influence and the Fear of Apprehension'; Meier, 'Jurisdictional Differences in Deterring Marijuana Use'; Paternoster and Iovanni, 'The Deterrent Effect of Perceived Severity'; Paternoster et al., 'Estimating Perceptual Stability and Deterrent Effects'; Paternoster et al., 'Perceived Risk and Social Control'; Williams, 'Deterrence and Social Control'; Bishop, 'Legal and Extralegal Barriers to Delinquency'.
[3] See Braithwaite, *Crime, Shame, and Reintegration*, 69–82.
[4] For a formal defence of this strategy, see Scholz, 'Cooperation, Deterrence, and the Ecology of Regulatory Enforcement'.
[5] See further Kagan and Scholz, 'The "Criminology of the Corporation" and Regulatory Enforcement Strategies', 74–9 (regulatory model of the corporation as citizen).

law), we will discuss guidelines as to the circumstances where state prosecutions of individuals should be launched. Ironically, it is conceivable that the capacity for the Accountability Model to expose the skeletons concealed in individual closets would mean not only more individual sanctioning through the medium of internal discipline systems but also conceivably more prosecutions of individuals under the restrictive guidelines we propose in Section 6. If we can succeed in transforming internal corporate resistance to state investigation by leveraging support for the state justice system from private justice systems, the result will be a sea change in the extent to which guilty individuals are subjected to public and private sanctions.

An objection should be anticipated. It is that reliance on internal discipline systems is no guarantee that those systems will in fact be used by corporate defendants in such a way as to deliver individual accountability. The sceptical will object that, whatever the possible theoretical appeal of the Accountability Model, in practice it amounts to leaving the fox in charge of the chicken coop. Worse, it will encourage corporate foxes to use their well-developed cover-up skills.

While there is always a risk of corporate deviousness, a number of major steps can be taken to minimise the risk. The first is to provide an array of sanctions that offer a powerful disincentive against corporate non-compliance with the terms of an internal discipline order. The second is to designate individual representatives of the company as parties responsible for complying with the terms of the internal discipline order. The third is to provide mechanisms for monitoring compliance, again as part of the order that requires internal disciplinary action to be taken.

The Accountability Model outlined in Chapter 5 makes it clear that a corporation that fails to undertake internal disciplinary action faces an array of sanctions (including punitive injunctions and adverse publicity orders) that can be escalated, if necessary, to the extent of imposing corporate capital punishment. This approach is a far cry from the present position under many regimes of corporate regulation, which lack a cogent pyramid of enforcement. Given the pyramid of enforcement proposed under the Model, it is not in the rational self-interest of corporations to feign compliance because the risks on the downside can be raised to a progressively intolerable level. If the corporate fox is a game theoretic animal, then the chickens will be preserved and warmed to their responsibilities, with only the irresponsible stragglers subject to prey. If the corporate fox is irrational or demented, then it will be placed in captivity or even exterminated.

A second important safeguard is the technique of pin-pointing senior as well as middle managers as responsible for ensuring compliance with the internal disciplinary program proposed. The aim is to make it quite clear that heads will roll in the event of non-compliance, and to facilitate the task of prosecution for contempt should that step be necessary. Empirical research has confirmed the importance of the attitude of top management toward compliance efforts.[6] In light of this research, a good approach might be to insist on

⁶ Clinard, *Corporate Ethics and Crime*; Braithwaite, 'Taking Responsibility Seriously'.

a task force comprised of designated representatives from senior and middle management to be responsible for assuring implementation of the remedial and disciplinary program. The use of a managerial task force for dealing with crises is not uncommon as a matter of self-regulation, one example being the 30-strong task force deployed by Ford in response to the emissions-testing fraud that occurred in 1971–72.[7]

A third safeguard, as canvassed in Chapter 5, is to equip courts with the power to insist upon monitoring and supervisory controls where necessary to deal with untrustworthy defendants. There are various possibilities, ranging from internal monitoring committees[8] to receivership, with the costs in all cases to be met by the corporation.[9] The underlying strategy is to exploit the spirit of voluntary co-operation within corporations, but to escalate the degree of intervention in a manner commensurate with any given level or type of intransigence. Thus, the more the level of intransigence, the greater the degree of interference, and the higher the consequential cost of compliance to the corporation. There will always be corporations that fail to respond to incentives of this kind, but under the pyramid of enforcement contemplated by the Accountability Model they face extinction through corporate capital punishment. Moreover, the corporation's directors and managers will have selected themselves as prime candidates for prison.

Notwithstanding these safeguards, it may be argued that corporations and their executives will be disinclined to comply because, if they do comply, they may be in breach of the terms of an insurance policy which covers them against civil liability. Disclosing the circumstances surrounding an offence and the role of those personnel who were implicated in it could easily amount to an admission of liability. Insurance policies typically provide that liability is not to be admitted without the prior consent of the insurance company, and an insurance company may be unwilling to give consent, at least where the exposure is large. Any such contractual term of insurance is overridden by a statutory or judicially imposed obligation which requires the insured to furnish information, even full information, about an alleged offence. Nonetheless, the Accountability Model fosters accountability agreements which are entered into voluntarily rather than as a matter of legal obligation. Where an insurance company refuses to consent to a corporation or its executives admitting liability in the context of an accountability agreement, an enforcement agency may thus be left with no choice but to formalise proceedings and thereby enable that constraint to be overridden. The main concern here is that responsibility for corporate offences and liability to compensate for resulting harms be governed by the public interest rather than by the self-interest of

---

[7] See Fisse and Braithwaite, *The Impact of Publicity on Corporate Offenders*, ch. 4.
[8] See further Gruner, 'To Let the Punishment Fit the Organization'.
[9] On institutional reform and judicial administration, see Chayes, 'The Role of the Judge in Public Law Litigation'; Brakel, 'Special Masters in Institutional Litigation'; Roach, 'The Limits of Corrective Justice and the Potential of Equity in Constitutional Remedies'; Schwartz, *Swann's Way*; Yarbrough, *Judge Frank Johnson and Human Rights in Alabama*. The Accountability Model seeks to minimise these difficulties by means of a pyramid of enforcement under which court supervision is threatened if necessary but rarely needs to be invoked.

insurance companies. The Accountability Model offers an incentive system where leverage is exerted on corporations to internalise the costs of harms they cause and where the price of insurance is left to be adjusted accordingly. Corporations or officers with an unsatisfactory record may face higher premiums. In setting rates, insurers may well need to become more active in checking the internal controls of the companies whose risks they assume; they can be expected to act as gatekeepers—no more, no less.

2 Recognition of Corporate Responsibility

Desideratum
A strategy for allocating responsibility for corporate crime should also accept that corporate action is not merely the sum of individual actions and that it can be just and effective to hold corporations responsible as corporations.

The Accountability Model gives a prominent role to corporate as well as individual responsibility. Corporate criminal liability is one of the main planks in the structure of legal liability envisaged. The concept of corporate blameworthiness, in the sense of corporate intentionality and negligence, is explicitly recognised. These matters have already been discussed in some detail. However, further clarification is required as to the circumstances where corporate criminal liability would be warranted under the Accountability Model. The most critical point is that corporate criminal responsibility can be imposed on two bases: first, initial fault, and second, reactive fault.

Situations can arise where a corporation is palpably at fault at or before the time when the *actus reus* of an offence is committed. Thus, Essence Corp may formulate a policy of non-compliance with a requirement imposed under antipollution or antitrust criminal law, as where the directors decide that the fines imposed for a violation are likely to fall well short of the savings from non-compliance. Alternatively, it may be the case that the corporation has behaved in a grossly negligent way, as by failing to heed complaints about similar violations in the past, or clear warnings that its operating systems were inadequate. Where there is sufficient evidence against a corporation of initial fault in the sense indicated, then the Accountability Model holds that liability should be imposed on that basis.

More typically, there will be insufficient evidence of initial corporate fault but ample evidence that the *actus reus* has been committed on behalf of the corporation. The Accountability Model recognises this fact of corporate regulation by providing a structure that allows corporate criminal liability to be imposed on the basis of reactive fault. The broader timeframe is more realistic because it takes into account everyday notions of corporate responsibility for what corporations do, or fail to do, after their activities lead to injury or harm. If a company sets in train an industrial process which exposes workers to asbestos or even intends to operate the process so that it sprays asbestos over workers, the company is not culpable unless it knew or should have known the risks involved. But if the company later found out the risks and failed to take corrective action, then plainly it is culpable given its reactive fault.

Under the Accountability Model, the corporation may be held responsible for the *actus reus* of the offence and then required to conduct a rigorous self-investigation which may lead to individual discipline, remediation of defective SOPs, compensation to victims, or other relevant responses. If the remedial and disciplinary measures documented in the self-investigation report are insufficient and inexcusable, then the court can proceed to criminal conviction and sentencing of the corporation. Corporate criminal sanctions should be imposed when the publicising of the self-investigation report, and the disciplinary, diagnostic, reformative and compensatory measures taken pursuant to it are insufficient to signify and expiate the level of responsibility that the corporation has as a corporation for the offence.

It is important, however, not to take an excessively legalistic or punishment-oriented view of corporate responsibility in the reactive framework contemplated under the Accountability Model. The publication by the court of the self-investigation report can itself provide a powerful form of corporate reprobation. On the other hand, if the corporation reacts to its offence with such exemplary remedial measures that it actually attracts more positive than negative publicity through the report, then so much the better. Both the negative and positive aspects of the publicity are warranted respectively by the irresponsibility and the responsibility that the corporation has shown.

These conceptions of corporate responsibility are latent in the present law in many jurisdictions, but have yet to be crystallised in the form laid out by the Accountability Model. Thus, existing concepts of personal and vicarious corporate responsibility represent rough and ready stages toward the development of concepts of corporate fault that more adequately reflect the foundational principle that corporate criminal responsibility should be predicated on corporate blameworthiness as compared with merely the fault of some individual representative. Likewise, the increasing attention paid to internal discipline and institutional reform in the context of corporate sentencing heralds the emergence of reactive corporate fault as a basis of corporate criminal liability. In Section 18 of this chapter, we have more to say on how corporate criminal responsibility should be tied not only to fault associated with the initial offence but also to reactive fault.

3 Imposing Responsibility on All Responsible Actors

Desideratum
A strategy for allocating responsibility for corporate crime should seek to maximise the allocation of responsibility to all who are responsible, be they individuals, subunits of corporations, corporations, parent corporations, industry associations, gatekeepers such as accountants and indeed regulatory agencies themselves. All responsible should be held responsible.

The Accountability Model reflects the desideratum, derived from the arguments in Chapters 2 and 3, that all who are responsible should be held responsible. The greatest strength of the Model is that it involves a practical strategy for implementing this ideal.

The Model accepts that individuals have individual responsibilities for corporate crime and collectivities have collective responsibilities for corporate crime. Collective responsibilities are imposed by means of corporate liability through public enforcement action. Individual responsibility is achieved mostly through private justice systems, with guidelines for special cases where public prosecutions of individuals are warranted.[10] Collectivities within the corporation would also be sanctioned by its private justice system. The capacity for private justice systems to bring to bear a wide variety of organisationally potent sanctions against subunits like research teams, divisions and sections is a major strength of the Model. The animating point here is that the public criminal justice system has found it impossible to provide suitable methods for dealing with subunit responsibility. Fining all individuals in the subunit would be an extreme or unworkable solution,[11] and collective subunit fines would merely be debited against the profit and loss account of the entire corporation.

The dual corporate and individual focus of the Accountability Model should not be taken to exclude simple individualism or simple corporate responsibility in business regulation. As explained below, situations will occur where the appropriate form of accountability is individual responsibility or corporate responsibility alone.

Where a small business which conforms to Mintzberg's Simple Structure[12] breaks the law as a result of a direct decision of its chief executive, and where that person rather than other shareholders is the primary beneficiary of the offence, there is clearly a case for prosecuting the chief executive and taking no action against the corporation. Where the corporate veil is used as a device to protect an individual criminal mastermind who tightly holds the corporation, it is that individual who is the appropriate subject of criminal liability.[13] Where corporations are bankrupted, individual liability for executives and directors responsible for the bankruptcy should and must be the objective.

Where a corporate offence is of a relatively minor nature involving low level penalties, simple collectivism is defensible. If an insurance company lodges a financial statement with the Insurance Commissioner a month late, fining the corporation might be desirable, but the costs of the state pursuing

---

[10] It is taken as axiomatic that indemnification of individual criminal liability is prohibited in law; see Bucy, 'Indemnification of Corporate Executives Who Have Been Convicted of Crimes'. It is also assumed that sanctions against individual offenders should be imposed in such a way as to minimise the risk of unlawful indemnification in practice (e.g., by means of community service orders, not fines).

[11] Pepinsky has considered the imposition of a fine for corporate crime consisting of a proportion of the salary of each employee, though he ultimately rejected it; Pepinsky, *Crime and Conflict*, 139.

[12] Mintzberg, *The Structuring of Organizations*, 305–13.

[13] See Freiberg, 'Abuse of the Corporate Form'.

the individuals who may have failed in their responsibilities within the corporation would be a waste of taxpayers' money. However, in major cases involving multiple actors in complex organisations—the cases which are the real challenge confronting corporate criminal law—neither simple individualism nor simple collectivism is likely to be adequate: organisational complexity compounds the problem of allocating responsibility and necessitates a dual individual/collective approach.

A further major dimension of the Accountability Model is the inclusion of parent–subsidiary relationships within the framework of responsibility. Where the indictment is against a subsidiary corporation, there may well be a need to consider the responsibility of the parent as well as that of the subsidiary.[14] It is notorious that offences by subsidiaries often occur against a background of parental connivance or pressure where the attitudes of those at group headquarters may permeate a whole string of subsidiary companies. As a general rule, parent corporations are not criminally or civilly liable for the conduct of their subsidiaries.[15] Only in exceptional cases will it be possible to establish liability against the parent, as where there is documentary evidence that the conduct of the subsidiary was expressly authorised by the parent's board of directors.[16] This is recognised under the Accountability Model, which fosters internal disciplinary inquiries into the part played by the parent corporation in the events leading to an offence by a subsidiary.[17] Thus, the court before which a subsidiary is charged with an offence would be able to urge the subsidiary voluntarily to include an analysis of the role of its parent company in its self-investigation and action report, and an account of the steps taken by the parent to take appropriate disciplinary and other action. Parental fault and subsidiary diligence in convincing the parent to make good its fault can then be allowed to mitigate subsidiary fault.

The Accountability Model can also take account of the contribution made to an offence by actors external to the corporation. A criminal trial is limited to the narrow issue of the guilt of those charged. In contrast, the internal investigation and action report involves a wider-ranging inquiry into what went wrong and what can be done to prevent it happening again. The dramaturgical model discussed in Chapter 4 indicated that the persons responsible for a play may be not only actors, directors, scriptwriters and producers;

---

[14] See Fisse, 'Sanctioning Multinational Offenders'; Blum, *Offshore Haven Banks, Trusts and Companies*; Osunbor, 'The Agent-Only Subsidiary Company and the Control of Multinational Groups'.

[15] Collins, 'Ascription of Legal Responsibility to Groups in Complex Patterns of Economic Integration'.

[16] Partly for this reason, the modern trend is toward group liability; see Blumberg and Strasser, *The Law of Corporate Groups*, ch. 1; Finzen and Walburn, 'Union Carbide Corporation's Liability for the Bhopal Disaster'; Walde, 'Parent–Subsidiary Relations in the Integrated Corporate System'.

[17] Another approach would be to pierce the corporate veil and to make a parent corporation liable for the *actus reus* of an offence committed by a subsidiary and then force the parent to use the internal disciplinary mechanism of the group. If the parent were liable for the *actus reus* in this way, then it would be subject to the jurisdiction of the courts where the *actus reus* occurred.

responsibility may also lie with critics and the audience. Likewise, a self-investigation report may reveal that a corporate offence was partly the result of external forces. Thus, it may emerge that the reason why a corporation committed manslaughter was that they consulted with a government regulatory official who advised that their course of action was safe. In the *Exxon Valdez* oil spill, for example, the US National Transportation Safety Board found that inadequate traffic control by the Coast Guard contributed to the spill.[18] Another possibility is that the report may reveal some responsibility on the part of a major customer which insisted that unless the corporation supplied a cheaper but less safe product they would put them out of business by going to another supplier.

The advantage of the self-investigation and action report process in this context is that it holds out some prospect of effecting informal social control against external actors who bear some responsibility (not necessarily criminal responsibility). Where the court is satisfied as to the accuracy of the assessment made in the self-investigation and action report (which may require the involvement of an outside counsel of impeccable integrity), it can order that the corporation send a copy of the report with an attached press release approved by the court to an agreed list of media outlets. The publicity thereby generated will mostly be damaging to the corporation, but it will also bring these outside organisations into the debate over their responsibility for what went wrong. Public criticism is, after all, the stuff of effective informal social control, as well as being at the heart of democratic, participatory problem-solving.

Finally, the Accountability Model further exploits the power of publicity and open public debate by using these forces of social control against gate-keepers. Sometimes gatekeepers will be partially under the effective control of the organisation conducting the self-investigation. Thus, the organisation can suggest to its accounting firm that, unless a certain culpable employee of the accounting firm is disciplined, it will lose a valued client. The organisation can suggest to a consumer group that nominates members of a consumer council (as, for example, in the case of Australia's Telecom and British Telecom as it formerly was) that members of that council who failed to perform their gatekeeping role are no longer acceptable to the organisation. This applies similarly to culpable lawyers, insolvency practitioners, contract toxicology laboratories and others employed from outside as gatekeepers. In cases where gatekeepers are beyond any direct control of the defendant corporation, then the appropriate mechanism under the Accountability Model is public identification of their culpability in the self-investigation report, and referral of the report to the relevant licensing authorities (for example, the medical licensing board where the gatekeeper is a consultant medical practitioner).

The risk, of course, is that the defendant corporation will seek to pass the buck to outsiders. We will return to the general issue of scapegoating below in

---

[18] *Chicago Tribune*, 14 July 1991, Section 1, 14.

Section 7. But some comment is in order about the danger of this special form of buck-passing and obfuscation of corporate blame. First, even if the court mistakenly accepts the fault of an innocent outsider, the court may still be deeply unimpressed by the reactive responsibility of a firm that uses this excuse. Second, the innocent outsider may persuade the court that it has been scapegoated by the defendant corporation, with even more disastrous consequences for the view taken by the court of the firm's reactive fault. Third, the innocent outsider may sue the defendant firm for defamation. Fourth, as we argue in Section 7, a defendant who makes deliberately misleading statements about the culpability of an outsider in a self-investigation report will be liable for perjury.

4 Cost-Efficiency

Desideratum
The maximisation of the allocation of responsibility to all who are responsible should be pursued cost-efficiently, and in a way that does not place unrealistic burdens either on corporations or on the public purse.

The Accountability Model proposed would not be at all cost-efficient for minor corporate offences or cases of simple individual culpability by the owners of tightly held or bankrupt corporations. We have already pointed out that in cases of the former type (for example, failure to lodge timely tax returns) the immediate imposition of a corporate fine or penalty makes sense and that individual liability alone is the appropriate response in cases of the latter kind.

The most costly investigations are those where:
(1) the harm associated with the offence is great;
(2) the offence is by or through a large and complex organisation; and
(3) there are multiple actors who bear responsibility for the offence.
This is where the Accountability Model comes into its own. In such cases, the traditional criminal enforcement model results in millions of dollars being spent by all sides in games of legal cat and mouse. The cost savings from the Accountability Model can be enormous for all parties involved.

For the state, the necessity to mount expensive raids on the premises of the organisations to seize truckloads of suspect documents may be obviated. Instead, it is the firm which is given the job of combing through the files (something it knows about and is therefore better equipped to do at low cost). Similarly this is the case with interrogatories, collecting forensic evidence, following paper trails through complex chains of corporate structures, conducting engineering tests, and the like. The state shifts a lot of its enforcement costs onto the firm (the corporation is required to bear the investigative costs; where outside counsel or other consultants are employed, their costs would also be met by the corporation). There is an economic efficiency rationale for making firms bear the costs of their externalities.[19] Moreover, our contention

---

[19] See generally Staaf and Tannian, *Externalities*; Mishan, *The Costs of Economic Growth*.

is that internal investigations collect the same information more cheaply than external investigations because the former occur in a context of voluntary co-operation rather than resistance and because insiders have the local knowledge to quickly sniff out the buried bodies.

The result is a major saving in state investigation costs, which means that the state can investigate more cases of known or suspected corporate crime than the small minority of such cases that are seriously investigated at present. The superior cost-effectiveness of voluntary self-investigations over resisted external investigations also produces a reduction in total investigation costs.

The effect on the corporate side is a major shift of resources from defensive litigation to actually solving the problem.[20] Instead of company lawyers burning the midnight oil briefing executives on how to give evasive answers, on legal delaying tactics, on manipulating legal professional privilege to obstruct state access to critical documentary evidence, or at worst, in organising the shredding of critical evidence, company lawyers are put to work on diagnosing exactly where the system broke down and on designing educational programs and improving procedural controls. Another possible effect is that resources otherwise spent on litigation will be used for voluntary compensation payments to victims. To the extent this happens, the economy is less subject to wasteful diversions of expertise, the lot of victims is eased, and the firm is better for having salvaged some goodwill from its consumers by using its scarce resources to compensate them voluntarily rather than to fight them in court.

State investigation costs are important, because they are the fundamental reason why regulatory agencies typically settle for corporate convictions, leaving individual liability in the too-hard basket. Consider the IBM antitrust case in the US. After 13 years of investigation, and five years of pre-trial discovery, the US Justice Department dropped its case against IBM and never got close to indicting any individual IBM employee. Ironically, the case ran for so long that by the end of the saga the problem had solved itself with the emergence of the Japanese computing giants and new American competitors such as Apple. How much better might it have been to have employed an enforced self-investigation and reform strategy that could have been in place to prevent IBM monopolisation during the 13 years when this monopoly power mattered? Imagine the antitrust litigation resources that could have been redeployed onto other cases. Imagine the savings to IBM. We do not know exactly how much IBM spent on legal defence during these years, but it certainly ran to an eight-figure sum.[21] IBM Chairman Frank Cary used to joke: 'Nick Katzenbach [the former Attorney General brought over as IBM general counsel] is the only guy at IBM with an unlimited budget ... and he always exceeds it'.[22] When we visited IBM headquarters during the pre-trial years,

[20] Where the costs of pursuing an investigation would be very high (e.g., pursuing records back over 20 years), then allowance can be made for that at the level of directions by court when ordering internal discipline or in working out what is a reasonable excuse for non-compliance with an internal discipline order.

[21] Fisse and Braithwaite, *The Impact of Publicity on Corporate Offenders*, 203.

[22] *Newsweek*, 24 August 1981, 45.

there was one facility in which 94 million documents relevant to the Justice Department suit were stored. The information management costs alone on both sides of this gladiatorial contest were enormous—and to what end?

The axe the US Attorney General could have credibly held over IBM's head was either a court case to break up IBM or a plea to Congress for legislative action to do so. In the shadow of this axe, there might have been:

(1) credible self-investigation of IBM's predatory practices;
(2) undertakings to desist from them and discipline the executives responsible for them;
(3) undertakings to eschew takeovers of specified types of competitors;
(4) voluntary compensation payments to competitors who were victims of its predatory practices and who remained viable competitors;
(5) undertakings to step up its internal education and disciplinary practices on antitrust compliance; and
(6) limited voluntary divestitures.[23]

Such a self-investigation and settlement with IBM in the 1960s might have given America a more competitive, cost-efficient computer industry during the lost 13 years of litigation, and it might have taken the US into the 1980s with both a larger stable of vigorous competitors to join IBM in taking on the Japanese and European computer firms and a leaner, more competitive IBM.[24] Instead, the US entered the 1980s with a computer industry that could still fairly be described as 'Snow White and the seven dwarfs'.[25]

5 Safeguarding Individual Interests

Desideratum
The maximisation of the allocation of responsibility to all who are responsible should be pursued justly in such a way as to safeguard the interests of individuals. Rights of suspects must be respected. Procedural justice must not be sacrificed on the altar of substantive justice.

The Accountability Model catalyses corporate justice systems so as to cause private justice systems to impose sanctions on individuals in a way that is beyond the grasp of state justice. As we have seen, this strategy offers considerable advantages, including the cost-efficiency considerations canvassed above. However, it would also privatise some sanctioning that presently occurs in the public sector. This is cause for concern. The state justice system provides a wide panoply of rights and due process safeguards that are not generally required in the private sector. Accordingly, there is a real worry that privatisation of criminal justice will undermine civil liberties.[26]

---

[23] Note that the Justice Department litigation was totally devoid of impacts on all these fronts. See Waldman, 'Economic Benefits in the IBM, AT&T, and Xerox Cases'.
[24] For the theory behind such an expectation, see Porter, *The Competitive Advantage of Nations*.
[25] Martin, 'The Computer Industry', 291.
[26] See generally Matthews, *Privatizing Criminal Justice*.

Little comfort can be taken from the possible reply that private corporations do not have the awesome power of the state. Like Ian Eagles,[27] we wonder if it might be an 'elegant and comforting legal conceit that limited liability companies are but citizens writ large, and not the state writ small, which empirical observation would tend to suggest'.[28] Corporate justice systems[29] already handle a massive volume of informal adjudication of criminal allegations, particularly in the domain of employee theft, and the adequacy or otherwise of the procedural protections now provided are open to serious question. By highlighting this concern, the Accountability Model may well stimulate inquiry into protections for defendants across the whole gamut of private corporate discipline.

It should be made clear from the outset that it is misleading to regard private discipline as 'second class justice' in contrast to the 'first class justice' administered by the state.[30] Stuart Henry's[31] study of disciplinary proceedings in the private sector revealed that some employees felt that they received fairer dealing from the company than from the state. In the words of one interviewee:

> It's better than prosecution in a court. The management consider your work record, how long you've been here, or if you might have done it before. In court they've got too much to do to consider all that. They just take you as another case. In the joint [internal disciplinary] tribunal you don't know what sentence you're going to get, but the chances are it will be considered fairly.[32]

Henry found evidence of employees viewing company justice as more individualised, and therefore fairer than court-administered justice, and more contextualised within an understanding of the world and of the accepted rules of the game within the company. This finding is consistent with a growing literature showing more generally that citizens who experience informal justice—court-annexed arbitration, plea bargaining and mediation—are more likely to come away with a perception that they have been treated fairly than are citizens who have been dealt with by a court.[33]

It may thus be accepted that corporate justice is more able to get to the bottom of what really happened, to reflect the culture of the organisation, and to be perceived as fair by those subjected to investigation or sanctions. However, we can hardly ignore the fact that private justice systems have

---

[27] See case-note, *Finnegan v New Zealand Rugby Union* (1985) 2 *New Zealand Universities Law Review*, 159, 181, 190.

[28] Eagles, 'Public Law and Private Corporations'.

[29] See the essays in Shearing and Stenning, *Private Policing*. Also Shearing and Stenning, 'Modern Private Security'.

[30] On the defence of adjudication in state courts and the need to avert 'second class' informal justice, see Alschuler, 'Mediation with a Mugger'; Fiss, 'Against Settlement'.

[31] Henry, *Private Justice*.

[32] Ibid., 146. See also Felstiner and Drew, *European Alternatives to Criminal Trials and Their Applicability in the United States*, 35–7; Findlay and Zvekic, *Analysing (In)Formal Mechanisms of Crime Control*, 145–77.

[33] See the review in Lind and Tyler, *The Social Psychology of Procedural Justice*.

weaker safeguards of procedural fairness. Superior fairness on average may be accompanied by outrageous instances of procedural unfairness at the extremes, abuses that would never be allowed to occur in the state justice system. So we require a theory of due process for private justice to constitutionalise it, and to guarantee rights within it.

There has been a substantial movement in all Western democracies toward legislating rights for employees in disciplinary proceedings which may lead to the termination of employment.[34] In the US, a laggard nation in moving on such reform, there nevertheless was a sharp increase in wrongful discharge litigation during the 1980s.[35] In 1966, the International Labour Organization adopted recommended standards for all affiliated nations. These standards include the right of employees to be given reasons for termination, to state their case, to be represented, and to appeal.[36]

This is not the place for a systematic treatment of the rights that employees should enjoy in disciplinary proceedings.[37] However, we cannot sensibly advocate a privatising of justice without at least suggesting the need for and the shape of a theory of due process in corporate justice.

An immediate and perhaps self-evident point is that there can be no automatic transplantation of state criminal justice rights into private disciplinary arenas. State criminal proceedings have the power to deprive citizens of their life and liberty; private justice systems do not. Many of the procedural protections in the criminal justice system have been defended by the courts on the

---

[34] By 1962, an International Labour Organization study found that 76 nations had some form or another of national regulation of the termination of the employment relationship at the initiative of the employer. International Labour Organization, 'Termination of Employment (Dismissal and Lay Off)'. For a recent example of increased procedural rights for workers, as advanced by a conservative government, see Industrial Arbitration (Unfair Dismissal) Amendment Act 1991 (NSW).

[35] The number of wrongful termination court filings in the Los Angeles Superior Court increased from 15 in March–April 1980 to over 100 in the same period in 1986. See Dertouzos, Holland and Ebener, *Introduction to the Legal and Economic Consequences of Wrongful Termination.* See also Westin, 'Employer Responses to New Judicial Rulings on At-Will Employment'.

[36] International Labour Organization, *Conventions and Recommendations 1919–1966*, 1060–1, Recommendation No. 119, 'Recommendation Concerning Termination of Employment at the Inititiative of the Employer'. See also Weyland, 'Present Status of Individual Employee Rights'.

[37] The literature on this question is vast. See Collins, *Justice in Dismissal*; McCulloch, *Termination of Employment*; McCarry, *Aspects of Public Sector Employment Law*; Stewart, 'Employment Protection in Australia'; Summers, 'Individual Rights in Collective Agreements and Arbitration'; Fleming, 'Some Problems of Due Process and Fair Procedure in Labor Arbitration'; Comment, 'Industrial Due Process and Just Cause for Discipline'; Silard, 'Rights of the Accused Employee in Company Disciplinary Investigations'; Jones, 'Evidentiary Concepts in Labor Arbitration'; Edwards, 'Due Process Considerations in Labor Arbitration'; Blades, 'Employment at Will vs. Individual Freedom'; Blumrosen, 'Legal Protection for Critical Job Interests'; Kanski, 'Employee Drug Testing'; Silver, 'Rights of Individual Employees in the Arbitral Process'; Spelfogel, 'Surveillance and Interrogation in Plant Theft and Discipline Cases'; M. Stone, 'Due Process in Labor Arbitration'; Burkey, 'Employee Surveillance'; Barbash, 'Due Process and Individual Rights in Arbitration'; Weyland, 'Present Status of Individual Employee Rights'; Craver, 'The Inquisitorial Process in Private Employment'; Carlson and Phillips, 'Due Process Considerations in Grievance Arbitration Proceedings'.

grounds of the potentially severe sanctions available to the state.[38] On the other hand, there may be contexts where the corporation wields more power than the state. Surveillance is one possible example. It may be easy for an employer to monitor every move or conversation of an employee, whether in the office, in the toilet, or on the telephone.[39] The state, in contrast, is likely to have much more difficulty in getting the same level or extent of access.

However, the employer does have investigative needs that transcend the interest of the state in punishing the guilty.[40] A right to silence is not defensible for an employee who is alleged by management to have sabotaged machinery. The company must be able to demand answers to questions about where the spanners had been put in the works (on pain of dismissal for noncompliance) so that it can get the machine going again and protect the safety of others. The employer, unlike the state, is properly a holder of rights. So in the sanctioning of employees by employers there are issues of balancing the rights of the latter against those of the former which do not arise when the state sanctions.

There is now an extensive literature on various employee rights in the context of employee discipline.[41] The more important rights that have been discussed are these: to remain silent,[42] to refuse drug tests,[43] to refuse lie-detector tests,[44] to refuse search or seizure,[45] to protection from electronic eavesdropping,[46] to notice of an investigation,[47] to a hearing,[48] to an unbiased tribunal,[49]

---

[38] See Packer, *The Limits of the Criminal Sanction*, 131.

[39] See Marx, 'The Interweaving of Public and Private Police in Undercover Work'; Marx, *Undercover*.

[40] Craver, 'The Inquisitorial Process in Private Employment'; Silard, 'Rights of the Accused Employee...'. See also Abrams and Nolan, 'Toward a Theory of "Just Cause" in Employee Discipline Cases'.

[41] Seminal contributions include Craver, 'The Inquisitorial Process in Private Employment'; Westin and Salisbury, *Individual Rights in the Corporation*.

[42] Carlson and Phillips, 'Due Process Considerations in Grievance Arbitration Proceedings', 538–41; Comment, 'Industrial Due Process and Just Cause for Discipline'; Jones, 'Evidentiary Concepts in Labor Arbitration', 1286–91; Silard, 'Rights of the Accused Employee ...'; Craver, 'The Inquisitorial Process in Private Employment', 7–13; Edwards, 'Due Process Considerations in Labor Arbitration', 155–9; Spelfogel, 'Surveillance and Interrogation ...', 184-5.

[43] Kanski, 'Employee Drug Testing'; McCulloch, *Termination of Employment*.

[44] Belair, 'Employee Rights to Privacy'; Craver, 'The Inquisitorial Process in Private Employment', 28–39; McCulloch, *Termination of Employment*; Spelfogel, 'Surveillance and Interrogation ...', 187–8; Burkey, 'Employee Surveillance', 211.

[45] Craver, 'The Inquisitorial Process in Private Employment', 43–9; Spelfogel, 'Surveillance and Interrogation ...', 180–2; Silard, 'Rights of the Accused Employee ...', 225–6; Burkey, 'Employee Surveillance'; Carlson and Phillips, 'Due Process Considerations in Grievance Arbitration Proceedings', 541.

[46] Marx, *Undercover*; Belair, 'Employee Rights to Privacy'; Spelfogel, 'Surveillance and Interrogation ...', 180-2; Craver, 'The Inquisitorial Process in Private Employment', 51–5; Burkey, 'Employee Surveillance', 204, 209.

[47] Carlson and Phillips, 'Due Process Considerations in Grievance Arbitration Proceedings', 525, 531–3; Summers, 'Individual Rights in Collective Agreements and Arbitration', 362, 408; Silard, 'Rights of the Accused Employee ...', 224–5; Fleming, 'Some Problems of Due Process ...', 236; Weyland, 'Present Status of Individual Employee Rights', 195. See generally Friendly, 'Some Kind of Hearing', 1280–1.

to call and/or confront witnesses,[50] to appeal,[51] to legal or union representation,[52] and to protection from retrospective application of regulations.[53]

None of these possible rights will be pursued here. While they appear to present rather intractable issues for classical liberalism, it would be a mistake to assume that they cannot be resolved. One normative framework which could be applied to this task is that advanced by Michael Bayles.[54] On Bayles' analysis the fundamental norm of procedural justice is to minimise the sum of economic and moral error costs less process benefits. Process values or benefits include participation, fairness, intelligibility, timeliness, and confidence in the procedure:

> Participation is based on the pervasive human desire to have a say in decisions that significantly affect one. Fairness requires equality of procedures applied in similar cases; it promotes comparative justice and is especially important in competitive contexts. Intelligibility involves making decisions perspicuous, especially to those persons to whom they apply. It can promote persons' ability to plan, regardless of whether a decision is favorable or unfavorable, correct or incorrect. Timeliness is making decisions within an appropriate time, not leaving affected persons hanging. Confidence in the procedure is a second order value based on people's belief that efficiency and the other process benefits are appropriately realized in the procedure. A failure of confidence can lead to demoralization and lack of voluntary compliance.[55]

A more reflexive normative framework that might usefully be applied is Braithwaite and Pettit's[56] republican theory of criminal justice. This theory implies a more participatory criminal justice system, with much reliance on reprobation in private spheres, just as in the proposal under consideration

---

[48] Robins, 'Unfair Dismissal'; Tepker, 'Oklahoma's At-Will Rule'; Carlson and Phillips, 'Due Process Considerations in Grievance Arbitration Proceedings', 536–8; Comment, 'Industrial Due Process and Just Cause for Discipline'; Blades, 'Employment at Will vs. Individual Freedom'. See generally Friendly, 'Some Kind of Hearing', 1267.

[49] Weyland, 'Present Status of Individual Employee Rights', 210–11; Comment, 'Industrial Due Process and Just Cause for Discipline', 622–3; Summers, 'Individual Rights in Collective Agreements and Arbitration', 370.

[50] Comment, 'Industrial Due Process and Just Cause for Discipline', 620; Carlson and Phillips, 'Due Process Considerations in Grievance Arbitration Proceedings', 536–8; Fleming, 'Some Problems of Due Process ...' 245–8.

[51] Robins, 'Unfair Dismissal'; Weyland, 'Present Status of Individual Employee Rights', 210; Comment, 'Industrial Due Process and Just Cause for Discipline'. See generally Friendly, 'Some Kind of Hearing', 1294–5.

[52] Barbash, 'Due Process and Individual Rights in Arbitration', 19; Weyland, 'Present Status of Individual Employee Rights', 211; Craver, 'The Inquisitorial Process in Private Employment', 16–21; Carlson and Phillips, 'Due Process Considerations in Grievance Arbitration Proceedings', 533; Summers, 'Individual Rights in Collective Agreements and Arbitration', 392; Silard, 'Rights of the Accused Employee...'; Spelfogel, 'Surveillance and Interrogation...', 188, 191–3; Edwards, 'Due Process Considerations in Labor Arbitration', 163-8.

[53] Weyland, 'Present Status of Individual Employee Rights', 194.

[54] Bayles, *Procedural Justice*.

[55] Ibid., 139.

[56] Braithwaite and Pettit, *Not Just Deserts*.

here. It is a consequentialist theory that sets the maximizing of 'dominion' as the goal the criminal justice system ought to pursue.

Dominion is freedom understood in the republican sense of citizenship. It differs from the standard liberal notion of freedom as absence of constraint. Instead of this asocial liberal conception of freedom, dominion is (1) the social status you perfectly enjoy when you are no more constrained than anyone else in your society; (2) when this absence of constraint is no accident, being assured by the protective apparatus of custom and law; and (3) when it is common knowledge among you and others that you enjoy that absence and that assurance. Further, you enjoy maximum dominion when you enjoy no less a prospect of liberty than the best that is compatible with the same prospect for all citizens. The key characteristic of dominion for our present purposes is the third one mentioned above—the requirement to encourage in citizens a subjective awareness of their enjoying an assurance against constraint. It follows that the state must be bound by rights and be seen to be bound by rights.

The republican theory is an example of a theory that can be applied to the task of deriving the rights to be imposed by the state on private justice systems and in deciding how those rights ought to be enforced. Dominion, Braithwaite and Pettit argue, is that which is threatened by paradigm cases of crime. There are forms of crime which invade the dominion we properly have over our persons, our property and our province. Of course, whenever we confer a right—such as a right to protection from phone tapping—there are costs to dominion. There will be crimes that might have been prevented had agents of the private justice system not honoured a right to protection from phone-tapping. What the theory requires us to weigh is the loss of dominion involved in these preventable crimes from the benefit in having a right to protection that cannot be trumped. If the latter outweighs the former, then we ought to support a right to protection from phone-tapping.

Interception of telephone conversations is an instructive case because it shows how we can use the theory to conditionalise the right. If there were a blanket legal prohibition against intercepting telephone calls, there would be substantial costs to dominion, perhaps so substantial as effectively to remove the freedom of citizens to use telephones. This is because it is necessary for telephone companies to intercept calls for mechanical and service quality control checks. Also, there may be legitimate acceptable grounds for corporate switchboard operators and service personnel to intercept calls[57] or there may be a telephone beside a machine dedicated to emergency breakdown calls which can be tapped into by any of the company's engineers. An interesting way of resolving these issues was formulated in *US v Carroll*:[58] to be protected from eavesdropping, a citizen must '(1) subjectively anticipate that his discussion will be confidential and (2) speak under circumstances warranting such a subjective expectation of privacy'.[59] Given the centrality of the

---

[57] See Craver, 'The Inquisitorial Process in Private Employment', 56–9.
[58] (1971) 337 F. Supp. 1260.
[59] Ibid., 1262.

subjective element of dominion, this is precisely the kind of conditionalising of rights commended by republican theory.[60]

The subjective element of dominion also means that we must attend closely to the work psychologists are doing on subjectively perceived procedural justice.[61] This follows from the goal of encouraging in citizens a subjective awareness of their enjoying assurance against constraint. Allan Lind and Tom Tyler's literature review shows that 'process control, impartiality, ethicality and the perceived quality of decisions are the major determinants of procedural justice judgments'.[62] Process control means 'voice', that citizens prefer procedures that give them considerable freedom in deciding how they present their viewpoint, including freedom to choose to be represented (by a lawyer, union representative or fellow worker). So the literature on the psychology of procedural justice suggests as a minimum that defendants in private justice systems be given an opportunity to a hearing of which they are given notice, where they can choose to be represented by whoever they wish, where they have a right to be heard, to call witnesses and a right to ask questions of those who testify against them. Interestingly, however, the literature counsels the need for hesitancy about excessive regulation of due process rights beyond this at the adjudication stage:

> Because procedural justice judgments are affected by a variety of procedural characteristics, and because the importance of each characteristic varies from one situation to another, there is probably no single procedure that maximizes procedural justice in all situations. Perhaps in recognition of this, recent work has shown less concern with the fairness of particular procedures and more concern with psychological, judgmental processes in procedural justice. The complexity of trying to describe a single fairest procedure is emphasized by recent studies (e.g., Barrett-Howard and Tyler, 1986, Tyler, 1987b) showing that the situation in which a procedure is encountered can change the emphasis given to various criteria for procedural justice. Given this state of affairs, we can design procedures on the basis of what we know generally concerning the factors that contribute to procedural justice, but we must carefully evaluate procedural innovations to make sure we have not ignored situation-specific considerations.[63]

The warning we read from the procedural justice empiricists here is the same as that transmitted by the Continental reflexive law theorists. It is the warning of Jurgen Habermas[64] about supplanting communicative action with legal norms. It is the warning of Niklas Luhmann[65] about the dangers of the

---

[60] This might only be true, however, if the society or the corporation which is the context for the honouring of the right is not a totalitarian one. In a totalitarian context, citizens may never speak with a subjective expectation of privacy, and such a conditionalised right would be an empty letter.

[61] Lind and Tyler, *The Social Psychology of Procedural Justice*.

[62] Ibid., 125.

[63] Ibid., 216–17. The two works cited in the quotation are Barrett-Howard and Tyler, 'Procedural Justice as a Criterion in Allocation Decisions'; Tyler, *Why People Obey the Law*. See also Michelman, 'Formal and Associational Aims in Procedural Due Process'.

[64] Habermas, 'Law as Medium and Law as Institution'.

[65] Luhmann, 'The Self-Reproduction of Law and Its Limits'.

rationality of the legal system destroying patterns of life in other social systems. It is the warning of Gunter Teubner[66] about the incompatibility of state law with the internal logic of the other subsystems it tries to regulate. And ironically it is the warning in Erhard Blankenburg's[67] critique of reflexive law. If the law becomes excessively interventionist in proceduralising private justice systems, it creates a hazardous mismatch between the design of private justice and the patterns of particular corporate cultures; it jeopardises that very contextual responsiveness that attracts disputants to informal justice.

At the same time, the psychological literature on procedural justice does more than inform us of certain very basic rights (like the right to an unbiased hearing) that the law should expect of private justice systems as substitutes for state justice. It also commends an approach to how other less foundational procedural safeguards ought to be formulated. This arises from the fundamental importance of 'voice' or 'process control' in studies that address the subjective sense of justice. If we take voice seriously, private justice procedures will be the product of democratic workplace decisionmaking; the procedural rules of adjudication will be imposed by neither the state nor by management, but decided collectively by the workforce.

So, within the normative framework of republican theory, we can read the procedural justice literature as recommending two things: first, a set of very basic due process rights to be imposed on all private justice systems which have the power to fire or fine employees; second, a meta-right to participatory process for the formulation of other less basic due process safeguards. Most Western democracies have labour relations inspectorates of some form. The implication would be that they should have the role not of rulebook regulation in this area, but of catalysing the participatory involvement of employees in constructing the rules of their own private justice system.[68] Then the inspector should be satisfied that the process that comes out of this workplace democracy satisfies in its own way the basic due process rights for private systems enshrined in state law. Further, appeal to the courts (at least of dismissal decisions) should be available when defendants believe that either the process inflicted on them did not satisfy these basic rights or did not comply with the fair procedures agreed democratically prior to the hearing. Moreover, a republican state would be actively involved in training unionists and other workplace advocates in how to demand their rights and to act effectively as advocates for employees accused of wrongdoing.

The approach considered above is hardly radical. The historical trends are very much in the same direction. The growth of private justice as a generally preferred alternative to state justice with respect to employee offences against the property of the employer has been accompanied by a trend toward constitutionalising private justice systems.[69] The position in Britain illustrates this

---

[66] Teubner, 'Substantive and Reflexive Elements in Modern Law'; Teubner, 'After Legal Instrumentalism?'
[67] Blankenburg, 'The Poverty of Evolutionism'.
[68] For an example of this kind of regulatory model, see Braithwaite, Grabosky and Fisse, *Occupational Health and Safety Enforcement Guidelines*.
[69] Habermas, 'Law as Medium and Law as Institution'.

trend. In 1969, only 2 per cent of firms with under 50 employees had formal procedures for disciplinary matters, and only 19 per cent for firms with over 500.[70] By 1979, another study found half of small firms to have procedures and 99 per cent of companies with over 500 employees.[71] Similarly, there was an increase in the percentage of procedures which were the outcome of consultation and negotiation with trade unions—from 20 per cent in 1969 to 65 per cent in 1979.[72] The Western world generally has seen an increase in legislation and litigation of the right of workers to have allegations of unjust dismissal adjudicated in courts.[73] The law thereby created increasingly enshrines the fundamental due process rights commended by a republican reading of the procedural justice literature.

While the procedures of adjudication in private justice systems tend to be headed in the direction indicated by republicanism, this cannot be claimed of the investigation and surveillance that goes hand in hand with private adjudication. The aggressiveness of the private security industry in using undercover and other intrusive tactics, and the new surveillance technology— electronic eavesdropping, periscopic prisms, computer data banks, 'spy dust'—render the private security industry a growing threat to civil liberties.[74] Constitutionalising the surveillance–investigative end of private justice systems is imperative. Proactive state regulation of the threat to civil liberties posed by private security is as much needed in Western polities as is independent regulation of intrusive operations mounted by state police.

Assuming that a commendable array of employee rights in internal discipline systems can be formulated, how would such rights be enforced? This is a large topic that embraces issues as diverse as class actions, measure of damages, and alternative dispute resolution. The only point that needs to be made here is that the Accountability Model contemplates that the court which has the carriage of an enforcement action against a corporation would also be empowered to deal with complaints by employees about the internal disciplinary action taken by the corporation. Thus, an accountability order could require a corporate defendant to spell out the procedural safeguards available to employees subject to investigation and to record and report any internal complaints about procedural injustice made in relation to the inquiry. By structuring accountability orders and assurances in such a way, it would be possible for the courts to maintain a watching brief and to intervene in cases where employees have been denied procedural justice.

---

[70] This comparison is drawn from Henry, *Private Justice*, 101. The data are drawn from Dawson, 'Disciplinary and Dismissals Practice and Procedures'.

[71] Dickens et al., 'A Response to the Government Working Papers on Amendments to Employment Protection Legislation'.

[72] Henry, *Private Justice*, 101.

[73] See Collins, *Justice in Dismissal*; Kidd, 'Disciplinary Proceedings and the Right to a Fair Criminal Trial Under the European Convention on Human Rights'; Lenard, 'Unjust Dismissal of Employees at Will'; Carlson and Phillips, 'Due Process Considerations in Grievance Arbitration Proceedings'; Tepker, 'Oklahoma's At-Will Rule', 373; Weyland, 'Present Status of Individual Employee Rights'.

[74] See Marx, 'The Interweaving of Public and Private Police in Undercover Work'.

6 Equal Application of Law

Desideratum
Those who are responsible for equal wrongs should be treated equally.

Legal positivists will object to the Accountability Model on the ground that it negotiates away the ideal of equal punishments for equal wrongs. According to this view, what the legal system does or should do is decide equitably on who to prosecute solely on the weight and seriousness of the evidence against each suspect and then punish the guilty in equitable proportion to the seriousness of their offences. That traditional view is sustained by a willingness among those who hold it to indulge a legalistic myopia, a willingness to ignore both the sanctioning capacity of private justice systems and the arbitrary exclusion from the state justice system of the activities of most of the persons responsible for known corporate crimes. The legalist conceit is to focus on the tip of the iceberg that can be formally processed and take pride in the equitable treatment administered by the courts in those cases.[75] To the legal pluralist, such pride is hollow. There is no substance in an approach that fails to grapple with the inequities that occur between the legally processed tip and the shadowy base of the iceberg. This is especially so given that a vast amount of private justice system sanctioning already occurs within the submerged bulk of the iceberg.

The Accountability Model is motivated by a legal pluralist vision of equality. This means that the desideratum is to do the best that is feasible to secure greater equality of treatment of those who are equally responsible for corporate crime—a very different objective from equal state punishments for equal wrongs. Our claim is that a strategy that suitably mobilises private justice systems will more justly sheet home responsibility to many more of those who are responsible than will a strategy that is preoccupied with state justice systems; equality will be promoted, not diminished. This is because the most profound inequality is between the few who are sanctioned and the many who are never called to account.[76] Second, the approach taken under the Accountability Model will increase oversight of private justice systems by the courts so as to ensure that:
(1) action is taken in cases of flagrant leniency by private justice systems;
(2) private justice systems are more systematic in holding those responsible accountable; and
(3) citizens' rights are not trampled under the cover of private justice systems.

In other words, a policy of the state system actively engaging with private justice systems is seen as the best route to a more equitable criminal justice system. Such engagement must be negotiated, flexible and plurally responsive to disparate regulatory orders. Otherwise the state will destroy private justice

---

[75] See further Braithwaite, 'Paradoxes of Class Bias in Criminal Justice'; Sargent, 'Law, Ideology and Corporate Crime'.

[76] Levi's reflections on the selectivity of applying the full force of the law against the Guinness four are interesting in this regard: Levi, 'Sentencing White-Collar Crime in the Dark?'

systems. If we destroy them, then we return to a world of pretend corporate crime enforcement where we chip away merely at the tip of the iceberg. We settle for a world where hardly any of those who are responsible are held responsible. As argued elsewhere,[77] the facts of life about corporate crime conduce to the theorem that 'where desert is least, punishment will be greatest'. Braithwaite and Pettit have pointed out that the upshot of a policy narrowly focused on imposing just deserts on convicted individuals will be just deserts for the poor and immunity for the rich.[78] They argue that abandoning such a policy is a necessary step to move toward a more equitable criminal justice system.

A policy of the state washing its hands of private justice systems is not as bad as a policy that destroys them. But washing our hands is a policy of pretend equality. We pretend that inequality between the cases dealt with by private justice systems and the cases processed by public justice systems do not matter, that inequality between the cases ignored by both systems and the cases processed by public justice systems do not matter. The Accountability Model, by contrast, postulates a public justice system that neither washes its hands of private justice systems nor seeks to take them over. The vision is of a public justice system that tolerates diversity in private justice systems, that nurtures them, but that constitutionalises them to ensure the protection of fundamental human rights.

It is certainly true that courts negotiating with private justice systems in ways that are plurally responsive to preserving their integrity will impose formally unequal punishments in the domain of public courts. Our claim, however, is that formally unequal punishments at this level can be a sign of a more fundamental underlying equality in the tendency of a plurality of justice systems to move toward the desideratum of holding responsible all who are responsible.

The crucial issue of grants of immunity needs to be resolved in this light. First, we must be willing to grant immunities to prosecution as an investigative means to the end of holding responsible more of those who are responsible. It is no objection to say that an immunity increases formal legal inequality if the effect of granting the immunity is to increase equality of treatment among the wider set of all those who are responsible.

Second, the legal pluralist views immunity from state punishment in a different light because immunity from state punishment does not confer immunity from sanctioning by a private justice system. The interesting question to consider is whether formal grants of state immunity are necessary if the court is to motivate full and frank disclosure of responsibility by private justice systems. We think generally they are not. However, where a court, after dialogue with the prosecution or a regulatory agency, judges that immunities for certain individuals should be granted, we see no objection in principle to granting them.

Why do we think widespread use of immunities is unnecessary? The evidence from public policing is that police intimations of the likelihood of

[77] Braithwaite and Pettit, *Not Just Deserts*, 182–201.
[78] Ibid.

non-prosecution or of merely 'favourable consideration' for suspects so long as they are full and frank in their disclosures can be effective in securing such disclosures. That is, the empirical evidence is that police do not generally have to offer iron-clad immunities to effectively trade off favourable consideration for full disclosure. The same, we are confident, would be true under the Accountability Model, where the courts could well say:

'You can expect that no individuals will be prosecuted criminally if your private justice system succeeds in reporting fully on the responsibility of all those who are responsible for this offence and succeeds in imposing private disciplinary measures suitably proportionate to the responsibility of each of those responsible. However, if you lack the will or capacity to impose suitably proportionate disciplinary action on any responsible individual, you can expect the court to prosecute that individual criminally.'

Our (empirically rebuttable) presumption is that this kind of offer will mostly motivate rigorous internal investigation, reporting of wrongdoing and disciplinary adjudication. Confidence in that presumption is based not only on the experience of public police in negotiating voluntary co-operation from guilty parties but also on the experience of regulatory agencies. The US SEC's handling of the Gulf Oil case bears this out, as does the Australian Trade Practices Commission's success in the Solomons Carpets case.[79]

It is important, on grounds of equity, that guidelines be issued to indicate the types of cases where criminal prosecutions are appropriate notwithstanding the good faith mobilisation of private justice systems against those responsible for an offence. Two guidelines we would suggest under the Accountability Model are as follows:

(1) Criminal prosecution of the corporation is usually warranted in cases where the reactions of the corporation in mobilising its private justice system, diagnosing the causes for the offence, acting to remedy those causes, disciplining those responsible, and making compensation for the harm done, are insufficient to identify publicly the fact that the corporation has remitted or discharged its liability for the *actus reus* of an offence.[80]

(2) Criminal prosecution of the corporation is usually called for where there is evidence that the *actus reus* of an offence was committed by the corporation in accordance with a calculated policy or an entrenched ethos or culture of non-compliance or by reason of defective organisational precautions grossly short of the standard of care expected of a corporation in its position.[81]

Guidelines for the prosecution of individuals would also be needed. As we envisage the Accountability Model, criminal prosecution of an individual would be called for where:

---

[79] See Chapter 7, 230–2.
[80] This reflects the concept of reactive fault discussed in Fisse, 'Reconstructing Corporate Criminal Law', 1197–213.
[81] On corporate policy see Fisse, 'The Attribution of Criminal Liability to Corporations'. On corporate ethos see Bucy, 'Corporate Ethos'.

(1) responsible individuals are beyond the disciplinary reach of corporations (for example, employees of outside accounting firms that are no longer retained by the corporation);

(2) the disciplinary action taken by the corporation against an individual is insufficient to reflect the level of responsibility that individual bears for the offence; or

(3) no level of disciplinary action by the corporation can be sufficient to remit/redeem the responsibility of an individual (that is, the reprobation of a criminal conviction is required to reflect the gravity of the offence or the blameworthiness of the offender).

Cases within (3) will arise where, for example: (a) a single individual bears most of the responsibility for the intentional commission of a serious offence (involving serious injury to persons or property), or (b) an individual bears a substantial part of the shared responsibility for a serious offence and where that individual is under a special duty in relation to that offence (for example, a director in relation to breach of a director's duties; the medical director and chief executive in relation to a fraud in the safety testing of a drug by a pharmaceutical company).

The case studies of corporate crime suggest that the circumstances in (3)(a) will not occur often in the large corporations that typically create problems of allocation of responsibility (they would of course be very common in small tightly held corporations that break the law). Most of the case studies in the literature, and certainly those where we have been able to interview key players, show that there are many responsible actors at many levels within and outside the organisation of large corporate defendants.[82] In most cases, this is not fault-based responsibility of the kind required for criminal liability (for example, recklessness or gross negligence), but responsibility nevertheless. The advantage of private justice systems here is their capacity to sheet home sub-criminal forms of responsibility in a suitable way. In comparison, existing corporate criminal law enforcement crudely polarises responsibility by fastening upon some vulnerable individuals. Other responsible actors are often pleased to co-operate in the prosecutor's crude simplification by shifting blame to the individuals that the prosecution chooses to vilify. Sadly, there can be a convergence of self-interest in this conspiracy of simplification between the enforcers who want to get a notch, any notch, on their gun and the responsible corporate agents who want to shift their responsibility onto the luckless target of prosecution. Go to a training course for complex fraud prosecutors and you will hear the instructor say: 'Simplify, simplify, then simplify the story again so that the jury will understand it'. So the problem of scapegoating, which we address below, is not just a problem of defendant evasion of culpability. It is also a problem of the way a traditional state enforcement system creates inequitable incentives for concentrating and crystallising blame. Private justice systems generally, though not invariably, are less about getting notches on guns. Certainly, if corporations are given strong incentives

---

[82] See, e.g., Fisse and Braithwaite, *The Impact of Publicity on Corporate Offenders.*

to report fully on internal responsibility for an offence (as by the threat of an escalated level of response in the event of non-co-operation), it is in their self-interest to comply rather than to ape the simple-minded personifications of responsibility that are apparent where the state crucifies a few 'evil' individuals.

Most fundamentally, the ability to ensure that equal wrongs are treated more equally depends on being able to get to the truth of who contributed to the wrongs, which is something corporate regulatory enforcement rarely accomplishes at present. Interacting state and private justice systems will usually get closer to a holistic grasp of the complexity than either the state justice system or a private justice system working alone. And getting closer to the truth of the responsibility of all who are responsible is an indispensable step toward more equitable treatment of all who are responsible. If no-one knows who is blameworthy, then it is impossible to ensure the equal application of law to those responsible.

A final point to be made about the equality of treatment desideratum is a mundane and conventional one. The point is that negotiation of any accountability agreement or assurance must be constrained by the right of any party to abandon the negotiation, to demand either that allegations against them be dropped or proved in a court of law, and to appeal to a higher court against any excessively severe court order. In our experience, corporate defendants are well advised of such rights by their legal advisers. Indeed, in Australia they tend to remind Trade Practice Commission negotiators of 'the worst that could happen if we went to court' at any point where they believe negotiated demands are becoming unreasonable. This rights-assertiveness hardly merits cynicism. On the contrary, the right not to be subjected to liability beyond the limits set by law is the most fundamental constraint upon inequality of treatment in negotiated settlements.

7 Control of Scapegoating

Desideratum
A strategy for allocating individual responsibility should remedy the scapegoating that has been endemic when individual accountability for corporate wrongdoing has been pursued.

The greatest problem with all strategies for calling individuals to account, including the strategy adopted under the Accountability Model, is scapegoating.[83] Prosecutors often walk away from prosecutions of individuals for corporate crime for fear that the smokescreen of confused accountability which organisations throw up will both render investigation costs prohibitive and mislead them into indicting scapegoats. Corporations, if left to their own devices, will try to deflect responsibility to a select group of sacrificial

---

[83] See generally Allport, *The Nature of Prejudice*, ch. 15.

personnel, often at a lower level than the actual source of skulduggery. How responsive is the Accountability Model to these problems of scapegoating?

The first and most obvious point to be made is that the Accountability Model gives prosecutors an avenue for unravelling individual responsibility within a corporation without committing themselves to a lengthy, resource-intensive investigation that might ultimately prove inconclusive. Although the state's investigatory resources are thin, this does not mean that the only individual targets are those who bob up on the surface as potential scapegoats. Under the Accountability Model the prosecution press for a compliance report that gives a concise but full picture of the roles played by all relevant corporate personnel in the events that led to commission of the *actus reus* of an offence. There is no need to rely upon corporate liability as a crude device for avoiding the hazard of indicting scapegoats. Rather, individual responsibility can be brought more fully out into the open by using corporate liability as a lever to activate a publicly constitutionalised internal discipline system of the defendant corporation.

The Accountability Model is also responsive to the risk of scapegoating at the level of corporate internal discipline. There are five basic safeguards:

(1) pyramidal enforcement where scapegoating or related forms of non-compliance with accountability agreements, orders, or assurances result in sanctions which are escalated, if necessary, to a point far beyond the tolerance of rational corporate or managerial self-interest;

(2) judicial scrutiny of corporate action when accountability reports are submitted pursuant to accountability agreements, orders or assurances;

(3) empowerment of employees with a right to complain about scapegoating to a court and, where relevant, to an internal accountability monitoring committee of the corporate defendant;

(4) legal recognition of private systems of justice so as to foster participatory self-determination of issues such as the allocation of responsibility for offences committed on behalf of a corporation; and

(5) minimum procedural protections for individuals exposed to internal disciplinary proceedings.

The concerns that have been expressed in the past about corporate scapegoating relate very much to present regulatory regimes where those who engage in scapegoating can usually get away with it. The most basic reason for this derangement of social control is that the problem has not been addressed in a systematic way. Little or no attempt has been made by legislators and enforcement agencies to provide a pyramid of enforcement where the consequences of scapegoating are clearly spelt out and where the severity of the consequences can be increased to the point where scapegoating is rarely worth the risk.[84] Added to that, we have lacked any well-designed scheme of

---

[84] This incentive appears to explain why the chief executive of Salomon Brothers Inc. in New York co-operated fully in the investigation of allegedly serious securities violations by Salomon Brothers and why the US Government did not not indict the firm on criminal charges, thereby saving the firm from a real risk of being driven out of business; see 'Salomon Seeks New Chief Executive', *SMH*, 29 May 1992, 24; 'Salomon: No Criminal Charge', *SMH*, 22 May 1992, 26.

accountability reports where the emphasis is on responsibility for corporate offences and on using the power of judicial scrutiny as a weapon against scapegoating. Nor have employees been given a specific express right to voice their concerns about scapegoating to the court before which their corporate employer is on trial or being sentenced. The failure of the legal system to recognise the nature and operation of private systems of justice within corporations has permitted scapegoating to flourish. This is partly because corporations have been allowed to allocate responsibility for breaches of their internal rules in an autocratic way that conduces to the self-protection of managers in power; there has been no requirement that all relevant participants be given a say in the process of determining accountability. Moreover, corporations have had a great deal of latitude in relation to procedural protections for persons subject to internal disciplinary inquiries. Even the most basic procedural protections that one would expect to find in an internal disciplinary system (for example, the right to particulars of the allegation and to reply to the case against one) are not always provided or, when provided, may be too costly for employees to act on.

In our view it is this pervasive neglect of the problem of corporate scapegoating that accounts for the intensity of the concern repeatedly voiced about it. Although scapegoating can never be entirely overcome, it is at least possible to provide an integrated set of safeguards to minimise it. The problem should also be seen in perspective. Scapegoating under the Accountability Model would amount to perjury: corporate officers who file an accountability report known to be false in so material a particular would plainly be lying under oath.

It is worth elaborating upon the particular significance of participatory self-determination of responsibility, coupled with minimum procedural protections for individuals exposed to internal disciplinary proceedings. One reason for encouraging the corporation itself to haggle over who is responsible is that the participants in the haggling will be persons who spend their lives participating in the symbolic world of the corporation concerned, who speak the same language of responsibility, who understand the extent to which the organisation chart really means something. We have argued already that insiders do tend to have clear understandings on who is responsible for what, or at least on what the rules are for deciding who is responsible, and clear interests in keeping those understandings from outsiders. These understandings arise from an informal corporate case law. When corporate actors choose to be open with you, they tell you that 'Fred should have known he was responsible because there was a near-disaster just like this once before and Fred was told in no uncertain terms that while he would be let off this time, if it happened again his head would roll'. This corporate case law overrides a formal corporate organisational chart which would suggest that it was not Fred's responsibility. Unfortunately, the case law is not usually written down, whereas the misleading corporate 'statute law' is written and accessible to outsiders. Insiders, in contrast, can sort the wheat from the chaff on the basis of general internal agreement on what is the wheat and what is the chaff. Organisational life is full of nudges and winks, of rules which are not really meant to be obeyed, of high-flown titles which are misleading as descriptors of what people really do.

Justice in the allocation of individual responsibility for organisational wrongdoing requires ascertainment of the agreed understandings of who was responsible for deciding to do something or for failing to do something in the terms of the symbolic world of the particular organisational culture. Both the unfamiliarity of outsiders, the stereotypes of organisational behaviour they bring to the task of understanding, and the cynical interests insiders have in confusing outsiders and pandering to their stereotypes when it suits them justify reliance on insiders. This is not to say that investigators from head office, while much better placed than total outsiders, will not have their own problems in coming to grips with shared understandings of responsibility. They need to recruit insiders from the relevant divisions to work with them.

The corporate scapegoating problem arises usually from those at the top of the organisation protecting themselves by sacrificing someone lower down. While insiders have the capacity to sheet home responsibility to those who are agreed to be responsible, when it is found that the boss (or someone the corporation cannot afford to lose) is responsible, an alternative scapegoat may be set up.

What can be done about this? Our suggestion is that courts refuse to agree to corporate self-investigations unless certain guarantees of due process are met. The critical guarantee required is this. At the stage of a draft report for the court being prepared, it should be widely circulated around the organisation and an open meeting held within the organisation to discuss it. All who wished to attend this meeting should be able to do so, with travel expenses met by the organisation. In particular, all persons subject to adverse comment in the draft report should be urged to attend and to invite any witnesses to speak on their behalf. A model for how such informal discussion on a draft report might be held is provided by pre-decision conferences on draft authorisations of anticompetitive conduct under the Australian Trade Practices Act.[85]

The conduct of the meeting would be in the hands of the corporation, but representatives of the court and the prosecution would be invited to attend this meeting to observe that principles of natural justice were observed. The court would communicate its wish that every person adversely reported upon in the report be called upon to speak in their own defence or otherwise challenge the report in this open forum. If the possibility of misconduct by the chief executive is an issue, then the open forum must be chaired by an outsider beyond the control of the chief executive (perhaps the outside investigator or an outside director).

---

[85] See Trade Practices Act (Cth.), ss. 90A, 93A. A draft determination is tabled in advance of these predecision conferences. All parties with an interest in the draft determination are able to attend and voice their criticisms of the draft in an informal atmosphere. Because the discussion is focused on criticism of a draft determination rather than on a wide-ranging reconsideration of all the issues, these conferences rarely occupy more than one day and usually only a half day.

If the meeting were conducted in an oppressive manner, if representatives of the court and the prosecution were not invited to attend, if evidence of scapegoating emerged at the hearing, this would be reported when the court resumed to consider the company's final report, redrafted in light of criticisms made at the in-house meeting. The prosecution might then choose to call some of those who complained at the meeting to give further evidence to the court.

Of course, a report which was a whitewash of top management responsibility would result in the court adopting the most punitive response possible and seeking to attract adverse publicity for the corporation and its top managers over both the offence and the cover-up. The literature on corporate crime provides many examples of corporations suffering more severe adverse publicity over a cover-up associated with an offence than they suffered from the offence itself.[86] This is one reason why, even under present unsatisfactory arrangements, corporations sacrifice their chief executives surprisingly often.[87] Thus, an open procedure which exposes the corporation to the risk of double jeopardy through adverse publicity is quite a potent safeguard against scapegoating.

It does not, however, eliminate the problem of an executive being 'bribed' to be a scapegoat voluntarily (as with the 'vice-president responsible for going to jail'). Even with consensual scapegoating, however, the open meeting exposes the corporation to some unpredictable risk that a whistle-blower will disclose the scapegoating in the presence of court-appointed observers. This risk would be further enhanced if the prosecutor gave his telephone number to all present at the meeting and invited them to speak or write to him in confidence should they feel intimidated about getting up at the meeting.

The Accountability Model thus tries to get to the truth of who was responsible by means of an internal inquiry conducted in the language of responsibility of the organisation by those who speak that language. That inquiry is followed by a further open informal hearing conducted in the responsibility language of the corporation rather than in the responsibility language of the law. The underlying framework is a pyramid of enforcement plainly indicating that the greater the level of co-operation, the less the risk of escalation of sanctions. For managers, the message is that there is little or no future in scapegoating others. For whistle-blowers, the signal is that an opportunity is provided for airing their grievances within the organisation without branding themselves as traitors.[88]

---

[86] Consider, e.g., the Air New Zealand, General Motors Corvair, and Coke and Cancer at BHP case studies in Fisse and Braithwaite, *The Impact of Publicity on Corporate Offenders*.

[87] The Solomons Carpets case, discussed in Chapter 7, is a case in point. Other cases of this nature occurred during the foreign bribery disclosures in the 1970s. See Fisse and Braithwaite, *The Impact of Publicity on Corporate Offenders*.

[88] Whistle-blowers currently face a real risk that if they go public they will be dismissed without effective means of redress; see generally Dworkin and Near, 'Whistleblowing Statutes'; Westin, *Whistle Blowing*; Finn, *Official Information*; Western Australia, *Report of the Royal Commission into Commercial Activities of Government*, Pt. II, Ch. 4. They may also be reluctant to blow the whistle given their feelings of loyalty (see McDowell, *Ethical Conduct and the Professional's Dilemma*, ch. 7) or lest their company be driven out of business by an ensuing prosecution. Under the Accountability Model, the emphasis is on upholding responsibility, but within a framework which fosters dialogue, institutional rehabilitation and continuity, and minimisation of the need for the law to invoke the threat of severe sanctions.

We have argued that, as compared with the criminal justice system, private justice systems are profoundly more capable, if not more willing, to make the buck stop at those whom insiders know to be the real decisionmakers, or those who neglected their clear and agreed responsibilities. The proposal advanced is one that attempts to make the corporation willing as well as able. It does so by the following set of incentives: the prospect of criminal non-prosecution; risks that scapegoating will be exposed in an open meeting of the organisation; the threat of escalated and severe punishment (for example, adverse publicity orders, punitive injunctions) unless the capacities of the private justice system to make the buck stop are mobilised; and the spectre of perjury charges against those individuals nominated as responsible for ensuring the accuracy of self-investigation reports.

We hardly maintain that the Accountability Model will entirely solve the problem of scapegoating. However, we do contend that it will result in the buck being made to stop more often in more of the right places than is possible by persisting with the traditional approach to the enforcement of the criminal law against corporate crime. It is impossible under any model to guarantee that corporate crime investigations will be done with absolute thoroughness and fairness, whether by state or private investigators. The question that makes sense here is a comparative empirical question: which corporate crime enforcement model guarantees the most thorough and fair investigations where scapegoating the powerless by the powerful is put at maximum risk? We think the Accountability Model does. That, however, is a claim which can be rebutted on empirical grounds by studying actual cases of the kind we discuss in Chapter 7.

8 Avoiding Unwanted Spillovers

Desideratum
A strategy for sanctioning the responsible should minimise spillovers of the effects of sanctions on actors who bear no responsibility for the wrongdoing.

A prime feature of the Accountability Model is the attempt to make all responsible actors responsible rather than using corporate liability for fines as a blunt weapon for indirectly achieving sanctioning effects on a wide range of persons irrespective of their connection with the offence. As Coffee, Gruner and Stone have suggested, the whole idea of the type of reform advanced here is to replace corporate sanctions which 'pound like bludgeons at the periphery of large corporations'[89] with more refined sanctions which strike like an épée at the vital sensitivities of responsible actors.[90] To bring the analogy into the domain of late twentieth-century warfare, the sanctions now deployed against

---

[89] Gruner, 'To Let the Punishment Fit the Organization'.
[90] Coffee, 'Beyond the Shut-Eyed Sentry', 1276; Fisse, 'Reconstructing Corporate Criminal Law', 1159.

corporations resemble Scud missiles. Usually they land harmlessly in the wilderness; when they get close to the target, they are mostly shot down by defensive systems; and when they do strike the target area, they often inflict unconscionable damage on the innocent. What we need instead are smart bombs, which, by bouncing beams of light back and forth between bomb and target, are able to make surgical strikes.

The interactive beams of light relevant under the Accountability Model are cast by the state on the work of private justice systems and by private justice systems back to the state in self-investigation reports. But the bombs can never be smart if we continue to lack a strategy for focusing and interactively refocusing our beams of light. Without a more creative approach to eliciting feedback from within the target organisation, there is no alternative to blasting our missiles at a black box. We have seen that hurling enough explosives at the black box to get the attention of powerful actors within it may cause extensive collateral damage to shareholders, creditors, to economic welfare generally and to workers who lose jobs.

In a self-investigation process run by the corporation itself, there is both a will and a capacity to avoid unnecessary collateral damage. On the other hand, we hope that we have shown that it is possible to give the self-investigation team incentives to thrust its épée into the responsible pockets of the organisation. We have seen that state investigators whose only interest is to claim scalps may find it appealing to hack away at the organisation with a broadsword. The self-investigation team can have no interest in collateral damage to actors other than those who can be shown to be responsible. The real problem, as we saw in the last section, is that while it will always be in the interest of self-investigators to use an épée rather than a broadsword, what we must watch for is that they do not strike their épée into the heart of a scapegoat.

Serious organisational crimes will often stem from responsible actors in positions of control.[91] Since the impact of sanctions under the Accountability Model will be borne primarily by managers in such positions, the prospects of preventive efficacy in sanctioning will be increased compared with a strategy of firing Scuds toward folks who are not in control.

Another advantage of the Accountability Model is that it switches away from monetary incentives to non-monetary impacts (internal discipline, managerial restructuring, reform of defective SOPs, improvement of internal compliance systems, and public reprobation of those responsible for the wrongdoing). These forms of sanction are more likely to penetrate the black box of corporations than the relatively blunt instrument of fines. Non-monetary impacts are also less readily transmitted to shareholders, workers and consumers. Unwanted overspill effects would thus be reduced. This way of minimising collateral damage is readily achievable, as is evident from the

---

[91] See Clinard, *Corporate Ethics and Crime*; Braithwaite, *Corporate Crime in the Pharmaceutical Industry*; Braithwaite, 'Taking Responsibility Seriously'; Bruck, *The Predators' Ball*; Hobson, *The Pride of Lucifer*.

simplicity of targeting managers and other key players in an organisation as a condition of corporate probation.[92]

9 Escaping the Deterrence Trap

Desideratum
A means must be devised to escape the deterrence trap—the situation where the only way to make it rational to comply with the law is to set penalties so high as to jeopardise the economic viability of corporations that are the lifeblood of the economy.

Readers will recall the deterrence trap. If the average returns from a corporate crime are a million dollars and if the chances of being punished for it are only one in a hundred, then a fine must be set at over $100 million dollars to deter the rational actor who gets average returns. Yet this may be so high as to deplete the liquidity of the corporation to such an extent that innocent creditors, consumers and workers will suffer.

One can of course take the view that escaping the deterrence trap is a bad idea. If a corporation is inflicting such large external costs on society that, if they were internalised, the corporation would fail, then it should fail: corporations which occasion more costs than benefits to society ought not to exist. The political reality in any economy, however, is that there are always some corporations which are 'too big to fail'. Imposing a fine that would bankrupt them is only a theoretical possibility. Yet even if such a fine were an option, one would not necessarily be justified in taking such a course. A corporation which has imposed more social costs than benefits in the past may well be changed to social advantage in the future. Assume, for argument's sake, that General Motors during some period in its history committed serious product safety offences at high social cost. Assume further that the fine required for rational deterrence would be of such an order as to send the company into bankruptcy. Few would opt in favour of an optimal fine. Bankruptcy would prejudice the chances of recovering the costs of the company's past wrongdoing. It makes far more sense to use non-monetary sanctions to insist upon changes to the company's practices as a going concern. Advantage can then be taken of the company's capability to rectify harm caused to victims in the past and at the same time generate jobs, produce useful products, and otherwise act in a socially beneficial way. It is therefore essential to have a corporate sanctioning system which can step over the deterrence trap.

The deterrence trap depends on the assumption that the corporation is a unitary actor. Second, it is set by reference to a rational economic actor model of corporate behaviour. The Accountability Model is not governed by these postulates. As explained below, this means that it can avoid the trap.

The Accountability Model can avoid the deterrence trap partly by striking many targets besides the unitary corporation: the aim is to reach personnel

---

[92] Gruner, 'To Let the Punishment Fit the Organization', 78–9.

within the organisation and external actors as well. The deterrence trap is also avoided by appealing to multiple motivational bases of corporate action rather than to the single-minded goal of corporate profit maximisation. Corporate profit maximisation may often be the most important motivating factor in corporations, but others are significant as well. These include corporate and individual repute, corporate social responsibility, the desire to compensate victims, the desire to be law-abiding, and the shame of demotion or dismissal. The question of motivational complexity will be discussed in the next section and need not be taken further for the moment.

The basic point is that the deterrence trap is a trap only if we attempt to deal with one actor (the unitary corporation) as if that actor has a single motivation (financial returns). The trap is avoidable by adopting an enforcement strategy that focuses on many responsible actors (unitary corporations, subunits, executives, board members, gatekeepers) on many different motivational bases. Thus, if we can deter an act of fraud in the safety testing of a drug by dismissing and disgracing a research scientist motivated by the pursuit of scientific glory, a sub-optimal fine that leaves the unitary corporation in a deterrence trap is surplus to what is required for deterrence. A multiplex strategy of seeking to hold responsible all who are responsible can by-pass the deterrence trap in many different ways. It can deter by appealing to the economic motivation of an executive who fears dismissal (and whose personal gain from the offence is small), to the motivation of the Chairperson of the Board to be seen to be head of a law-abiding corporation,[93] to the research division's desire to be seen as a group of scientists with scientific integrity and professional standing,[94] to the outside auditor's wish to be seen as someone who does their job,[95] and so on. Moreover, change is effected not only or mainly by deterrence. Appeal to more positive motivational foundations to put things right is also important, as is installing monitoring and other controls designed to prevent further offending. In short, the legal pluralism of the Accountability Model resolves the problem of the deterrence trap.

10 Heeding Motivational Complexity

Desideratum
A strategy for sanctioning the responsible must recognise that actors are motivationally complex. Profit maximisation is an important motivation for many private corporate actors, but the maintenance of individual and corporate repute, dignity, self-image and the desire to be responsible citizens are also important in many contexts, as are various more idiosyncratic motivations. A good strategy will not be motivationally myopic.

[93] As in the Solomons Carpets case, discussed in Chapter 7.
[94] See Braithwaite, *Corporate Crime in the Pharmaceutical Industry*, ch. 3.
[95] As in the Lockheed bribery scandal; see Boulton, *The Grease Machine*. See generally Grabosky, 'Professional Advisers and White Collar Illegality'.

Many business regulatory scholars assume that business firms and their executives are motivated only by profit maximisation. Our own empirical work in many industries—pharmaceuticals, coal, oil, aerospace, nursing homes—calls this into question. We need not repeat this evidence here;[96] those who are committed economistic thinkers are unlikely to be swayed by empirical evidence in any case. Nor are they likely to be interested in contemplating what motivates non-profit organisations to break the law. The question that matters for most who read this book is simply whether the Accountability Model appeals to a sufficient plurality of motivations.

The strength of the Accountability Model in this regard is its reliance on local justice. Local justice understands that what the Glasgow research group wants more than anything else is to establish dominance over the Birmingham R. & D. group, to become *the* centre of R. & D. excellence in the firm. Consequently, local justice comprehends that halving the Glasgow group's budget to shift those resources to Birmingham would be the cruellest cut of all. The point is that what is motivationally important to actors is organisationally idiosyncratic in a way that may be beyond the creative capacity of state justice.

This, of course, is a double-edged sword. Private justice systems can impose sanctions that look devastating to outsiders (thereby being useful for general deterrence) yet which are easy to live with locally (thereby being useless for specific deterrence). Watchfulness against specific deterrence failures of this sort is one reason why it is important for a representative of the court or the enforcement agency to attend the open meeting within the organisation to hear the discussion of the draft internal investigation and action report and to follow up suspicions of such failures with individuals who evince cynicism at that meeting. The hope is that a procedure that gives ample opportunities to whistle-blowers will make it seem an unwarranted risk to dress up soft options as tough solutions. Increasing this risk is also another reason why it is desirable to involve non-court outsiders such as union representatives in the process.

It seems to us that the very process of naming those who are responsible for wrongdoing in a report that is made public has the strength of motivational appeal that can be multiplex and therefore can have more than one chance at success. Being named in such a report can hold back an executive's career or cost an annual bonus, thus appealing to monetary motivations. It can reduce the person's professional stature, thus appealing to professional values. It can cause shame in the eyes of one's family, church or neighbours. It can cause guilt of a personal kind to individuals who have no family and who care not about the views of churchgoers or neighbours. For individuals who feel no guilt, it can undermine their pride in being a consummate corporate gamesman who never allows a blot on his copybook. And this list could be expanded in other ways.

---

[96] See particularly, Ayres and Braithwaite, *Responsive Regulation*, ch. 2; Fisse and Braithwaite, *The Impact of Publicity on Corporate Offenders*; Braithwaite, *To Punish or Persuade*; Braithwaite, *Corporate Crime in the Pharmaceutical Industry*.

Similarly, when collectivities are held responsible, there can be collective costs in money, reputation, pride and shame. And even if all of these individual and collective motivations fail to hit the spot, the Accountability Model can still play upon the managerial motive to clear away the aggravation and distraction that nosy outsiders investigating the firm can cause. The easiest way to make the problem go away may be to grab the problem by the horns and fix it in a way that will totally satisfy the court. It is hard to underestimate the importance of this motivation, as is illustrated by the Solomons Carpets case, which is discussed in more detail in the next chapter. When the lawyer representing Solomons sat down with officials from the Trade Practices Commission, he said that his brief was, within reason, to do what needed to be done to put the problem right and get this episode behind the corporation. One reason for such a stance is that nagging allegations of illegality are often seen as a threat to employee morale and often do in fact undermine morale, as we found empirically in an earlier study.[97] Perhaps, more critically, they distract top management from their normal job of scanning the firm's horizon looking for new business opportunities.[98]

Here we see a nice feature of the Accountability Model, namely the ability to exploit the fix-it motivational set by giving the firm a chance to seize the agenda and get the problem out of the way expeditiously. Corporations who find it a terrible aggravation to have their timetable set by courts over which they have no control will sometimes (as in the Solomons case) run the extra mile and do much more than the court would ever demand of them. Managerial freedom, independence and self-control are deeply engrained in the managerial psyche, as is hatred of the idea of being pushed around by lawyers, especially hostile lawyers from the government.

It may be that the multiplex motivational appeals inherent in the self-investigation report stage of the Accountability Model will fail. In that event, the full panoply of motivational appeals available from traditional criminal enforcement can be swung into action. These include monetary appeals by means of fines or disqualification from acting as a director or accountant, reputational appeals through the medium of adverse publicity orders, appeals to freedom by threatening imprisonment (not to mention the fear of rape and other acts of violence in prison),[99] and appeals to the desire to avoid outside interference through corporate probation. In other words, a range of criminal sanctions is available to ensure that the court is itself not locked into responding to corporate motivation at a narrowly economistic level. Elsewhere, we have argued that a variety of arrows is needed in the corporate sentencer's quiver if the non-monetary motivations for corporate offending are to be targeted effectively.[100] The court must be in a position to use sanctions which can achieve some control of corporate crime by deterrence and by rehabilitation. But when the prospects of both deterrence and rehabilitation

---

[97] Fisse and Braithwaite, *The Impact of Publicity on Corporate Offenders.*
[98] Ibid.
[99] It is the inescapable reality that this is part of the fear of imprisonment that makes imprisonment seem to us among the most morally dubious of punishments.
[100] Fisse and Braithwaite, 'Sanctions against Corporations'.

seem forlorn (as when the corporation is an incorrigibly irrational ideological opponent of a regulatory law), the court must also have available incapacitative options like corporate capital punishment (revocation of charter or licence, seizure of assets). In other words, the criminal law must be equipped to respond preventively to the corporation that is not only incorrigibly irresponsible but also incorrigibly economically irrational.

To ensure that our incapacitative axe stays sharp to deal with the worst cases of irrational corporate action, positive motivations for reform and restitution should be at the cutting edge.[101] The Accountability Model steels corporations to the need for positive action without destroying their motivation for reform: the axe is ground and poised, but is not swung until the corporation has been given the opportunity to design and implement a program of voluntary reform and self-discipline.

In Chapter 4, the point was made that organisational action is so motivationally complex that rational actor models will frequently have highly imperfect explanatory power. Our alternative is to favour a methodology that requires the firm to do its own ethnography of responsibility in a way that is attuned to the motivational complexity of its corporate life. The critic might say, however, that in motivating the firm to do its own ethnomethodology with a poised axe, our model is ultimately reducible to a rational actor model of deterrence. This criticism would be wrong, however, because the axe is more motivationally complex than might initially meet the eye. It may be the deterrent threat of the axe that appeals to rational self-interest. But the axe might also be a symbol of shame. Most crucially, the axe that lops the corporate head can be a weapon to incapacitate an irrational actor, as compared to the deterrent threat it holds for rational decisionmakers. The axe can either motivate the rehabilitation of a corporate cancer or cut it out if rehabilitative motivation fails.

11 Recognising and Using Internal Justice Systems

Desideratum
A strategy for sanctioning the responsible should avoid myopia about which agents will dispense sanctions against those responsible with the greatest justice and effectiveness. Often, it will be enforcement agents of the state who will do the best job. Yet we should not privilege the state as the only law-enforcer that matters. In particular, corporate internal disciplinary systems must be taken seriously as legal orders with realised and unrealised potential for justice and effectiveness.

The Accountability Model that we have outlined is animated directly by this desideratum. The existence of corporate disciplinary systems[102] is fully

---

[101] For a more extensive discussion of the theory of reform under the shadow of the axe, of how punishment contingently encourages and discourages reform, see Ayres and Braithwaite, *Responsive Regulation: Transcending the Deregulation Debate*, ch. 2.

[102] See generally Shearing and Stenning (eds), *Private Policing*; Henry, *Private Justice*; Lakoff and Rich (eds), *Private Government*.

recognised and those systems are harnessed to dispense sanctions against those who are responsible for offences committed by or on behalf of corporations. At the same time, it is recognised that there will be situations where the public system of enforcement is likely to be more effective, and earlier in this chapter we have suggested guidelines which clarify the range of cases where, in our view, individual criminal liability or corporate criminal liability should be sought by enforcement agencies rather than relying exclusively on individual or corporate accountability at the level of internal disciplinary systems. We have also addressed the risks of injustice that arise where internal discipline is exercised against individuals within organisations, and the steps that are needed to protect the rights of employees when confronted by a corporation that is forced to produce a compliance report detailing what it has done to impose accountability.

The further question arises whether private systems of justice are best conducted by insiders, or whether some degree of outside intervention is needed. The proposal put forward by John Coffee advocated the use of outside counsel for conducting internal disciplinary inquiries. Although this approach has often been used in the US (the E. F. Hutton fraud case is one example, the Gulf Oil bribing inquiry another), and although it provides a degree of independence, we have serious reservations about mandating any such requirement.

An outside counsel foisted on the corporation by the court may in many cases be able to get to the bottom of who was responsible for what with the active co-operation of the corporation. But in many cases the outside counsel may not. First, as an outsider he or she may not get the co-operation required; second, he or she may bring to the corporation commonsense assumptions (for example, that the job is to find only the responsible individuals) that are insensitive to the culture of the organisation.

In our view, the corporation and a task force of designated personnel, and not an independent outside counsel or a court-appointed probation officer, normally should be made responsible for investigating and reporting upon internal responsibility for the offence. The reasons for this are as follows:

(1) Placing responsibility with the corporation for determining who and what was responsible maximises the chance of a just allocation of responsibility.
(2) The criminal law should communicate the message that accountability, remediation and organisational reform are the responsibility of the corporation, and not outsiders.
(3) Corporate fault for the offence should be assessed on the basis of how the corporation reacts to the offence as well as on the basis of its responsibility in causing the offence.[103]

---

[103] The timeframe within which one assesses responsibility influences how one sees the role of insiders and outsiders in conducting internal disciplinary inquiries. If the timeframe is taken to be merely the period covered by the commission of the *actus reus* and the prior interval available for taking preventive action, then there seems nothing odd about court-appointed outsiders taking the lead role in investigating internal accountability for the offence. However, if the timeframe is taken to include conduct in response to having committed the *actus reus* of

We are not opposed to corporations employing outside counsel to conduct McCloy-style investigations. Indeed, in certain situations, as where there are major issues of outsider responsibility, we believe them to be sorely needed. Rather, the point is that the corporation should decide whether to hire outside counsel or whether to use its own personnel. In other areas of management, corporations make their own judgement as to whether they can get better advice from an outside consultant or from their in-house experts, and so it should be with this area of management. At the end of the day, if the court successfully persuades the corporation that it is in its interests to discover who and what was responsible, it will make the choice of using in-house or outside investigators on the basis of who is most likely to establish an allocation of responsibility which is just and which will be seen to be just by the court. Sometimes, however, it may be appropriate for the court to say to the corporation that the circumstances of the case were such that the corporation will have difficulty persuading the court that internal corporate justice has been done in the absence of independent outside advice. We are simply submitting that the corporation should ultimately be responsible for its internal private justice system, and face the consequences if that system is judged deficient by the court in the protection it offers the public and the fairness with which it disciplines those alleged to be responsible.

One of the traps to be avoided is assuming that private justice systems serve only to locate culpable individuals. In Section 10 of this chapter, we have illustrated the phenomenon of motivational complexity with an example of competing research groups within a corporation. A transnational pharmaceutical company may have three research divisions, each run as Adhocracies— one in Australia, one in France and one in the US. Each of these research divisions might be attempting to innovate within a free-floating matrix management system in a way that renders unjust individual responsibility for a failure to report fairly all of the side-effects associated with a new drug. Instead, collective blame fairly lies with the French team as a collectivity. Accordingly, corporate headquarters may sanction the French research team by cutting their budget, allocating to the French team all of the hack-work research for the next year, and saving the exciting projects for the Australians or Americans; they might give away the pet project of the French to the Americans. Alternatively, they might impose a sanction in the Bureaucratic Politics tradition—the French might lose their seat on the Corporate Research and Development Planning Committee to their arch enemies, the Australians. Insiders might know what would hurt the culpable individuals or subunit most without damaging the productive efficiency of the whole corporation. Outsiders are unlikely to understand this. They do not have the knowledge base either to grasp what creative options there are for sanctioning the guilty research team in a way which would make them stop and think about the irresponsibility of their collective behaviour, or to assess whether the socially

---

an offence, then it is more natural for the primary role to be played by insiders. In other words, the model of empowering private justice systems is a strategy for taking reactive fault seriously in addition to causally prior fault.

useful productive work of the corporation will be inhibited by the internal sanctioning recommended.

Outsiders do not understand the culture of the organisation. Investigators imbued in the corporate culture will be quick to grasp that X is an area of corporate accountability guided by collective responsibility requiring a collective sanction, or while Y might seem on paper to be a committee decision, 'everyone knows' that a key individual really made the decision, with the committee being a rubber stamp. Given the time pressures a court would be likely to impose under the Accountability Model or any other practical model, it is difficult to imagine an outsider genuinely coming to grips with the subtleties of an unfamiliar corporate culture. Thus, the risks will be enhanced of the buck being made to stop at the wrong place. By the wrong place, we mean a place which the shared understandings of actors in the organisation would not define as the locus of responsibility. The corporate culture, partly on the basis of formal lines of authority and partly on the basis of informal understandings, defines which individuals and groups are responsible. It is they who should be sanctioned because it is they who had been put on notice within the corporate culture that it was their responsibility.

Compared with insiders, outside investigators face many practical handicaps in getting to the truth. They have a rather limited capacity to arrive unannounced or to surreptitiously inspect a workplace without arousing suspicion. Outsiders can rarely match the technical knowledge insiders have of unique production or documentation processes. Internal investigators' specialised knowledge of their employer's product lines make them more effective probers than outsiders who are more likely to be generalists. Their greater technical capacity to spot problems is enhanced by a greater social capacity to do so. Internal compliance personnel are more likely than outsiders to know where the bodies have been found buried after earlier crises, and to be able to detect cover-ups. As discussed in Chapter 2, this is evident from the difference between the capacity of government inspectors and that of internal compliance staff in the pharmaceutical industry to get answers.[104]

Private justice systems have a superior capacity to finger the culpable partly because of their capacity to trap suspected wrongdoers. The quality assurance manager of a pharmaceutical company gave a telling illustration. His assay staff was routinely obtaining test results showing the product to be at full strength. When they found a result of 80 per cent strength, the laboratory staff would assume that the assay was erroneous, simply mark the strength at 100 per cent, and not recalculate the test, or so the manager suspected. The manager's solution was periodically to 'spike' the samples with understrength product to see whether his staff would pick out the defects. If not, they could be dismissed or sanctioned in some other way.

Another example of the greater effectiveness of internal inspectors concerns a medical director who suspected that one of his scientists was 'graphiting' safety testing data. His hunch was that the scientist, whose job was to

[104] See Chapter 2 in this book, 38–9, citing Braithwaite, *Corporate Crime in the Pharmaceutical Industry*, 137.

run 100 trials on a drug, instead ran 10 and fabricated the other 90 so they would be consistent with the first 10. The medical director possessed investigative abilities that would have been practically impossible for an outside investigator. He could verify the number of animals taken from the animal store, the amount of drug substance that had been used, the number of samples that had been tested, as well as other facts. His familiarity with the laboratory made this easy. As an insider, he could probe quietly without raising the kind of alarm that might lead the criminal to pour an appropriate amount of drug substance down the sink.

For all these reasons, inside investigation teams are generally more capable of putting the right heads on the chopping block than are outsiders. But being more capable, they are not necessarily more willing. Inside investigators will be much more susceptible than outsiders to pressures from top management to get themselves or the corporation off the hook by crucifying a convenient scapegoat. The superior capacities of private justice systems to deliver just sanctioning of individuals and subunits within the corporation will only be delivered in practice if creativity is applied to the design of external checks and balances against scapegoating, as discussed in Section 7.

There are other reasons for putting the emphasis on internally conducted investigations. Traditions of corporate independence from government and non-interference in the internal affairs of corporations impel the law to communicate the message that it is the responsibility of the corporation, not the state, to put its house in order. When the law imposes onerous expectations of responsibility on corporations, most of them will rise to the challenge of meeting those expectations. If, on the other hand, the law treats corporations as unworthy of trust to put their houses in order, then that will be a self-fulfilling prophecy. Most companies have both a strong animus toward being good corporate citizens and a strong resentment of governments which assume them to be otherwise. Courts which operate from starting assumptions that corporations have good faith to right the wrongs of the past will mostly have that trust rewarded. Moreover, in the case where the axe of sanctions for non-compliance is poised over the corporation, the detection of abused trust can be readily remedied by allowing the forces of gravity to operate on the axe. On the other hand, when the state treats corporations as incorrigible, it creates managerial resentment and the rather effective forms of resistance and cover-up discussed in the next section. The community has little to lose from trust in the shadow of the axe, and a lot to gain.

The corporation also often has something to gain from seizing an opportunity to put its own house in order rather than risk the court doing it for them. If part of the reality of the axe is a management restructuring order, the corporation knows it can come up with new policies and new lines of responsibility which will do less violence to productive efficiency than that likely to be imposed by an unsympathetic court. Second, there are psychic rewards for executives who see themselves as responsible citizens freely choosing reforms to put things right for the future and to compensate for past wrongs. There are also morale advantages for top management to be able to say to employees that, although the corporation may have erred, it has voluntarily taken extraordinary steps to remedy the wrong.

More fundamentally, the law should foster cultural traditions where citizens, be they individual or corporate, take responsibility for their own rehabilitation rather than have it dictated to them. A law which imposes expectations of responsible reaction to wrongdoing encourages social responsibility; a law which strips corporate citizens of such obligations by telling them how to reform encourages abrogation of responsibility.

A further reason for initially trusting the corporation to formulate its own reaction to the offence is the well-established psychological datum that actors are more committed to solutions which they impose on themselves than they are to actions which are directives from others.[105] Compliance with the law in a complex organisation requires sustained commitment to internal compliance systems. Getting the rehabilitative measures right is important; but so is sustaining enthusiasm to continue enforcement of the measures in the long term. Only the corporation, not the court or the probation service, can deliver sustained commitment to compliance. Hence, the objective of the state should be to create the conditions for the corporation to own the solution to its problem.

12 Averting Cultures of Resistance

Desideratum
Special care must be taken to ensure that the state does not cause private justice systems to become organised against the state justice system. The state should have enforcement policies that avert the formation of organised business cultures of resistance to regulatory law.

Eugene Bardach and Robert Kagan have suggested that one of the problems with a single-mindedly punitive business regulatory strategy is that it can lead to an 'organised culture of resistance'—a business culture which resists the authority of the state to secure compliance with its laws by sharing knowledge about the methods of legal counterattack, and by other means.[106] The Accountability Model proposal that the courts rely more heavily on private justice systems can be seen as part of a wider philosophy of monitored self-regulation[107] which puts responsibility for learning from mistakes and fixing them squarely in the hands of business.

This philosophy contends that an organised culture of resistance is less likely to the extent that the state operates from starting assumptions of trust in business as responsible corporate citizens. Giving offenders a second chance

---

[105] See the conclusion of Vroom's review that 'the participation of individuals or of groups in decisions which affect them appears to be positively related to their acceptance of decisions and to the efficiency with which decisions are executed': Vroom, 'Industrial Social Psychology', 196, 237.

[106] Bardach and Kagan, *Going by the Book*.

[107] See Ayres and Braithwaite, *Responsive Regulation;* Braithwaite, 'Enforced Self-Regulation'; Braithwaite, *To Punish or Persuade*; Mitnick, 'The Two-Part Problem of Regulatory Compliance'.

to put their house in order can build a commitment to try harder to ensure compliance in future. The self-inspection and action report can be seen as such a second chance. If the court treats a corporation as if it is trustworthy and responsible, then that will often be a self-fulfilling prophecy. If the court or regulatory agency from the outset demeans a corporation as unscrupulous and manipulative, then that too may be a self-fulfilling prophecy, especially when managers are involved who deeply regret what some of their colleagues have done and wish to do everything possible to ensure responsible behaviour in future. A regulatory process which prematurely treats the corporation and its officers as evil persons, rather than as persons who perpetrated a prohibited act for reasons yet to be established, runs the risk of driving responsible managers within the organisation into the camp of irresponsible executives who advocate an organised culture of resistance to regulatory law.

It is also true that corporations which have no socially responsible managerial constituencies within them will abuse and exploit assumptions of good faith. When this is the case, there is a remedy under the Accountability Model. The remedy is that the court will strike the corporation with a highly publicised corporate sanction, will prosecute individual executives as well when the evidence can be found and will maintain ongoing intervention in the corporation's affairs through corporate probation or punitive injunctions.[108]

Thus, we see the proposal to catalyse private justice systems as part of a response to the downward spiral of protracted litigiousness in government–business relations. Our proposal attempts to counter the organised culture of resistance to regulatory law by putting the onus on business to come up with the solution to the problem of non-compliance. This is a better first approach than setting out to coerce a solution which becomes a rallying cry for corporate resistance.

13 Reflecting the Diverse Aims of the Criminal Justice System

Desideratum
A strategy for sanctioning the responsible should also avoid myopia about the aims of the criminal justice system. Narrowly focused utilitarianism or retributivism are prescriptions for disastrous corporate criminal enforcement policies. Criminal liability is not merely a matter of paying a price for crime, but has a prohibitory function which is reflected by the denunciatory emphasis of the criminal process. Nor should criminal liability be viewed simply as a matter of retribution. The harms protected against by corporate criminal law are too serious for us to indulge in retribution at the cost of increasing corporate harm-doing.

---

[108] It is the publicity and the ongoing intervention in the internal affairs of the company which are sometimes more feared by business than the size of the penalty, though the size of the penalty can help foster publicity. See Fisse and Braithwaite, *The Impact of Publicity on Corporate Offenders*.

The myopia that we are most anxious to avoid with the Accountability Model is an economistic one that orients the justice system to a pricing system for harm-doing. We have seen in Section 9 how this approach can lead into a deterrence trap and how a more plural responsibility model can lead us out of that trap. In the last section, we indicated how a narrowly retributive model can fuel a business subculture of resistance. Such a model would require us to pursue the objective of state criminal punishment of all who are criminally responsible. We have seen that this is an impossible objective,[109] the pursuit of which would result in a massively cost-inefficient corporate criminal law (see Section 4). Short of adopting the full pricing model or the full retributive model, our approach does heed and reflect the core ideas that underpin both models. These are respectively that the capacity to deter economically rational actors is crucial to any strategy of corporate criminal law, and that just reprobation for all of those who are responsible for corporate crime is needed. Two philosophies of punishment that are irreconcilable if either is pushed to the limit (insistence that just reprobation can only be delivered by determinate state criminal punishment is at odds with insistence on always imposing the 'economically efficient' price on crime) can be reconciled under the Accountability Model.

The Model also differs from retributive and deterrence pricing models in the strong emphasis it places on incapacitation and rehabilitation. We assume that in some circumstances the deterrence trap or the economically irrational tenacity of some subcultures of resistance to law will mean that incapacitative controls are needed. These will range from corporate capital punishment and director disqualification to corporate probationary conditions that incapacitate, as by putting electronic seals on nuclear materials that will trigger an alarm at the nuclear regulatory agency if the seals are broken, or by putting a full-time government safety inspector in the coal mine for the duration of the probation order,[110] and so on.

Most distinctively, however, the Accountability Model puts great store in the possibility of corporate rehabilitation. It is based on the belief that if one treats corporations as deserving only retribution, they are likely to act as corporations deserving only retribution. If corporations are treated as actors motivated only by threats to their profits, they are likely to obey the law only when it is profitable to do so. The Accountability Model avoids such counterproductive assumptions by giving corporations a chance to accept and act upon the proposition that law-abidingness is an obligation of corporate citizenship. It is not based on the assumption that corporations will always or even generally accept these obligations of corporate citizenship; it simply gives them a chance to do so. There is a good deal of empirical evidence that corporations often do rise to the challenge of voluntary reform when

---

[109] See also Braithwaite and Pettit, *Not Just Deserts*.
[110] The US Mine Safety and Health Administration did this with its resident inspector program, a program that was effective in improving safety in the targeted mines. See Braithwaite, *To Punish or Persuade*, 82–3.

confronted with allegations of law-breaking.[111] In our view, any model of corporate criminal law which fails to embody this factor is misguided.

The policy of seeking to hold responsible all who are responsible means that there will always be some deterrent costs, because the investigation itself will have significant costs, and systematic reprobation of the responsible will have substantial reputational costs. It also means a principled attempt to allocate denunciation to the responsible in proportion to their responsibility. The retributivist must view this as a positive step, even if it falls far short of his or her desideratum of proportionate state punishment of all who are responsible. Similarly, either the voluntary or the mandatory accountability order will almost always involve some incapacitative elements (such as extra auditing, shifting irresponsible personnel, or new technology that reduces the risk of further offending).

The main advantage of the Accountability Model in integrating the competing objectives of criminal justice policies, however, is its dynamic quality—the way it shifts the balance of these competing objectives depending on corporate responsiveness. The initial thrust of the Model is a major emphasis on the objective of corporate rehabilitation. But if the move in that direction fails, the emphasis then shifts toward deterrence and judicial denunciation. The latter shift, as argued in Section 18, is justified because there are compelling reasons why reactive fault should be a central basis of criminal liability.

If, then, there is still evidence of regulatory failure, further escalation up the enforcement pyramid will occur toward sanctions that rely more heavily on incapacitation than on deterrence or denunciation. The slippery slope down which corporations are ultimately led when they show themselves to be beyond rehabilitation, beyond shame, and beyond deterrence is corporate capital punishment. Corporations, unlike human beings, do not have inviolate rights to existence. In the rare cases where corporations are found to be incorrigible criminals after they are given chances to prove themselves otherwise, there is no compelling reason to put up with the social costs they impose on us; we are best to insist on the sale of their assets to other enterprises with better management.[112]

14 Varieties of Responsibility and Organisational Diversity

Desideratum
A strategy for allocating responsibility should be in harmony with the varieties of structures, cultures, decisionmaking and accountability principles in large and small organisations.

---

[111] Hopkins, *The Impact of Prosecutions under the Trade Practices Act*; Waldman, *Antitrust Action and Market Structure*; Fisse and Braithwaite, *The Impact of Publicity on Corporate Offenders*; Braithwaite et al., *Raising the Standard*.

[112] Of course, if they are not only so incorrigible but also so valueless that no other firm will buy them at any price, then there is no social loss in forcing them into bankruptcy.

Chapter 4 revealed the diversity of ways in which organisations can structure their decisionmaking, their accountability principles, their role allocation and their internal and external environments. Positivist organisation theory, as we saw, is unable to provide practical guidance on how the law ought to allocate responsibility for organisational crime.

There is no unifying theory waiting to be discovered by sociologists for jurisprudential recycling. Every organisation is different in the way responsibility is defined and decided within it. Yet within every organisation shared understandings exist as to what is a just and effective way of assigning responsibility. Imposing reifications of how responsibility works from organisation theory, from the law, or from moral philosophy, does such violence to particularistic conceptions of responsibility as to foster cynicism about the need to behave responsibly. Imposition of these externally derived reifications of responsibility means that those held responsible by the outside world will be viewed as scapegoats by the insiders to whose behaviour social control is meant to be directed.

Instead of the usual route of confronting jurisprudence with positivist organisation theory, the Accountability Model confronts jurisprudence with ethnomethodology. As Harold Garfinkel conceives it, the project of ethnomethodology is to 'analyse ... the formal properties of commonplace, practical common sense actions, 'from within' actual settings, as ongoing accomplishments of those settings'.[113] The proposal is that the corporation conduct its own ethnomethodology, with outside consultants if it chooses, and thereby to unfold how actors are held responsible for action within the organisation. The conduct of the ethnomethodological study, the particularistic responsibility principles revealed by it, and the way these principles are acted upon to respond to the offence under consideration would all be subject to critical scrutiny by the court.

We make the assumption, based on our own fieldwork, that all organisations will have some agreed responsibility principles which can be revealed by this process. Organisations which fit Mintzberg's definition of an Adhocracy are settings where a particularistic ethnomethodology is most needed and yet where even this approach may fail to reveal shared meanings over who or what is responsible.[114] Yet we doubt that even the most fluid, chaotic Adhocracy can survive, certainly not in a competitive market, unless it can reach agreement on how to make actors responsible for that which is accepted as within their span of control.

We also take the position that a Machine Bureaucracy will be able to mobilise its private justice system in a way that is tolerably just and effective for its kind of machine bureaucracy, and certainly in a way that is more sensible than imposing the accountability systems of, say, other Machine Bureaucracies with their different histories. Similar observations can be made for all of the diverse types of organisations discussed in Chapter 4. In short, the approach is one which highlights the importance of comprehending that

[113] Garfinkel, *Studies in Ethnomethodology*, vii–viii.
[114] Mintzberg, *The Structuring of Organizations*, 431–67.

identical structures do not imply identical understandings for allocating responsibility because the sediment of how human agency is exercised over the history of the organisation can result in unpredictable agreements being struck over who will be responsible for what.

The process adopted under the Accountability Model avoids a forced choice between simple-minded alternative models of organisational life. To think in terms of Kriesberg's three models,[115] the internal investigation and action report might well contain an analysis which lays part of the blame with the corporation as a rational actor striving to maximise profits, part of the blame with defective SOPs, and part of the blame with individuals and sub-units pursuing their own political agendas within the bureaucracy.

Moreover, when it comes to the 'action' part of the self-investigation and action report, responsible individuals and subunits can be portrayed (1) as 'amoral calculators' who need 'deterrence'; (2) as 'political citizens' who offended because they needed 'persuasion' as to the reasonableness or rationality of the law; (3) as 'incompetent' actors who need assistance from the regulatory agency or the internal compliance group as 'consultants', or some combination of the three. This is the typology of the regulator–business interface proposed by Robert Kagan and John Scholz.[116] It follows that our strategy enables the court to acquire a more variegated appreciation of what went wrong. The problem with the externally imposed criminal law model of responsibility is that it is locked into an image of business as amoral calculators who must be deterred or given their just deserts.

By catalysing a self-investigation report the state can leave itself more open to the possibility that instead of responding to the crime by setting up the regulatory agency as police, it would be better to put the agency in the role of politician persuading corporate citizens of the need to comply, or in the role of consultant assisting the corporation in redesigning compliance systems. In other words, a strategy based on the self-investigation and action report not only allows the law to respond to the diversity of corporate culture, it also fosters a more diverse conceptualisation of the state's regulatory mission than arises from the punitive obsessions of traditional criminal law. Courts are as capable of delusion by their simple models into losing sight of the multi-faceted nature of the goals shared by the state they represent as they are capable of counterproductivity by simplifying the diverse meanings of corporate behaviour.

The Accountability Model provides a process of investigation which opens up both complexity and subtlety in the understanding of what happened, and a diversity of approaches to remediation. In contrast, the traditional criminal process tends to straightjacket investigations within one assumption—amoral calculation—and to channel investigations toward one kind of resolution—punishments calibrated according to the degree of moral failure. Jurists tend to resent the incursion of 'extraneous' issues because they undermine the

---

[115] Kriesberg, 'Decisionmaking Models and the Control of Corporate Crime'.
[116] Kagan and Scholz, 'The 'Criminology of the Corporation' and 'Regulatory Enforcement Strategies'.

integrity of the calibration processes of their narrowly punitive model. Under the influence of this mind-set, interventions to remedy defective SOPs, for example, must be assessed in terms of how they will affect the proportionality of deserved sentences.

The courts need to learn that social control by court-ordered punishment is not the most important form of social control.[117] Just as economists must be wary of their propensity to allow the more measurable to drive out the more important, lawyers need to be on guard against their propensity to allow the more formalistic to drive out the more effective. Care is thus needed when applying the Accountability Model not to destroy informal social control by administering traditional notions of punitive justice. At the same time, there is no denying the value of the universalistic protections that the courts are accustomed to providing. Where, for example, the rights of employees in internal disciplinary inquiries are violated by a corporate defendant then, as we have seen in Section 5, those rights need to be protected. The role of the courts here is to intervene and to ensure that rights are upheld.

15 Nuanced Imaginings of Corporate Action

Desideratum
A strategy for allocating responsibility should be capable of nuanced response to the likelihood that the same corporate action can be usefully understood in many different ways. Our mechanisms for allocating responsibility should not be so calibrated that the ambiguous and paradoxical nature of corporate action eludes us. In other words, we should be able to avoid the traps of narrowness of vision through institutions that are able to imagine corporate action in multiple ways. Our methodology for allocating responsibility should foster a dialogue that brings these multiple interpretations of responsibility into the open.

Why do so many of those individuals who are convicted of corporate crimes feel that, while they might not be lilywhite, they have been unfairly victimised? Why do they tend to feel anger rather than shame at their conviction, or to feel mad rather than bad?[118] One plausible reason is that, as insiders of the offending organisation, they can see the offence from a number of different viewpoints that were not seriously considered during their trial. Under those alternative understandings of what led to the offence, others seem to the convicted offender to be just as responsible as they are. In the responsibility discourse of the criminal law, the person who intentionally commits the *actus reus* of the offence is clearly guilty. Now it may be that certain other individuals set up decisionmaking practices so that 'if someone had to do what had to

---

[117] See Braithwaite, *Crime, Shame and Reintegration*; Fisse and Braithwaite, *The Impact of Publicity on Corporate Offenders*.

[118] For empirical evidence on this question, see Benson, 'Emotions and Adjudication: Status Degradation among White Collar Criminals'.

be done', it would be the person who was in fact convicted. Once convicted, the person will naturally feel that these other individuals are responsible too, perhaps more responsible, and he or she will be bitter that the criminal process allows no adequate opportunity for seeing things as they happened.

We do not regard it as inevitable that the criminal process must remain blind to all responsibility discourses other than those that warrant a criminal conviction. Hence the desideratum that the process be opened up to bring multiple interpretations of responsibility into the open. Gareth Morgan[119] argues that sophisticated understandings of organisations involve 'imaginising' organisational action as many things at once. Our model must be able to reveal responsibility through multiple patterns of significance; we must acquire a nuanced picture of who did what and why through trying a variety of metaphors of organisational action.

A conspicuous strength of the Accountability Model is that it opens up the possibility of doing just this. It does so by nurturing alternative imaginings of what happened organisationally. The Model does not preclude or inhibit a nuanced understanding of responsibility, nor does it translate wrongdoing merely into the rudimentary responsibility discourse of the criminal law. The rudimentary approach now taken by the criminal law should be seen for what it is. There are usually some potential criminal hands at work on the surface. Evidence sufficient to stamp their responsibility as criminal can often be obtained without much ado. Beneath the surface, other persons may share in the responsibility for the offence, but they are let go because it would be difficult to turn their responsibility into a story of criminal responsibility. Better still, they can be transformed into white knights who co-operate with the prosecution to blacken the ill-fated chosen defendant.

Our hope for the internal investigation and action report under the Accountability Model is that it would allow a multiplex understanding of responsibility. Consider the following imaginary investigation and action report, which is suggested by a case on which we have done fieldwork:

Bribes were paid to many influential foreign government officials to secure sales of military equipment [details of offences are given].

A and B, who arranged the transfer of moneys, were not aware that they were paying bribes. Nor did these officers ask questions about certain transactions that were clearly unusual. They failed to draw the attention of the auditors to these transactions; they were negligent or wilfully blind [*fault-based responsibility*].

The auditors, in turn, failed to educate finance staff about the need to red flag such unusual transactions [*responsibility for compliance system failure*] and were themselves negligent in failing to detect them [*gatekeeper responsibility*].

Executive A was responsible for approving these bribes [*decision-making responsibility*], and knew they were bribes arranged by a foreign sales agent to guarantee sales [*external actor responsibility*].

---

[119] Morgan, *Images of Organization*. See Chapter 4, 118-22.

The sales agent regularly acceded to hints from foreign defence officials B, C and D for kickbacks [*foreign actor responsibility*].

The defence attaché in the Foreign Office encouraged the corporation to 'take good care' of B, C and D because they were political supporters of foreign policy objectives and critical to a positive ongoing defence relationship [*government responsibility*]. Knowing this, Executive A's immediate superior frequently spoke to him in these terms: 'B, C and D are vital political connections and vital to sustaining our goodwill with our own defence department—so keep them happy' [*responsibility for tacit approval of bribery*]. Executive A was also under pressure from his competitor in the corporation, Executive X. X denigrated A as too 'soft' to be effective in the world of defence sales [*responsibility for sustaining a corporate culture conducive to bribery*]. A knew that, if he put any obstacles in the way of corrupt payments, X would seize upon this in gossip about A being weak, a threat to the collective secrecy of the system of corruption, and someone who should be demoted. A believed on good grounds that if he did not play the game, he would be demoted and that someone more unscrupulous (like X) would take his job.

Some of the payments that A believed to be bribes went into the pocket of the sales agent, who exaggerated the pay-offs demanded by the foreign defence officials. He used some of the money which A took to be for foreign bribes on expensive dinners with prostitutes for A's superior [*external actor and top management responsibility*]. A did not understand that this was the reason why his superior had said to him: 'It is best to follow the advice of our sales agent on these foreign sales. He knows what he is doing and I trust him completely'.

Under the responsibility discourse of the criminal law, if any individual is indicted, it will almost certainly be A and no one else. The prosecutor will call on various of the other responsible actors to turn state's evidence and to incriminate A. We can readily understand why A would feel scapegoated.

Under the Accountability Model, the self-investigation and action report process would result in others being sanctioned besides A. All of those responsible would suffer from the shame of exposure of their part in the offences described in the report. Perhaps those who made the payments would be censured for their wilful blindness, held back in their careers or sent on a training course devoted to the detection and prevention of questionable payments. At the other extreme, perhaps A's boss and the sales agent would be dismissed in circumstances of abject disgrace.

The point is that the different types of responsibility will drop out of the picture unless the process of allocating responsibility is open to different metaphors of organisational decisionmaking. It may be useful to see the organisation (as the criminal law may previously have seen it) as a machine bureaucracy in which A has responsibility within the decisionmaking structure for deciding to pay the bribes. However, if we apply Morgan's metaphor of the organisation as a system of domination, we very quickly uncover the responsibility of A's boss. If we apply Morgan's political system metaphor or

Kriesberg's political actor model, we quickly see the crucial role of X's reprehensible politicking as well as the responsibility of the defence attaché from the Foreign Office. If we think about organisations as cultures, we investigate the responsibility of the chief executive for cultivating a culture of moral ambivalence and wilful blindness concerning corruption. If we apply Kriesberg's organisation process model, we are likely to identify many defective SOPs in the corporation's accounting system that allowed the off-books accounts and kickbacks to occur unnoticed by the auditors.

If we apply Morgan's metaphor of the organisation as an organism in an environment (or Lawrence and Lorsch's environmental contingency theory), we see that changes to the culture of this organisation and/or imposing criminal responsibility on individuals within it will have limited effects because we are dealing with an environment in which organisations will find it difficult to survive if they refuse to pay bribes. To change that environment, the first step is to make the criminogenic nature of that environment a matter of public knowledge. The complicity of a system of defence attachés, sales agents with connections to powerful ruling families, and foreign defence officials must be exposed. The self-investigation and action report is an ideal instrument for doing just this. But it is only a step toward an international political crackdown on transnational corruption, backed by extraterritorial application of national corruption laws, with each nation supporting another's corruption case through its own criminal laws and industry-wide anticorruption codes of corporate conduct.[120] The metaphor of organisations as organisms in an environment causes us to identify that those who are responsible for the failure of all of these things to happen are largely external to the organisation.

Finally, a dialectical understanding of the organisation might lead us to conclude that A was right. Given the realities of the corporate culture and the environment within which it survives, an attempt by A to refuse to pay bribes would result in A's replacement by someone more ruthless. A might achieve more by working quietly to change the culture of the organisation and by trying to persuade the organisation to talk with its competitors about informal agreements to reduce the need for them to pay bribes. The dialectical metaphor thus prompts us to ponder whether the traditional criminal law model of responsibility might do more harm than good in this context.

The self-investigation and action report creates a space where such analysis of the causes of an offence and the multiple responsibilities for it can be brought into the open. Dialogue is the best methodology for bringing about such a change. This means simply giving everyone involved a chance to expose their account of how and why the offence occurred. Traditional criminal investigations are preoccupied with acquiring evidence and obtaining criminal convictions; dialogue is seen as a diversion from that goal. Private justice systems, which are designed to move on from decisions about what

---

[120] The codes may be informal as well as formal; thus, Braithwaite found evidence of such informal agreement among American and European pharmaceutical companies in Latin America following the enactment of the US Foreign Corrupt Practices Act: Braithwaite, *Corporate Crime in the Pharmaceutical Industry*, ch. 2.

and who was responsible to decisions about what should be done to prevent a recurrence, are much better placed to foster the dialogue needed. Private justice systems, however, are at risk of domination by the ruling elite of the organisation, a domination which will censor some readings of the offence and which may steer the investigation to a narrow and hierarchically self-serving interpretation of the incident.

This is where the public justice system can intervene to prevent the private justice system from chilling unwanted dialogue. It can do this by sending a representative to an open meeting within the corporation to discuss a draft self-investigation report, by talking privately to people after this meeting about whether they felt free to speak out and by encouraging the involvement of outside directors and representatives of independent parties (unions, environmental groups, consumer groups) in the investigation. Finally, it can encourage the involvement of outside consultants with outstanding track records of integrity and expertise in providing a nuanced understanding of the diverse responsibilities underlying the offence. This approach can readily be stimulated by a court, as by making it plain to a corporate defendant that an investigative report is more likely to be accepted if independent scrutiny is built into the self-investigation process.

16 Redundancy

Desideratum
A strategy for allocating responsibility in a complex corporate world where the motivations of actors are multiple and where no single model of corporate action grasps the whole story should be based on redundancy. If the intervention fails for one reason, there should be other features of the intervention which might enable it to succeed. Redundancy should be built into interventions, while the inefficiencies of costly redundancies are avoided.

It should be clear by now that the Accountability Model is based on giving multiple sources of social control—corporate or industry association self-regulatory systems, regulatory agencies, courts—a chance to exercise their creativity in fashioning controls that will help to prevent corporate crime by systematically improving the allocation of responsibility for it. The Model thus embodies redundancy at the level of control agencies.[121] The enforcement pyramid also involves redundancy by increasing the array of controls available to the particular agency of regulation. So the court that fails to trigger voluntary corporate reform is able to issue an accountability order; if that fails to mandate reform in this way, deterrent sentences can be imposed; if deterrence fails, the court can resort to a variety of incapacitative strategies

---

[121] On redundancy and regulation see generally Bendor, *Parallel Systems*; Landau, 'Redundancy, Rationality, and the Problem of Duplication and Overlap'.

the ultimate of which is corporate capital punishment. The enforcement pyramid is thus based on a fail-safe strategy.

There are three basic ways in which the Accountability Model exploits redundancy in its approach to crime control:

(1) It eschews the notion that there is a single ideal or static approach to social control by allowing a plurality of public and private justice system controls to flourish. It is a platform for fostering innovation in social control.
(2) Credence is given to the possibility of successful control through denunciation, deterrence, rehabilitation and incapacitation and all of these bases of control are given an opportunity to do their work. However, each of these is viewed as a rather weak basis of control unless placed in a creative synergy with the others.
(3) The implementation of these redundant modalities of control is left to different types of agents—corporate compliance staff, industry association compliance staff, state regulatory agency compliance staff, outside directors, unions, public interest groups, prosecutors and judges.

In the abstract, redundancy may seem costly or even grossly inefficient. However, the Accountability Model minimises and seeks to avoid these problems by using a dynamically responsive mode of redundancy. The redundancy in an enforcement pyramid is hardly static. Corporate compliance staff are initially trusted to use their best endeavours to secure compliance; if they fail, the first preference may be to give an industry self-regulatory system a chance to secure compliance; if that fails, regulatory agency administrative interventions are triggered; if they fail, the courts come into action. In the enforcement pyramid, efficiency is pursued by trying cheaper interventions first and only escalating to more costly interventions when these break down or prove insufficient. A similar approach is apparent in relation to the different modalities of control in the Model. As explained in Section 13, denunciation, rehabilitation, deterrence and incapacitation are pursued dynamically and sequentially. The Model is designed to avert the danger of all barrels being discharged loosely, much less simultaneously.

17 Preserving Managerial Flexibility

Desideratum
A strategy for allocating responsibility should ensure that the law does not inefficiently straightjacket management systems into conformity with legal principles.

In Chapter 4, we pointed out that one of the solutions to the problem of mismatch between organisational accountability systems and the accountability required by the law is for the law to require that certain accountability mechanisms be put in place. For example, the law can mandate that all manufacturing corporations above a certain size have a vice-president for environmental affairs and that this officer must see monthly reports on a variety of matters of environmental concern. A disadvantage of this solution is that it mandates management systems that may not be the most efficient way of dealing with the problem for some types of organisations. Moreover, clumsy intervention to secure one type of control may compromise the integrity or coherence of other existing control systems.

The Accountability Model minimises this danger by allowing problem organisations ample opportunity to design and implement their own account-ability solutions through the self-investigation and action report. This reflects the assumption, as expressed in Section 7, that corporations are more likely to be committed to programs of action that they have developed themselves. Moreover, self-tailored solutions are likely to be more effective and cost-efficient when they are designed by managers familiar with all the likely organisational consequences than when they are designed by outside lawyers or imposed as a universal requirement by regulatory officials or courts. Under the Model, mandated requirements are imposed only when organisations fail to come up with their own credible accountability assurances.

A secondary agenda of regulatory agencies in promoting accountability agreements and assurances is to foment a more educative and innovative com-pliance culture. Innovative internal compliance systems are likely to come from triggering the managerial creativity of the private sector. When a respected corporate leader unveils a new type of corporate compliance pro-gram pursuant to an accountability agreement or assurance, this can become a model for other companies to consider. From several angles there is educative potential in respected companies (1) publicly admitting and apologising for breaking the law,[122] (2) explaining to the business community the nature of the management breakdowns that allowed this to happen, and (3) unveiling path-breaking internal compliance systems or technologies to prevent this from happening again.

18 Coping with the Dynamics of Corporate Behaviour

Desideratum
A strategy for allocating responsibility should operate with a conception of fault that is not time-bound, but copes with the dynamic nature of cor-porate action.

One philosophical foundation of the Accountability Model is the concept of reactive corporate fault, by which is meant an unreasonable corporate failure to devise and undertake satisfactory preventive or corrective measures in response to the commission of the *actus reus* of an offence by personnel acting on behalf of the organisation. In Chapter 2, we explained what this

---

[122] See Wolfe's discussion of the importance of corporate apology to victims of corporate law-breaking so as to counter the notion that business is just a game, as opposed to an activity with very human consequences: Wolfe, 'The Corporate Apology'. See also Braithwaite, *Crime, Shame and Reintegration,* on the power of apology, repentance and forgiveness in building moral commitment to the law.

concept means and how it offers a practical way of reflecting corporate blameworthiness in cases where a corporation has compliance policies and systems in place and where the gravamen of corporate fault lies in the unresponsive nature of the corporation's reaction to having caused harm. In Section 2 above, we have recommended that reactive corporate fault be an explicit basis of corporate criminal liability. This is a cardinal step if corporate criminal liability is to be workable and rebuilt on the foundation of corporate blameworthiness. There is, however, more to the concept of reactive fault than its ability to reflect the phenomenon of corporate blameworthiness at the post-offence stage of corporate behaviour. Reactive fault also provides the key to structuring legal liability in a way that can handle dynamic changes in the corporate environment. A frequent criticism made of the legal regulation of business is that precedent and backward-looking assessments of liability project a static model of corporate behaviour, whereas innovation and change within corporations require a more dynamic and forward-looking approach.[123] As explained below, the reactive fault element built into the Accountability Model allows the law to move in pace with changes that occur within a corporate defendant's organisation, and to insist on higher standards on a case-by-case basis, without injustice.

The defence of reasonable precautions is a good example of the difficulty that the law faces in keeping step with rapidly changing social and corporate conditions. The tension has been described as follows:

> The gravitation of law toward conformity and stability pulls the standard of due diligence down to a customary level and exerts a field of minor incremental change. If this is allowed to happen, the law puts its power behind existing compliance technology and provides little or no incentive for corporations to develop more innovative solutions, or apply state-of-the-art techniques. Furthermore, if social assessments of the gravity of pollution undergo a marked change, as they have over the past two decades, adherence to preexisting standards of due diligence is at best an exercise in social irrelevance. Yet, if the law ties itself to a proactive timeframe for the assessment of liability, it can easily be faced with an invidious choice: to impose a demanding new standard and thereby take a defendant unfairly by surprise, or to retain a lax old standard and thereby deprive potential victims of more adequate protection.[124]

One solution lies in the adaptive mechanism built into the Accountability Model. Take the case where a company is charged with a pollution offence and pleads a defence of due diligence on the strength of having installed an industry-approved waste treatment plant. A defence of proactive due diligence would impose a relatively static and undemanding standard of care. In comparison, a defence of reactive due diligence lends itself to a more dynamic and demanding standard of care. Far from being confined to *ex ante* due diligence, the reactive due diligence standard would extend to the care that should be taken by a corporation to learn from and respond to a violation.

---

[123] See generally Schon, *Beyond the Stable State*.
[124] Fisse and French, 'Corporate Responses to Errant Behavior'.

Thus, a reactive standard of due diligence might well require the company to install a state-of-the-art backup treatment facility and not merely a treatment plant previously accepted as customary within the industry. Provided that notice of the higher standard expected was given (as by a court when imposing an accountability order), that higher standard could be imposed without occasioning unfair retrospective application. New benchmarks in compliance technology and innovation in compliance management might well be achieved, voluntarily wherever possible. Unlike the present law, which is relatively static, this approach has a progressive impetus toward improvement of existing practice and learning quickly from experience.

Apart from the standards expected of operating plants and procedures, reactive fault allows a dynamic approach in cases where individual criminal liability is inadequate because of changes that have occurred within the corporate organisation. In Chapter 2, we drew attention to the way in which transnational or multi-state corporations can and sometimes do transfer individuals out of the jurisdiction by giving them a job at an overseas or interstate subsidiary. More significantly, it was noted that individual criminal liability is inadequate where, as is often the case, personnel change places so that those responsible for a past offence are no longer responsible for compliance in the same area of the company's activities. Plainly, the prevention of similar offences in the future requires an approach that is directed at the managers who have taken over the relevant zone of control. Corporate criminal liability, as currently structured, can exert some pressure on the organisation to guard against repetition of the offence, but falls well short of focusing on the individuals who were implicated in the offence committed or who are in a position to prevent that kind of offence from recurring in the future. How should liability be restructured so as to provide that focus? Again, the key lies in the concept of reactive corporate fault. The relevance of this concept where guilty personnel are exported to another jurisdiction is explained in Section 19. The discussion below concerns the more important question of what can be done to deal with the problem of shifts in the composition of management.

An approach based on reactive fault can readily focus on the managers who have taken over control in the area where an offence previously occurred. The reactive duty to provide an adequate self-investigation report is not met unless the corporation explains exactly what measures have been taken to minimise the risk of repeating the offence. This requires an explanation of what has been done to advise and train the new managers in light of the unsatisfactory performance of their predecessors. It also requires an account of what has been done to enhance the internal disciplinary controls over the new managers should they step out of line. In other words, pressure can be put on the corporation and its new managers to learn specifically from past breakdowns and to revise the compliance system accordingly. The form of responsibility relevant here is fault-based in so far as the corporation and the new managers are liable if they inexcusably fail to take the precautions needed. However, the approach is hardly backward-looking. On the contrary, the emphasis is on the power and function of the new managers to take the steps necessary for the future.

This forward-looking conception of responsibility bears out a point that we have stressed earlier, namely that it is a mistake to view internal disciplinary systems in a narrow legalistic way as if they clone the criminal justice system. Internal discipline within organisations cannot sensibly be approached as if the employees are suspects charged with offences. The ongoing place of the employee in the organisation is critical; at least in private corporations it is not in the interests of shareholders that resources be spent persecuting the past sins of personnel. Private systems of justice embody more diverse and richer forms of responsibility, including the future-directed conception of responsibility indicated above. By using the framework of reactive fault to exploit this future-directed capacity, the Accountability Model gives the state legal system a parallel capacity to move forward and keep abreast of organisational change. Instead of assuming that corporations will adjust to the pace of the law, the hypothesis is that the law can adjust to the pace of corporations only by recognising how private systems of justice themselves adapt to organisational change and how they modify their own conceptions of responsibility accordingly.

19 Transnationality

Desideratum
A strategy for allocating responsibility should not be bound by a national jurisdiction; it should be capable of responding to the increasingly international nature of corporate action.

As previously mentioned, transnational corporations can move individuals at risk of prosecution beyond jurisdiction to a foreign subsidiary, parent, or associated company. This is one facet of the problem of organised cultures of resistance, as discussed in Section 12. Even if there is no such calculated protective move, it can often happen that the individuals responsible for offences will be in a country other than that in which criminal proceedings are launched.[125] Fraud in the safety testing of a pharmaceutical product, bribery, and money laundering are typical contexts in point. Extradition and mutual assistance arrangements may not always be in place and in any event are cumbersome. Fining the local corporation in such a case will not necessarily be effective, partly because there is no guarantee that the defendant will do more than write a cheque, and partly because a fine levied according to the wealth of the local corporation may fall well short of what is needed to make an

---

[125] Consider, e.g., the problems the Australian government would confront were it to prosecute the American transnational A. H. Robins for assault against the 3,000 Australian victims of the Dalkon Shield intra-uterine device. None of the individuals subject to allegations of responsibility would be in Australia; see Cashman, 'The Dalkon Shield'. Consider also the role of foreigners in the foreign bribery scandals of the 1970s (e.g., McCloy, *The Great Oil Spill*; Boulton, *The Grease Machine*). See generally Fisse, 'Sanctioning Multinational Offenders'; Walde, 'Parent–Subsidiary Relations in the Integrated Corporate System'.

impression on a large, well-heeled parent.[126] This is a difficult problem that calls for a new international legal order of transnational controls. However, the Accountability Model does at least provide a partial solution by equipping the local state system of justice with a useful additional means of transnational enforcement.[127]

The private justice systems of transnational corporations can reach across international borders in a way that the public justice system of the state cannot. As capital becomes increasingly internationalised and executives increasingly mobile, this emerges as a good reason for catalysing private justice systems. Moreover, there is no doubt that this can be done. The heads of many foreign executives and agents of American transnationals rolled as a result of the spate of self-investigatory reports that the US SEC secured from companies involved in foreign bribery in the 1970s.[128]

The Accountability Model deploys the same strategy as that used by the US SEC but refines and toughens the means of implementation. As we have seen, a feature of the Accountability Model is the reactive duty that it imposes on corporate defendants to undertake an internal disciplinary inquiry and to sanction those responsible. A company that transfers guilty personnel to another jurisdiction can be asked voluntarily to repatriate the culprits or to have them disciplined abroad through the internal disciplinary mechanism of the subsidiary or other related corporation. If necessary, it can be required by an accountability order to take whatever steps are practicable to achieve the same end. Conceivably there will be cases where the corporation responds that it is unable to secure the return of the personnel concerned, or that the related corporation refuses to co-operate and insists that the issue of discipline is none of its business. In that event, a court proceeding under the Accountability Model would be empowered to freeze any of the suspects' assets or entitlements that are under the control of the corporation (for example, unpaid bonuses, rights to shares or dividends under an employee share-holding scheme), and to prohibit the corporation from using the services of the suspects until such time as satisfactory disciplinary action is taken. More importantly, the failure of the corporation to secure effective disciplinary action would be publicised as a result of the self-investigation report it must file, and the report would be circulated to news media and enforcement agencies in the jurisdiction to which the suspects have flown.

A further order could be made insisting upon stringent precautions against repetition of the offence. Thus, the fact that the corporation's internal disciplinary system broke down may well warrant insistence on monitoring and supervisory precautions that go beyond what would be expected of well-run corporations that do maintain effective internal disciplinary controls. One

---

[126] Compare *R. v Hoffmann-La Roche Limited* (No. 2) (1980) 56 CCC (2d) 563 at 569 (Ontario High Court of Justice); *T.P.C. v Bata Shoe Co. of Australia Pty. Ltd.* (1980) 44 FLR 145 (Federal Court of Australia).

[127] Timberg, 'The Corporation as a Technique of International Administration'.

[128] See, e.g., the Exxon and Lockheed case studies in Fisse and Braithwaite, *The Impact of Publicity on Corporate Offenders*, 168–81, 144–60.

possibility would be to insist on the appointment of a vigilance committee, with outside representation, and to require that committee (1) to submit regular audits to the court that the conditions that led to the offence have been rectified, and (2) to provide a clean bill of health for any manager in the same area of operations who is to be transferred to an affiliated corporation beyond the jurisdiction. The Accountability Model thus allows progressively escalated responses that can counter transnational corporate attempts to cut employees free from the normal bonds of internal discipline.

20 Public and Private Organisations

Desideratum
A strategy for allocating responsibility should be workable with public as well as with private organizations.

The proposal for catalysing private justice systems under the Accountability Model is well suited to government organisations. While the threat of a heavy corporate fine might hang over their head with less trepidation than with a private organisation which will not be bailed out by the taxpayers, the more anxiety-provoking threats in both cases are management restructuring orders (as might be made by way of probationary conditions)[129] or organisational capital punishment. Moreover, it is possible, though we have no persuasive empirical evidence on the matter, that public organisations are even more sensitive to the public denunciation of their wrongdoing enabled by the scheme of self-investigation and action reporting.

Technically, there is little or no difficulty in applying the Accountability Model to public organisations. While in most jurisdictions the state enjoys immunity from criminal prosecution, this doctrine is steadily eroding.[130] The trend toward corporatisation and shared ownership of public organisations increasingly blurs the private–public distinction. In any case, the Accountability Model does not require a threshold finding of organisational criminal responsibility: it is sufficient that the *actus reus* of the offence has been committed by the organisation, and the removal of immunity in relation to this form of liability would be only a small step removed from the extinction of Crown immunity that has already occurred in relation to civil liability.

One might argue that the Accountability Model is unduly redundant in this context because very similar approaches are already in place; public reports of auditors-general, inspectors-general, parliamentary committees, and other controls are a well-known feature of public organisational life. We take a

---

[129] Probation makes more sense than a fine in the context of governmental instrumentalities. The focus is on internal organisational controls, as opposed to the quixotic spectacle of one arm of government paying a fine into general revenue and then being reallocated the funds to allow it to continue to perform its public function.

[130] See further Hogg, *Liability of the Crown*; Barack, *Crimes by the Capitalist State*; Fisse, 'Controlling Governmental Crime'; Thompson, 'Criminal Responsibility in Government'.

contrary view. Existing controls leave much to be desired because they are top-down and outside-in as compared with the interactive bottom-up/top-down approach of the Accountability Model. Public organisations have private justice systems and internal disciplinary and compliance mechanisms comparable with those in private organisations. Current strategies for regulating public organisations do not engage in a sufficiently constructive way with these internal systems. Take the practice of auditors-general, who in our view regularly make two kinds of mistakes. Sometimes they ride roughshod over the internal compliance or quality assurance systems of the public organisation. More commonly, they take the internal investigations of such groups and put them in their reports as if they were their own findings, thus undermining the incentive for internal compliance and quality assurance groups to be diligent. The Accountability Model, in contrast, gives internal investigation groups full credit for their work, provides rewards when the task is done well, and holds out the threat of punishment when it is done badly.

Another critical factor is that corporate criminal law loses legitimacy in the eyes of the private sector if the public sector is exempted. This is borne out by a research project on the regulation of health care institutions in Australia and Britain.[131] In both countries, the private sector resents the inspection and accountability strictures which apply to them and yet not to government hospitals and nursing homes. This incites the private sector to use the well-known technique of neutralising non-compliance by 'condemning the condemners'.[132] As one British nursing home proprietor commented, 'Who are the Health Authority to tell us about not respecting patients' rights when you see the way they treat patients in their own long-stay wards'. In our view, therefore, the Accountability Model can and should be applied to public as well as private organisations.

Conclusion: Accountability for Corporate Crime in Theory and Practice

The Accountability Model that we have advanced foreshadows a very different world of corporate criminal justice from the present. All collectivities and individuals responsible for a corporate crime would be exposed to publicly accountable sanctioning administered either by public or private justice systems. This exposure would occur whether the responsible actors are corporations, divisions of corporations, foreign parents of the corporations, employees of the corporation in any part of the world, lawyers and other gatekeepers, or even government enforcement agencies. It would also be a world in which responsible actors who hide behind the corporate veil or behind their power to scapegoat will be forced to give an account of themselves to their

---

[131] Braithwaite et al., *Raising the Standard*.
[132] Sykes and Matza, 'Techniques of Neutralization'. For an account of the 'games' played by crisis-prone corporations, see Mitroff and Pauchant, *We're So Big and Powerful Nothing Bad Can Happen to Us*, ch. 3.

associates at work and, ultimately, to their neighbours and family. This vision, we believe, is straightforward and consistent with everyday ideas about accountability and responsibility. It is a way of beginning to think about how to design a criminal justice system that is both more effective and more just in grappling with the challenge of complex organisational crime.

But is the Accountability Model feasible in practice? In the next chapter, we try to answer this question by spelling out exactly how we think the Model should be deployed in practice.

7 The Possibility of Responsibility for Corporate Crime

Corporate Crime Control: Complexity and Multiplexity

Corporate crime is a greater threat to humankind today than at any time in the past. Our planet is more fragile than ever and therefore more at risk from the predations of environmental criminals. Our economy is more internationalised, and therefore more vulnerable to sophisticated criminals who use the corporate form to run an international law evasion game—playing one set of laws off against another. Worse, as in the BCCI case, large corporations can effectively avoid national laws by setting themselves up in such a way that no national regulator is their home regulator.

Our economies are also more in flux than ever. The marketplace is more open to radical new ideas about how to organise business and, as evidenced by leveraged buyouts, poison pills, and junk bonds, those ideas can sweep through capitalist markets overnight. We have now learnt that when the organisation that invents an idea like junk bonds is a systemic law-breaker, and when the junk-bond 'king' (Michael Milken) is a criminal, the entrepreneurship that can fundamentally transform the face of capitalism (as junk bonds did in the 1980s) can also be a dire threat to its health.[1]

In a dynamic corporate economy, criminal law models that were designed to stabilise individual criminal liability are doomed to fail. The more flux there is in the economy, the more the uncertainty about the likely efficacy of any control strategy. Given the escalating uncertainty, the more imperative it becomes to have a dynamic and diversified strategy. A dynamic strategy is one that tries remedy after remedy, abandoning each one if experience proves it a failure. This is an assumption underlying the Accountability Model we have described in Chapter 5 and elaborated upon in Chapter 6. The diversified strategy of the Accountability Model relies on multiple points of leverage to secure social control. A crucial part of that strategy is to eschew a narrowly criminal model of responsibility for corporate crime. Thus, the engineer who settles for a third-best solution, when the second-best solution might have prevented an oil spill, has a certain kind of professional responsibility for the spill, but not criminal responsibility.

[1] Bruck, *The Predators' Ball.*

We have explored the strategy of redesigning corporate criminal law so as to cast the net of responsibility further around the actors, individual and collective, that share some responsibility for a violation of law. We do not advocate universal application of this net-widening strategy. Experiments that move us in this direction are required, coupled with empirical evaluation of them. The criminal justice system is a rather loose and chaotic system that allows considerable scope for innovation. This is perhaps a blessing in disguise given that any attempt to lock the system into uniform pursuit of a single narrow objective, such as just deserts, rehabilitation or incapacitation, or even deterrence, would have disastrous consequences.[2]

Philip Pettit and John Braithwaite have argued that a monolithic policy of just deserts is untenable in the context of corporate crime.[3] Such a policy inevitably means just deserts for the poor and comparative immunity for the powerful. The point need not be laboured that sole reliance on rehabilitation or incapacitation to control corporate crime also would be a recipe for failure;[4] no modern society has the resources to try to regiment corporate activities in the way that such a strategy would require. Deterrence is more plausible as a monolithic objective but, as we have shown in this book, we cannot rely solely on deterrence to secure corporate crime control. Sometimes corporate crime does not fit the rational actor model. Sometimes corporations break the law out of ignorance, incompetence or to symbolically resist the regulatory order of the state. There will always be many kinds of fraud in a capitalist economy that will remain economically rational no matter how much we improve the effectiveness of enforcement or the size of penalties. Alternatively, a policy of increasing penalties to the level needed to render certain types of crime irrational will bankrupt firms and close factories, thereby harming innocent workers and communities. Sole reliance on rational deterrence would simply leave us defenceless against cost-effective crimes.

Fortunately, there is a way out of the deterrence trap. As indicated in previous chapters, a solution is to open up multiple deterrence targets. Some targets are softer than others. Perhaps many corporations have such deep pockets that they cannot be deterred by penalties provided in the law. Perhaps many chief executives are such tough and brutish human beings as to be both shameless and protected by 'vice-presidents responsible for going to jail' on their behalf. But these are not the only targets of a strategy of holding responsible all who are responsible. The shameless chief executive may have a chairperson who is highly sensitive to his or her own reputation and the reputation of the organisation he or she heads. There may be an accountant

---

[2] Braithwaite and Pettit, in *Not Just Deserts*, have argued that all of these objectives can be satisfactorily pursued if dominion is set as an appropriately nuanced target for the criminal justice system.

[3] Ibid., 183–201.

[4] There are good grounds for believing that rehabilitation and incapacitation are more promising for the control of corporate crime than for the control of street crime (Braithwaite and Geis, 'On Theory and Action for Corporate Crime Control'). However, when powerful corporate actors have the will to resist rehabilitation and incapacitation, they have a formidable capacity to do so. Hence the folly of singleminded reliance on corporate rehabilitation or incapacitation.

who takes pride in his or her reputation for ethical conduct. No large criminal sanctions may be needed to prod such actors to take steps which are in their power to prevent organisational crime from occurring. This is important because, while only a small number of people may be involved in committing a corporate crime, a much larger number of people usually have the power to prevent it.[5] The crime, as some philosophers would say, is 'overdetermined' by the acts and omissions of the many people with such power.[6]

In a complex corporate offence there can be three types of actors who bear some level of responsibility for the wrongdoing or capacity to prevent the wrongdoing:

(1) hard targets who cannot be deterred by maximum penalties provided in the law;
(2) vulnerable targets who can be deterred by maximum penalties; and
(3) soft targets who can be deterred by shame, by the mere exposure of the fact that they have failed to meet some responsibility they bear, even if that is not a matter of criminal responsibility.

A strategy of seeking to hold all responsible who are responsible avoids the risk, inherent in more narrowly focused strategies, of deterrent appeals failing on hard targets.[7] When all who are responsible are held responsible, there is a much better chance that vulnerable and soft targets will also be struck. If the commission of a corporate crime is overdetermined by the acts and omissions of a number of such targets, a deterrent impact on just one of them could be sufficient to prevent the crime. Vulnerable and soft targets in other companies will heed the cautionary tale of the misfortune inflicted on those responsible in a convicted corporation. So general deterrence may be possible on a wide front.

The purpose of opening up the corporate criminal process to detailed public reporting on the responsibility and sanctioning of all who are responsible runs much deeper than simply deterring executives, directors, accountants, brokers, legal advisers and sloppy regulators who observe the public accountability spectacle with trepidation. The process we propose seems to us less important as a deterrent process, and more important as a cultural process of solemnly having the court signify the unacceptability of certain types of conduct. Put another way, the activities of courts can and do constitute corporate

---

[5] Consider, for example, former NSW Attorney General John Dowd's account of the power of the legal adviser in 'The Responsibility of Lawyers for the Prevention, Detection and Rectification of Client Fraud', 70–1.

[6] On the concept of overdetermination in the theory of causation and prevention, see Lewis, 'Causation' and 'Postscript E: Redundant Causation'.

[7] One of the reviewers of the manuscript for this book commented: 'one is left unclear about what should happen to the "hard targets" described as being unamenable to maximum penalties'. Under the Accountability Model they are subject to the dynamic strategy and the individual prosecution guidelines canvassed in Chapter 6 (Section 6). This Model avoids the difficulty of trying to predict who will be soft and who will be hard targets. For those who turn out to be hard targets, application of the prosecution guidelines will probably have little effect on them but, in terms of the strategy of corporate deterrence discussed in the text, it is unnecessary to hit those targets.

consciences. The best protection the community has against any form of crime is not deterrent threats that can never be mobilised with satisfactory certainty. The best protection, we contend, is that large numbers of those who might be rationally tempted are brought to the view that criminal conduct (or failure to prevent criminal conduct) would be shameful or irresponsible.

The public reporting on responsibility that we favour also transcends individual or corporate deterrence as a control strategy in that it conceives of the need for a community to be constantly attending to institutional failures as a cause of corporate crime: regulatory failures, failures in the professional standards of accountants, lawyers or brokers, breakdowns in conventions that sustain a fabric of business ethics, failures of industry self-regulation, defective SOPs, technological failures, defective voluntary industry standards, defective laws, structural facts about an industry that make criminality almost inevitable, community apathy or indifference about a problem it should be taking seriously. Our proposal is oriented to a constant public re-examination of the institutional and structural reforms needed to make it more difficult for organisations to make criminal choices.

A sensible criminal justice policy is one that recognises the weakness of all the weapons at its disposal. It therefore hedges its bets in the hope that the weaknesses of some weapons can be covered by the strengths of others. Sometimes implementation of the model we favour would lead to institutional reform of a type that would reduce the incidence of this offence across the board; more typically it would not. Sometimes it would have a significant impact in constituting the shamefulness of harmful practices; often it would not. Sometimes it would effect corporate reform and rehabilitation; often it would not. Sometimes it would incapacitate evildoers by removing them from positions of economic power; often it would not. Sometimes it would deter vulnerable targets; often it would not. But when it fails to deter vulnerable targets, it may still deter soft targets with the fear of exposure of their irresponsibility.

Sometimes it would fail on all these fronts. But perfect and complete control should not be our objective. We can live with a certain amount of crime. Past a certain point, further crime-fighting will cost us more in freedom and in dollars than it is worth. At the end of the day, we want policies for dealing with crime which attack the problem from a number of different directions so as to give us a level of crime we are prepared to live with.

We should not be prepared to tolerate the level of organisational crime now present in contemporary Western societies. However, we reject the view that it is impossible to reduce organisational crime to a more tolerable level. Impossibility is our lot only if we think in terms of control by rational corporate deterrence or if the desired level of crime is pitched near zero. Countenancing radical reform to the corporate criminal process makes greater control of corporate crime entirely conceivable. Moreover, a corporate criminal process that is considerably less prone to the scapegoating and injustice of contemporary practices is also possible. The aspiration of this book has been to contribute to the debate about the best way to move toward these objectives.

The Accountability Model in Action

In the last chapter, we outlined how the application of our preferred model might have resulted in a more beneficial and less costly handling of the IBM antitrust cases of the 1960s and 1970s. To conclude, we provide four more detailed illustrations of the Accountability Model in action: the BCCI case, the Zeebrugge ferry disaster, the Solomons Carpets two-price advertising case, and the CML insurance selling scam.

BCCI: Responsibility reconstructed

In the 1980s, BCCI became banker to the world's biggest criminals: it specialised in laundering dirty money through accounts fraudulently dedicated to that purpose. BCCI at one time was the seventh largest commercial bank in the world. Its crime had tragic effects, such as wiping out the social security fund of the nation of Gabon, leaving pensionless people who had worked all their lives.[8] Five BCCI executives were indicted in 1988 and subsequently convicted for laundering drug money after a successful sting operation by the US Customs and other federal agencies in Florida. As part of its plea agreement, BCCI fired these individuals, though it continued to pay for their legal representation.[9] Subsequent to the Florida indictment, two junior BCCI employees were convicted for money laundering in Britain, where BCCI had its operating centre. The conviction of these comparatively junior employees did nothing in either country to address the systematic culture of criminality[10] that pervaded the bank at its highest levels and to prevent the subsequent looting of billions of dollars of investors' funds.

Worse than that, the Florida plea agreement prohibited the US Attorney from charging BCCI with other crimes. The truth of the corporate responsibility from the very top of the organisation was obscured by a press release from BCCI headquarters in London after the plea agreement, saying that the actions of the convicted individuals were 'contrary to the express written policies of BCCI' and had taken place without the knowledge of the bank's management or Board.[11]

While there is no doubt that the New York District Attorney is one of the heroes in correcting the head-in-the-sand attitude of federal law enforcement officials, we have deep doubts about the cosy plea agreement of the New York District Attorney in 1992 with the recidivist corporate criminal, Kamal Adham, the former intelligence chief of Saudi Arabia, fourth biggest individual shareholder in the bank, and a central actor in and beneficiary of the fraud. While we understand the usefulness of the co-operation of Adham in proceeding criminally against Clark Clifford and Robert Altman, we also understand

---

[8] Passas, 'I Cheat, Therefore I Exist? The BCCI Scandal in Context'.

[9] Fialka and Truell, 'Rogue Bank', *WSJ*, 3 May 1990, A1.

[10] This is the description of BCCI provided by the Governor of the Bank of England before the Treasury and Civil Service Committee of the British Parliament: *Financial Times*, 24 July 1991, 6.

[11] Adams and Frantz, *A Full Service Bank*, 290.

why Clifford and Altman bitterly claim that they had become 'the most visible, convenient targets' for prosecutors who had made 'deals ... with true scoundrels'.[12]

A better way to have proceeded with either the British or US cases, we contend, would have been to hold BCCI civilly liable for having engaged in money laundering and to proceed on that platform to fix the responsibility of those implicated in the web of illegality. The top management of BCCI would have then been brought in and required by the court to complete a full internal investigation of money laundering in all the bank's international operations, not just those in the country of the detected offence. Preferably, this would have been conducted with the assistance of an *independent* outside accounting firm.[13] More critically, the court would have required specified top management officials to certify (under threat of imprisonment for contempt) that the bank had disclosed all of its international money laundering activities. Perhaps the top management team therefore might have refused to co-operate: the extent and seriousness of BCCI's money laundering was so breathtaking that no top management officer might have been prepared to put their neck in this disclosure noose; alternatively, a tactical decision might have been made to resist disclosure on the basis that the court lacked jurisdiction to obtain details relating to the bank's operations abroad. Such a response would have sounded the alarm bells that should have been rung.[14]

A full-scale investigation, as opposed to a targeted sting operation designed to get some notches on a prosecutor's gun, would have then swung into action under the Accountability Model. We can be absolutely certain that this would have turned up insiders who were willing to reveal the complex story of the illegal bank within a bank (as they subsequently did when the Bank of England, the US Congress and New York District Attorney Robert Morgenthau finally revealed wider-ranging investigations in 1991).[15] As soon as the wider investigation showed that the reason for the refusal to co-operate with a self-investigation report was the enormity of the top management fraud, one of the governments concerned could then have gone over top management's head to the shareholders—the ruler and government of Abu Dhabi. This would have been followed by inexorable political pressure for

---

[12] Truell and Gurwin, *False Profits*, 409, 411.

[13] In fact, the Bank of England subsequently did require Price Waterhouse to conduct an 'independent' investigation. But Price Waterhouse was far from independent. It had been BCCI's sole auditor since 1987 and may deserve some of the blame for the fiasco: *Australian Financial Review*, 17 Sept. 1991, 14. See also *Financial Times*, 15 May 1992, 7; 12 March 1992, 8. See also Kerry Report, *The BCCI Affair*, 14: 'BCCI provided loans and financial benefits to some of its auditors, whose acceptance of these benefits creates an appearance of impropriety...'. '[There was also the] possible acceptance of sexual favors provided by BCCI officials to certain persons affiliated with the firm [Price Waterhouse].'

[14] In fact, however, what BCCI top management did was to co-operate with the investigations that did occur, while using a variety of stalling tactics.

[15] District Attorney Morgenthau explained why getting the co-operation of insiders was not difficult once the truth started becoming apparent... 'A lot of them were angry. They were told they were shareholders. They were going to get their share through ICIC. Then they found out they weren't': Adams and Frantz, *A Full Service Bank*, 298.

government-to-government demands for co-operation, with full disclosure of the malfeasance of the bank.

Whether by voluntary disclosure, by government investigation or by inter-governmentally-forced disclosure, the court would have ended up with a document revealing that there was a secret bank within a bank at BCCI that engaged in massive fraud and bribery itself and that moved money for other major international fraudsters, for the very biggest drug empires, for terrorist groups, for Manuel Noriega and Saddam Hussein, for Peru's central bank to hide a quarter of the nation's hard currency from foreign bank creditors, for covert nuclear programs, and for illegal arms sales to Iran.[16] The court would have learned that by 1988 the then CIA director's nickname for the bank—the 'Bank of Crooks and Criminals International'—had wide currency and that US federal enforcement agencies had received literally hundreds of tips concerning BCCI crimes over the years.[17] It would have become clear to the court that a possible reason for this extraordinary nest of international criminality was that the bank was set up in such a way that it had no home regulator. It was effectively offshore in every country in which it operated. In response, the court could have opened up a more searching inquiry, conducted by honest elements within the bank working with outside consultants, to reveal to the public the full story of the regulatory failures that had occurred. What were the loopholes in the 1983 Basle Concordat on shared international regulation of banks that allowed BCCI to be effectively offshore everywhere?[18] Why did BCCI provide free travel to the Secretary-General of the United Nations, to Jimmy Carter, and more extravagant benefits to many other prominent international political figures?[19] How should the international banking system and the international banking regulatory system be reformed to prevent latter-day BCCIs from springing up?

If responsibility for corporate crime is to be imposed at all effectively, the courts need to impel the publication of Accountability Reports which document the responsibility of all who are responsible and which examine the institutional responses necessary to thwart repetition of offences. In a case like that of BCCI, where the Governor of the Bank of England is among those who share some responsibility,[20] along with the government of Abu Dhabi,[21] and even possibly the British Prime Minister (who had been briefed on the matter by the Governor and was arguably irresponsible in failing to pick up

[16] In 1986, the CIA advised several other US government agencies that BCCI was a criminal organisation (*Financial Times*, 2 August 1991, 6). When Benazir Bhutto became Prime Minister of Pakistan in 1988, she was so advised by 'friends in America' (*WSJ*, 5 August 1991, A11).
[17] Truell and Gurwin, *False Profits*, 348.
[18] *Financial Times*, 22 July 1991, 12. The Basle Concordat has now been amended with a view to having large international banks regulated on a worldwide basis by a single bank regulator (*Financial Times*, 7 July 1992, 3).
[19] *Financial Times*, 27–28 July, 1991, 4; Kerry Report, *The BCCI Affair*, 11, concluded: 'BCCI systematically bribed world leaders and political figures throughout the world'.
[20] Kerry Report, 18–20.
[21] Kerry Report, 20–22.

his telephone to register his concern with the Sheik of Abu Dhabi),[22] the court would have a role that can stand independently above the failings of the international club of regulators. The regulators claim that they had to sit on their hands to prevent a run that would harm depositors. The critics point out that their inaction brought more innocent victims into the web and that 'the Bank [of England] might have been more concerned about Middle East relations than protecting depositors'.[23] Stronger critics allege that key players in the central banks or finance ministries of a dozen nations took bribes from BCCI.[24]

Courts in Florida and England had opportunities to exert independent scrutiny long before the British and US congressional inquiries began to do so effectively in late 1991. Even before the Florida indictment, in 1987 BCCI was fined in Kenya for breaches of foreign exchange regulations over coffee exports,[25] and was implicated in a Philadelphia case as a result of financing the illegal purchase of US materials for the Pakistan Atomic Energy Commission.[26] BCCI was also formally charged with violating foreign exchange controls in Mauritius (1983), the Sudan (1985), India (1986), Colombia (1989), and Brazil (1989).[27] We do not criticise these courts for failing to open up the whole can of worms.[28] Rather, the problem is that liability has yet to be conceived and structured in such a way as to encourage courts to pursue the issue of allocation of responsibility in complex corporate cases and to achieve the wide measure of accountability that is often required.

The features which make the BCCI case so depressingly beyond the control of national legal positivist strategies[29] leave it somewhat vulnerable to our legal pluralist strategy. The Bank of England and the British Chancellor of the Exchequer, John Major, who were in the best position to strike at BCCI, acted like jellyfish in the face of the enormity and diplomatic sensitivity of the problems. But all it needed was one national regulator or one court to show some entrepreneurship with the Accountability Model and the international crooked empire of BCCI could have been unravelled. In this case, there were many national regulators and at least nine courts which had that opportunity. Perhaps national banking regulators are too mutually subservient to trigger a process that would expose each other as jellyfish. If so, the objective is to persuade individual judges to apply the Accountability Model. A judge in Florida

---

[22] See 'Senate Accuses Bank and Government over BCCI', *Guardian Weekly*, 11 Oct. 1992, 18. Early indications from the Bingham inquiry suggest that it may exonerate John Major.

[23] *Financial Times*, 12 March 1992, 8;

[24] Truell and Gurwin, *False Profits*, 166.

[25] *Financial Times*, 13 Nov. 1991, 13.

[26] *WSJ*, 5 Aug. 1991, A11.

[27] Truell and Gurwin, *False Profits*, 168.

[28] Nikos Passas has pointed out to us, however, that Senator Kerry, together with other US Senators, did write to the Florida judge urging him to reject the plea agreement with BCCI.

[29] For a critique of the present limits of sovereign regulatory powers in the BCCI case, see Reiss, 'Detecting, Investigating and Regulating Business Law-Breaking'.

is unlikely to be overly worried about the prospect of triggering a report which reveals weak-kneed conduct on the part of a Bank of England or a John Major.

Faced with cases of the enormity of BCCI, the criminological tradition has been to evince a policy analysis of despair. Nikos Passas has provided the most incisive analysis we have seen of the reasons for pessimism about controlling such corporate crime.[30] Four difficulties were identified by Passas as particularly intransigent in the BCCI case:

(1) *Inter-agency conflicts, miscommunications and inertia.* The most critical failure here was that the CIA's 1986 report on the criminality of BCCI was distributed to some but not all federal enforcement agencies (critically, not to the FBI, the Justice Department, the DEA, and the Federal Reserve). Investigations were compartmentalised in a way that missed the big picture of systemic criminality. So the Bank of England naively and incompetently allowed itself to believe that BCCI simply had a few rotten apples that were being removed from the barrel.

(2) *Inadequate resources.* An integrated investigation would have been impossibly costly for most enforcement agencies in most countries.

(3) *BCCI's power.* Partly this was the power of cultivating and bribing some of the most influential political figures in the world. But it was also the power of harbouring the secrets of the CIA, British, French, and Swiss intelligence and other such clients who had used the services of the bank. Then there was the power of the major shareholders, the Sheik of Abu Dhabi and his government. Ultimately, the most persuasive power was the fear of disrupting Western–Arab relations and even of touching the White House through opening up the bank's role in the Iran-Contra affair.

(4) *Legal restraints.* Secrecy provisions in many national banking and tax laws and the difficulties of extraterritorial enforcement were an effective last line of defence for the bank.

The Accountability Model is no simple panacea for these massive difficulties, but it supplies an analysis of how these and many other related problems may be approached. Points (1) and (2) above are tackled under the Model by motivating the defendant corporation to pay for independent counsel to pull together all the threads of the entire tapestry of responsibility. The fact that Price Waterhouse, in spite of its non-independence,[31] could successfully perform this role, all too late in June 1991,[32] indicates that the strategy could have worked. A company that deluded the world about the reality of its operations as a giant Ponzi scheme was always vulnerable to a holistic international investigation of its operations. Such a comprehensive investigation was bound to discover two simple mechanisms for sustaining the illusion of solvency: (a) being off-shore to every national enforcement agency so that each of them missed the big picture; and (b) having 'two legally separate holding companies, each based in an offshore banking haven, each with separate auditors',[33]

---

[30] Passas, 'Regulatory Anaesthesia or the Limits of the Criminal Law?'
[31] See fn. 13.
[32] Adams and Frantz, *A Full Service Bank*, 317–19.
[33] Ibid., 313.

so that bad assets were hidden from their own auditors. On Nikos Passas' point (2), the June 1991 Price Waterhouse investigation, because it was not conducted by the state, did not involve demands on taxpayer resources. A court-initiated integrated self-investigation report would have been paid for by the bank's creditors and depositors, but it would have saved them much more than it cost. Administrative solutions can improve the 'inter-agency conflicts, miscommunications and inertia' (point 1) that foiled holistic understanding of the crookedness of the bank.[34] But because administrative solutions will not eliminate co-ordination problems caused by political cor-ruption, we should want judges who refuse to tolerate co-ordination failure by demanding holistic self-investigation reports, and when they do not get them, who call for holistic governmental investigations. In the BCCI case, the desire to prevent a precipitate collapse of all the bank's operations or withdrawal of all the bank's operating licences as a result of court-ordered publicity might have been a potent motivation for co-operation. While BCCI was powerful, it was also vulnerable to a court that could easily have caused the collapse of the entire bank. Hence, it would have co-operated and negotiated with a court in an attempt to avoid this outcome (just as it later did with the Bank of England).

Point (3) can be tackled because of the separation of powers between the courts and the state in a functioning democracy: an independent judge has less reason to worry about what the White House, John Major, the CIA or the Bank of England thinks than does the head of a US government agency.

Point (4) can be tackled because the Accountability Model does not directly rely on national laws to empower investigators; it relies on the self-investigative and internal disciplinary capacities of the defendant corporation. These capacities are no more limited by the sovereignty of national law than is the corporation's capacity to commit transnational crime. If the company has the will to find out what happened through its international transactions, it generally has the capacity to do so. The Accountability Model might have succeeded with BCCI where traditional courts, internal auditors and the inter-national club of regulators failed because of the critical capacity of the Accountability Model to hold the regulators themselves accountable, not to mention other courts that had failed to take a hard look at the total web of criminality.

The Zeebrugge disaster: Salvaging responsibility from The Herald of Free Enterprise

The Zeebrugge ferry disaster is another instructive vehicle for understanding how the Accountability Model could extend responsibility for corporate crime across a broader front than is possible under the present law.

The disaster, in which 189 persons died, stemmed from a failure to ensure that the bow doors of the ferry were securely closed before sailing out to sea.

---

[34] The CIA probably had that holistic understanding from early 1985. Its problem was inertia for reasons that are still to be fully revealed. See Kerry Report, 16.

A coronial inquiry ensued[35] and led to an unsuccessful prosecution[36] of the company, P&O European Ferries (Dover) Limited, and seven individuals, including the assistant bosun who failed to close the doors, the first officer, the master, the senior master, two directors, and a senior manager. There was also an official inquiry by Mr Justice Sheen under the Merchant Shipping Act.[37] Mr Justice Sheen made a number of adverse findings against the company and its safety systems and procedures. He also suspended the certificate of the ship's master for one year, and that of the first officer for two years. In addition to the criticism voiced in Mr Justice Sheen's report and in the media,[38] the company was liable civilly for compensation to those injured and to the relatives of the victims who perished.

The process of allocating responsibility within the company was rather uneven. The ship's master was subjected to internal disciplinary action, but the matter was settled when he resigned. The first officer was dismissed. The directors of the ferry company at the time of the disaster moved on to other ventures. The assistant bosun resigned on medical grounds. However, nothing appears to have happened to other persons who were the subject of Mr Justice Sheen's finding that the whole of the company had been 'infected with the disease of sloppiness'.[39] Numerous managers or employees fell into this category, including the onshore management responsible for seeing that clear orders about the closure of the bow doors were given on board. Britannia palpably failed to rule these waves.

Under the Accountability Model, the task of imposing responsibility in such a case would not be dispersed through diverse channels of legal action, but co-ordinated and managed initially as one case. The case would start as a civil proceeding against the company for committing the *actus reus* of manslaughter. Establishing that the company, acting through its officers, employees or agents, caused the death of the 189 victims would be relatively straightforward and hardly a matter requiring protracted proceedings. Upon being found liable for having caused the deaths of the victims, the company and designated officers of the company would be required to investigate and prepare a report detailing exactly what disciplinary, precautionary, and compensatory initiatives it proposed to take. In terms of accountability and disciplinary action, one would expect to find a more comprehensive and even-handed outcome than what in fact ensued. Thus, the adequacy or otherwise of the performance of the directors and managers in the area of safety would need to be assessed in detail, with particulars given as to the disciplinary steps taken or to be taken. One would also expect deficiencies of design by the ship's architects to be documented, together with failings within the Department of Transport to provide regulations adequately covering the

---

[35] See *R v HM Coroner for East Kent, ex parte Spooner* (1989) 88 Cr App R 10.
[36] The jury was directed to acquit all accused: *R v Stanley and Others*, CCC No 900160, 19 Oct. 1990.
[37] UK, Department of Transport, *mv Herald of Free Enterprise*, Report.
[38] See, for example, 'P&O Ferries Charged with Manslaughter', *The Times*, 23 June 1989, 1.
[39] UK, Department of Transport, *mv Herald of Free Enterprise*, Report, 14.

special dangers associated with roll-on/roll-off ferries. There would also need to be a specific indication of what exactly the company was going to do to improve the safety systems on board in light of the lessons to be learned from the calamity (for example, warning lights on the bridge to indicate if bow doors had not been shut).

If the report was palpably deficient, the company and the persons designated as responsible for preparing it would be liable for contempt and the matter would be referred back for immediate corrective action. If the report was accepted, the action proposed or taken in relation to internal discipline, reform of safety procedures, and compensation would provide a basis for prosecutors to decide whether criminal prosecution was necessary under the guidelines in place for making that decision.[40] Conceivably, it would be unnecessary to prosecute any individuals, assuming that internal corporate sanctions had been administered in relation to all who were accountable for the pervasive sloppiness found by Mr Justice Sheen. Perhaps a prosecution against the company for manslaughter by criminal negligence would be warranted, on the basis that it had been criminally negligent in failing to run a tight ship. In the event of such a prosecution, the test of corporate liability would not be the discredited *Tesco* principle of corporate liability for a 'directing mind', but a broader test of corporate blameworthiness: had the company grossly failed to achieve the standard of care expected of a *company*[41] in its position?

Even if no-one were ultimately held criminally liable, the Accountability Model would foster social control by ensuring that all who had a hand in bringing about the disaster would be publicly identified and, in the case of officers or employees of the company, subjected to some publicly stated and independently scrutinised regime of internal sanctions and re-education. This is a far cry from the limited efforts in fact made under English law to achieve responsibility in the wake of the Zeebrugge case. In effect, the fundamental issue of responsibility dropped between the cracks in the system of coronial inquiry, criminal prosecution, and official inquiry under the Merchant Shipping Act. Processes like coronial inquiries, official inquiries into shipping disasters, and royal commissions have their uses and can be reformed but, as illustrated by the Zeebrugge case, are not currently designed to achieve responsibility for corporate crime. A different model—the Accountability Model—is needed to achieve that end, and legal procedures should be revised in the way indicated above. Had this type of procedure been

---

[40] See Chapter 6 in this book, 180–1.
[41] See Chapter 2 in this book; Field and Jörg, 'Corporate Liability and Manslaughter'. Compare *R v Stanley and Others*, CCC No 900160, 19 Oct. 1990, at 8, where Mr Justice Turner ruled that corporate criminal liability depends on the attribution to the company of the individual criminal liability of a directing mind; aggregation of the fault on the part of various representatives, or corporate fault in a corporate sense was ruled to be insufficient. This ruling reflects an individualistic preoccupation rather than a reasoned attempt to define corporate liability in the corporate terms required to reflect the corporate nature of the defendant. Nonetheless, there may still have been difficulties establishing corporate criminal negligence given the degree of risk of such a mishap occurring; see Bergman, 'Recklessness in the Boardroom'.

in place, cross-channel ferry users would by now have been assured that those responsible for the Zeebrugge disaster had been called to account and either removed from their positions of trust or exposed to a rigorous program of retraining. Audited information to this effect could well have been published, by court mandate, on the most obvious and relevant repositories: the ferries and their ticket offices. As things stand, who is to tell whether or not the 'disease of sloppiness' remains?

The Australian Trade Practices Commission and the wisdom of Solomons

Consideration of the IBM, BCCI and Zeebrugge cases might lead to the mistaken conclusion that the Accountability Model is only useful for thinking about very major cases. To remedy this impression, we will consider a case of rather small significance that few readers will have heard of—the action taken by the Australian Trade Practices Commission against Solomons Carpets for two-price advertising.

Solomons ran advertisements claiming that certain carpets were on sale for up to $40 per metre off the normal price. This representation was false; some of the carpets were no cheaper than the normal price. The matter came before the Trade Practices Commission in 1991 at a time when John Braithwaite was a member of the Commission. The Commission had difficulty deciding what action to take on this alleged breach of its act. It was a less serious matter than others that were putting demands on its scarce litigation resources; it was also an area that the Commission did not regard as a top enforcement priority.

The Commission decided to offer Solomons an administrative settlement which included voluntary compensation for consumers in an amount exceeding the criminal fine that was likely should they be convicted. The facts of the matter made it fairly unlikely that any court would order compensation for consumers, but likely that a modest criminal fine would be imposed. All the commissioners felt that Solomons would reject the administrative settlement because it would be cheaper for them to face the consequences of litigation. Even so, in the interests of consumers it was decided that the idea was worth a try. The commissioners (including Braithwaite) turned out to be wrong in assuming that such decisions are necessarily made by companies according to a deterrence cost-benefit calculus. Unknown to the Commission at the time, there was also a 'soft' target within the company, namely the Chairman of the Board, the retired patriarch of this family company. For him, as a responsible businessman, it made sense to accept the Commission's argument that resources should be spent on correcting the problem for the benefit of consumers rather than on litigation and fines.

The Chairman of the Board was dismayed at the prospect of allegations of criminality against his company, and was concerned for its reputation and his family reputation. He was also angry with his chief executive for allowing the situation to arise and for indulging in such a marketing practice. He sought the resignation of his chief executive and instructed his remaining senior management to co-operate with an administrative settlement that included the following seven requirements:

(1) Compensation to consumers (legal advisers on both sides were of the opinion that the amount was considerably in excess of what was likely to be ordered by a court).

(2) A voluntary investigation report to be conducted by a mutually agreed law firm to identify the persons and defective procedures that were responsible for the misleading advertising.

(3) Discipline of those employees and remediation of those defective procedures.

(4) A voluntary Trade Practices education and compliance program within the firm and among its franchisees directed at remedying the problems identified in the self-investigation report on an ongoing basis and at improving Trade Practices compliance more generally.

(5) An industry-wide national Trade Practices education campaign funded by Solomons to get its competitors to also improve their compliance with regard to advertising of carpets.

(6) Auditing and annual certification of completion of the agreed compliance programs by an agreed outside law firm at Solomons' expense.

(7) A press release from the Commission advising the community of all of the above and of the conduct by Solomons that initially triggered the investigation. (The press release attracted significant coverage in most major Australian newspapers.)

In addition, although it was not part of the deed of agreement, Solomons volunteered to conduct an evaluation study of the improvement (or absence thereof) in compliance with the Act by its competitors as a result of the industry-wide education campaign that it funded.

The deed of agreement with Solomons was not free from difficulty. Solomons' solicitors advised the company against having the agreement approved by a court as this would expose management to imprisonment for contempt should there be a failure to satisfy all the terms of the agreement (a more severe sanction than that to which the company was exposed for the original breach). The Commission wanted court approval in order to strengthen the enforceability of the agreement and also to render the Commission accountable to the court for its exercise of discretion in negotiating the deed.[42] Debate with the Commission's Consultative Committee (which includes representatives of business, legal and consumer groups) on the problems in getting Solomons to agree to court approval of the agreement led to a recommendation to the government that the Trade Practices Act be amended to allow administrative settlements to be registered with the court in a way that renders them enforceable, provides for judicial scrutiny, and removes the

---

[42] In relation to a previous deed, the Commission had been subjected to some criticism for failing to obtain the sanction of a court for the agreement. The rather weak clause that was included in the Solomons deed (cl. 8) read: 'The parties acknowledge that it is intended that Solomons' obligations under this Deed are enforceable in an appropriate Court by action for specific performance.'

hazard of imprisonment for executives where there is non-compliance with the terms of an agreement. Ultimately, this proposal was not implemented, but the enforceability of undertakings to the Commission was considerably strengthened under an amendment in December 1992.

At low cost to taxpayers, the Commission adopted an approach that appears at this point to have improved consumer protection in a major Australian market. The company was required to undertake disciplinary action and to report the steps taken. The company was also required to provide compensation which victims would not otherwise have received (without compromising their right to take further private action).[43] Added to these advantages, the Commission was able to promote general deterrence by publicising the nature and costs of the settlement.

The Colonial Mutual Life insurance selling case: Taming the wild colonial boys

The Australian Trade Practices Commission has taken the basic Solomons Carpets strategy much further by using it successfully in the largest consumer protection cases in Australian history. A number of insurance companies engaged in a widespread and systematic pattern of deceptive or unconscionable conduct which involved selling insurance policies to people living in remote Aboriginal communities in North Queensland. After an eight-month investigation, the Trade Practices Commission exerted pressure on the companies to enter into deeds of compliance under which they agreed to pay compensation, take internal disciplinary action, and revise their operating procedures so as to guard against repetition. The first company to enter into such a deed was Colonial Mutual Life Assurance Society Ltd (CML), one of Australia's largest insurance firms. The second was Norwich Union Life Insurance Society (now Norwich Union Life Australia Limited), another major. At least three other insurance companies have been under investigation concerning misrepresentations at remote Aboriginal communities.

The conduct of insurance agents in these cases had been abominable. They had misrepresented the terms of the investment policies sold, and had used unconscionable selling tactics. The vulnerability of poorly educated remote Aboriginal people to exploitation by authoritative business people from the city in white shirts became clear during the Commission's investigation. Victims tended to assume that it must have been them who had done something wrong. On occasions when the Commission investigators knocked on the front door, the victims would flee out the back door. Many shook continuously throughout their interviews and some cried with fear. The insurance agents cashed in on this vulnerability, a product of two centuries of white oppression and destruction of self-assurance. In one case, the customer was even told that he would go to jail unless he signed the policy, an apparently credible threat to Aboriginal males, a majority of whom have been locked up

---

[43] The deed provides: 'The parties to this agreement further note and affirm that this agreement in no way derogates from the rights or remedies available to any other person arising from the said conduct'.

at some time in their lives. False representations were made to Aboriginal people that they would need to commit some of their existing unemployment benefits to a savings investment plan because when they turned 65 they would no longer be eligible for government welfare support. The saddest false representation was that the policy would pay generous funeral benefits. This is a matter of profound religious importance to Aboriginal people who live in communities away from their special part of the country. When they die, they must be taken back to be part of their country forever. Readers will recall from Chapter 2 that Aboriginal people reject the Western view of the physically bounded individual, seeing the person as part of the land. Unfortunately, for indigent people, it can be prohibitively expensive to transport a body long distances along bush tracks. Hence the appeal of the false representations about funeral benefits.

Other particular cases were equally heart-rending. One family had been putting money into a special bank account for their young daughter's education. The agent secured a fat commission fee out of this account by persuading the family to provide for their daughter by taking out a policy. What kind of policy? A death benefit!

There were many types of misrepresentations. The most common was that policy-holders would get their money back in two years. In fact, administration costs absorbed all the premiums paid during the first two years. Another unfair practice was the failure to inform policy-holders that their policies would lapse unless the premiums were paid regularly. In most instances, the policies sold to the Aboriginal people lapsed because deductions from their wages could no longer be made when their temporary employment ceased. In many cases, the deductions from wages continued to be made notwithstanding that the policies had previously lapsed.

Aboriginal people were often not given copies of their policies by agents whose defence was that they would only lose them and it would be better if the agent held them. Letters of complaint from policy-holders in remote communities were ignored. Many of these people did not have ready access to a telephone. When they did get access, calls were not returned.

In the first round of settlements negotiated by the Trade Practices Commission, the local Aboriginal Community Council participated actively in the negotiation process and advanced a number of the key terms ultimately included in the subsequent deeds of settlement. Under the CML deed, refunds totalling $1.5 million have been paid to some 2,000 policy-holders affected, even where claims were barred by the three-year limitation period. Victims received 15 per cent compound interest on their investments, a considerably higher rate than those prevailing at the time of the deed. Some victims have received payouts well in excess of $10,000. CML also undertook to pay $715,000 into an Aboriginal Assistance Trust Fund for the benefit of Aboriginal people, including those in the communities affected by CML's unfair practices.

A further requirement of the deed was that CML conduct an internal investigation to discover any failings in the company's compliance program and to identify the officers, employees or agents who had engaged in or who had contributed to the unfair practices. The company was then required to undertake appropriate remedial and disciplinary action and to report the action taken to the Trade Practices Commission. Another clause in the deed required specific action to be taken to ensure that disadvantaged persons understood the nature and content of any insurance policy offered to them. CML was also required to put a senior manager in charge of compliance with the Trade Practices Act and to identify to the Commission the person who would report annually on progress.

The Commission and CML released a jointly prepared media statement summarising the terms of the deed and called a press conference. The release spelt out CML's willingness to co-operate in resolving the matter. It also indicated the joint view of the signatories that the arrangement was in the best interests of the company, the Commission and the community. The more critical question for our purposes is what happened within CML as a result.

Although a cynic might be tempted to say that the CML deed largely left the company free to return to unconscionable sales tactics, the outcome within the organisation has been cathartic. Members of the CML Board insisted on a purge. Over 80 employees or agents have been dismissed, including a national sales manager, two state sales managers for Queensland and NSW, and Tri-Global, a major corporate agency that is contesting its termination in the courts.

One question mark surrounding the CML deed of settlement is the confidential nature of the compliance and internal disciplinary report required to be filed with the Trade Practices Commission. Under the Accountability Model outlined in Chapter 5, such a report is publicly available and it is open to a court to order its publication in specified media. The power of adverse pub-licity is particularly important where, as is so often the position, scarce enforcement resources preclude criminal or civil proceedings against those responsible. Moreover, these documents can be a resource for compliance educators who wish to help their companies to learn from the mistakes of others in their industry. This issue was not squarely addressed in the negotiations leading up to the CML deed.

A deeper concern raised by the CML case is the inadequacy of internal disciplinary proceedings alone where the conduct of those disciplined is blatantly and callously unlawful. CML's agents resorted to a range of egregiously unfair tactics. Apart from the conduct of the agents in the field, the question arises whether senior management was seriously at fault in allowing the pattern of unfair selling practices to develop. The idea of ensnaring the support of Aboriginal community councils to sell policies to the majority of the members of impoverished communities hardly passes the smell test, and there have been suggestions in the news media that senior management had ample reason to suspect that violations of the Trade Practices Act were occurring. A warrant has been issued for the arrest of one selling agent who has absconded and thereby impelled criminal proceedings for that reason alone. However, there has been no initiation of criminal proceedings in relation to senior management.[44] The exercise of prosecutorial discretion needs to be watched closely in this context, and there is a need, as we have discussed in Chapter 6, for guidelines which focus on this issue.

The CML case and the related settlements in train represent a landmark in the development of enforcement strategies geared to achieving accountability for corporate law-breaking. The Commission built upon the experience gained from the Solomons Carpets affair and negotiated its way to success in a complex and large-scale matter, involving multiple major corporations, numerous corporate and individual agents of those corporations and thousands of largely illiterate victims located in some of the most inaccessible locations in a vast continent. There were legion evidentiary and procedural problems, particularly time limits on actions under the Trade Practices Act. Although some features of the CML deed of settlement and its aftermath are troubling, these problems can be addressed and are tackled under the Accountability Model we propose.

Beyond managing the sheer complexity and size of the case, the Trade Practices Commission's approach in the CML operation involved an advance over the Solomons strategy in a number of ways. Accountability was improved by having the agreed facts formally endorsed by a court of law. There was a quantum leap in the number of people compensated, in the educational commitment enshrined in the deed, in the rigour of the internal investigation, and in the number of people who lost their jobs as a result of the investigation. Most importantly, however, the case has triggered a wider community campaign to reform insurance practices. Media coverage has been extensive. All levels of the Australian polity have been touched by the shocking practices publicly revealed by the case. Even the Prime Minister asked for a briefing on it. The Minister for Justice has given a ministerial direction to the Commission to conduct a wider inquiry into the insurance industry and its sales practices.[45] State consumer affairs agencies are examining their neglect of Aboriginal consumer education. Certain weaknesses which have been revealed in the Insurance Contracts Act and the Trade Practices Act are likely to be remedied by parliament. Feverish deliberations are underway within the industry itself about how to prevent such a damaging public relations debacle from happening again. Thus, the possibility of regulation through a licensing regime for agents is back on the insurance industry's agenda.

The Trade Practices Commission has also felt compelled to re-examine its own position on some important matters. One of the forms of exploitation discovered by Commission staff involved 'twisting'. A client who had been sold one policy would some months later be asked to twist this policy over to another one, often with a different company. Some Aboriginal policy-holders were twisted twice, without understanding that for each twist they were committing a big slice of their meagre savings to a new commission for the agent. Years ago, on antitrust grounds, the Commission had insisted on deletion of insurance industry ethics policies which outlawed twisting. The Commission

---

[44] The possible bases of liability include complicity (under s. 75B(a) of the Trade Practices Act) and failure to exercise reasonable care and diligence as a corporate officer (under s 232(4) of the Corporations Law).

[45] See Australia, Trade Practices Commission, *Superannuation and Life Insurance*.

saw twisting narrowly as a means of shifting business from one company to a competitor who might offer a better deal. Now the Commission is wondering whether it bears some responsibility for discouraging the industry from cracking down on forms of twisting that exploit disadvantaged consumers.

In other words, the CML case and its relatives brought out multiple levels of responsibility: the responsibility of the insurance companies, its directors and executives, of their agents, of Aboriginal community councils, of parliament to write better laws, of the Life Insurance Federation of Australia, of state consumer affairs agencies, of the Insurance and Superannuation Commission, and even of the Trade Practices Commission itself for its regulatory failures.

For some participants, responsibility was brought home in a particularly compelling way. Top management found themselves directly confronted with the shame of the practices from which they and their companies had benefited. The media and the courts were not the only forums in which some found themselves exposed. The top management of Norwich were pressed into immediate contact with the victims as part of the process leading up to settlement. This was an exacting and conscience-searing experience. They had to take four-wheel-drive vehicles into Wujal Wujal (in tropical North Queensland) to participate in dispute negotiations in which the victims were given an active voice. Living for several days under the same conditions as their victims, Norwich's top brass had to sleep on a mattress on a concrete floor, eat tinned food, and survive at times without electricity.

Processes of dialogue with those who suffer from acts of irresponsibility are among the most effective ways of bringing home to us as human beings our obligation to take responsibility for our deeds.[46] Traditional courts, where victims are treated as evidentiary cannon fodder rather than given their voice, have tended to be destructive of this human way of eliciting responsibility. There is also the danger of corporate techniques of neutralisation of wrongdoing, such as 'denial' in the sense of refusal to recognise the nature and extent of wrongs occasioned by corporate activities.[47] Boardrooms and executive suites are hardly the frontiers where victims are harmed, but provide a haven conducive to cosy rationalisations and distorted pictures of actual corporate impacts. As the recent Australian insurance cases illustrate, the Accountability Model heeds these dangers by leaving space for directors and managers to have encounters with victims. Encountering the victims allows the shame of the wrongdoing to be communicated directly to those responsible. The process of encounter also helps to pre-empt or counter efforts by directors or managers to deny the existence of the problem or to neutralise it by means of some self-serving rationalisation. Beyond these salutary effects, encounters with victims provide an opportunity for healing through acceptance of responsibility and putting right the wrong.

---

[46] See further Day and Klein, *Accountabilities*, 249; Wolfe, 'The Corporate Apology'.
[47] See generally Sykes and Matza, 'Techniques of Neutralization'; S. Cohen, 'Human Rights and Crimes of the State'.

Another important feature of the negotiation process leading to the CML settlement was the role played by the Aboriginal community councils. Although some councils initially had supported particular sales agents in their sales drives, their stance radically changed as complaints were made about what the agents had done. Later, these councils vigorously assisted the Commission by bringing forward the victims to give evidence. Councils also held out for stringent terms of settlement and made detailed suggestions as to the contents of the deed. The role played was thus consistent with a strategy of tripartite enforcement in which consumer or other representative groups have a voice in the course of enforcement action taken.[48] One advantage of the tripartite model is that it helps to reduce the danger of enforcement agencies entering into cosy deals. Single victims or even groups of victims may have limited bargaining power compared with that of a corporate defendant. That imbalance can be overcome or partly offset if, as in these insurance cases, a representative group capable of protecting the interests of the victims participates in the negotiations. In these cases, this process was also salutary from the standpoint of accountability. By advancing and protecting the interests of the victims, members of Aboriginal community councils were able to make up for their initial mistake in encouraging and facilitating insurance sales campaigns. They accepted their responsibility in the matter and sought to rectify the harms done. The most direct and constructive method of making up for their mistake was to intervene in the enforcement process and to see to it that the wrongs were righted by the Trade Practices Commission.

The Future of Responsibility for Corporate Crime: Experimentation and Empiricism

Our reform prescription is that there should be more experiments of the kind envisaged above, with massively complex cases like BCCI and small and relatively simple cases like Solomons followed by empirical evaluation studies of the impact of the Accountability Model.[49] The empirical research would address a variety of questions. Were the agreements complied with? Did the voluntary compliance programs improve compliance? Did disciplined employees change their ways? How much adverse publicity did the case attract and what was its impact? Did targeted audiences re-examine their business, professional or bureaucratic ethics in light of the case? Did institutional change occur as a result of making the investigation public? Did the institutional changes make a difference to the effectiveness of internal controls?

It is trite to end a book with a call for empirical research to evaluate approximations at implementing a proposed reform. Calls for praxis and evaluation research are cheap. We shall try to make it more expensive by doing some ourselves in the years ahead. Praxis, as we have seen, is already underway in Australia.

---

[48] Ayres and Braithwaite, *Responsive Regulation*, ch. 3.
[49] There is also room for further and more detailed scenario writing; see Bardach, *The Implementation Game*, ch. 10.

It should also be realised that the Accountability Model is itself a self-learning device.[50] The more that the Accountability Model is put into practice, the richer the legal system's understanding of corporate behaviour and the role of responsibility as a mechanism of social control. Where non-compliance occurs, the corporations and persons responsible are subject to escalated and more intrusive responses, thereby providing courts and enforcement agencies with a further range of experience. Moreover, self-learning and adaptive change are inherent in the Accountability Model's strategy of trying to hold all responsible who are responsible. Thus, courts, legislators, or enforcement agencies who fail to take corrective action to repair breakdowns in the operation of the Accountability Model would thereby implicate themselves in the crimes they allow off the hook. In the world of accountability, the perpetually re-examined proposition is that no-one passes the buck.

---

[50] See further Fisse, 'Community Service as a Sanction against Corporations', 1016.

Bibliography of Cited Works

Abrams, R. I. and Nolan, D. R., 'Toward a Theory of "Just Cause" in Employee Discipline Cases' [1985] *Duke Law Journal*, 594–623.

Ackerman, B. A. and Hassler, W. T., 'Beyond the New Deal: Coal and the Clean Air Act' (1980) 89 *Yale Law Journal*, 1466–571.
  Clean Air, Dirty Coal (New Haven: Yale University Press, 1981).

Adams, J. R., *The Big Fix: Inside the S & L Scandal* (New York: John Wiley & Sons, 1990).

Adams, J. R. and Frantz, D., *A Full Service Bank: How BCCI Stole Billions Around the World* (New York: Pocket Books, 1992).

Adams, S., *Roche Versus Adams* (London: Jonathan Cape, 1984).

Adler, M. J., *Ten Philosophical Mistakes* (New York: Macmillan, 1985).

Akers, R. L., Krohn, M. D., Lanza-Kaduce, L. and Radosevich, M., 'Social Learning and Deviant Behavior: A Specific Test of a General Theory' (1979) 83 *American Sociological Review*, 114–53.

Alchian, A. A., 'The Basis of Some Recent Advances in the Theory of Management of the Firm' (1965) 14 *Journal of Industrial Economics*, 30–41.

Alexander, C. P., 'Crime in the Suites', *Time*, 10 June 1985, 52–3.

Allison, G. T., *Essence of Decision: Explaining the Cuban Missile Crisis* (Boston: Little, Brown, 1971).

Allport, F. H., *Institutional Behavior: Essays Toward a Re-Interpreting of Contemporary Social Organization* (Chapel Hill: University of North Carolina Press, 1933).

Allport, G. W., *The Nature of Prejudice* (Cambridge, Mass.: Addison-Wesley, 1954).

Alschuler, A. W., 'Mediation with a Mugger: The Shortage of Adjudicative Services and the Need for a Two-Tier Trial System in Civil Cases' (1986) 99 *Harvard Law Review*, 1808–59.
  'Ancient Law and the Punishment of Corporations: Of Frankpledge and Deodand' (1991) 71 *Boston University Law Review*, 307–13 .

Altrogge, P. and Shughart, W. F., 'The Regressive Nature of Civil Penalties' (1984) 4 *International Review of Law and Economics*, 55–66.

American Bar Association, 3 *Standards for Criminal Justice* (Boston: Little, Brown, 1980).
  Final Report, *Collateral Consequences of Convictions of Organizations* (Chicago: ABA, 1991).

American Law Institute, *Model Penal Code, Tentative Draft No. 4* (Philadelphia: ALI, 1955).

Andenaes, J., *Punishment and Deterrence* (Ann Arbor: University of Michigan Press, 1974).

Anderson, F. R., Kneese, A. V., Reed, P. D., Stevenson, R. B. and Taylor, S., *Environmental Incentives* (Baltimore: Johns Hopkins University Press, 1977).

Anderson, L. S., Chiricos, T. G. and Waldo, G. P., 'Formal and Informal Sanctions: A Comparison of Deterrent Effects' (1977) 25 *Social Problems,* 103–14.

Aoki, M., *The Co-Operative Game Theory of the Firm* (Oxford: Oxford University Press, 1984).

Apps, P. F. and Rees, R., 'Taxation and the Household' (1988) 33 *Journal of Public Economics,* 355–69.

Arkin, S., *Business Crime* (New York: Matthew Bender, 1985).

Arrow, K. J., *Social Choice and Individual Values* (New Haven: Yale University Press, 2nd edn, 1963).

Ashford, N. M., *Crisis in the Workplace: Occupational Disease and Injury, A Report to the Ford Foundation* (Cambridge, Mass.: MIT Press, 1976).

Australia, Commonwealth Director of Public Prosecutions, *Prosecution Policy of the Commonwealth* (Canberra: AGPS, 1990).

Australia, Draft White Paper, *Reform of the Australian Taxation System* (Canberra: AGPS, 1985).

Australia, Law Reform Commission, Report No. 60, *Customs and Excise* (Canberra: AGPS, 1992).
  Sentencing Penalties, Discussion Paper No. 30 (Canberra: The Law Reform Commission, 1987).

Australia, Senate Standing Committee on Constitutional Affairs, *The Social and Fiduciary Duties and Obligations of Company Directors* (Canberra: AGPS, 1989).

Australia, Standing Committee of Attorneys-General, Criminal Law Officers Committee, *Model Criminal Code, Discussion Draft,* ch. 2, 'General Principles of Criminal Responsibility' (Melbourne: Criminal Law Officers Committee, 1992).

Australia, *The Trade Practices Act: Proposals for Change* (Canberra: AGPS, 1984).

Australia, Trade Practices Commission, Annual Report 1980–1981 (Canberra: AGPS, 1981).

Australia, Trade Practices Commission, *Superannuation and Life Insurance* (Canberra: Trade Practices Commission, 1992).

Ayers, K. A. Jr, *The Processing and Prosecution of White Collar Crime by the States' Attorney Generals* (Ann Arbor, Michigan: University Microfilms International, 1984).

Ayers, K. A. Jr and Frank, J., 'Deciding to Prosecute White-Collar Crime: A National Survey of State Attorneys General' (1987) 4 *Justice Quarterly,* 425–39.

Ayres, I. and Braithwaite, J., *Responsive Regulation: Transcending the Deregulation Debate* (New York: Oxford University Press, 1992).

Bailey, M., *The Oilgate Scandal* (Sevenoaks, UK: Coronet, 1979).

Baker, D. I., 'To Indict or Not to Indict: Prosecutorial Discretion in Sherman Act Enforcement' (1978) 63 *Cornell Law Review,* 405–18.

Barack, G. (ed.), *Crimes by the Capitalist State: An Introduction to State Criminality* (Albany, NY: State University of New York Press, 1991).

Barbash, J., 'Due Process and Individual Rights in Arbitration' (1964) *17th NYU Conference on Labor,* 7–25.

Bardach, E., *The Implementation Game: What Happens After a Bill Becomes Law* (Cambridge, Mass.: MIT Press, 1977).

Bardach, E. and Kagan, R. A., *Going by the Book: The Problem of Regulatory Unreasonableness* (Philadelphia: Temple University Press, 1982).

Barnard, C. I., *The Functions of the Executive* (Cambridge, Mass.: Harvard University Press, 1938).

Barrett-Howard, E. and Tyler, T. R., 'Procedural Justice as a Criterion in Allocation Decisions' (1986) 50 *Journal of Personality and Social Psychology,* 296–304.

Bateson, G., *Steps to an Ecology of Mind* (London: Intertext, 1972).

Baumrind, D., 'Current Patterns of Parental Authority' (1971) *Developmental Psychology Monograph* 4, 1 Pt. 2.
'Parental Disciplinary Practices and Social Competence in Children' (1978) 9 *Youth and Society*, 239-76.

Baxi, U., *Mass Disasters and Multinational Liability: The Bhopal Case* (Delhi: Indian Law Institute, 1986).
'Evidence from Bhopal', *Multinational Monitor*, 3 July 1985, 1–7.

Bayles, M. D., *Procedural Justice: Allocating to Individuals* (Dordrecht: Kluwer Academic Publishers, 1990).

Baysinger, B. D., 'Organizational Theory and the Criminal Liability of Organizations' (1991) 71 *Boston University Law Review*, 341–76.

Becker, G., 'Crime and Punishment: An Economic Approach' (1968) 76 *Journal of Political Economy*, 169–217.

Belair, R. L., 'Employee Rights to Privacy' (1981) *NYU 33rd Conference on Labor*, 3–19.

Bell, D., 'Models and Reality in Economic Discourse' in D. Bell and I. Kristol (eds), *The Crisis in Economic Theory* (New York: Basic Books, 1981), ch. 4.

Bellah, R. N., Madsen, R., Sullivan, W. M., Swindler, A. and Tipton, S. M., *Habits of the Heart: Individualism and Commitment in American Life* (Berkeley: University of California Press, 1985).

BellSouth Corporation, *Antitrust Compliance Guidelines* (Atlanta: BellSouth, 2nd edn, 1989).

Bendor, J., *Parallel Systems: Redundancy in Government* (Berkeley: University of California Press, 1985).

Benedict, R., *The Chrysanthemum and the Sword: Patterns of Japanese Culture* (Boston: Houghton Mifflin, 1954).

Benn, S. I. and Mortimore, G. W. (eds), *Rationality and the Social Sciences* (London: Routledge & Kegan Paul, 1976).

Bennis, W. G., *Beyond Bureaucracy: Essays on the Development and Evolution of Human Organization* (New York: McGraw-Hill, 1973).

Benson, M., 'Emotions and Adjudication: Status Degradation among White Collar Criminals' (1990) 7 *Justice Quarterly*, 515–28.

Bequai, A., *White Collar Crime: A 20th Century Crisis* (Lexington, Mass.: Lexington Books, 1978).
Organized Crime (Lexington, Mass.: Lexington Books, 1979).

Bergman, D., 'Recklessness in the Boardroom' (1990) 140 *New Law Journal*, 1496–501.

Berle, A. A. and Means, G. C., *The Modern Corporation and Private Property* (New York: Harcourt, Brace & World, 1932).

Bernstein, M. H., *Regulating Business by Independent Commission* (Princeton, NJ: Princeton University Press, 1955).

Bierce, A., *The Devil's Dictionary* (New York: T. Y. Crowell, 1979).

Bingham, T. H. and Gray, S. M., *Report on the Supply of Petroleum and Petroleum Products to Rhodesia* (London: HMSO, 1978).

Bishop, D. M., 'Legal and Extralegal Barriers to Delinquency: A Panel Analysis' (1984) 22 *Criminology*, 403–20.

Bittel, L. R., *Management by Exception: Systematizing and Simplifying the Managerial Job* (New York: McGraw-Hill, 1964).

Bittker, B. I., *The Case for Black Reparations* (New York: Random House, 1973).

Black, T., 'The Erebus Inquiry' [1981] *New Zealand Law Journal*, 189–90.

Blades, L. E., 'Employment at Will vs. Individual Freedom: On Limiting the Abusive Exercise of Employer Power' (1967) 67 *Columbia Law Review*, 1404–35.

Blankenburg, E., 'The Poverty of Evolutionism: A Critique of Teubner's Case for "Reflexive Law" ' (1984) 18 *Law and Society Review,* 273–89.

Block, A. A. and Scarpitti, F. R., *Poisoning for Profit* (New York: William Morrow, 1985).

Block, D. J. and Barton, N. E., 'Internal Corporate Investigations: Maintaining the Confidentiality of a Corporate Client's Communications with Investigative Counsel' (1979) 35 *Business Lawyer,* 5–53.

Blum, R. H., *Offshore Haven Banks, Trusts and Companies* (New York: Praeger, 1982).

Blumberg, P. I. and Strasser, K. A., *The Law of Corporate Groups: Statutory Law— Specific* (Boston: Little Brown, 1992).

Blumrosen, A. W., 'Legal Protection for Critical Job Interests: Union-Management Authority Versus Employee Autonomy' (1959) 13 *Rutgers Law Review,* 631–65.

Boonin, L. G., 'Man and Society: An Examination of Three Models' (1969) XI *Nomos,* 69–84.

Bosk, C. L., *Forgive and Remember: Managing Medical Failure* (Chicago: University of Chicago Press, 1979).

Bosly, H. D., 'Responsibilité et Sanctions en Matière de Criminalité des Affairs' (1982) 53 *Revue Internationale du Droit Penal,* 125–43.

Boulding, K., *The Organizational Revolution* (New York: Harper, 1953).

Boulton, D., *The Grease Machine* (New York: Harper & Row, 1978).

Bower, J. L., *When Markets Quake: The Management Challenge of Restructuring Industry* (New York: Harper & Row, 1986).

Box, S., *Power, Crime, and Mystification* (London: Tavistock, 1983).

Braithwaite, J., 'Challenging Just Deserts: Punishing White-Collar Criminals' (1982) 73 *Journal of Criminal Law and Criminology,* 723-63.
'Enforced Self-Regulation: A New Strategy for Corporate Crime Control' (1982) 80 *Michigan Law Review,* 1466–507.
'Paradoxes of Class Bias in Criminal Justice' in H. E. Pepinsky (ed.), *Rethinking Criminology* (Beverly Hills: Sage, 1982), 61–85.
'The Limits of Economism in Controlling Harmful Corporate Conduct' (1982) 16 *Law & Society Review,* 481–504.
Corporate Crime in the Pharmaceutical Industry (London: Routledge & Kegan Paul, 1984), 117.
'Taking Responsibility Seriously: Corporate Compliance Systems' in B. Fisse and P. A. French (eds), *Corrigible Corporations and Unruly Law* (San Antonio: Trinity University Press, 1985), ch. 3.
To Punish or Persuade: Enforcement of Coal Mine Safety (Albany, NY: State University of New York Press, 1985).
Crime, Shame and Reintegration (Cambridge: Cambridge University Press, 1989).
Book Review of 'Interactive Corporate Compliance' (1990) 27 *American Business Law Journal,* 629-31.

Braithwaite, J. and Fisse, B., 'Varieties of Responsibility and Organizational Crime' (1985) 7 *Law and Policy,* 315–43.

Braithwaite, J. and Geis, G., 'On Theory and Action for Corporate Crime Control' (1982) 28 *Crime and Delinquency,* 292–314.

Braithwaite, J., Grabosky, P. and Fisse, B., *Occupational Health and Safety Enforcement Guidelines: A Report to the Victorian Department of Labour* (Melbourne: Department of Labour, 1986).

Braithwaite, J. and Makkai, T., 'Testing an Expected Utility Model of Corporate Deterrence' (1991) 25 *Law & Society Review,* 7-40.

Braithwaite, J., Makkai, T., Braithwaite, V. and Gibson, D., *Raising the Standard*:

Resident Centred Nursing Home Regulation in Australia (Canberra: AGPS, 1993).

Braithwaite, J. and Pettit, P., *Not Just Deserts: A Republican Theory of Criminal Justice* (Oxford: Clarendon Press, 1990).

Brakel, S. J., 'Special Masters in Institutional Litigation' [1979] *American Bar Foundation Research Journal*, 543-569.

Bratton, W. W. Jr, 'The New Economic Theory of the Firm: Critical Perspectives from History' (1989) 41 *Stanford Law Review*, 1471–527.

'The "Nexus of Contracts" Corporation: A Critical Appraisal' (1989) 74 *Cornell Law Review*, 407–65.

Brickey, K. F., 'Criminal Liability of Corporate Officers for Strict Liability Offenses: Another View' (1982) 35 *Vanderbilt Law Review*, 1337–81.

Corporate Criminal Liability (Willmette, Ill.: Callaghan, 1984).

Brodbeck, M. (ed.), *Readings in the Philosophy of the Social Sciences* (New York: Macmillan, 1968).

Bruck, C., *The Predators' Ball: The Inside Story of Drexel Burnham and the Rise of the Junk Bond Raiders* (Harmondsworth: Penguin, 1989).

Brudney, V., 'Corporate Governance, Agency Costs, and the Rhetoric of Contracts' (1985) 85 *Columbia Law Review*, 1403–44.

Bruns, N., 'Corporate Preventive Law Programs' (1985) 4 *Preventive Law Reporter*, 30–40.

Bucy, P., 'Corporate Ethos: A Standard for Imposing Corporate Criminal Liability' (1991) 75 *Minnesota Law Review*, l095–184.

'Indemnification of Corporate Executives Who Have Been Convicted of Crimes: An Assessment and Proposal' (1991) 24 *Indiana Law Review*, 279–356.

Bullock, A. and Stallybrass, O. (eds), *The Fontana Dictionary of Modern Thought* (London: Fontana Books, 1977).

Bureau of National Affairs, *White-Collar Justice* (Washington, DC: BNA, 1980).

Burkett, S. and Jensen, E. 'Conventional Ties, Peer Influence and the Fear of Apprehension: A Study of Adolescent Marijuana Use' (1975) 16 *Sociological Quarterly*, 522–33.

Burkey, L. M., 'Employee Surveillance: Are There Civil Rights for the Man on the Job?' (1969) *21st NYU Conference on Labor*, 199–214.

Burns, T., 'On the Plurality of Social Systems' in J. R. Lawrence (ed.), *Operational Research and the Social Sciences* (Oxford: Pergamon, 1966), 165–77.

Burns, T. and Stalker, G. M., *The Management of Innovation* (London: Tavistock, 1961).

Burrell, G. and Morgan, G., *Sociological Paradigms and Organizational Analysis* (London: Heinemann, 1979).

Burrough, B. and Helyar, J., *Barbarians at the Gate* (London: Jonathan Cape, 1990).

Byam, J. T., 'The Economic Inefficiency of Corporate Criminal Liability' (1982) 73 *Journal of Criminal Law & Criminology*, 582–603.

Byrne, J. and Hoffman, S. M., 'Efficient Corporate Harm: A Chicago Metaphysic' in B. Fisse and P. A. French (eds), *Corrigible Corporations and Unruly Law* (San Antonio: Trinity University Press, 1985), 101–36.

Campbell, D. N., Fleming, R. L. and Grote, R. C., 'Discipline without Punishment— At Last' (July–Aug. 1985) *Harvard Business Review*, 162–78.

Canada, Law Reform Commission, Working Paper 16, *Criminal Responsibility for Group Action* (Ottawa: Information Canada, 1976).

Recodifying Criminal Law (Ottawa: Law Reform Commission of Canada, 1986) .

Carlson, A. and Phillips, B., 'Due Process Considerations in Grievance Arbitration Proceedings' (1975) 2 *Hastings Constitutional Law Quarterly*, 519–45.

Caroline, M. W., 'Corporate Criminality and the Courts: Where are They Going?' (1985) 27 *Criminal Law Quarterly,* 237–54.

Carpenter, D. S. and Feloni, J., *The Fall of the House of Hutton* (New York: Henry Holt & Company, 1989).

Carr, E. H., *A History of Soviet Russia: The Bolshevik Revolution* (London: Macmillan, 1950).

Carson, W. G., 'White-Collar Crime and the Enforcement of Factory Legislation' (1970) 10 *British Journal of Criminology,* 383–98.

Cashman, P., 'The Dalkon Shield' in P. Grabosky and A. Sutton (eds), *Stains on a White Collar: Fourteen Studies in Corporate Crime or Corporate Harm* (Sydney: The Federation Press, 1989), 92–117.

Cass, R., 'Sentencing Corporations: The Guidelines' White Collar Blues' (1991) 71 *Boston University Law Review,* 291–305.

Chapman, B. and Trebilcock, M., 'Punitive Damages: Divergence in Search of a Rationale' (1989) 40 *Alabama Law Review,* 741–829.

Charles, D. and Lennon, K. (eds), *Reductionism Explanation and Realism* (Oxford: Oxford University Press, 1992).

Chayes, A., 'The Role of the Judge in Public Law Litigation' (1976) 89 *Harvard Law Review,* 1281–316.

Clark, R., *The Japanese Company* (New Haven: Yale University Press, 1979).

Clark, R. C., 'Agency Costs Versus Fiduciary Duties' in J. W. Pratt and R. J. Zeckhauser (eds), *Principals and Agents: The Structure of Business* (Boston: Harvard Business School, 1985), 55–79.

Clinard, M., *Corporate Ethics and Crime: The Role of Middle Management* (Beverly Hills: Sage Publications, 1983).

Clinard, M. B. and Yeager, P. C., *Corporate Crime* (New York: Free Press, 1980).

Coffee, J. C. Jr, 'Beyond the Shut-Eyed Sentry: Toward a Theoretical View of Corporate Misconduct and an Effective Legal Response' (1977) 63 *Virginia Law Review,* 1099–278.

'Corporate Crime and Punishment: A Non-Chicago View of the Economics of Criminal Sanctions' (1980) 17 *American Criminal Law Review,* 419–76.

'"No Soul to Damn No Body to Kick": An Unscandalized Inquiry into the Problem of Corporate Punishment' (1981) 79 *Michigan Law Review,* 386–459.

'Shareholders Versus Managers: The Strain in the Corporate Web' (1986) 85 *Michigan Law Review,* 1–109.

'Liquidity Versus Control: The Institutional Investor as Corporate Monitor' (1991) 91 *Columbia Law Review,* 1227–368.

Coffee, J. Jr, Gruner, R. and Stone, C. D., 'Standards for Organizational Probation: A Proposal to the United States Sentencing Commission' (1988) 10 *Whittier Law Review,* 77–102.

Coffee, J. C. Jr and Whitbread, C. K., 'The Convicted Corporation: An Outline of the New Federal Remedies' in O. G. Obermaier (ed.), *Corporate Criminal Liability* (New York: Practicing Law Institute, 1986), 318–60.

Cohen, A. K., 'Criminal Actors, Natural Persons and Collectivities' in School of Justice Studies, Arizona State University, *New Directions in the Study of Justice, Law and Social Control* (New York: Plenum Press, 1990), 101–25.

Cohen, M. A., 'Corporate Crime and Punishment: An Update on Sentencing Practice in the Federal Courts, 1988–1990' (1991) 71 *Boston University Law Review,* 247–80.

'Environmental Crime and Punishment: Legal/Economic Theory and Empirical Evidence on Enforcement of Federal Environmental Statutes' (1992) 82 *Journal of Criminal Law & Criminology,* 1054–108.

Cohen, M. A., Ho, C., Jones, E. D. and Schleich, L. M., 'Organizations as Defendants in Federal Court: A Preliminary Analysis of Prosecutions, Convictions, and Sanctions, 1984–1987' (1988) 10 *Whittier Law Review*, 103.

Cohen, S., 'Human Rights and Crimes of the State: On the Politics of Denial', John Barry Memorial Lecture, University of Melbourne, 30 Sept. 1992.

Coleman, J. L., 'Crime, Kickers, and Transaction Structures' in J. R. Pennock and J. W. Chapman (eds), *Criminal Justice* (1985) 27 *Nomos*, 313–28.

Coleman, J. S., *Power and the Structure of Society* (New York: Norton, 1974).

The Asymmetric Society (Syracuse, NY: Syracuse University Press, 1982).

Individual Interests and Collective Action (Cambridge: Cambridge University Press, 1986).

Foundations of Social Theory (Cambridge, Mass.: Harvard University Press, 1990).

Collier, N. C., 'Impolicy of Modern Decision and Statute Making Corporations Indictable and the Confusion in Morals Thus Created' (1910) 71 *Central Law Journal*, 421–7.

Collins, H., 'Ascription of Legal Responsibility to Groups in Complex Patterns of Economic Integration' (1990) 53 *Modern Law Review*, 731–44.

Justice in Dismissal: The Law of Termination of Employment (Oxford: Oxford University Press, 1992).

Comment, 'Industrial Due Process and Just Cause for Discipline: A Comparative Analysis of the Arbitral and Judicial Decisional Processes' (1959) 6 *UCLA Law Review*, 603–77.

Compte, A., *Systeme de Politique Positive* (Paris: Carilian-Goeury Et Vor Dalmont, 1851).

Conard, A. F., 'A Behavioral Analysis of Directors' Liability for Negligence' [1972] *Duke Law Journal*, 895–919.

Conklin, J. E., *'Illegal But Not Criminal': Business Crime in America* (Englewood Cliffs, N J: Prentice Hall, 1977).

Cook, J. D., *Results of the Toxicology Laboratory Inspection Program* (Jan.–March 1979) (Washington, DC: Food and Drug Administration Office of Planning and Evaluation, 1979).

Cooper, D., 'Responsibility and the "System"' in P. A. French (ed.), *Individual and Collective Responsibility* (Cambridge, Mass.: Schenkman Publishing Company, 1972), 81–100.

Cooper, G., 'The Taming of the Shrewd: Identifying and Controlling Income Tax Avoidance' (1985) 85 *Columbia Law Review*, 657–727.

Cooter, R. and Ulen, T., *Law and Economics* (Glenview, Ill.: Scott, Foresman & Company, 1988).

Copetas, A. C., *Metal Men: Marc Rich and the 10-Billion Scam* (London: Harrap Limited, 1986).

Craver, C. B., 'The Inquisitorial Process in Private Employment' (1977) 63 *Cornell Law Review*, 1-64.

Cressey, D., 'The Poverty of Theory in Corporate Crime Research' (1988) 1 *Advances in Criminological Theory*, 31–56.

Cullen, F. T. and Dubeck, P. J., 'The Myth of Corporate Immunity to Deterrence: Ideology and the Creation of the Invincible Criminal' (1985) 49 *Federal Probation*, 3–9.

Cullen, F. T., Link, B. G., and Polanzi, C. W., 'The Seriousness of Crime Revisited: Have Attitudes Toward White-Collar Crime Changed?' (1982) 20 *Criminology*, 83-102.

Cullen, F. T., Maakestad, W. J. and Cavender, G., *Corporate Crime under Attack: The Ford Pinto Case and Beyond* (Cincinatti: Anderson Publishing, 1987).

Curtler, H., *Shame, Responsibility and the Corporation* (New York: Haven Publishing, 1986).

Dallas, L. L., 'Two Models of Corporate Governance: Beyond Berle and Means' (1988) *University of Michigan Journal of Law Reform*, 19–116.

Dalton, M., *Men Who Manage* (New York: Wiley, 1959).

Dan-Cohen, M., *Rights, Persons, and Organizations* (Berkeley: University of California Press, 1986).

Dawson, S. J., Disciplinary and Dismissals Practice and Procedures, Unpublished British Government social survey, 1969.

Day, P. and Klein, R., *Accountabilities: Five Public Services* (London: Tavistock Publications, 1987).

Deal, T. E. and Kennedy, A. A., *Corporate Cultures: The Rites and Rituals of Corporate Life* (Reading, Mass.: Addison-Wesley, 1982).

Delatte, P., 'La Question de la Responsibilité Penale des Personnes Morales en Droit Belge' (1980) 60 *Revue de Droit Penal et de Criminologie*, 191–223.

Demb, A. and Neubauer, F.-F., *The Corporate Board: Confronting the Paradoxes* (New York: Oxford University Press, 1992).

DeMott, D. A., 'Beyond Metaphor: An Analysis of Fiduciary Obligation' [1988] *Duke Law Journal*, 879–924.

Dennett, D. C., *The Intentional Stance* (Cambridge, Mass.: MIT Press, 1987).

Derrida, J., *Limited Inc* (Evanston, Ill.: Northwestern University Press, 1988).

Dershowitz, A., 'Increasing Community Control over Corporate Crime: A Problem in the Law of Sanctions' (1961) 71 *Yale Law Journal*, 280–306.

Dertouzos, J. N., Holland, E. and Ebener, P., *Introduction to the Legal and Economic Consequences of Wrongful Termination* (Santa Monica: Institute of Civil Justice, Rand Corporation, 1988).

'Developments in the Law: Corporate Crime; Regulating Corporate Behavior through Criminal Sanctions' (1979) 92 *Harvard Law Review*, 1227–375.

'Developments in the Law: Injunctions' (1965) 78 *Harvard Law Review*, 994–1093.

Dewey, J., *Individualism Old and New* (New York: Capricorn, 1962).

Dickens, L. et al., 'A Response to the Government Working Papers on Amendments to Employment Protection Legislation' (mimeo, Coventry: University of Warwick, Industrial Relations Unit, 1979).

Doig, J. W., Phillips, D. E. and Manson, T., 'Deterring Illegal Behavior by Officials of Complex Organizations' (1984) 3 *Criminal Justice Ethics*, 27–56.

Donaldson, L. and Davis, J. H., 'Stewardship Theory or Agency Theory: CEO Governance and Shareholder Returns' (1991) 16 *Australian Journal of Management*, 49–64.

Donaldson, T., *Corporations and Morality* (Englewood Cliffs, NJ: Prentice-Hall, 1982).

Doré, R., *British Factory–Japanese Factory: The Origins of National Diversity in Industrial Relations* (Berkeley: University of California Press, 1973).

Dowd, J. 'The Responsibility of Lawyers for the Prevention, Detection and Rectification of Client Fraud' in P. Grabosky (ed.), *Complex Commercial Fraud* (Canberra: Australian Institute of Criminology, 1992), 65–71.

Downs, A., *Inside Bureaucracy* (Boston: Little, Brown, 1967).

Drane, R. W. and Neal, D. J., 'On Moral Justifications for the Tort/Crime Distinction' (1980) 68 *California Law Review*, 398–421.

Duguit, L., *Law in the Modern State* (London: Allen & Unwin, 1921).

Duke, S., 'Conspiracy, Complicity, Corporations, and the Federal Code Reform' in

A. Abramovsky (ed.), *Criminal Law and the Corporate Counsel* (New York: Law & Business, 1981), 147–79.

Durkheim, E., *De la Division du Travail* (Paris: Alcan, 5th edn, 1926).

The Rules of Sociological Method (New York: Free Press, 1964).

Dworkin, R., *Law's Empire* (Cambridge, Mass.: Belknap Press, 1986).

Dworkin, T. and Near, J., 'Whistleblowing Statutes: Are They Working?' (1987) 25 *American Business Law Journal*, 241–64.

Eagles, I., 'Public Law and Private Corporations' (1986) 45 *Cambridge Law Journal*, 406–13.

Edwards, J. Ll., *The Attorney General, Politics and the Public Interest* (London: Sweet & Maxwell, 1984).

Edwards, H. T., 'Due Process Considerations in Labor Arbitration' (1970) 25 *The Arbitration Journal*, 141–69.

Eells, R., *The Government of Corporations* (New York: Free Press of Glencoe, 1962).

Ellickson, R. C., 'Bringing Culture and Human Frailty to Rational Actors: A Critique of Classical Law and Economics' (1989) 65 *Chicago-Kent Law Review*, 23–55.

Ellis, D. D., 'Fairness and Efficiency in the Law of Punitive Damages' (1982) 56 *Southern California Law Review*, 1–78.

Elzinga, K. G. and Breit, W., *The Antitrust Penalties: A Study in Law and Economics* (New Haven: Yale University Press, 1976).

Emery, F. E. (ed.), *Systems Thinking* (Harmondsworth: Penguin, 1969).

Emmet, D., *Rules, Roles and Relations* (Boston: Beacon Press, 1975).

Ermann, M. D. and Lundman, R. J., *Corporate Deviance* (New York: Holt, Rinehart & Winston, 1st edn, 1978).

Corporate Deviance (New York: Holt, Rinehart & Winston, 2nd edn, 1982).

Etzioni, A., *The Moral Dimension: Toward A New Economics* (New York: Macmillan, 1988).

Ewing, D., *Freedom Inside the Organization* (New York: McGraw-Hill, 1977).

Ezorsky, G., 'On "Groups and Justice"' (1977) 87 *Ethics*, 182–85.

(ed.), *Philosophical Perspectives on Punishment* (Albany, NY: State University of New York Press, 1972).

Facolta Di Giurisprudenza, Universita Degli Studi Di Messina, *La Responsabilita Penale Delle Persone Giuridiche in Diritto Comunitario* (Milano: A. Giuffre, 1981).

Falls, M. M., 'Retribution, Reciprocity, and Respect for Persons' (1987) 6 *Law and Philosophy*, 25–51.

Fauconnet, P., *La Responsabilité* (Paris: Librarie F. Alcan, 1928).

Feeley, M., *The Process is the Punishment* (London: Russell Sage Foundation, 1990).

Feinberg, J., *Doing and Deserving* (Princeton: Princeton University Press, 1970).

Felstiner, W. L. F. and Drew, A. B., *European Alternatives to Criminal Trials and Their Applicability in the United States* (Washington, DC: Law Enforcement Assistance Administration, US Department of Justice, 1978).

Fialka, J. J. and Truell, P., 'Rogue Bank', *Wall Street Journal*, 3 May 1990, A1.

Fiebach, H. R.,'The Constitutional Rights of Associations to Assert the Privilege against Self-Incrimination' (1964) 112 *University of Pennsylvania Law Review*, 394–416.

Field, S. and Jörg, N., 'Corporate Liability and Manslaughter: Should We Be Going Dutch?' [1991] *Criminal Law Review*, 156–171.

Findlay, M. and Zvekic, U., *Analysing (In)Formal Mechanisms of Crime Control: A Cross-Cultural Perspective* (Rome: United Nations Social Defence Research Institute, 1988).

Fine, S., 'The Philosophy of Enforcement' (1976) 31 *Food, Drug and Cosmetic Law Journal*, 324–28.

Finkelstein, J. J., 'The Goring Ox: Some Historical Perspectives on Deodands, Forfeitures, Wrongful Death and the Western Notion of Sovereignty' (1973) 46 *Temple Law Quarterly*, 169–289.

Finn, P., *Official Information*, Integrity in Government Project, Interim Report 1 (Canberra: ANU, 1991).

Finnis, J., 'The Restoration of Retribution' (1972) 32 *Analysis*, 131–5.

Finzen, B. A. and Walburn, R. B., 'Union Carbide Corporation's Liability for the Bhopal Disaster: Multinational Enterprise Liability' in W. M. Hoffman, W. R. Frederick, and E. S. Petry, Jr (eds), *The Corporation, Ethics, and the Environment* (New York: Quorum Books, 1990).

Fiss, O., *The Civil Rights Injunction* (Bloomington: Indiana University Press, 1978).
    'The Supreme Court 1978 Term—Foreword: The Forms of Justice' (1979) 93 *Harvard Law Review*, 1–58.
    'Against Settlement' (1984) 93 *Yale Law Journal*, 1073–90.

Fisse, B., 'Consumer Protection and Corporate Criminal Responsibility: A Critique of Tesco Supermarkets Ltd. v. Nattrass' (1971) 4 *Adelaide Law Review*, 113–29.
    'Responsibility, Prevention and Corporate Crime' (1973) 5 *New Zealand Universities Law Review*, 250–79.
    'Probability and the Proudman v Dayman Defence of Reasonable Mistaken Belief' (1974) 9 *Melbourne University Law Review*, 477–512.
    'The Social Policy of Corporate Criminal Responsibility' (1978) 6 *Adelaide Law Review*, 361–412.
    'Criminal Law and Consumer Protection' in A. J. Duggan and L. W. Darvall (eds), *Consumer Protection Law and Theory* (Sydney: Law Book Company, 1980), 182–99.
    'Community Service as a Sanction against Corporations' [1981] *Wisconsin Law Review*, 970–1017.
    'Reconstructing Corporate Criminal Law: Deterrence, Retribution, Fault, and Sanctions' (1983) 56 *Southern California Law Review*, 1141–246.
    'Sanctioning Multinational Offenders' (Dec.–Jan. 1985) *Multinational Monitor*, 16–18.
    'Controlling Governmental Crime: Issues of Individual and Collective Liability' in P. Grabosky (ed.), *Government Illegality* (Canberra: Australian Institute of Criminology, 1986), 121–43.
    'Corporate Compliance Programmes: The Trade Practices Act and Beyond' (1989) 17 *Australian Business Law Review*, 356–99.
    Howard's Criminal Law (Sydney: Law Book Company, 5th edn, 1990).
    'Recent Developments in Corporate Criminal Law and Corporate Liability to Monetary Penalties' (1990) 13 *University of New South Wales Law Journal*, 1–41.
    'The Attribution of Criminal Liability to Corporations: A Statutory Model' (1991) 13 *Sydney Law Review*, 277–97.
    'The Punitive Injunction as a Sanction against Corporations' [forthcoming].

Fisse, B. and Braithwaite, J., *The Impact of Publicity on Corporate Offenders* (Albany, New York: State University of New York Press, 1983).
    'Sanctions against Corporations: Dissolving the Monopoly of Fines' in R. Tomasic (ed.), *Business Regulation in Australia* (Sydney: CCH Australia, 1984), 129–45.
    'The Allocation of Responsibility for Corporate Crime: Individualism, Collectivism and Accountability' (1988) 11 *Sydney Law Review*, 469–513.

Fisse, B. and French, P. A., 'Corporate Responses to Errant Behavior: Time's Arrow, Law's Target' in B. Fisse and P. A. French (eds), *Corrigible Corporations and Unruly Law* (San Antonio: Trinity University Press, 1985), 187–215.

Fleming, R. W., 'Some Problems of Due Process and Fair Procedure in Labor Arbitration' (1961) 13 *Stanford Law Review*, 235–51.

BIBLIOGRAPHY OF CITED WORKS   249

Florman, S. C., *Blaming Technology: The Irrational Search for Scapegoats* (New York: St Martin, 1981).
Francis, J. J., 'Criminal Responsibility of a Corporation' (1923) 18 *Illinois Law Review*, 305–23.
Freiberg, A., 'Monetary Penalties under the Trade Practices Act 1974 (Cth)' (1983) 11 *Australian Business Law Review*, 4–26.
    'Enforcement Discretion and Taxation Offences' (1986) 3 *Australian Tax Forum*, 55–91.
    'Abuse of the Corporate Form: Reflections from the Bottom of the Harbour' (1987) 10 *University of New South Wales Law Journal*, 67–102.
    'Reconceptualizing Sanctions' (1987) 25 *Criminology*, 223–55.
French, P. A. (ed.), *Individual and Collective Responsibility: The Massacre at My Lai* (Cambridge, Mass.: Schenkman Publishing, 1972).
    'Types of Collectivities and Blame' (1975) 56 *The Personalist*, 160–9.
    'The Corporation as a Moral Person' (1979) 16 *American Philosophical Quarterly*, 207–15.
    'Commentary' (1983) 2 *Business and Professional Ethics Journal*, 89–93.
    Collective and Corporate Responsibility (New York: Columbia University, 1984).
Friedman, H. M., *Securities and Commodities Enforcement* (Lexington, Mass.: Lexington Books, 1981).
Friedman, L. M., *The Legal System: A Social Science Perspective* (New York: Russell Sage, 1975).
Friendly, H. J., 'Some Kind of Hearing' (1975) 123 *University of Pennsylvania Law Review*, 1267–317.
Frug, G., 'The City as a Legal Concept' (1980) 93 *Harvard Law Review*, 1059–154.
Gaines, S. E., and Westin, R. A. (eds), *Taxation for Environmental Protection: A Multinational Study* (Westport, Conn.: Quorum Books, 1991).
Galbraith, J. K., *The New Industrial State* (London: Hamish Hamilton, 1967).
Garet, R. R., 'Communality and Existence: The Rights of Groups' (1983) 56 *Southern California Law Review*, 1001–75.
Garfinkel, H., *Studies in Ethnomethodology* (Englewood Cliffs, NJ: Prentice-Hall, 1967).
Geertz, C., *The Interpretation of Cultures* (New York: Basic Books, 1973).
    Local Knowledge (New York: Basic Books, 1983).
Geis, G., 'The Heavy Electrical Equipment Antitrust Cases of 1961' in G. Geis (ed.), *White-Collar Criminal* (New York: Atherton Press, 1968), 103–18.
Geis, G. and DiMento, J., 'Is it Sound Policy to Prosecute Corporations Rather Than or in Addition to Human Malefactors?', Paper presented at conference, Corporate Crime: Ethics, Law and the State, Queen's University, Kingston, Ontario, 12–14 Nov., 1992.
Gelb, H., 'Director Due Care Liability: An Assessment of the New Statutes' (1988) 61 *Temple Law Review*, 13–50.
Geraghty, J. A., 'Structural Crime and Institutional Rehabilitation: A New Approach to Corporate Sentencing' (1979) 89 *Yale Law Journal*, 353–75.
Gerber, J., 'Enforced Self-Regulation in the Infant Formula Industry: A Radical Extension of an "Impractical Proposal"' (1990) 17 *Social Justice*, 98–111.
Gerth, H. H. and Mills, C. W. (eds), *From Max Weber: Essays in Sociology* (London: Routledge & Kegan Paul, 1967).
Geyelin, P., 'Under Reagan, a Dismaying Trend to "Headlessness"', *International Herald Tribune*, 8 Oct. 1985, 4.
Gibbons, T., 'The Utility of Economic Analysis of Crime' (1982) 2 *International Review of Law and Economics*, 173–91.

Gibney, F., *Japan: The Fragile Super Power* (New York: Norton, 1979).

Gibson, W., *Burning Chrome* (London: Grafton, 1988).

Giddens, A., *Central Problems in Social Theory* (London: Macmillan, 1979).
    The Constitution of Society (Berkeley: University of California Press, 1984).

Ginzberg, E. and Reilly, E. W., *Effecting Change in Large Organizations* (New York: Columbia University Press, 1957).

Goff, C. H. and Reasons, C. E., *Corporate Crime in Canada* (Scarborough, Ont.: Prentice-Hall of Canada, 1978).

Goldberg, A. M., 'Corporate Officer Liability for Federal Environmental Statute Violations' (1991) 18 *Environmental Affairs,* 357–79.

Goldring, J. and Maher, L. W., *Consumer Protection Law in Australia* (Sydney: Butterworths, 1979).

Goodin, R. E., *Political Theory and Public Policy* (Chicago: University of Chicago Press, 1982).
    'Responsibilities' (1986) 36 *Philosophical Quarterly,* 50–6.
    'Apportioning Responsibility' (1987) 6 *Law and Philosophy,* 167–85.

Goodpaster, K., 'The Concept of Corporate Responsibility' (1983) 2 *Journal of Business Ethics,* 1–22.

Goodwin, S. D., 'Individual Liability of Agents for Corporate Crimes under the Proposed Federal Criminal Code' (1978) 31 *Vanderbilt Law Review,* 965–1016.

Gordon, R. A., *Business Leadership in the Large Corporation* (Washington, DC: Brookings Institute, 1945).

Gouldner, A. W., *Patterns of Industrial Bureaucracy* (Glencoe, Ill.: Free Press, 1954).

Grabosky, P., 'Professional Advisers and White Collar Illegality: Towards Explaining and Excusing Professional Failure' (1990) 13 *University of New South Wales Law Journal,* 73–96.

Grabosky, P. and Braithwaite, J., *Of Manners Gentle: Enforcement Strategies of Australian Business Regulatory Agencies* (Melbourne: Oxford University Press, 1986).
    (eds), *The Future of Business Regulation in Australia* (Canberra: Australian Institute of Criminology, 1992).

Grabosky, P. N., Braithwaite, J. B. and Wilson, P. R., 'The Myth of Community Tolerance Toward White-Collar Crime' (1987) 20 *Australia and New Zealand Journal of Criminology,* 33–44.

Great Britain Law Reform Commission, *Report No. 143, Codification of the Criminal Law* (London: HMSO, 1985).
    Report of the Public Inquiry into the Accident at the Hixon Level Crossing (Cmnd. 3706, 1968).
    Report of the Tribunal to Inquire into the Disaster at Aberfan (HL 316, 1966).

Green, M. J., Moore, B. C. and Wasserstein, B., *The Closed Enterprise System* (New York: Grossman, 1972).

Grippando, J. M., 'Caught in the Non-Act: Expanding Criminal Antitrust Liability for Corporate Officials' [1989] *Antitrust Bulletin,* 713–57.

Groening, W. A., *The Modern Corporate Manager: Responsibility and Regulation* (New York: McGraw-Hill, 1981).

Gruner, R., 'To Let the Punishment Fit the Organization: Sanctioning Corporate Offenders through Corporate Probation' (1988) 16 *American Journal of Criminal Law,* 1–106.

Grupp, S. E. (ed.), *Theories of Punishment* (Bloomington: Indiana University Press, 1971).

Gunningham, N., *Pollution, Social Interests and the Law* (London: Martin Robertson, 1976).

Habermas, J., 'Law as Medium and Law as Institution' in G. Teubner (ed.), *Dilemmas of Law in the Welfare State* (Berlin: Walter de Gruyter, 1985), 203–20.

Haddock, M. D., McChesney, F. S. and Spiegel, M., 'An Ordinary Economic Rationale for Extraordinary Legal Sanctions' (1990) 78 *California Law Review*, 1–51.

Hallis, F., *Corporate Personality: A Study in Jurisprudence* (London: Oxford University Press, 1970).

Hans, V., 'Attitudes Toward Corporate Responsibility: A Psycholegal Perspective' (1990) 69 *Nebraska Law Review*, 158–89.

Hans, V. and Ermann, D., 'Responses to Corporate Versus Individual Wrongdoing' (1989) 13 *Law and Human Behavior*, 151–166.

Hans, V. and Lofquist, W. S., 'Jurors' Judgments of Business Liability in Tort Cases: Implications for the Litigation Explosion Debate' (1992) 26 *Law and Society Review*, 85–116.

Hare, T., 'Reluctant Soldiers: The Criminal Liability of Corporate Officers for Negligent Violations of the Clean Waters Act' (1990) 138 *University of Pennsylvania Law Review*, 935–78.

Hart, H. L. A, *Punishment and Responsibility* (New York: Oxford University Press, 1968).

Hart, O., 'An Economist's Perspective on the Theory of the Firm' (1989) 89 *Columbia Law Review*, 1757–74.

Hart, O. and Holmstrom, B., 'The Theory of Contracts' in T. F. Bewley (ed.), *Advances in Economic Theory: Fifth World Congress* (Cambridge: Cambridge University Press, 1987).

Hawkins, K., *Environment and Enforcement: The Social Definition of Pollution* (Oxford: Clarendon Press, 1984).

Hay, G., 'Review of Elzinga and Breit, *The Antitrust Penalties*' (1978) 31 *Vanderbilt Law Review*, 427–44.

Hayek, F. A., *Individualism and the Economic Order* (London: Routledge & Kegan Paul, 1949).

Hedberg, B. L. T., Nystrom, P. C. and Starbuck, W. H., 'Camping on Seesaws: Prescriptions for a Self-Designing Organization' (1976) 21 *Administrative Science Quarterly*, 41–65.

Heilbroner, R. L., *Behind the Veil of Economics: Essays in the Worldly Philosophy* (New York: W. W. Norton & Company, 1988).

Heimer, C. A., *Reactive Risk and Rational Action: Managing Moral Hazard in Insurance Contracts* (Berkeley: University of California Press, 1985).

Henry, S., *Private Justice: Towards Integrated Theorising in the Sociology of Law* (London: Routledge & Kegan Paul, 1983).

Herlihy, E. D. and Levine, T. A., 'Corporate Crisis: The Overseas Payment Problem' (1976) 8 *Law and Policy in International Business*, 547–629.

Herling, J., *The Great Price Conspiracy* (Washington, DC: Luce, 1962).

Herman, E. S., *Corporate Control, Corporate Power* (Cambridge: Cambridge University Press, 1981).

Hessler, C. A., 'Command Responsibility for War Crimes' (1973) 82 *Yale Law Journal*, 1274–404.

Hill, M., 'Recent Developments in Corporate Criminal Law in England' (1991) 3 *Current Issues in Criminal Justice*, 122–42.

Hindess, B., 'Classes, Collectivities and Corporate Actors' in S. R. Clegg (ed.), *Organization Theory and Class Analysis* (Berlin: Walter de Gruyter, 1989), 157–71.

Hobson, D., *The Pride of Lucifer* (London: Hamish Hamilton, 1990).

Hodgkinson, C., *Towards a Philosophy of Administration* (Oxford: Blackwell, 1978).
Hogg, P. W., *Liability of the Crown* (Sydney: Law Book Company, 2nd edn, 1989).
Honoré, A. M., 'Groups, Laws, and Obedience' in A. W. B. Simpson (ed.), *Oxford Essays in Jurisprudence* (Oxford: Clarendon Press, 1973).
Hopkins, A., *The Impact of Prosecutions under the Trade Practices Act* (Canberra: Australian Institute of Criminology, 1978).
Horster-Philipps, U., *Im Schatten Des Grossen Geldes* (Cologne: Pahl-Rugenstein, 1985).
Horwitz, M., 'The History of the Public/Private Distinction' (1982) 130 *University of Pensylvania Law Review*, 1423–8.
Hovenkamp, H., 'Antitrust's Protected Classes' (1989) 88 *Michigan Law Review*, 1–48.
Hrebiniak, L. G., *Complex Organizations* (St Paul: West Publishing Company, 1978).
Hurley, A., 'Section 76 of the Trade Practices Act: Are Pecuniary Penalties Alone an Effective Sanction?' (1986) 18(3) *Commercial Law Association of Australia Bulletin*, 19–31.
Hutchinson, T. W., *Knowledge and Ignorance in Economics* (Oxford: Basil Blackwell, 1977).
Hwang, C.-L. and Lin, M.-J., *Group Decision Making under Multiple Criteria* (Berlin: Springer-Verlag, 1987).
Hyde, W. W., 'The Prosecution and Punishment of Animals and Lifeless Things in the Middle Ages and Modern Times' (1916) 64 *University of Pennsylvania Law Review*, 696–730.
International Labour Organization, 'Termination of Employment (Dismissal and Lay Off)', 46th Sess., Rep. VII (1) (Geneva: ILO, 1962).
    Conventions and Recommendations 1919–1966 (Geneva: ILO, 1966).
Irwin, W. A. and Liroff, R. A., *Economic Disincentives for Pollution Control: Legal, Political and Administrative Dimensions* (Springfield, Va.: Environmental Protection Agency, National Technical Information Service, 1974).
Iseman, R. H., 'The Criminal Responsibility of Corporate Officials for Pollution of the Environment' (1972) 37 *Albany Law Review*, 61–96.
Jackall, R., *Moral Mazes* (New York: Oxford University Press, 1988).
Jacobs, F., *Criminal Responsibility* (London: Weidenfeld and Nicolson, 1971).
Jacoby, N. H., Nehemkis, P. and Eells, R., *Bribery and Extortion in World Business* (New York: Macmillan, 1977).
Janis, I. L., *Victims of Groupthink* (Boston: Houghton, Miffin, 1972).
Janis, I. L. and Mann, L., *Decision Making* (New York: Free Press, 1977).
Jensen, G. F. and Erickson, M., 'The Social Meaning of Sanctions' in M. Krohn and R. Akers (eds), *Crime, Law and Sanctions: Theoretical Perspectives* (Beverly Hills: Sage, 1978), 119–36.
Jensen, C. M. and Meckling, W. H., 'Theory of the Firm: Managerial Behavior, Agency Costs and Ownership Structure' (1976) 3 *Journal of Financial Economics* 305–60.
Jescheck, H.-H., *Lehrbuch des Strafrechts: Allgemeiner Teil* (Berlin: Duncker & Humboldt, 3rd edn, 1978).
Jevons, W. S., *The Theory of Political Economy* (London: Macmillan, 1879).
Johnson, R. and Brown, G. M. Jr, *Cleaning Up Europe's Waters* (New York: Praeger, 1976).
Jones, E. A., 'Evidentiary Concepts in Labor Arbitration: Some Modern Variations on Ancient Legal Themes' (1966) 13 *UCLA Law Review*, 1241–97.
Josephson, M., *The Robber Barons: The Great American Capitalists 1861-1901* (New York: Harcourt Brace Jovanovich, 1962).

Jung, H. and Krause, F., *Die Stamokap-Republik der Flicks* (Frankfurt: VMB, 1985).

Kadish, S., 'Some Observations on the Use of Criminal Sanctions in Enforcing Economic Regulations' (1963) 30 *University of Chicago Law Review*, 423–49.

Kafka, F., *The Castle* (New York: Random House, 1985).

Kagan, R. A. and Scholz, J. T., 'The "Criminology of the Corporation" and Regulatory Enforcement Strategies', in K. Hawkins and J. M. Thomas (eds), *Enforcing Regulation* (Boston: Kluwer-Nijhoff, 1984), 67–95.

Kahan, J. S., 'Criminal Liability under the Food, Drug, and Cosmetic Act—The Large Corporation Perspective' (1981) 36 *Food, Drug, and Cosmetic Law Journal* 314–31.

Kanski, A. M., 'Employee Drug Testing: Balancing the Employer's Right to Know with the Employee's Right to Privacy' (1987) 1 *Detroit College of Law Review*, 27–63.

Kant, I., *The Metaphysical Elements of Justice* (Cambridge, New York: Cambridge University Press, 1965).

Kanter, R. M., *The Change Masters: Corporate Entrepreneurs at Work* (London: Unwin Paperbacks, 1983).

Katz, D. and Kahn, R. L., *The Social Psychology of Organizations* (New York: Wiley, 1966).
The Social Psychology of Organization and Management (Chicago: Science Research Associates, 1973).

Kaufman, H., *The Limits of Organizational Change* (University, Alabama: University of Alabama Press, 1971).

Kennedy, C., 'Criminal Sentences for Corporations: Alternative Fining Mechanisms' (1985) 73 *California Law Review*, 443–82.

Kerry Report, *The BCCI Affair*, Report to the Senate Foreign Relations Committee, Subcommittee on Terrorism, Narcotics, and International Operations (Washington, DC: Government Printing Office, 1992).

Kerse, C. S., *EEC Antitrust Procedure* (London: European Law Centre, 1981).

Kidd, C. J. F., 'Disciplinary Proceedings and the Right to a Fair Criminal Trial Under the European Convention on Human Rights' (1987) 36 *International and Comparative Law Journal*, 856–72.

Kilz, H. W. and Preuss, J., *Flick: Die Gekaufte Republik* (Hamburg: Spiegel Buch, 1983).

Kirkpatrick, W. W., 'The Adequacy of Internal Corporate Controls' (1962) 343 *Annals of the American Academy of Political and Social Science*, 75–83.

Klevorick, A. K., 'On the Economic Theory of Crime' in J. R. Pennock and J. W. Chapman (eds), *Criminal Justice* (1985) 27 *Nomos*, 289–309.

Knightley, P., Evans, H., Potter, E. and Wallace, M., *Suffer the Children: The Story of Thalidomide* (New York: Viking Press, 1979).

Komarow, G., 'Individual Responsibility under International Law: The Nuremberg Principles in Domestic Legal Systems' (1980) 29 *International and Comparative Law Quarterly*, 21–37.

Koprowicz, K. M., 'Corporate Criminal Liability for Workplace Hazards' (1986) 52 *Brooklyn Law Review*, 183–227.

Kraakman, R. H., 'Corporate Liability Strategies and the Costs of Legal Controls' (1984) 93 *Yale Law Journal*, 857–98.
'Gatekeepers: The Anatomy of a Third-Party Enforcement Strategy' (1986) 2 *Journal of Law Economics & Organization*, 53–104.

Kramer, R. C., 'Corporate Criminality: The Development of an Idea' in E. Hochstedler (ed.), *Corporations as Criminals* (1984), 13–37.

Kraut, R., 'Deterrent and Definitional Influences on Shoplifting' (1976) 23 *Social Problems*, 358–68.

Kreimer, S. F., 'Reading the Mind of the School Board: Segregative Intent and the De Facto/De Jure Distinction' (1976) 86 *Yale Law Journal,* 317–55.

Kriegler, R. J., *Working for the Company* (Melbourne: Oxford University Press, 1980).

Kriesberg, S. M., 'Decisionmaking Models and the Control of Corporate Crime' (1976) 85 *Yale Law Journal,* 1091–129.

Kruse, S. V., Erhvervslivets Kriminalitet: Studier i det Objective Strafansvar, Unpublished PhD thesis, 1983, copy held in Max Planck Institute for Criminal Law Library, Freiburg, Germany.
  'Criminal Liability for Negligence of Business Leaders' [1984] *Commonwealth Law Bulletin,* 971–87.

Ladd, J., 'Morality and the Ideal of Rationality in Formal Organizations' (1970) 54 *Monist,* 488–516.

Lahti, R., 'Finland National Report' (1982) 54 *Revue Internationale de Droit Penal,* 249–62.

Lakoff, S. A. and Rich, D. (eds), *Private Government* (Glenview, Ill.: Scott, Foresman & Company, 1973).

Landau, M., 'Redundancy, Rationality, and the Problem of Duplication and Overlap' (1969) 29 *Public Administration Review,* 346–58.

Lareau, W., *American Samurai: Why Every American Executive Must Fight for Quality* (New York: Warner Books, 1991).

Latham, E., 'The Body Politic of the Corporation' in E. S. Mason (ed.), *The Corporation in Modern Society* (Cambridge, Mass.: Harvard University Press, 1960), 218–36.

Lawrence, P. R. and Lorsch, J. W., 'Differentiation and Integration in Complex Organizations' (1967) 12 *Administrative Science Quarterly,* 1–47.
  Organization and Environment (Boston: Graduate School of Business, Harvard University, 1967).
  Developing Organizations: Diagnosis and Action (Reading, Mass.: Addison-Wesley, 1969).

Lederman, E., 'Criminal Law, Perpetrator and Corporation: Rethinking a Complex Triangle' (1985) 76 *Journal of Criminal Law & Criminology,* 285–340.

Leigh, L. H., *The Criminal Liability of Corporations in English Law* (London: Weidenfeld & Nicolson, 1969).
  'The Criminal Liability of Corporations and Other Groups' (1977) 9 *Ottawa Law Review,* 247–302.
  'The Criminal Liability of Corporations and Other Groups: A Comparative View' (1982) 80 *Michigan Law Review,* 1508–28.

Lenard, P. M., 'Unjust Dismissal of Employees at Will: Are Disclaimers a Final Solution?' (1987) 15 *Fordham Urban Law Journal,* 533–65.

Levi, M., 'Sentencing White-Collar Crime in the Dark? Reflections on the Guinness Four' (1991) 30 *Howard Journal of Criminal Justice,* 257–79.

Lewis, D. R., 'A Proposal to Restructure Sanctions under the Occupational Safety and Health Act: The Limitations of Punishment and Culpability' (1982) 91 *Yale Law Journal,* 1446–73.

Lewis, D., 'Causation', and 'Postscript E: Redundant Causation' in *Philosophical Papers,* vol. II (Oxford: Oxford University Press, 1986), 159–94.

Lewis, H. D., 'The Non-Moral Notion of Collective Responsibility' in P. A. French, (ed.), *Individual and Collective Responsibility: The Massacre at My Lai* (Cambridge, Mass.: Schenkman, 1972), 119–44.

Lewis, J. R., *Uncertain Judgment: A Bibliography of War Crimes Trials* (Santa Barbara, California: ABC-Clio, 1979).

Lind, E. A. and Tyler, T. R., *The Social Psychology of Procedural Justice* (New York: Plenum Press, 1988).

Lipsey, R. G. and Lancaster, K., 'The General Theory of Second Best' (1956) 24 *Review of Economic Studies,* 11–32.

Loasby, B. J., *Choice, Complexity and Ignorance: An Enquiry into Economic Theory and the Practice of Decisionmaking* (Cambridge: Cambridge University Press, 1976).

Lofquist, W. S., 'Organizational Probation and the US Sentencing Commission' (1993) 525 *Annals of the American Academy of Political and Social Science,* 157–69.

Loomis, C. J., 'White-Collar Crime' *Fortune,* 22 July 1985, 91.

Luban, D., Strudler, A., and Wasserman, D., 'Deeds Without Doers: Individual Responsibility in Organizational Settings' [forthcoming].

Lucas, J., *The Principles of Politics* (Oxford: Clarendon Press, 1966).

Luhmann, Niklas, 'The Self-Reproduction of Law and Its Limits' in G. Teubner (ed.), *Dilemmas of Law in the Welfare State* (Berlin: Walter de Gruyter, 1985), 111–27.

Lukes, S., *Individualism* (Oxford: Basil Blackwell, 1973).

Macey, J. R., 'Agency Theory and the Criminal Liability of Corporations' (1991) 71 *Boston University Law Review,* 307–40.

Mackie, J. L., 'Morality and the Retributive Emotions' (1982) 1 *Criminal Justice Ethics,* 3–11.

Mangham, I., *Interactions and Interventions in Organizations* (New York: Wiley, 1978).

Mann, K., *Defending White-Collar Crime: A Portrait of Attorneys at Work* (New Haven: Yale University Press, 1985).

Mannheim, H., *Group Problems in Crime and Punishment* (London: Routledge & Kegan Paul, 1955).

Manning, R., 'The Random Collectivity as a Moral Agent' (1985) 11 *Social Theory and Practice,* 97–105.

Marris, R. and Wood, A., *The Corporate Economy: Growth, Competition and Innovative Power* (London: Macmillan, 1971).

Martin, D. D., 'The Computer Industry' in W. Adams (ed.), *The Structure of American Industry* (New York: Macmillan, 1977), 285–311.

Marx, G. T., 'The Interweaving of Public and Private Police in Undercover Work', in C. D. Shearing and P. C. Stenning (eds), *Private Policing* (Beverly Hills: Sage, 1987), 172–93.

Undercover: Police Surveillance in America (Berkeley: University of California Press, 1988).

Mathews, A. F., 'Internal Corporate Investigations' (1984) 45 *Ohio State Law Journal,* 655–702.

Matthews, R., *Privatizing Criminal Justice* (London: Newbury Park, Sage, 1989).

May, L., *The Morality of Groups: Collective Responsibility, Group-Based Harm and Corporate Rights* (Notre Dame, Ind.: University of Notre Dame Press, 1987).

Mayer, M., *The Greatest Ever Bank Robbery: The Collapse of the Savings and Loan Industry* (New York: Charles Scribner's Sons, 1990).

McAdams, T. and Tower, C. B., 'Personal Accountability in the Corporate Sector' (1978) 16 *American Business Law Journal,* 67–82.

McCarry, G. J., *Aspects of Public Sector Employment Law* (Sydney: Law Book Company, 1988).

McCarthy, C., 'American: It's a Flying Shame', *Washington Post,* 13 Oct. 1985, O2.

McCloy, J. J., *The Great Oil Spill: The Inside Report* (New York: Chelsea House, 1976).

McConnell, G., *Private Power and American Democracy* (New York: Alfred A. Knopf, 1966).

McCormack, D. R., 'The Tightening White Collar: Expanding Theories of Criminal Liability for Corporate Executives, Directors, and Attorneys' (1986) 49 *Texas Bar Journal*, 494–6.

McCulloch, K. J., *Termination of Employment: Employer and Employee Rights* (Englewood Cliffs, NJ: Prentice-Hall, 1984).

McDonald, M., 'Collective Rights and Tyranny' (1986) 56(2) *University of Ottawa Quarterly*, 115–23.

'The Personless Paradigm' (1987) 37 *University of Toronto Law Journal*, 212–26.

McDonnell, M., *Challenger: A Major Malfunction—A True Story of Politics, Greed, and the Wrong Stuff* (London: Simon & Schuster, 1987) .

McDowell, B., *Ethical Conduct and the Professional's Dilemma* (New York: Quorum Books, 1991) .

McVisk, W., 'Toward a Rational Theory of Criminal Liability for the Corporate Executive' (1978) 69 *Journal of Criminal Law and Criminology*, 75–91.

Meier, R. and Johnson, W., 'Deterrence as Social Control: The Legal and Extra-Legal Production of Conformity' (1977) 42 *American Sociological Review*, 292–304.

Meier, R. F., 'Jurisdictional Differences in Deterring Marijuana Use' (1982) 12 *Journal of Drug Issues*, 61–71.

Mendeloff, J., *Regulating Safety: An Econometric and Political Analysis of Occupational Safety and Health Policy* (Cambridge, Mass.: MIT Press, 1979).

Michelman, F. I., 'Formal and Associational Aims in Procedural Due Process' in J. R. Pennock and J. W. Chapman (eds), *Due Process* (1977) 18 *Nomos*, 126–71.

Michels, R., *Political Parties* (New York: Free Press, 1949 [first published 1915]).

Miester, D. J., 'Criminal Liability for Corporations That Kill' (1990) 64 *Tulane Law Review*, 919–48.

Milan, V., *The Cybernetic Samurai* (New York: Arbor House, 1985).

Mill, J. S., *Considerations on Representative Government* in J. Gray (ed.), *John Stuart Mill: On Liberty and Other Essays* (Oxford: Oxford University Press, 1991).

Millon, D., 'Theories of the Corporation' [1990] *Duke Law Journal*, 201–62.

Mills, E. B., 'Perspectives on Corporate Crime and the Evasive Individual' (1986) 8 *Criminal Justice Journal*, 327–61.

Ming, W. W. C.,'The Recovery of Losses Occasioned by Corporate Crime—Suits Against Officers Who Involve Their Company in a Crime' (1983) 25 *Malaya Law Review*, 271–94.

Mintzberg, H., *The Structuring of Organizations* (Englewood Cliffs, NJ: Prentice-Hall, 1979).

Mintzberg on Management (New York: Free Press, 1989).

Mishan, E. J., *The Costs of Economic Growth* (Harmondsworth: Penguin, 1969).

Mitchell, E., 'A Theory of Corporate Will' (1945) 56 *Ethics*, 96–105.

Mitnick, B. M., *The Political Economy of Regulation* (New York: Columbia University Press, 1980).

'The Two-Part Problem of Regulatory Compliance: Compliance Reform and Strip Mining' in *Research in Corporate Social Performance and Policy*, vol. 4 (Greenwich, Conn.: JAI Press, 1982), 215–42.

'The Theory of Agency and Organizational Analysis' (1987) Working Paper Series, Graduate School of Business, University of Pittsburgh.

Mitroff, I. and Pauchant, T., *We're So Big and Powerful Nothing Bad Can Happen to Us* (New York: Birch Lane Press, 1990).

Monks, R. A. G. and Minow, N., *Power and Accountability* (New York: Harper Collins, 1991).

Moore, C. A., 'Taming the Giant Corporation? Some Cautionary Remarks on the Deterrability of Corporate Crime' (1987) 33 *Crime & Delinquency*, 379–403.

Moore, S. F., 'Legal Liability and Evolutionary Interpretation: Some Aspects of Strict Liability, Self-Help and Collective Responsibility' in M. Gluckman (ed.), *The Allocation of Responsibility* (Manchester: Manchester University Press, 1972), 51–107.

Morgan, G., *Images of Organization* (Beverly Hills: Sage, 1986).

Morvillo, R. G., 'Voluntary Corporate In-House Investigations—Benefits and Pitfalls' (1981) 36 *Business Lawyer*, 1871–5.

Mouzelis, N. P., *Organisation and Bureaucracy: An Analysis of Modern Theories* (London: Routledge & Kegan Paul, 1975).

Muchlinski, P. T., 'The Bhopal Case: Controlling Ultrahazardous Industrial Activities Undertaken by Foreign Investors' (1987) 50 *Modern Law Review*, 545–87.

Mueller, G. O. W., '*Mens Rea* and the Corporation' (1957) 19 *University of Pittsburgh Law Review*, 21–50.

Muller, E., *Die Stellung der Juristischen Person im Ordnungswidrigkeitenrecht* (Köln: Dr Peter Deubner verlag GmbH, 1985).

Murphy, J., *Retribution, Justice and Therapy* (Dordrecht: D. Reidel Pub., 1979).

NSW, Independent Commission against Corruption, *Report on Unauthorised Release of Government Information*, vol. 1 (Sydney: ICAC, 1992).

NZ, *Report of the Royal Commission to Inquire into the Crash on Mount Erebus, Antarctica of a DC10 Aircraft Operated by Air New Zealand* (Wellington: NZ Government Printer, 1981).

Neilson, W. A., 'Administrative Remedies: The Canadian Experience with Assurances of Voluntary Compliance in Provincial Trade Practices Legislation' (1981) 19 *Osgoode Hall Law Journal*, 153–98.

Nemerson, S. S., 'Criminal Liability Without Fault: A Philosophical Perspective' (1975) 75 *Columbia Law Review*, 1517–77.

Nonet, P., 'The Legitimation of Purposive Decisions' (1980) 68 *California Law Review*, 263–300.

Noonan, J. T., *Bribes* (New York: Macmillan, 1985).

Note, 'Indemnification of the Corporate Official for Fines and Expenses Arising from Criminal Antitrust Litigation' (1962) 50 *Georgetown Law Journal*, 566–85.

Nozick, R., *Anarchy, State and Utopia* (New York: Basic Books, 1974).

O'Neill, J. (ed.), *Modes of Individualism and Collectivism* (London: Heinemann, 1973).

Ogren, R. W., 'The Ineffectiveness of the Criminal Sanction in Fraud and Corruption Cases: Losing the Battle against White-Collar Crime' (1973) 11 *American Criminal Law Review*, 959–88.

Ohmae, K., 'Japanese Companies Are Run from the Top', *Wall Street Journal*, 21 April 1982, 26.

Olson, M. Jr, *The Logic of Collective Action* (Cambridge, Mass.: Harvard University Press, 1965).

Orland, L., 'Reflections on Corporate Crime: Law in Search of Theory and Scholarship' (1980) 17 *American Journal of Criminal Law*, 501–20.

Osunbor, O., 'The Agent-Only Subsidiary Company and the Control of Multinational Groups' (1989) 38 *International and Comparative Law Quarterly*, 377–87.

Ouchi, W. G., *Theory Z: How American Business Can Meet the Japanese Challenge* (Reading, Mass.: Addison Wesley, 1982).

Packer, H. L., *The Limits of the Criminal Sanction* (Stanford: Stanford University Press, 1968).

Page, J. A. and O'Brien, M.-W. *Bitter Wages: Ralph Nader's Study Group Report on Disease and Injury on the Job* (New York: Grossman, 1973).

Parker, J. S., 'Criminal Sentencing Policy for Organizations: The Unifying Approach of Optimal Penalties' (1989) 26 *American Criminal Law Review*, 513–604.

Parsons, T., *Structure and Process in Modern Society* (New York: Free Press, 1960).

Pascale, R. T. and Athos, A. G., *The Art of Japanese Management* (New York: Simon and Schuster, 1981).

Passas, N., 'I Cheat, Therefore I Exist? The BCCI Scandal in Context' in W. F. Hoffman, J. Kamm and R. E. Frederick (eds), *International Perspectives on Business Ethics* (New York: Quorum Books [in press]).

'Regulatory Anaesthesia or the Limits of the Criminal Law? The Prosecution of BCCI for Money Laundering in Tampa, Florida' (Washington, DC: Drug Policy Foundation [forthcoming]).

Paternoster, R. and Iovanni, L., 'The Deterrent Effect of Perceived Severity: A Reexamination' (1986) 64 *Social Forces*, 751–77.

Paternoster, R., Saltzman, L., Chiricos, T. and Waldo, G., 'Estimating Perceptual Stability and Deterrent Effects: The Role of Perceived Legal Punishment in the Inhibition of Criminal Involvement' (1983) 74 *Journal of Criminal Law and Criminology*, 270–97.

'Perceived Risk and Social Control: Do Sanctions Really Deter?' (1983) 17 *Law and Society Review*, 457–79.

Patterson, G. R., *Coercive Family Process* (Eugene, Oregon: Castalia Publishing, 1982).

Pearce, D., Markandya, A. and Barbier, E. B., *Blueprint for a Green Economy* (London: Earthscan Publications, 1989).

Pearce, D. W. and Turner, R. K., *Economics of Natural Resources and the Environment* (Baltimore: Johns Hopkins University Press, 1990).

Pennington, R. R., *Directors' Personal Liability* (London: Collins, 1987).

Pepinsky, H. E., *Crime and Conflict: A Study of Law and Society* (London: Martin Robertson, 1976).

Perrow, C., 'A Framework for the Comparative Analysis of Organizations' (1967) 32 *American Sociological Review*, 194–208.

Normal Accidents: Living With High-Risk Technologies (New York: Basic Books, 1984).

Pettit, P. and Goodin, R. E., 'The Possibility of Special Duties' (1986) 16 *Canadian Journal of Philosophy*, 651–76.

Pizzo, S., Fricker, M. and Muolo, P., *Inside Job: The Looting of America's Savings and Loans* (New York: Harper Perennial, 1989).

Polinsky, A. M. and Shavell, S., 'Should Employees be Subject to Fines and Imprisonment Given the Existence of Corporate Liability?' (1992) Program in Law and Economics, Harvard Law School, Discussion Paper No. 105.

Popper, K., II *The Open Society and Its Enemies* (London: Routledge & Kegan Paul, 1945).

Porter, M., *The Competitive Advantage of Nations* (New York: Free Press, 1985).

Posner, R. A., *Antitrust Law: An Economic Perspective* (Chicago: University of Chicago Press, 1976).

Economic Analysis of Law (Boston: Little Brown, 2nd edn, 1977).

'An Economic Theory of the Criminal Law' (1985) 85 *Columbia Law Review*, 1193–231.

Pugh, D. S. and Hinings, C. R., *Organizational Structure: Extensions and Replications—The Aston Programme II* (London: Saxon House, 1976).

Ramsay, I. M., 'Liability of Directors for Breach of Duty and the Scope of Indemnification and Insurance' (1987) 5 *Company and Securities Law Journal*, 129–56.

Reel, A. F., *The Case of General Yamashita* (Chicago: University of Chicago Press, 1949).

Rees, R., 'The Theory of Principal and Agent' in J. D. Hey and P. J. Lambert (eds), *Surveys in the Economics of Uncertainty* (Oxford: Basil Blackwell, 1987), 46–90.

Reiman, Jeffrey H., *The Rich Get Richer and the Poor Get Prison* (New York: Wiley, 1979).

Reiss, A., 'The Institutionalization of Risk' (1989) 11 *Law & Society Review*, 392–402.

'Detecting, Investigating and Regulating Business Law-Breaking' in P. Grabosky and J. Braithwaite (eds), *Business Regulation and Australia's Future* (Canberra: Australian Institute of Criminology, 1993), 189–200.

Ricketts, M., *The Economics of Business Enterprise: New Approaches to the Firm* (Brighton, Sussex: Wheatsheaf Books, 1987).

Roach, K., 'The Limits of Corrective Justice and the Potential of Equity in Constitutional Remedies' (1991) 33 *Arizona Law Review*, 859–905.

Robins, E., 'Unfair Dismissal: Emerging Issues in the Use of Arbitration as a Dispute Resolution Alternative for the Nonunion Workforce' (1984) 12 *Fordham Urban Law Journal*, 437–57.

Romano, R., 'Metapolitics and Corporate Law Reform' (1984) 36 *Stanford Law Review*, 923–1016.

'Theory of the Firm and Corporate Sentencing' (1991) 71 *Boston University Law Review*, 377–82.

Rorty, A. O. (ed.), *The Identities of Persons* (Berkeley: University of California Press, 1976).

Rose-Ackerman, S., 'Effluent Charges: A Critique' (1973) 6 *Canadian Journal of Economics*, 512–28.

Rudge, P. F., *Order and Disorder in Organizations* (Kambah, ACT: CORAT, 1990).

Russell, B., *Human Knowledge* (London: Routledge, 1992 [first published 1948]).

Sadurski, W., *Giving Desert Its Due: Social Justice and Legal Theory* (Dordrecht: D. Reidel, 1985).

Safire, W., 'On Sutton and Hutton', *New York Times*, 9 May 1985, 31.

Sagoff, M., 'At the Shrine of Our Lady of Fatima or Why Political Questions Are Not All Economic' (1981) 23 *Arizona Law Review*, 1283–98.

Sand, P. H., 'The Socialist Response: Environmental Protection Law in the German Democratic Republic' (1973) 3 *Ecology Law Quarterly*, 451–90.

Sargent, N., 'Law, Ideology and Corporate Crime: A Critique of Instrumentalism' (1989) 4 *Canadian Journal of Law & Society*, 39–75.

Sawyer, M. C., *Theories of the Firm* (London: Weidenfeld & Nicolson, 1979).

Schelling, T. C., *The Strategy of Conflict* (Cambridge, Mass.: Harvard University Press, 1963).

'The Strategy of Inflicting Costs' in R. M. McKean (ed.), *Issues in Defense Economics* (New York: Columbia University Press, 1967), 105–27.

'Command and Control', in J. W. McKie (ed.), *Social Responsibility and the Business Predicament* (Washington, DC: Brookings Institution, 1974), 79–108.

Micromotives and Macrobehavior (New York: Norton, 1978).

Schlegel, K., *Just Deserts for Corporate Criminals* (Boston: Northeastern University Press, 1990).

Schneider, K., 'Faking It: The Case against Industrial Bio-Test Laboratories' [1983] (Spring) *The Amicus Journal*, 14–26.

Schneider, M. W., 'Criminal Enforcement of Federal Water Pollution Laws in an Era of Deregulation' (1982) 73 *Journal of Criminal Law and Criminology*, 642–74.

Schneyer, T., 'Professional Discipline for Law Firms' (1991) 77 *Cornell Law Review*, 1–46.

Scholz, J. T., 'Cooperation, Deterrence and the Ecology of Regulatory Enforcement' (1984) 18 *Law and Society Review*, 179–224.

'Voluntary Compliance and Regulatory Enforcement' (1984) 6 *Law and Policy*, 385–404.

Schon, D., *Beyond the Stable State* (New York: Norton, 1973).

Schrager, L. S. and Short, J. F., 'Toward a Sociology of Organizational Crime' (1978) 25 *Social Problems*, 407–19.

Schwartz, B., *Swann's Way: The School Busing Case and the Supreme Court* (New York: Oxford University Press, 1986).

Sciamanda, J., 'Preventive Law Leads to Corporate Goal of Zero Litigation, Zero Legal Violations' (1987) 6(1) *Preventive Law Reporter*, 3–8.

Scott, R., *Muscle and Blood* (New York: E. P. Dutton, 1974).

Scott, W. G. and Hart, D. K., *Organizational Values in America* (Boston: Houghton Mifflin, 1979).

Screvens, R., 'Les Sanctions Applicables aux Personnes Morales dans les États des Communautés Européenes' (1980) 60 *Revue de Droit Pénale et de Criminologie*, 163–90.

Segerson, K. and Tietenberg, T., 'Defining Efficient Sanctions' in T. Tietenberg (ed.), *Innovations in Environmental Policy* (Aldershot, Hants, England: E. Elgar, 1992), 53–73.

Selznick, P., 'Foundations of the Theory of Organizations' (1948) 13 *American Sociological Review*, 25–35.
TVA and the Grass Roots: A Study in the Sociology of Formal Organization (Berkeley: University of California Press, 1949).

Sen, A., *On Ethics & Economics* (Oxford: Basil Blackwell, 1988).

Seney, H. W., 'The Sibyl at Cumae: Our Criminal Law's Moral Obsolescence' (1971) 17 *Wayne Law Review*, 844–53.

Settle, R., The Welfare Economics of Occupational Safety and Health Standards, PhD Dissertation, University of Wisconsin, 1974.

Shackle, G. L. S., *Epistemics and Economics: A Critique of Economic Doctrines* (Cambridge: Cambridge University Press, 1972).
Imagination and the Nature of Choice (Edinburgh: Edinburgh University Press, 1979).

Shapiro, S. P., 'Policing Trust' in C. D. Shearing and P. C. Stenning (eds), *Private Policing* (Beverly Hills: Sage, 1987), 194–220.
'The Social Control of Impersonal Trust' (1987) 93 *American Journal of Sociology*, 623–58.

Shavell, S., 'Criminal Law and the Optimal Use of Nonmonetary Sanctions as a Deterrent' (1985) 85 *Columbia Law Review*, 1232–62.

Shaver, K. G., *The Attribution of Blame: Causality, Responsibility, and Blameworthiness* (New York: Springer-Verlag, 1985).

Shearing, C. and Stenning, P., 'Modern Private Security: Its Growth and Implications' in M. Tonry and N. Morris (eds), *Crime and Justice: An Annual Review of Research*, vol. 3 (Chicago: University of Chicago Press, 1981), 193–245.
(eds), *Private Policing* (Beverly Hills: Sage, 1987).

Sher, G., 'Groups and Justice' (1977) 87 *Ethics*, 174–81.

Shirk, W. B., Greenberg, B. D. and Dawson, W. S., 'Truth or Consequences: Expanding Civil and Criminal Liability for the Defective Pricing of Government Contracts' (1988) 37 *Catholic University Law Review*, 935–91.

Sigler, J. A. and Murphy, J. E., *Interactive Corporate Compliance: An Alternative to Regulatory Compulsion* (New York: Quorum Books, 1988).
Corporate Lawbreaking and Interactive Compliance: Resolving the Regulation-Deregulation Dichotomy (New York: Quorum Books, 1991).

Silard, J., 'Rights of the Accused Employee in Company Disciplinary Investigations' (1970) *NYU 22nd Annual Conference on Labor,* 217–32.

Siliciano, J. A., 'Corporate Behavior and the Social Efficiency of Tort Law' (1987) 85 *Michigan Law Review,* 1820–64.

Silk, L. and Vogel, D., *Ethics and Profits: The Crisis of Confidence in American Business* (New York: Simon & Schuster, 1976).

Silver, E., 'Rights of Individual Employees in the Arbitral Process' (1959) *NYU Conference on Labor,* 53–62.

Simon, H. A., *Models of Man: Social and Rational* (New York: John Wiley & Sons, 1957).

Administrative Behavior (New York: Free Press, 2nd edn, 1965).

Singer, R., *Just Deserts: Sentencing Based on Equity and Desert* (Cambridge, Mass.: Bollinger, 1979).

Sjostrom, H. and Nilsson, R., *Thalidomide and the Power of the Drug Companies* (Harmondsworth: Penguin, 1972).

Smith, R. A., *Corporations in Crisis* (Garden City, NY: Anchor Books, 1963).

Solomon, L. D. and Nowak, N. S., 'Managerial Restructuring: Prospects for a New Regulatory Tool' (1980) 56 *Notre Dame Lawyer,* 120–40.

South Australia, Criminal Law and Penal Methods Reform Committee, Fourth Report, *The Substantive Criminal Law* (Adelaide: South Australian Government Printer, 1977).

Spelfogel, E. J., 'Surveillance and Interrogation in Plant Theft and Discipline Cases' (1969) *NYU Conference on Labor,* 171–98.

Spiegelhoff, T. L., 'Limits on Individual Accountability for Corporate Crimes' (1984) 67 *Marquette Law Review,* 604–40.

Staaf, R. J. and Tannian, F. X. (eds), *Externalities: Theoretical Dimensions of Political Economy* (New York: Dunellen Publishing, 1972).

Stanbury, W. T., 'Public Policy Toward Individuals Involved in Competition Law Offences in Canada', Paper presented at conference, Corporate Crime: Ethics, Law and the State, Queen's University, Kingston, Ontario, 12–14 Nov. 1992.

Steiner, I. D., 'Heuristic Models of Groupthink' in H. Brandstatter, J. H. Davis, and G. Stocker-Kreichgauer (eds), *Group Decision Making* (London: Academic Press, 1982), 503–24.

Stewart, A., 'Employment Protection in Australia' (1989) 11 *Comparative Labor Law Journal,* 1–47.

Workplace Disciplinary Rules and Procedure: Australia, Unpublished ILO Working Paper, 1991.

Stewart, J. B. *Den of Thieves* (New York: Simon & Schuster, 1991).

Stewart, R. B., 'Regulation, Innovation, and Administrative Law: A Conceptual Framework' (1981) 69 *California Law Review,* 1256–377.

'Organizational Jurisprudence' (1987) 101 *Harvard Law Review,* 371–90.

Stiglitz, J. E., 'Approaches to the Economics of Discrimination' (1973) 63 *American Economic Review,* 287–95.

Stoljar, S. J., *Groups and Entities* (Canberra: ANU Press, 1973).

Stone, C. D., *Where the Law Ends: The Social Control of Corporate Behavior* (New York: Harper, 1975).

'A Slap on the Wrist for the Kepone Mob' (1977) 22 *Business and Society Review,* 4–11.

'The Place of Enterprise Liability in the Control of Corporate Conduct' (1980) 90 *Yale Law Journal,* 1–77.

'A Comment on "Criminal Responsibility in Government"' in J. R. Pennock and J. W. Chapman (eds), *Criminal Justice* (1985) 27 *Nomos,* 241–66.

'Corporate Regulation: The Place of Social Responsibility' in B. Fisse and P. French (eds), *Corrigible Corporations and Unruly Law* (San Antonio: Trinity University Press, 1985), 13–38.

Stone, M., 'Due Process in Labor Arbitration' (1972) *24th NYU Conference on Labor*, 11–25.

Stretton, H., *Capitalism, Socialism and the Environment* (Cambridge: Cambridge University Press, 1976).

Stubbing, R. A., *The Defense Game* (New York: Harper & Row, 1986).

Summers, C. W., 'Individual Rights in Collective Agreements and Arbitration' (1962) 37 *New York University Law Review*, 362–410.

Sunga, L. S., *Individual Responsibility in International Law for Serious Human Rights Violations* (Dordrecht: Martinus Nijhoff, 1992).

Surber, J., 'Individual and Corporate Responsibility: Two Alternative Approaches' (1983) 2 *Business and Professional Ethics Journal*, 67–89.

Sutton, A. and Wild, R., 'Corporate Crime and Social Structure', in P. R. Wilson and J. Braithwaite (eds), *Two Faces of Deviance: Crimes of the Powerless and Powerful* (Brisbane: University of Queensland Press, 1978), 177–98.

Sykes, A. O., 'The Economics of Vicarious Liability' (1984) 93 *Yale Law Journal*, 1231–80.

Sykes, G. and Matza, D., 'Techniques of Neutralization: A Theory of Delinquency' (1957) 22 *American Sociological Review*, 664–70.

Taylor, S. W., 'Criminal Liabilities of Ships' Masters' [1981] *Lloyds Maritime and Commercial Law*, 499–505.

    'The Criminal Liability of Ships' Masters: Provisions and Changes' [1984] *Lloyds Maritime and Commercial Law Quarterly*, 446–58.

Temby, I., 'Some Observations on Accountability, Prosecution Discretions and Corporate Crime', Paper presented to The Commercial Law Association of Australia, Sydney, 28 October 1986.

Tepker, H. F., 'Oklahoma's At-Will Rule: Heeding the Warnings of America's Evolving Employment Law?' (1986) 39 *Oklahoma Law Review*, 373–426.

    'Enterprise Corporatism: New Industrial Policy and the "Essence" of the Legal Person' (1988) 36 *American Journal of Comparative Law*, 130–55.

Teubner, G., 'Substantive and Reflexive Elements in Modern Law' (1983) 17 *Law and Society Review*, 239–85.

    (ed.), *Dilemmas of Law in the Welfare State* (Berlin: Walter de Gruyter, 1986).

    (ed.), *Autopoietic Law: A New Approach to Law and Society* (Berlin: Walter de Gruyter, 1988).

    'After Legal Instrumentalism?   Strategic Models of Post-Regulatory Law' in G. Teubner, *Dilemmas of Law in the Welfare State* (Berlin: Walter de Gruyter, 1986), 299–326.

Thompson, D. F., 'Criminal Responsibility in Government' in J. R. Pennock and J. W. Chapman (eds), *Criminal Justice* (1985) 27 *Nomos*, 201–40.

Thompson, J. D., *Organizations in Action* (New York: McGraw-Hill, 1967).

Tiedemann, K., 'Antitrust Law and Criminal Law Policy in Western Europe' in L. H. Leigh (ed.), *Economic Crime in Europe* (London: Macmillan, 1980), 39–56.

Tigar, M. E., 'It Does the Crime But Not the Time: Corporate Criminal Liability in Federal Law' (1990) 17 *American Journal of Criminal Law*, 211–34.

Timberg, S., 'The Corporation as a Technique of International Administration' (1952) 19 *University of Chicago Law Review*, 739–58.

Tittle, C. R., *Sanctions and Social Deviance* (New York: Praeger, 1980).

Toffler, A., *Future Shock* (New York: Bantam Books, 1970).

Tombs, S., 'Corporate Crime and "Post Modern" Organizations', Paper presented at conference, Corporate Crime: Ethics, Law and the State, Queen's University, Kingston, Ontario, 12–14 Nov. 1992.

Truell, P. and Gurwin, L., *False Profits: The Inside Story of BCCI, The World's Most Corrupt Financial Empire* (Boston: Houghton Mifflin, 1992).

Tundermann, D. W., 'Personal Liability for Corporate Directors, Officers, Employees and Controlling Shareholders under State and Federal Environmental Laws' (1985) 2 *Proceedings Rocky Mountain Mineral Law Institute*, 2-1–2-48.

Turner, J. C., *Rediscovering the Social Group: A Self-Categorization Theory* (Oxford: Basil Blackwell, 1987).

Tyler, T. R., *Why People Obey the Law* (New Haven: Yale University Press, 1990).

UK, Department of Transport, *mv Herald of Free Enterprise*, Report of Court No. 8074 (London: HMSO, 1987).

US, HR, Committee on the Judiciary, Subcommittee on Crime, *White-Collar Crime*, Hearings, 95th Cong., 2nd Sess., 1978.

US, HR, Committee on the Judiciary, Subcommittee on Crime, *Corporate Crime*, Hearings, 96th Cong., 2nd Sess., 1980.

US, HR, Committee on the Judiciary, Subcommittee on Crime, *E. F. Hutton Mail and Wire Fraud Case*, Hearings, Pt 1, 99th Congress, 1st Sess., 1985, Pt 2, 99th Cong., 2nd Sess., 1986, Report, 99th Cong., 2nd Sess., 1986.

US, National Commission on Reform of Federal Criminal Laws, I Working Papers (Washington, DC: US Government Printing Office, 1970).

US, President's Commission on Coal, Staff Findings (Washington, DC: US Government Printing Office, 1980).

US, SEC, *Report of the Securities and Exchange Commission on Questionable and Illegal Foreign Payments*, Submitted to the Senate Committee on Banking, Housing and Urban Affairs, 94 Cong., 2nd Sess., 1976.

US, Senate, *Administered Prices*, Pts 27 & 28, Hearings Before the Subcommittee on Antitrust and Monopoly of the Committee of the Judiciary, 87th Cong., 2nd Sess., 1961.

US, Sentencing Commission, 'Discussion Draft of Sentencing Guidelines and Policy Statements for Organizations' (1988) 10 *Whittier Law Review*, 7–75.

US, Sentencing Commission, *Discussion Materials on Organizational Sanctions* (Washington DC: Sentencing Commission, 1988).

US, Sentencing Commission, Preliminary Draft, *Sentencing Guidelines for Organizational Defendants* (Washington, DC: Sentencing Commission, 1991).

Van de Ven, A. H. and Delbecq, A. L., 'A Task Contingent Model of Work Unit Structure' (1974) 19 *Administrative Science Quarterly*, 183–97.

van der Haas, H., *The Enterprise in Transition: An Analysis of European and American Practice* (London: Tavistock Publications, 1967).

Vaughan, D., *Controlling Unlawful Organizational Behavior: Social Structure and Corporate Misconduct* (Chicago; University of Chicago Press, 1983).

'Autonomy, Interdependence and Social Control: NASA and the Space Shuttle Challenger' (1990) 35 *Administrative Science Quarterly*, 225–57.

Velasquez, M., 'Why Corporations Are Not Morally Responsible for Anything They Do' (1983) 2 *Business and Professional Ethics Journal*, 1–18.

Victoria, *Royal Commission into the Failure of the West Gate Bridge, Report* (Melbourne: Victorian Government Printer, 1970).

von Burchardt, R. and Schlamp, H. -J. (eds), *Flick-Zeugen* (Hamburg: Rowolt, 1985).

Von Hirsch, A., *Past or Future Crimes: Deservedness or Dangerousness in the Sentencing of Criminals* (New Brunswick, NJ: Rutgers University Press, 1985).

Vroom, Victor H., 'Industrial Social Psychology' in G. Lindzey and E. Aronson (eds), *Handbook of Social Psychology*, vol. V (Reading, Mass.: Addison-Wesley, 2nd edn, 1968), 196–268.

Walde, T. W., 'Parent–Subsidiary Relations in the Integrated Corporate System: A Comparison of American and German Law' (1974) 9 *Journal of International Law and Economics*, 455–506.

Waldman, D. E., *Antitrust Action and Market Structure* (Lexington, Mass.: Lexington Books, 1978).
'Economic Benefits in the IBM, AT&T, and Xerox Cases: Government Antitrust Policy in the 70s' (1979) 12 *Antitrust Law and Economics Review*, 75–92.

Walsh, W. M., 'Pride, Shame and Responsibility' (1970) 20 *Philosophical Quarterly*, 1–13.

Walt, S. and Laufer, W. S., 'Corporate Criminal Liability and the Comparative Mix of Sanctions' in K. Schlegel and D. Weisburd (eds), *White Collar Crime Reconsidered* (Boston: Northeastern University Press, 1992).

Walter, C. and Richards, E. P. Jr, 'Corporate Counsel's Role in Risk Minimization: Lessons from Bhopal' (1986) 2 *Preventive Law Reporter*, 139–54.

Walton, C. C. and Cleveland, F. W. Jr, *Corporations on Trial* (Belmont, California: Wadsworth, 1964).

Warbrick, C. J. and Sullivan, R., 'Ship Routeing Schemes and the Criminal Liability of the Master' [1984] *Lloyds Maritime and Commercial Law*, 23–9.

Warner, M., *Organizational Choice and Constraint* (Westmead, Hants., England: Saxon House, 1977).

Warnick, L., 'The Investigation of Fraud' in P. Grabosky (ed.), *Complex Commercial Fraud* (Canberra: Australian Institute of Criminology, 1992), 97–119.

Watkins, M., 'Electrical Equipment Antitrust Cases: Their Implications for Government and for Business' (1961) 29 *University of Chicago Law Review*, 97–110.

Wells, C., 'The Decline and Rise of English Murder' [1988] *Criminal Law Review*, 788–801.

Western Australia, *Report of the Royal Commission into Commercial Activities of Government and Other Matters* (Perth: Government Printer Western Australia, 1992).

Westin, A. F., 'Employer Responses to New Judicial Rulings on At-Will Employment: A Warning About the "Legal Armourplate" Approach' (1983) *NYU 36th Annual Conference on Labor*, 1–24.
(ed.), *Whistle Blowing: Loyalty and Dissent in the Corporation* (New York: McGraw-Hill Book Company, 1981).

Westin, A. F., and Salisbury, S. (eds), *Individual Rights in the Corporation* (New York: Pantheon Books, 1980).

Weyland, R., 'Present Status of Individual Employee Rights' (1970) *22nd NYU Conference on Labor*, 171–216.

'White-Collar Crime: A Survey of Law' (1980) 18 *American Journal of Criminal Law*, 169–386.

Whiting, R. A., 'Antitrust and the Corporate Executive' (1961) 47 *Virginia Law Review*, 929–87, (1962) 48 *Virginia Law Review*, 1–49.

Williams, F. P. III, 'Deterrence and Social Control: Rethinking the Relationship' (1985) 13 *Journal of Criminal Justice*, 141–51.

Williams, G., *Criminal Law: The General Part* (London: Sweet & Maxwell, 2nd edn, 1961).

Williamson, O., 'The Modern Corporation: Origins, Evolution, Attributes' (1981) 19 *Journal of Economic Literature*, 1537–68.
'Corporate Governance' (1984) 93 *Yale Law Journal*, 1197–230.

Wilson, B. (ed.), *Rationality* (Oxford: Basil Blackwell, 1977).

Wilson, L. C., 'The Doctrine of Wilful Blindness' (1979) 28 *University of New Brunswick Law Journal*, 175–94.

Wilson, S. V. and Matz, A. H., 'Obtaining Evidence for Federal Economic Crime Prosecutions: An Overview and Analysis of Investigative Methods' (1977) 14 *American Criminal Law Review*, 651–716.

Wishart, D. A., 'A Conceptual Analysis of the Control of Companies' (1984) 14 *Melbourne University Law Review*, 601–33.

Wolf, S., 'The Legal and Moral Responsibility of Organizations' in J. R. Pennock and J. W. Chapman (eds), *Criminal Justice* (1985) 27 *Nomos*, 267–86.

Wolfe, A. 'The Corporate Apology' (1990) 33 *Business Horizons*, 10–14.

Wolff, J. C., 'Voluntary Disclosure Programs' (1979) 47 *Fordham Law Review*, 1057–82.

Wolff, M., 'On the Nature of Legal Persons' (1938) 54 *Law Quarterly Review*, 494–521.

Wray, C. A., 'Corporate Probation under the New Organizational Sentencing Guidelines' (1992) 101 *Yale Law Journal*, 2017–42.

Wylie, M. I., 'Corporations and the Non-Compellability Right in Criminal Proceedings' (1991) 33 *Criminal Law Quarterly*, 344–63.

Yarbrough, T. E., *Judge Frank Johnson and Human Rights in Alabama* (University, Alabama: University of Alabama Press, 1981).

Yeager, P. C., *The Limits of Law: The Public Regulation of Private Pollution* (Cambridge: Cambridge University Press, 1991).

Yoder, S. A., 'Criminal Sanctions for Corporate Illegality' (1978) 69 *Journal of Criminal Law and Criminology*, 40–58.

Young, H., 'Where Does the Buck Stop?' *Guardian Weekly*, 18 Oct. 1987, 1.

Zimring, F. E. and Hawkins, G. J., *Deterrence: The Legal Threat in Crime Control* (Chicago: University of Chicago Press, 1973).

Index